WINSTON CHURCHILL

THE YEARS OF PREPARATION

WINSTON CHURCHILL

THE YEARS OF PREPARATION

A BIOGRAPHY

BY

Lewis Broad

HAWTHORN BOOKS, INC. *Publishers*

New York

© 1958 by Hawthorn Books, Inc., 70 Fifth Avenue, New York City 11.
Copyright under International and Pan-American Copyright Conven-
tions. All rights reserved, including the right to reproduce this book,
or portions thereof, in any form, except for the inclusion of a brief
quotation in a review. This book was manufactured in the United
States of America. Library of Congress Catalog Card Number 58-11830.

First Edition, November, 1958

Cartoons: Culver; Bettman; H. U. Steger, *Bei Whisky und Zigarre* (Diog-
enes Verlag); Illustrated London News; Pictorial Parade, Inc.; Oscar Berger
(New York Times); © Punch, London; Cummings (London Express); Vicky,
Up the Poll (Turnstile Press); Western Mail; Hynes (London Herald).

CONTENTS

BOOK FOUR

FIGHTING THE SOCIALISTS

BOOK FIVE

FIGHTING THE DICTATORS

WINSTON CHURCHILL

THE YEARS OF PREPARATION

PREFACE

FIRST, I should express my appreciation to my American publishers who have made it possible for me to carry out this final revision of my biography of Sir Winston Churchill. For long enough it had been clear that drastic revision would be necessary, but I was unable to undertake what I knew must be a considerable task. It has proved to entail not the revision but the rewriting of a great part of the book.

I now complete a biography which has engaged me, on and off, for twenty-five years. It was in the early thirties that I began first to accumulate the material. In an abbreviated form, the book appeared early in World War II as one of a series concerning Britain's leaders. As a full-length biography it was published in 1941, bringing the record of events up to the meeting with President Roosevelt and the signing of the Atlantic Charter. It was republished in 1946, carrying the story to Sir Winston's fall from power; three further chapters were added in 1951; a further extension in 1952 enabled me, with satisfaction, to restore him to his place in Downing Street. In 1956 appeared the edition marking the close of the long public career.

Publication by installments of the biography of a still living statesman has its drawbacks. With the appearance of each edition, its predecessors become progressively out of date. The accumulation of knowledge about Sir Winston and the war, the disclosures of official papers, and the abundance of memoirs have produced a wealth of material embarrassing to a biographer in its copiousness. Matters that fifteen years ago could only be deduced are now established. Facts not to be guessed at have become known. The part played by Sir Winston at the various crises of the war has been

described by his own and other pens. It is this abundance of information, sufficient for a work ten volumes long, that sets the
biographer his problems of assimilation and selection.

Into the portmanteau of his life he packed material enough to
serve for three careers. He was already engaged in making history
when the generation that fought the last war was in the process of
being born. His services in the first war against the Germany of
the Kaiser were little less spectacular, and certainly no less controversial than those he rendered in the second.

Had the mischances of fortune cut short his career in 1918, he
would still have had his place in history. Between the wars, before
the fight with Hitler began, he played a leading part in the events
of twenty troubled years. It is these two phases of his life that form
the subject of the first of the two volumes of my biography. A
second volume is required to give an account of his widely ranging
services in the second war.

England's politics do not, as far as I can discover, furnish a parallel to Churchill's record of service to the State. Having begun the
twentieth century as servant of the old Queen, Victoria, he faced
the opening years of the second half of the century in the service
of the young Queen, Elizabeth II. Search the records, and you
will find no parallel to the case of this man who served under a
queen, under a king her son, under that king's son, under his son
in turn, and finally under the daughter of that son. In and out of
office, he did his duty to the Sovereign in five generations.

History will see in Winston Churchill the man of action engaged in what has been called the endless adventure of governing
men. This book might well be subtitled "A Narrative Biography."
By this I mean that I have sought to record what Churchill did
and what Churchill said without attempting, for the most part, to
analyze or judge. Content to leave the judgment to history, I have
found it sufficient to tell the story of this man's incomparable adventure and achievement. I have sought to set down the facts as
accurately as I have been able to discover them, without distortion
or suppression.

In my first edition I laid claim to impartiality. Since then, with
some mental pain, we have become conscious that there is no such
thing as impartiality outside mathematical tables. Any record of

events must be regarded as partial or distorted on one side or other of the Iron Curtain.

When I set out twenty-five years ago to write on Churchill I did so with the intention of exposing a demagogue. Honest men, I thought, should know this self-seeking, unscrupulous politician for what he was. Such was my thesis, but the further I investigated the more insubstantial it was seen to be. I had postulated an astute politician guilty of many errors. His errors, on investigation, largely disappeared. The astuteness of the politician was dubious. The figure of the patriot Minister emerged.

I have many acknowledgments to make, for I have incurred a debt to any author I could discover who had made a contribution to the Churchill saga. Above all, I must acknowledge the abundant indebtedness that I, in common with every one of his biographers, have incurred to Sir Winston himself. I do not call to mind any statesman so extensively autobiographical. Since, over the years, he provided such copious records of his activities, biographers might be tempted to leave the telling of his life story to the man who wrote (as he did most things) so much better than others. For playing the biographer I can find one sufficient reason and one alone—that he could not without blush of modesty pay to himself the tribute that is his due for his part in the history he helped to fashion.

In closing the story that must be an inspiration to the free peoples down the ages, I end on a note of wistful envy. In the years to come, a writer—having at his disposal all of Winston Churchill's vast store of papers—will be privileged to tell in its completeness the tale of his illustrious life. I envy him his task. I console myself with the thought that I have contrived to scratch my name in the wrappings of Winston Churchill's immortality.

As to the privileged author to whom I have referred, it would be pleasant to think the Churchill tradition was to be maintained. Winston wrote the biography of Lord Randolph, his father. How agreeable it would be were Mr. Randolph Churchill, in his generation, to become the official biographer of his father.

I was engaged in my final chapters when I came across a statement made by Lord Rosebery on the writing of biography. "The life of any man that ever lived on earth is far more than his public career. To set forth the annals of the time in which the hero existed and to note his contact with them is only a part of his life, though it is often held to be the only part that is worth remembering. But the life of a man is not only his public life." Lord Rosebery spoke with the authority of one who had a public career as Prime Minister, and he pronounced on literary matters with the authority of one who was a better author than he was a Prime Minister. I came to conclude that to meet Lord Rosebery's requirements something needed to be added to a biography designed as a narrative of events. To the record of what my hero did, there should be added some account of the nature of the man who wrought the deeds. It is for this reason that I begin, as a prologue, with a profile.

PRELUDE

Let all
Who knew me well, what they know freely speak
So those (the greatest curse I meet below)
Who know me not may not pretend to know.

Let none of those
Pretending friendship to give malice weight
Publish my life; let no false sneaking peer
(Some such there are) to win the public ear
Hand me to shame with some vile anecdote . . .
Let one sprig of bay around my head
Bloom while I live and point me out when dead
Let it (may Heaven indulgent grant my prayer)
Be planted on my grave nor wither there;
And when on travel bound some rhyming guest
Roams through the Churchyard whilst his dinner's drest
Let it hold up this comment to his eyes—

Life to the last enjoyed, here Churchill lies
Whilst (O what joy that pleasing flattery gives)
Reading my works he cries—
Here Churchill lives.

—CHARLES CHURCHILL, The Candidate

WINSTON CHURCHILL—A PROFILE

W E SAW HIM in the plenitude of his powers when in 1940 our world seemed to be falling to pieces about us. It was then that the diverse strands of his character were fused together and he emerged as the indomitable leader of the British people. It was then that his massive figure seemed to absorb in his own person the shock of successive calamities, breaking their force as the breakwater receives and breaks the force of the tempest. We drew comfort and inspiration from him at the time of our peril. Without need to brace himself to meet the emergency of catastrophe he stood there in his solid strength. By his bearing, resolute, unflinching, imperturbable, he gave an example that steadied us in the hour of our adversity, showing us the way to survive and to prevail.

The qualities in the repertory of greatness were displayed by Winston Churchill in those days. The man and the hour were matched. His life, it seemed, had been directed to prepare him for the occasion of that supreme emergency. What he did could have been performed only by a man in whom strength of character was joined to vast capacity. When all was over and the record of his services made fully known it seemed incredible that one man, in his single person, could have achieved so much.

Greatness needs no bellman and Winston Churchill no introduction. He made his introduction for himself on the world's stage. For nearly sixty years of his public life the spotlights played upon him, dazzling in their intensity. But the brighter the light the deeper the shadow cast. Limelight is the worst light in which to observe the niceties of a man's make-up.

There are great men whose characters have been a challenge to the understanding of their posterity. In our own day Stanley

15

Baldwin was an enigma and Anthony Eden will doubtless provide problems for the psychoanalysts. Winston Churchill will disappoint the seekers after human mysteries. It is the weak and confused characters who provide the greater psychological interest.

When the magic forces of heredity fashioned him, they made a character that was all of a piece. With those who are less fortunate, qualities ill-combined and antagonistic produce lifelong inner tension and conflict. With Winston it was contrived that inner harmony should not be marred. The psychological pieces produced a character of simplicity made strong by the depth of its parts. A river flows deepest where its channels are narrowest. It was the concentration of his qualities in narrow compass that gave Churchill his strength. How fortunate to be blessed with such endowments: courage, honesty, magnanimity, loyalty—the classic virtues. He was able to live according to his own ideal, which found expression in the couplet he used to pay tribute to those who had won his respect:

> He nothing common did, or mean,
> Upon that memorable scene . . .

Churchill did not fall below the level of the great events in which he played his part. He emerged from fifty years in politics with his integrity intact. I do not remember that he was reproached for trickery or double-dealing, for disloyalty to a friend or for disclosing an undertaking to an opponent. To the qualities of character, the life force added a fine brain, inexhaustible energy and an iron constitution. Thus equipped, he was able to find the physical strength to sustain the activities of the supercharged engine of his mind.

In the prime of his life fatigue seemed unknown to him. A fellow M.P., newly returned in a by-election, was seated in the smoking room of the House declaring himself exhausted by his exertions. Churchill broke in upon his lamentations.

"You have no business to be tired, a young man like you," Churchill chided him. "I have never been tired in my life."

To complete his make-up Churchill was invested with a fighting spirit, unbounded confidence in himself, insatiable intellectual curiosity, an indomitable will and an outstanding capacity for the conduct of affairs.

Here was one who plainly was fashioned to make a stir in the world. But, when he took to politics it could have been foretold that no easy path lay before him. Who with ambition to succeed as politician would have chosen to handicap himself with the classic virtues? Loyalty. The cynic says that at the top there is no loyalty in politics. Honesty. Churchill, according to a friend, showed himself to be so strictly honest and truthful that he would not even tell a "dinner lie" to get out of a distasteful engagement. But honesty carried to this degree would be the ruin of lesser men in politics. Courage. It can take men into dangerous places which, in politics, the ambitious do well to avoid. Iron determination. Suppleness serves better to conform with the shifts of public feeling. Fighting spirit. That, too, can be an embarrassment. The young politician should seek the good opinion of others. Churchill earned the reputation for an infinite capacity for making enemies.

A man's character shapes his destiny. Churchill in common with lesser folk had to accept the consequences that flowed from his qualities. Viewed from the personal aspect his career in all its varied turns of fortune is seen as a drama resulting from the interplay of his qualities and the political forces of his time. Always he had a taste for drama, not so fastidiously formed that melodrama was excluded. The drama of his public life was to his liking. It was played as he would have conceived it—on the grand scale.

Life, for Winston Churchill, was an adventure, but it was not to be lightly undertaken. He was not born for the age of the common man. For him the old values persisted. Do we see here the influences of his first environment? A ducal mansion was his birthplace. He was cradled in the stately apartments of Blenheim, a place that is monumental among England's stately homes. Its creator, the architect and dramatist John Vanbrugh, was light in his wit but grandiose in his designs, so that on his death the wits gave him for epitaph the lines:

> Lie heavy on him, Earth! for he
> Laid many heavy loads on thee!

Life on the grand scale came naturally enough to a child cradled in the magnificence of Blenheim.

For the aspiring politician it does not do to set too heroic a standard for the electors. Except in time of crisis, John Doe and Mrs. Doe prefer the comfortable to the heroic. It is an advantage for the politician to share the prejudices and fears of the common man, his caprice, his bursts of envy and of spite. Churchill was built to another pattern, free from envy and rancor and uncharitableness. It was his handicap that he had no instinctive awareness of emotions he did not share. Not that he was lacking in human feeling—far from it. Remember how he rebuked a high-ranking officer for thinking in abstract, inhuman terms of the troops in his command? It was at one of the wartime conferences. A major-general made reference to soldiers as "bodies," the term in use by staff officers. Churchill chided him for what he called cold-blooded inhumanity. Soldiers were men; to call them bodies seemed as though they were freight or, what was worse, corpses.

Emotional, stirred by the thought of human suffering, Churchill was easily moved to display his feelings. During the Blitz he was often seen standing with tears fast falling, as he brooded over the losses and sufferings of the victims of the bombs.

He won the successes of a man of surpassing ability and he suffered the setbacks of an impolitic politician. I can think of no statesmen who experienced in like degree the extremes of good and evil fortune. He was little more than thirty when he was appointed Minister of the Crown, ranking high among the leaders of his party. At forty he had been sent toppling from his place. Within a couple of years he had restored himself and was back in office as the right-hand man of Lloyd George, Britain's leader in World War I. Again Fortune frowned and he found himself without a party, a place in the Government, or a seat in the House of Commons. Beginning once more at the beginning, he rose for a third time, to high Cabinet office; and challenging fortune for the third time, he paid the penalty. For ten years he was in the political wilderness, so badly placed that he was tempted to leave the uncertainties of politics for the board room and the director's recompense. It was then that the call came and he was swept onward to the highest place.

His character stood the tests to which he was exposed. He knew days of exaltation and of despair, but he schooled himself so that, meeting triumph and disaster, he could "treat those two impostors just the same." Mark how he bore himself at the time of his most dramatic reverses. In 1945 victory in Europe had been won. With her allies to East and West, Britain had emerged triumphant over Hitlerism. Then, before the echoes of exultant applause had died away, he was dismissed by the people he had led. Gratitude and admiration, we know, are no permanent emotions in politics, but no man who had served his countrymen so faithfully was ever so summarily dismissed. Harsh as was his treatment, he maintained his composure. No word of protest or reproach escaped him. The architect of victory took his place among the fallen on the political field as if it were part of the accustomed daily round. Perhaps, indeed, he drew a certain grim satisfaction from the distinction. A rebuff so stupendous was no common guerdon for the victor's brow. As a Frenchman reflected: *"Il existe des services si grands qu'ils ne peuvent se payer que par l'ingratitude."*

It was a bitter reverse, robbing him of the opportunity of taking a lead in planning the new world after the victory to which his leadership had so greatly contributed. But keenly though he felt the disappointment, he had lived through days of more intense personal anguish. There are storms that shake the stoutest oak. The reverse that sent Churchill from the Admiralty in 1915 was one that shook the oak of his manhood.

It was the height of World War I. Churchill was playing a conspicuous part. As First Lord of the Admiralty he was responsible, politically, for the direction of the fleets upon which Britain's survival depended. He had been the strategic prompter in the Cabinet of the Prime Minister. He had been the inspiration of the Dardanelles expedition, then in progress, that energetically pursued might have knocked out the Turks and turned the enemy flank in the Balkans. The most vigorously active minister of the Asquith Ministry, he conceived himself to be bearing a weight of responsibility for which, under Providence, he had been specially prepared. He was also the member of the Government team most hated by their opponents, the Tories. They had old scores to settle with him. Taking advantage of a crisis in affairs, they delivered an ultimatum to Asquith—he must dismiss Churchill from the Admiralty. So great was the pressure they brought to bear that Asquith was forced to yield to their demands.

Winston Churchill was ejected from the Admiralty. Downgraded in ministerial rank, he lost his authority to influence, as he had before, the conduct of the war. It was a devastating shock, the most shattering humiliation in all his career. Lucifer's was a greater fall, but Lucifer found his consolations—"better to rule in hell than serve in heaven." Churchill suffered the agonies of a tortured soul. Having found minor relief in painting, he soon left the scene of politics to go a'soldiering in the trenches.

The political analyst will linger here to point the moral of the fall and apportion the blame among Churchill's various short-comings as politician—his dash and rashness, his overmastering ways, the mistrust and anatgonism he aroused, his failure to take the essential precaution of making his political base secure, for at that time he had neglected the politician's home base, which is the House of Commons, in his single-minded devotion to his duties at the Admiralty. He himself put the matter differently and the lesson he drew was that it was inexpedient to attempt to direct a major military operation, the Dardanelles, from a subordinate ministerial position.

Twenty-four years passed before the black stain of that humili-ation was wiped out. It was September 1939. Churchill had dropped behind in the political race. Excluded from the succes-sive Governments, he had been unable to save the country from the consequences of national weakness. As he had foreseen and forewarned, Hitler was setting the war drums beating as he strove to make Germany dominant over the world. In this hour, on every hand, there were cries for "Winnie."

The summons came from the Prime Minister, Neville Cham-berlain. Would Churchill take office? Naturally he would. The definite offer followed—a seat in the War Cabinet and the post of First Lord of the Admiralty. Jubilantly he accepted. It was a mo-ment of supreme gratification. After his long exclusion he was to be admitted once again to the Cabinet. Having for so long been powerless to influence events, he was to take a hand in the conduct of affairs in the place that by experience of old he knew best. And beyond these things there was cause for exquisite satisfaction. The office he had forfeited in 1915 was the one to which, by public acclaim, he was now recalled. The chagrin of the past was wiped out in the magnificence of his vindication. And the stone the builders had rejected then became the pillar of national defense.

A few months later came the call to the premiership. The greatest distinction of his career was marked by the slightest celebration. That May day in the year 1940 he was too concerned with the burden of events to find time to savor the satisfaction of the fulfillment of a life's ambition and he took his appointment to the premiership in his stride, just one more incident of the twenty-four hours of history. Nor, in 1951 when he began his third term as Prime Minister, was he over-elated—by then he had been glutted by moments of success.

In the emotional highlights of his career there was an earlier occasion that stood out for the personal gratification it gave him. This was in 1924 when he was summoned by Stanley Baldwin, newly made Prime Minister, to be offered the post of Chancellor of the Exechequer in his Conservative Government. That was a day to lift his spirits by the fulfillment of the hopes of his youth. Chancellorship of the Exchequer was the job his father had thrown up, to the ruin of his career. As a young M.P. Winston Churchill had raised his father's tattered flag in the House of Commons. Now the Churchill banner was to be proudly displayed once again at the Exchequer. In the person of the son it seemed that reparation was being done to the father. Nor did this exhaust the tally. By this appointment Churchill was proving himself, posthumously, in his father's eyes. Lord Randolph had looked on his son as a mental lightweight. How much Winston would have given to have caused the parent to reverse his judgment. That was not possible, for Randy had long since joined the statesmen of the ages. But maybe his spirit, haunting the chamber in which his speeches had made his fame, could note that Winston in his turn had succeeded to the Exchequer, showing himself to be as good a man as his father. There were not many moments in his sixty years of service that gave Winston cause for greater elation.

From his wardrobe Churchill brought out the Chancellor's robe he had inherited with Randy's tattered flag. It had a distinction among political mantles. Not only Randy, but the great Gladstone himself, had worn this gown of silk. It is usual for a Chancellor, on quitting the Exechequer, to sell his robe to his successor for the sum (in those days) of £150. The garment is costly to produce and once his term of office is over a Chancellor has no use for it. Randy, however, declined to follow tradition. Goschen, a political nonentity, was nominated to the Exchequer to succeed Lord

Randolph. He might have the place but Randy was damned if he should have the uniform. Goschen had to provide for himself and Randy's robe of office passed down to his son. Not even Elijah's mantle was worn with greater pride.

Courage, physical and moral, must be ranked high among Winston Churchill's qualities. In battle or in politics he showed himself to be endowed with that virtue prized above others by men of action. No soldier, according to Napoleon, is proof against cowardice. If that be so, Churchill was wondrously successful in mastering and masking his feelings. In hand-to-hand fighting on the Indian frontier, as a lancer riding in the cavalry charge against the Dervishes across the desert sands, or in the trenches in World War I, he gave every appearance of relishing the excitement and danger. In World War II he showed the same spirit. Touring the London streets during the Blitz, he made his friends and family anxious for his safety. In this he differed from his predecessor, Lloyd George, who showed the impulse of the average man to seek the safety of the shelter when the bombs began to fall.

In politics the average man is shy of championing the unpopular cause. Not so Winston. For years he campaigned against pacifism and appeasement when the opinion in the House of Commons and in the country was set against him. When he denounced the betrayal of Czechoslovakia in the settlement at Munich his words raised a storm of dissent in the House of Commons. For a time he could not make himself heard above the clamor. He waited till the demonstration was ended and, unperturbed, completed what he had to say.

His courage stood out in the crisis of the Abdication when, to the last, he spoke up for his Sovereign who had also been his friend. Opinion was hostile and indignant when it became known that King Edward VIII proposed to make a twice-married American woman his wife and Queen. The leaders of the country, archbishops and the Church, Prime Minister and Parliament, Dominion governments, influential newspaper owners—all were against him. Men who had been proud of the privilege of the company of the popular Prince of Wales dissociated themselves from the unpopular King. Churchill stood by the Sovereign who had need of a counselor. He rose in a hostile House to state the

King's case. He conceived it to be his duty. No personal consideration could turn him from the path where his duty lay.

Having considered some aspects of the man as he was born, we must, to complete our understanding of him, inquire a little into the influences that molded him. There is a personal problem every biographer must attempt to solve—he must explain the processes of development that bridge the gap between birth and the achievements of maturity. How, in the case of Winston Churchill, did it come about that the child born in 1874 was in a position, in 1914, to have charge of the British Navy and, in 1940, to be entrusted with the leadership of the British nation? As the infant lay in his cradle in the stately halls of Blenheim, a mathematician might have calculated the odds against any baby of that year's vintage reaching any one particular appointment were not less than a quarter of a million to one. How was it that this long shot came off and the Blenheim baby reached 10 Downing Street? Churchill himself would have been in no wise baffled by the problem, but would have explained that it was his destiny brought about by the workings of a beneficent Providence.

He was endowed with an unfaltering belief in his own mission and drew support from the conviction that he was the instrument of a higher purpose. He shared this faith with others charged with the responsibility for great affairs. Haig, Commander in Chief in France in World War I, was sustained by the simple assurance that he directed his armies under divine guidance—"It is God's battle and I am not dismayed by the numbers of the enemy." Gladstone, greatest of Liberal Prime Ministers, drew comfort from a vivid sense of continued relation with the unseen world— "I do believe that the Almighty has employed me for His purposes in a manner larger and more special than before and has strengthened and led me accordingly." They are words that imply personal protection such as was given to their protégés by Homer's goddesses.

Winston Churchill expressed the matter differently as might be expected from one whose life was not governed by Gladstone's all-pervading religious sense; but though otherwise expressed, the basic idea was the same. Churchill conceived himself to have been walking with destiny—"I had the sense of being used, however unworthy, in some appointed plan." That was a confession during his premiership. Nearly thirty years before, when he was first appointed to take charge of the Admiralty, he had been inspired to take down his Bible and open it at random as a man seeking divine pronouncement on his affairs. His eyes lighted on the passage in Deuteronomy that includes the verse "Understand therefore this day, that the Lord thy God is He which goeth ever before thee: as a consuming fire He shall destroy them, and He shall bring them down before thy face; so shalt thou drive them out, and destroy them quickly, as the Lord hath said unto thee." He might pardonably conclude that he had received a message of reassurance. At no time would Churchill have classed himself with the devout, or with those men moved strongly by religious feeling. He took his religion quietly—the soldier's uncomplicated faith, based on a few simple facts. Nothing moved him so much as the old, familiar hymns that children learn at their mother's knee.

Accept that the Churchill premiership is to be attributed to the divinity that shapes men's ends, and it is still necessary to explore the means by which the designs of Providence were accomplished. To become Prime Minister, Churchill had necessarily to turn politician. How was that determined? There was no compelling reason. True, his father had been brilliant in politics, but Randy did not consider his first-born to have brains enough to be other than a soldier. Winston was sent to learn the soldier's trade, one pre-eminently suitable for a man of action. Had he remained in the Army he would have won fame with Britain's death-or-glory generals, but not one to be long confined by the cramping routine of regimental life, he quitted the Army.

A man so versatile might have won distinction in one of several walks of life. In the law he would have made a compelling advocate though not, I think, a particularly judicial judge. On the stage he would have shone in drama and melodrama. As an amateur of the brush he revealed talent that would have made his reputation as a professional artist. Not these avocations, but journalism, was his second choice after soldiering.

Beginning as war correspondent he had a spectacular career, combining the roles of reporter and combatant. Later he gained the distinction of being the only British Minister of the Crown to occupy at the same time the editor's chair of a national newspaper. It was a short-lived editorship, lasting no longer than the ten-day emergency of the General Strike in 1926 when he ran the government organ, *The British Gazette.*

He had the qualities that make the journalist—insatiable curiosity, grasp of a situation, an eye for the human detail and an ear for the telling phrase. He could see copy in any situation. Look, for instance, at the use he made of the accident he suffered while visiting New York in 1932. Knocked down by a passing car in the street, his injuries were grave. Fifteen bones were broken, there was internal hemorrhage and for two days life itself was in danger. He was, as he said, "very tough and very lucky," and so survived. Before he had left his sickbed he had dictated a graphic and detailed record of his impressions, complete with a mathematical estimate of the forces involved. He wrote:

> There was one moment—I cannot measure it in time—of a world aglare, of a man aghast. I certainly thought quickly enough to achieve the idea *"I am going to be run down and probably killed."* Then came the blow. I felt it on my forehead and across the thighs. But besides the blow there was an impact, a shock, a concussion indescribably violent. It blotted out everything except thought.
>
> A friend of mine of mathematical predilections has been kind enough to calculate the stresses involved in the collision. The car weighed some 2,400 pounds. With my evening coat on I could not have weighed much less than 200 pounds. Taking the rate of the car at thirty-five miles an hour—I think a moderate estimate—I had actually to absorb in my body 6,000 foot-pounds. It was the equivalent of falling thirty feet on to a pavement. The energy absorbed, *though not, of course, the application of destructive force,* was the equivalent of stopping ten pounds of buckshot dropped 600 feet, or two charges of buckshot at point-blank range.
>
> I do not understand why I was not broken like an egg-shell or squashed like a gooseberry. I have seen that the poor policeman who was killed on the Oxford road was hit by a vehicle traveling at very much the same speed, was completely shattered. I certainly must be very tough or very lucky, or both.

Few even among the professionals would have chosen to turn to account an experience involving such grievous personal suffering.

As Prime Minister he proved himself, once again, to be outstanding as a war correspondent. Self-appointed reporter extraordinary to the House of Commons, he delivered the war speeches that, battle by battle, traced the course of hostilities. His sources of information were exceptional. He exploited them with brilliance. Ranging the battle-fields himself, he gained at first hand the color that brings scenes to life, and he had the journalist's knack of seizing on the vivid detail in reports received at second hand. Who, for instance, could forget in his account of the Battle of Libya, his reference to the young officer who reported that he had reached the second "B" in "Buq Buq"? In the entire range of Parliamentary oratory there is no parallel to Winston's war reports, nor will you find any series of speeches attaining the same pitch of dramatic interest.

As author no less than journalist he won his place in the front rank, and had he so chosen he might, turning historian, have become the Macaulay of the twentieth century. As it was he added new luster to the literary traditions of Britain's Prime Ministers— Gladstone, Beaconsfield, Russell, Rosebery, Balfour, Baldwin. Which of them surpassed him as master of language? Beaconsfield, the novelist, alone compared with him in popular and lasting interest. In *The World Crisis* Winston produced one of the finest contemporary records of war.* In *The Second World War,* he wrote in incomparable fashion the history he had helped to make. His biography of his father, Lord Randolph, was one of the outstanding lives written of a father by a son. His *Marlborough* was a contribution to history as well as a vindication of the great ancestral figure, genius among British military commanders.

Forcefulness, lucidity and majesty, the characteristics of his style, were founded on Gibbon and Macaulay. In book or speech the style was the same—much of the books can be delivered as speeches and the speeches will be read in books. He wrote as he spoke and as he lived, in the heroic manner.

* A great admirer of *The World Crisis* was the late King George V, who would pause in his reading of the account of the Battle of Jutland to work out the courses of the ships mentioned in the text. The King's librarian, Mr. Owen Morshead, recorded that of *Marlborough* His Majesty remarked: "There's Winston's life of his ancestor—no doubt everything he did was right! A bit too highbrow for me I expect, but I shall take it down to Sandringham to have a try; I dare say I shan't get far. Beautiful writer he is and a wonderful good fellow, too, into the bargain."

Always he found self-expression in words to be a necessity. Physical and mental impressions acting on the sensitive instrument of his brain released forces that set words in motion. Until they had discharged themselves in the orderly sequence of writing, peace and harmony were not restored within him.

Returning to my question, I ask again: Why was it, with so many alternative paths to success and fame open before him, that Winston Churchill should have chosen the uncertainties and disappointments of a politician's career? With no fortune to support him he had his living to earn and the financial rewards of politics are inconsiderable. When he was first returned, M.P.s were still unpaid. Nor had he more than a superficial knowledge of political affairs. Roving the outskirts of the Empire in search of the adventure of battle, he knew next to nothing about the topics of the hour that were rousing the electors of Wigan and Pudsey. Yet, without hesitation, he turned to politics.

He was, I conclude, impelled toward the House of Commons by the inner force that moves strong men to the fulfillment of their destinies. He was born with the urge to rule. Only through politics could the purpose of his life be realized. And so, twenty-five years of life gone by, he took the essential step that was to bring the baby cradled in Blenheim to 10 Downing Street.

He got off to a characteristic start. The spotlight shone on him then as it continued to shine on him down the years. He was the national hero of the moment, the young fellow who had got the better of the Boers. His brilliance was soon conceded—and his lack of judgment. One of the first to sum it up was William Harcourt, veteran Liberal leader. There was, Harcourt conceded, a great deal of force in Churchill's oratory, but, he added "The want of judgment in the fellow is despairing." The Tory leader, Arthur Balfour, also found him wanting—"I thought he was a young man of promise, but it appears he is a man of promises."

Lack of political judgment was to be the complaint that ran like a refrain through the pattern of the fifty years. It was echoed when he had reached the top and, victory in Europe achieved, he launched his appeal to the people in the 1945 general election. To discredit the Socialist leaders, lately his colleagues in the wartime Coalition Government, he suggested that if returned to power they would seek to establish in Britain a government on the Gestapo model. This was designed to make the electors' flesh creep. It was not likely to have affected the most timid minds. Mild-mannered Clement Attlee simply could not be pictured in the sinister role of a Gestapo chief. The speech lost Churchill and his party many votes. Lack of judgment, muttered the critics as they had said previously on innumerable occasions. Winston Churchill could sum up a military situation, and his judgment on foreign affairs was one of the soundest—but on politics he was fallible.

In the choice of his family Churchill showed excellent judgment. He came of a line of dukes that began with the celebrated military commander John Churchill, created Duke of Marlborough for his victories over the French in the reign of Queen Anne. Dukes were still dukes and personages when Winston was born, and there were advantages in the relationship. The grandson of a duke, he had his established place (if he chose to take it) in what was still known as the governing class. What today might be thought a handicap was then an indubitable asset. A fellow pushing his way in from the outside was looked on with suspicion. He might be an adventurer! Benjamin Disraeli, with no family background, was classed as one. It was years before Disraeli was accepted and became, as "Dizzy," the pillar of Toryism, venerable founder of the Primrose League, highly favored among Queen Victoria's Prime Ministers. Churchill was to be called ambitious, but at least he escaped the taunt of "adventurer."

Of the parents who gave him to the world, the father, Lord Randolph, had the greater influence upon him and was the inspiration of his career. Randy was a star (first magnitude) in the firmament of Victorian politics. Winston resolved to scintillate. Randy was a speaker of genius. Winston aspired to win the orator's crown, although he suffered the impediment of a stutter that took him years to overcome. Randy was wayward and erratic, and here, too, Winston followed the parental model.

His mother, the American-born beauty, fascinated him in her loveliness—"She shone for me like a star." Descended through her from several generations of American forebears, he must be credited with the possession of American characteristics, but it is not easy to identify them. It might be suggested that the union in him of the New World and the Old, produced a rejuvenation of the old, effete stock of the dukes of Marlborough and that Winston Churchill acquired his energy, even his brilliance, through his American mother. The supposition falls before the personality of his father. Lord Randolph was as striking a figure as his son, was moved by the same dash, displayed the same recklessness of spirit, had a greater astuteness as politician and, according to older Parliamentarians, surpassed the son in his nimbleness of mind.

Winston's American grandfather was one who gave consideration to the effect on the boy of the parental strains. He brought to bear the interest of a horse breeder and through a friend he received the verdict given in appropriate terms: "Interesting breeding; stamina goes through the dam, pace through the sire." It may be so.

Occasionally I have speculated further about this mixing of American and Briton. What, for instance, would have been the consequences had the parental arrangements been $b + a$ instead of $a + b$? He stated the proposition himself in his introductory remarks to Congress: "If my father had been American and my mother British instead of the other way round I might have got here on my own." It is a thought that opens up vistas of speculation. They are not to be explored by one like myself, imperfectly informed about the American political scene, but I should be ready to hazard the guess that as a United States citizen he would not have reached the foremost place. As an Englishman it required forty years of politics and a national emergency to make him Prime Minister, and without the urgency of the emergency he would never have reached Downing Street. In the United States the White House was already occupied when the emergency arose; and in the race for the Presidential stakes I cannot conceive that Winston Churchill could possibly have taken the lead over Franklin Roosevelt, who, in the skill and craft of politics, was incomparably his superior. In Britain, Churchill escaped the handicaps that befall the unsuccessful politician in the United States. His choice of Parliamentary constituency was not limited to the county of his birth, nor did he suffer any restriction on his candidatures. Defeated at Leicester in 1923, he was free to stand for the City of Westminster in 1924 and, failing there, for Epping a few months later. In the United States his political reverses would have involved him in heavier disabilities.

Among the influences that shaped him, I should not assign high place to his school. Like half-a-dozen Prime Ministers, including Stanley Baldwin, he was sent to Harrow, but I cannot find that his speeches contain many references to "the place on the Hill" until, during the war, he began to attend the Speech Day celebrations and joined in singing the school songs. A verse was added to "Forty Years On," the Harrow song, to mark the school's association with her most celebrated son.

His years in the Army were powerful in their effect, giving him a conception of Britain's role in the world that was the source of his imperialism, one of the fundamentals of his political faith. He served in India, the India that inspired the tales of Rudyard Kipling, the India of the heyday of the British Raj. The band of British officials and officers who ran the country could be regarded as the agents of a benevolent despotism. Churchill's imagination was fired. Others might come to see India's subject races rightly struggling to be free. His vision was of an enlightened imperialism bringing to backward peoples the boon of British justice and ordered government.

Active service on the North-West frontier and in the Sudan gave added force to the impressions formed by young Churchill the subaltern. He was never a jingo. When the war in South Africa was over he pleaded and worked for a generous settlement with the Boers. But his faith had been formed in the might, majesty, dominion and power of the British Empire as a world force making for justice and freedom. In his later years there might be difficulties over the application of the imperial principle in a changing world. He remained unaffected. With the English prophet he could say: "Ten thousand difficulties do not make one doubt." His faith in the beneficent results of British imperialism remained undiminished. The Victorians celebrated their last magnificent festival on the occasion of the old Queen's Diamond Jubilee (1897). It marked the peak of British imperialism, which passed thereafter into its slow decline. Others might suffer their imperial faith to fade. Not so Churchill. He carried the ideas of the Diamond Jubilee into the public life of the succeeding sixty years. Here was the inspiration of his angered, scornful protest that he had not become Prime Minister to preside over the liquidation of the British Empire.

He was the child of the Liberalism no less than the imperialism of the Victorians. He received the Liberal tradition sitting in Cabinet with the men in whom liberalism was seen in its final and most brilliant blossoming. The Cabinet served him for his university, his fellow ministers were his tutors. Never was there such a galaxy of political professors. The last Cabinet provided by the Liberal Party, it was the most distinguished intellectually. At its head was Herbert Henry Asquith, the just man in politics, by consent the greatest parliamentarian of the time. Augustine Birrell imparted wit to politics; John Morley, philosophy. Haldane excelled Asquith in sheer brain power; Edward Grey, the Foreign Secretary, in character. To sit in council with these minds was a *liberal* and a *Liberal* education. Winston expanded under their urbane humanity and learned from them to uphold the principles of which they were the repositories, the very ark and covenant of liberalism and liberty.

Imperialist and democrat, he combined beliefs that can easily become opposed in conflict. He maintained them in harmony and equipoise. He had been soundly indoctrinated by his ministerial tutors in democratic Liberalism. With the imperious tendencies of his nature, he might easily have been induced during his premiership to turn dictator as a means of fighting the dictators. There were times in the war when the niggling critics angered him by their factious opposition. Once or twice he was given sufficient provocation to tempt him into disposing of the Parliamentary mosquitoes. You could imagine him, the Cromwell of a later day, striding across Whitehall to the House of Commons to order the removal of the mace, that bauble, from the table, and to close the place of wrangling. But his task was to defeat the dictators, not to imitate them and he never wavered in his profound respect for the institutions of Parliamentary democracy. He had been nursed by the Mother of Parliaments. For the cause of democracy it was as well.

Some men enter politics to serve a cause. Churchill gave his powerful support to many causes, but it was not to serve a cause that he became a politician. Other men enlist to advance a party. Churchill served in turn the opposing parties, Conservative and Liberal, engaging with zest in the party fight on either side, but as I have several times suggested, his qualities were not those that produce the party politician. Your good party man accepts a program or a creed. Apart from a few fundamentals concerned in the main with his country's greatness, Churchill was fluid in his opinions. Within ten years after entering the House of Commons, he had boxed the political compass, passing from Conservative to Liberal, from Radical to Liberal Imperialist. In twenty-five years his pendulum had swung back and he was folded once again with the Conservatives. Political parties prefer rigidity in their chiefs.

Churchill was not so greatly concerned with parties or causes. His urgent desire was to get his hands on the levers of the machinery of government. It was then that his capacity was demonstrated. No more able administrator took charge of a government department. In his early years there seemed to be no exhaustion point for his energy, physical and mental. In the opening months of World War I, his vigor and versatility were superbly displayed. He was then First Lord of the Admiralty, an office that carries in time of war as great a responsibility as any in the government. Yet, in addition to his departmental duties, he undertook the air defense of London, inspired the invention of the tank, promoted the development of the bomb and, in a week-end visit to the Continent, took charge of the defenses of Antwerp. Later, it was his drive and direction that produced order out of chaos in the newly established Ministry of Munitions, "that jungle" as he called it.

At last, in World War II, his destiny was fulfilled and the child of Blenheim took the Prime Minister's chair at Number Ten. The entire machinery of government awaited his direction. He took over with the ease and assurance of a master. His drive made itself felt through all the departments of state. In never ceasing flow his directives flowed outward, chiding, exhorting, ordering, inspiring. No detail was too small to escape his attention. A memorandum concerned with a major problem in Allied strategy would be followed by orders to provide sugar for beehives, flowers for housewives, and rations for the back-yard hen. For sheer massiveness in capacity Churchill was incomparable. My second volume is the record of his indefatigable endeavors, of his skill in handling relations with the United States, of his prescience in dealing with the Russians. Plaguing the professionals of the services by his interventions in military matters, he was scarcely less prolific in strategic suggestions than the entire Chiefs of Staff.

When he had advanced to supreme power, the qualities that had been his weakness became his strength. The fumblings and uncertainties of the past dropped away. All the parts of the man locked together to produce the leader of the people at war. Force of character was matched with capacity. It was this that gave him his pre-eminence among the leaders of Britain.

Winston Churchill has been weighed in the balance with Lloyd George—the comparison is inevitable. In the days when his fame shone brighter than it does now, Lloyd George was the "man who won the war," World War I against the Kaiser's Germany. Perhaps, as an inspiration to the British people, he did. Of Churchill in World War II they say that he was the architect of victory, and he was little less. Each man in his turn rendered service that none other could have performed and without which victory might not have been achieved. In leadership their contributions were as different as their characters. In a broad sense you might say that Lloyd George was an inspiring, Churchill a dominating influence. Churchill was the more solid, Lloyd George the more mercurial. Lloyd George knew how to bring the best out of other men. Churchill was prepared to direct them into the best way of doing things or, if so permitted, undertake the thing himself. He had a knowledge of military affairs not possessed by Lloyd George, who was always the civilian. Churchill, ranking himself as chief of staff with the chiefs of staff, intervened over strategy and tactics to a degree Lloyd George would never have attempted—he would not have been rash enough to risk his reputation.

The qualities of the two men showed in their oratory. The impassioned Celt had greater fire as a speaker. His words could lift his hearers to the summits of his own Welsh hills. To the note of political passion he could add the fervor of the prophet. Reason rather than passion gave Churchill his hold over the minds of men. The sustained logic of the great war speeches brought conviction by the force of their argument. Lacking the lighter and more varied tones of the orator from Wales, Churchill excelled him in sustained power, in the marshaling of facts, in command of language, and in matchless phrase.

Lloyd George, without doubt, was the shrewder politician. He was more successful in handling men, Churchill of greater capacity in coping with affairs. No minister equaled Lloyd George in wooing others to his way and converting opponents into supporters. "He could charm the bark off a tree," pronounced Margot Asquith and her judgment of the man who supplanted her husband as Premier may be accepted. In the business of Cabinet and of committees, through which so much public work has to be done, Lloyd George was supremely effective. He could play upon others as a Welsh harpist upon his strings. He was quick to obtain the opinions and suggestions of other men and adapt them to his own uses. Churchill's method was quite different. In committee he sought not plans from other minds but support for his own. Lloyd George seemed to be persuasive. Churchill could not disguise that he was masterful. Where Lloyd George charmed, Winston Churchill imposed himself.

The magic of the charmer, for a time irresistible, comes at length to be suspect. The point was reached where any man who had to negotiate with him viewed Lloyd George with suspicion. J. H. Thomas, the Labour leader who met him many times, said that you dared not "turn your head to blow your nose or L.G. would trick you."

Churchill in all his dealings inspired the trust of other men, of President Roosevelt, even of the mistrustful Joseph Stalin. Churchill might be vexatious in pressing his opinions, but once his word was given there was no doubting its fulfillment. With his colleagues there were bonds of loyalty not common in politics. L.G. retained the admiration of his fellow ministers while they remained colleagues, but when he dismissed them the partings were marked by mutual and unedifying disparagement. His shafts were wounding as when he pronounced Neville Chamberlain fit to be no more than Lord Mayor of a provincial city—"in a lean year." I do not remember Churchill being concerned in any such quarrel. Such was his loyalty that he was said to promote ministerial failures rather than dismiss them.

Which of these two was the greater man? History will make her choice. We who lived with them may give our verdict, which according to their fashion the historians will ignore. Lloyd George and Winston Churchill were magnificent in their service. But, if a man were to set an example for his son to follow, it would be Churchill not Lloyd George who would serve as the pattern for most to follow. In the alloy of Lloyd George's nature there were flaws. Churchill was seen as a man possessed of the Roman qualities—massive, serene, lofty in spirit.

Even the burdens of a world war seemed not to exhaust Churchill's capacity for leadership. Imagination roving free, I see him as one of the antique Romans whose qualities he shared. In my mind's eye I invest him with the robes of Caesar. I can imagine him conducting the Gallic Wars with dash and spirit, flinging his legions across the Rhine. Certainly I can hear him in his tent, fighting for the day being done, dictating the opening lines of his commentaries—*Gallia est omnia divisa in partes tres.*

I have my doubts whether the memoirs of Churchillius would have conformed with the model of Caesar's chaste and restrained prose. I have no difficulty in following Churchillius across the Rubicon—it was a process with which Winston grew to be reasonably familiar—lording it in Rome, gaining before the Senate the orator's triumphs to add to the laurels won in battle. Thereafter, perhaps, history might have been improved upon, for Churchillius would have been magnanimous in his dictatorship, conducting affairs so far as was permitted him according to the best traditions of the House of Commons. Still, at the last, with the Ides of March, Churchillius would have suffered the fate of Caesar, for jealousy is persistent through the ages and Brutus is always waiting to add his stab to those of the lesser men whose envy greatness has aroused. The orator would come forth to mourn:

> But yesterday the word of Caesar might
> Have stood against the world; now lies he there,

There is need to add the epitaph of antique prose:

> His vertues and happiness being his tutors, he got about him a world of goodwills of certain valiant captains and soldiers together, whom he ordered so well, that he made them ready to perform what he commanded, and having such an unmatchable carriage towards them, he made them invincible with him: and in the middest of his continual troubles he did read, meditate, spake, wrote and left behind him the goodliest book that a martial man, and one that entertaineth the muses, can devise to take in his hands. His orations were a long time held in great reputation. . . . His magnanimity weighed more than any other vertue they could note in him.

Caesar and Churchill—the likeness in their qualities is no idle imagining. My fancy ends with the verdict of Plutarch: "Each is in manner the flower and epitome of a great nation." The lives of the great are an inspiration to their posterity. Winston Churchill will remain an inspiration while the English people survive to continue the fight in freedom's cause. There was an Elizabethan worthy who pledged himself to quit the port o' Heaven if England in her peril required his aid. Drake's drum, the Nelson touch, the Churchill spirit. Even as he lived, Winston Churchill took his place among the immortals of our history. We who lived with him through the anxious days were proud to render him our homage and acclaim him one of the Freemen of England.

The Winston Churchill story opened in what are already seen as the far-off times of the great-grandfathers of the present generation—indeed of the great-great-grandmother of England's present Queen. He was born—it is verging on the incredible—a Mid-Victorian, into a different society, and a vaster world, which still retained a little of the mystery of the unknown. The Poles had not been reached, much of Central Africa was unexplored. The world seemed to be a larger place before its compass had been reduced by the airplane, one of the inventions that, within the term of his years, gave the new look to civilization. When he was a child, the railway was the fastest and the horse the most general means of locomotion. There were no motor cars, no airplanes, no radio sets, no atom bombs. Electricity was not available for public lighting, neither electric train nor motor bus for public transport, nor the telephone for public communication.

In the villages and countryside of England the pattern of life had undergone no radical change since the times of the Stuart Kings. Had Churchill's great ancestor, the Duke of Marlborough, returned to his home in Oxfordshire, he would have had no difficulty in adjusting himself to new Victorian ways, once he was accustomed to the plaguey innovations in male attire. The ancestral homes of England were as uncomfortable as the ancestral families had left them. Water men in green baize aprons walked stately corridors with enormous cans yoked to their shoulders to supply water to tapless apartments. Lamp men spent their days tending the wicks of the paraffin lamps and candles needed to break the gloom of apartments once the sun had set. The stately halls were still the homes and not the mere showplaces of England, with house steward, groom of the chambers, butler, under-butler, footmen, in their liveries, plush-breeched, silk-stockinged and powdered, elegant but still engaged in useful services. Life, for the dwellers in the halls, was spacious and untroubled in the days before the motor coaches and the tourists came to Penshurst, to Longleat or to Wilton. And, by contrast, life pressed oppressively on the poor. The Duke of Marlborough could have adjusted himself easily enough to nineteenth-century Blenheim. But, were the hands of the clock to be reversed, no self-respecting trade unionist of today would accept for an hour the wages and conditions of his mid-Victorian predecessors.

How poor the poor could be, and how powerless, with farm hands drawing no more, in bad times, than ten shillings a week and the right to vote in the country's affairs often denied them. In the twenties they debated whether Labour was fit to govern. The mid-Victorians were scarcely prepared to concede that labor was fit to vote. The Labour (or Socialist) Party was beginning its political life. Churchill and the Labour Party were cradled together, for 1874, his birth year, saw the return to the House of Commons of the first two working men, officials of the Miners' Union. He had been several years an M.P. before the Parliamentary Labour Party began its existence with the 1906 general election.

Winston's long career saw the passing of the old order and the emergence of Labour as one of the dominating influences in the country. When he entered public life, the political struggle was waged, as it had been for centuries, between the older parties, as the lines of Gilbert remind us with a flavor that is already of Victorian antiquity

> . . . nature always does contrive
> That every boy and every gal,
> That's born into the world alive,
> Is either a little Liberal,
> Or else a little Conservative!

Liberals and Conservatives (Tories) were the ins and outs at Westminster. The statesmen who held the stage joined the majority many years ago. They are no more to most people than names in the history book, but in their day they were powerful and exciting figures. Leaders of the opposing parties in the fury of the tournament, they were men with whom young Churchill was to cross swords and with whom, by the time he had fought a couple of elections, he was to take his place on level terms. The great Gladstone had not long passed from the scene, a parliamentary patriarch. The Gladstone mantle had been draped at first on the inadequate and unhappy figure of Lord Rosebery and then on Campbell-Bannerman, the pawky Scot, who first gave Churchill ministerial office. Herbert Henry Asquith (Lord Oxford) was the up and coming man among the Liberals, and an eloquent Welsh solicitor, Lloyd George, was making his name in the radical (and pacifist) wing of liberalism.

The Tory chieftain was Lord Salisbury, head of the house of Cecil, whose record of service to the state eclipses that of the Churchills. The Cecils had been making the throne safe for Queen Elizabeth I, last of the Tudors, a hundred years and more before the Duke of Marlborough made the name of Churchill celebrated in the reign of Queen Anne, last of the Stuarts. Salisbury was one of the veterans and his place as Premier was taken by his nephew Arthur Balfour, who brought into the House the elegant detachment of the philosopher. The most vigorous figure in politics was the Birmingham businessman, Joseph Chamberlain. Old Joe had been a Liberal and republican but joining the Tories he devoted his last years to championing the cause of Empire, advocating tariffs to keep out foreign imports, with preferences to encourage Empire products.

The party fight was much the same then as now, but the participants raised different flags and different cries. The rights and wrongs of Ireland was the principal matter to engage the attention of young Mr. Churchill and the House of Commons. For years past, British politics had been bedeviled by the Irish Party, struggling to free their country from the Anglo-Saxon yoke, for Ireland was one of the four constituents of the United Kingdom. The Liberals supported, the Tories opposed Home Rule for Ireland, and Churchill was to be hotly engaged in a struggle that came to threaten civil war, so furious were the contestants in their folly. In the final stage, as I relate, he was one of the leading negotiators of the settlement that gave independence to Eire.

In his first Parliament young Churchill was also instructed in the advantages and drawbacks of tariffs. It is a problem debated afresh by each Parliamentary generation, without conclusive decision being reached. He numbered himself with the Free-Traders but later, with the changes brought by the years, it was seen that he was no bigot in his economic faith.

His political career coincided with the introduction of the successive measures of social reform that resulted in the establishment of the Welfare State. He was one of the pioneers and he initiated the final steps. When he was born the Welfare State was scarcely an idealist's dream. The free-for-all scramble to live was unrelieved in its harsher effects save for voluntary charity, with the workhouse as the last hope and refuge for the destitute. Compulsory elementary education had not even begun in 1874. There was no state insurance to provide aid for the sick and the workless, no state medical service, no pensions for the aged. There was poverty and destitution. At the other end of the social scale, the more fortunate were free to enjoy their possessions and pass them on to their heirs. Income tax was no more than eightpence on the pound (about three per cent), supertax had not been invented. Not until the budget of 1894 were inheritance taxes imposed on a modest scale.

In the fifty years that followed, Britain suffered a social revolution in which the extremes of wealth and destitution were removed. Churchill played his part in the changes. As President of the Board of Trade he set up the first labor exchanges. He gave the weight of his support to the launching of the scheme of state insurance for sickness and unemployment. Thirty years or so later he, as Prime Minister, set going the plans that, when the war was won, brought the Welfare State into being. During his premiership taxes were increased to the point that rendered it impossible for great fortunes to be accumulated on the former scale, while death duties entailed the breakup of estates that still survived.

Churchill the progressive was his father's son, for Lord Randolph was a social reformer ahead of his party, exponent of a brand of conservatism to appeal to the working man, but there were Tory elements in the Churchill creed. In the twenties the great question agitating the country arose from the emergence of the new party in the state. Was Labour fit to govern? The Tories declared emphatically: No. And Winston devoted himself to the formation of a political front against Socialism. The Socialists were not to be denied. They ousted the Liberals from their old position among the ins and outs of politics. Fit or not, Labour provided the country with its government.

In the press of great events Winston the politician tends to be forgotten in the figure of Churchill the War Minister. The twenties and the thirties were the years of his political failure. In the seventeen years between the fall of the Lloyd George Coalition in 1922 and the opening of the war in 1939, he served as Minister of the Crown for less than five years, although in that period the Conservatives held office for fourteen. It was in those years that the handicaps of character and the limitations of Winston the politician were made apparent. After their exertions in World War I, the people wished to live in untroubled comfort. The easy-going Baldwin was their man, and neither he nor the electors wished for tranquility to be broken by the disturbing force of a Churchill. Churchill lost touch with his party. His Toryism grew to be somewhat dated. His political decline set in with his term as Chancellor of the Exchequer in the Baldwin Government of 1924. He held the office that is supposed to carry with it the right of succession to the premiership, but he lost ground in the political race. Lesser men moved up, and by the time the Government fell in 1929 Churchill was no longer looked upon as Baldwin's heir-at-politics.

Thereafter, through the thirties, he played a lone hand. You may see him in his strength and weakness as he opposed two cardinal features of Conservative policy. First there were the India reforms. He fulminated against them in a series of speeches, somber, splendid and unavailing. He spoke against the stream of current opinion, powerless to check the process that before many years had gone by was to end in the partition of India into two states, sovereign and independent.

Still more somber and splendid, in his oratory Winston sought to rouse Government and people to a sense of their peril as Hitler set Germany on the road to war. For a long time his was a solitary voice in the wilderness, as he again opposed the flowing tide of opinion. Again he was powerless to change the course of events, although when the emergency of war came, his speeches were seen to have produced their effect in preparing the people for the efforts needed of them. In his campaign against disarmament and appeasement Winston Churchill deployed all his forces. The might and majesty of his oratory was not more superbly displayed even in time of war, but he had to acknowledge the failure of a mission. It was Britain's failure, too.

Ending my first volume at this point, I leave for the second the tale of how the British people rose from the errors of their past to achieve victory under Winston Churchill's guidance and inspiration.

BOOK ONE

FIGHTING THE LITTLE WARS

Plays, in the many games of life, that one
Where what he most doth value must be won:
Whom neither shape of danger can dismay,
Nor thought of tender happiness betray;
Who, not content that former worth stand fast,
Looks forward, persevering to the last,
From well to better, daily self-surpast;
Who, whether praise of him must walk the earth
For ever, and to noble deeds give birth,
Or he must go to dust without his fame
And leave a dead unprofitable name,
Finds comfort in himself and in his cause;
And, while the mortal mist is gathering, draws
His breath in confidence of Heaven's applause;
This is the happy warrior.

—WILLIAM WORDSWORTH

CHAPTER ONE

DESCENDANT OF DUKES

1874–1894

W INSTON CHURCHILL, three times Prime Minister of England,
was born at Blenheim Palace, the Churchill family home
which lies in the heart of England, eight miles from the city of
Oxford. It was a fitting birthplace for one who was to make English history, with traditions going back long before the Churchills
came.

Here, in ancient times, stood the palace of Woodstock, with the
bower built for Fair Rosamond by King Henry II. It gave the
name to one of Sir Walter Scott's romances of which Fair Rosamond's well was a reminder long after the mediaeval palace had
crumbled into ruins. A new tradition began when the place was
granted by Queen Anne to her illustrious commander, John
Churchill, Duke of Marlborough, to be the house of his heirs for
ever. Parliament added a sum of just under a half-million pounds
for the building of the grandiose mansion that stands amid a
park thirteen miles round.

Here down the generations, seven dukes passed their lives with
varying degrees of credit to themselves and service to the state.
Here Lord Randolph, son of the seventh Duke brought his bride,
the American beauty, to make her home with her mother-in-law.
And here Lord Randolph's heir was born.

He was impetuous at birth, impatient to begin the business of living, by the calendar a seven-and-a-half-month child. His mother was taken unawares. There was a small party that evening at which Lady Randolph was dancing, when she found it necessary to withdraw. Her room was many stately apartments and corridors distant and she had no time to reach it. The baby was born in a small cloak room on the ground floor amid the coats and cloaks of the women dancers.

"Most unconventional," remarked the Duchess, which we, with after knowledge would change to "most characteristic," for this was the arrival of one who would disdain the common path and would never wait upon time. So to the world of fashion *The Times* of London made the announcement: "On the 30th of November at Blenheim Palace, the Lady Randolph Churchill, of a son." The bells rang out a peal from Woodstock Church and there was rejoicing that the line of Marlborough was provided for to the third generation. The child received the names of Winston Leonard Spencer-Churchill each of which, together with the hyphen, told of his ancestral past.

Consider first the "Churchill," the name that will ring down the corridors of the ages. They were a West-of-England family, associated with the village in East Somerset that lies at the foot of the Mendip hills. Sir Winston Churchill was first introduced to history in the person of a Dorset lawyer who fought for King Charles in the civil wars and was knighted for his services. This poor Cavalier placed posterity in his debt by fathering two children—a daughter Arabella and a son, John. The boy was to rise to a dukedom, but let not the daughter be forgotten. The Churchills, like several other ducal houses, owed their initial fortunes to a woman's fall. Arabella, a maid-of-honor in the Court of Charles II, was no beauty—a tall, pale-faced creature, we are told, nothing but skin and bone. She was out riding one day, and being of an indolent nature, was sitting her horse so ill that the King's brother, the Duke of York, turned his horse beside hers to chide her for her bad seat. Then came the fall, deliciously described for us by old Grammont.

Her countenance had almost completed the Duke's disgust when her horse set off in a gallop whereat she lost her seat, screamed out and fell. A fall in so quick a pace must have been violent; and yet it proved favourable to her in every respect; for, without receiving any hurt, she gave the lie to all unfavourable suppositions that had been formed of her person, in judging from her face. The Duke alighted in order to help her; she was so greatly stunned, that her thoughts were otherwise employed than about decency on the present occasion; and those who first crowded around her found her in rather a negligent posture: they could hardly believe that limbs of such exquisite beauty could belong to Miss Churchill's face. After this accident, it was remarked that the Duke's tenderness and affection for her increased every day; and towards the end of the winter, it appeared that she tyrannised not over his passions, nor made him languish with impatience.

Through the Duke of York's favor, by whom she bore three children (one of them the Duke of Berwick), her brother John was given his chance. Rising in the royal service, he gained under Queen Anne the victories over the French of Blenheim, Ramillies, Oudenarde and Malplaquet, made his fame as a military genius of the age, and, by the indulgence of his sovereign and parliament, established himself with the title of Duke in the mansion in the parish of Woodstock that commemorates the name of the first of his famous victories. He had brains and his wife, the celebrated Sarah, had character, being for years the dominating force over the Queen whom her husband served at the wars.

Much has been written of late about the ancestral link between the eighteenth-century soldier and the twentieth-century statesman. I would wager that a stronger hereditary influence was that of Duchess Sarah, a woman of charm and high spirits, determined, imperious, domineering. John and Sarah were the great-great-great-great-great-great-great-great-grandparents of Sir Winston.

So much for the Churchill. Next for the "Spencer" in Winston's name, and the hyphen. Properly speaking he should be known to fame as Winston Spencer rather than by the more familiar style. As the first Duke of Marlborough left no son to follow him, his title passed in the female line through his daughters—first Henrietta (wife of Lord Godolphin) and second Anne, wife of Charles, Lord Spencer. It was through the line of Anne and the Spencers that the Marlborough dukedom has descended to our own times. Spencers they have been, and are. The hyphen came in with

George, fourth Duke of Marlborough, who lived in the reign of King George III. He received the royal license to join the name of Churchill with his own, thus bringing in the Spencer-Churchills. It was this Duke's further distinction to indulge his taste for gambling to the extent that he reduced himself to poverty so that he had to sell his art treasures and live in "complete but not reputable" seclusion in a corner of Blenheim Palace. The seventh Duke, "sensible, honorable and industrious" according to the national biographer, was one of those reliable figures in politics, who did duty to complete, with men of greater ability, the Cabinets of Queen Victoria.

Through the Spencer connection, Winston Churchill was ancestrally linked with famous figures in British politics, one of them Chief Minister to King George I. Through his grandmother, the Duchess of Marlborough he could trace his descent from a line of Marquises. Popularly known as "Fanny by the Grace of God," the Duchess was Lady Frances Anne Emily, daughter of the third Marquis of Londonderry, another family rich in associations with England's history. The Londonderrys trace their descent from the Vanes, the most famous of whom is remembered by Cromwell's outburst: "Sir Harry Vane, Sir Harry Vane—the Lord deliver me from Sir Harry Vane."

But, it is enough. The Churchill baby was well enough connected. Through Marlborough, Londonderry and Spencer, duke, marquis and earl and their ramifications, he was related to half the peers in the kingdom. His ancestral tree was ripe with distinguished figures of the past. There were rich strains that contributed to the making of him. But hereditary riches are not enough. The same strains went to the production of his brother John who made no stir in the world at all. Provide the strains as well as you may and there is still something needed, the individual spirit to spark off genius.

Let us offer the bow of respect to beauty in the person of Winston's mother. She was one of the leading beauties in a society of beauties. Professional beauties they were called, such women as Lillie Langtry, "the Jersey Lily," whom to see the crowds mounted the seats in Hyde Park. Today, I suppose, they would serve as pin-up girls and their statistics would be known to millions. In their own generation the reticences were still preserved and what was not measured won the more devoted admiration. To beauty Lady Randolph added charm, and distinction. She fascinated her son who wrote of her, "My mother made a brilliant impression upon my childhood's life. She shone for me like an evening star. I loved her dearly but at a distance. She always seemed to me a fairy princess."

To supplement his own tribute, Winston quoted the description given of Lady Randolph by Lord D'Abernon. A diplomat of the old school who served as Ambassador to Berlin, D'Abernon had known everybody worth knowing and the outstanding personages he portrayed in his recollections so vividly that they spring to life from his pages. Of Lady Randolph he wrote:

> ... I have the clearest recollection of seeing her for the first time. It was at the Vice-Regal Lodge at Dublin. She stood on one side to the left of the entrance. The Viceroy was on a dais at the farther end of the room surrounded by a brilliant staff, but eyes were not turned on him or on his consort, but on a dark, lithe figure, standing somewhat apart and appearing to be of another texture to those around her, radiant, translucent, intense. A diamond star in her hair, her favourite ornament—its lustre dimmed by the flashing glory of her eyes. More of the panther than of the woman in her look, but with a cultivated intelligence unknown to the jungle. Her courage not less great than that of her husband—fit mother for the descendants of the great Duke.

Through his mother, Winston could claim brotherhood with the Americans. Jennie Jerome by name, she was descended through five generations of Americans, men and women who played their part with the pioneers. They sprang from a Huguenot ancestor who, leaving France to avoid persecution, found freedom for himself and fortune for his descendants. One of these, Leonard Jerome, Jennie's father, was a gentleman of force, ability and character. At the time of his daughter's marriage to Lord Randolph, Mr. Jerome was proprietor and editor of *The New York Times*. He had already lost one fortune and made another. One of the "fathers of the turf" in America, he founded the first two race courses in the United States. His forcefulness was attested during the Civil War when mobs attacked the office of his paper. He had taken the precaution of arming his staff with rifles and had even purchased a battery of cannon. He had no hesitation in ordering the arms to be turned on the mob, who were beaten off, not without bloodshed.

The web of destiny was cast over the Atlantic. The Jeromes and the Churchills were brought to meet in the persons of their two most brilliant representatives. It was the month of August in the year 1873. Society had gathered at Cowes for the yachting festival, Lord Randolph Churchill among the rest. Mrs. Jerome had brought her two elder daughters to join in the gaieties of the regatta. They were presented to the Prince of Wales at the Royal Yacht Squadron Ball. It was delightful.

Then, in that romantic setting, Jennie and Randolph met. She was nineteen, he was twenty-three. It was a case of love at first sight. On the second night of their acquaintance each confided to a friend that their fates had been decided. On the third day Lord Randolph—but the happy tale is told by their son himself, who described the match in the biography of his father:

> Next day they met again "by accident"—so runs the account I have received—and went for a walk. That night—the third of their acquaintance—was a beautiful night, warm and still with the lights of the yachts shining on the water and the sky bright with stars. After dinner they found themselves alone together in the garden and—brief courtship notwithstanding—he proposed and was accepted.

The course of true love did not run smooth and I should like to tell you of how the plighted lovers overcame parental and ducal obstacles. But this is the life of Winston, not of his parents; and if you want to read this very Victorian and charming love story you must find it in the son's admirable biography.

Their trials at last over, Lord Randolph and Jennie were married on April 15, 1874, at the British Embassy in Paris, the bride being then resident in Paris with her mother. The following November young Winston came hurrying into the world.

Of Winston's father, Lord Randolph, I need only say here that he was a political meteor who flashed brilliantly upon the scene about the year 1880. He was termed, not inaptly, a "great elemental force in British politics."

He gained for himself the position of Chancellor of the Exchequer and was on the point of challenging the authority of Lord

Salisbury as Prime Minister and leader of the Conservative Party. Then, meteorlike, he fell; and as he fell he was smitten by illness that robbed him slowly of his mental powers and then of life itself.

Lady Randolph outlived her husband by a quarter of a century. When she had been five years a widow, she married Cornwallis West, from whom she obtained a divorce in 1913. Then in the evening of her life she became the wife of a former colonial administrator. She died in 1921.

Of Winston Churchill's genius there was little evidence in his childhood days. Had those capabilities, indeed, been more apparent his career would have been in the law and he might have sat in wig and ermine upon the judge's bench. But Fate decided otherwise and tin soldiers were in this case Fate's instrument.

Tin soldiers were the chief amusement of Winston's boyhood. He commanded one army, and his brother Jack another. They were forces on a continental scale, fifteen hundred men in all, organized as an infantry division with a cavalry brigade. By a treaty for the limitation of armaments, his brother Jack was only allowed colored troops. Even these were not given artillery—a very important point, since Winston's army could muster eighteen field guns, besides fortress pieces.

One day Lord Randolph came, like a field marshal, on a visit of inspection. All the troops were drawn up ready for immediate attack. Lord Randolph spent twenty minutes studying the scene.

He then turned toward Winston and asked him if he would like to become a soldier. The boy thought it would be splendid to command an army, so he said "yes" at once.

It was a fateful answer. His father took him at his word and Winston henceforth was committed to an army career.

How strangely the minor and the major things are linked across the years—the small chances of the individual's life and the turning points in the lives of nations. Had Paul who was called Saul never ridden one day to Damascus, had Hitler never gone as a housepainter to Vienna, how different history would have been.

And had Winston Churchill never played with tin soldiers he would have gone to the Bar and not to the Army; he would not then have found fame in the Boer War, become a figure in public life before he was thirty, and been First Lord before 1914 came.

Even the tin soldiers might not have been the instruments of fate had Lord Randolph had a higher opinion of his son's abilities. But he had considered that Winston was not clever enough for a career at the Bar—and so tin soldiers and the Army.

He reached the Royal Military College at Sandhurst by way of Harrow. Eton was the family tradition; but Winston had a weak chest and it was considered that the school on the hill would be better for him than the rival establishment by the river.

But for the discerning eye of Dr. Weldon, then headmaster, Harrow's doors would have been closed to him after the limitations of his learning had been disclosed by the papers he sent in at the entrance examination.

There was the terrible Latin prose paper—a blot, a smudge, and a pair of brackets as the total output for two hours' effort.

"It was from these slender indications of scholarship," wrote Winston in his later years, "that Mr. Weldon drew the conclusion that I was worthy to pass into Harrow. It is very much to his credit. It showed that he was a man capable of looking beneath the surface of things: a man not dependent upon paper manifestations. I have always had the greatest regard for him."

Harrow days were not happy days, but days of work that Winston found anything but congenial, an unending spell of worries that did not seem trivial. It was not only that school tasks were difficult—they seemed purposeless.

He sighed for something practical. If only he had had to run errands as a messenger boy, or to toil as a bricklayer's mate—that would have been something real. Better to have been the son of a grocer and to have helped dress the front windows of the shop— "it would have taught me more and I should have got to know my father, which would have been a great joy to me."

There is a cry straight from the heart in those words of regret that he did not get to know his father better, that father of meteoric brilliance who in Winston's school days thrust himself into the front ranks of politics and then threw all away.

Winston did get to know his father, but only after his father's death when he came to tell the story of his career.

In life he had no more than three or four long, intimate conversations with Lord Randolph, who died when Winston was twenty-one.

All my dreams of comradeship with him, of entering Parliament at his side and in his support were ended. There remained for me only to pursue his aims and vindicate his memory.

Harrow days and Sandhurst days—no release from school for the proper business of life was ever more welcome. The schoolboy who for all his terms was bored to tears because he had hardly ever been asked to learn anything which seemed to be of the slightest use to him, found life transformed as a cavalry cadet. Now there was use in everything he had to learn.

Gone were the tedium of Latin and Greek. In their place were the enchantments of military studies with a purpose. He had now to learn tactics, fortification, topography, military law, and military administration. In place of the games which failed to amuse, there were gymnastics, and above all riding. There were some curious blanks in the military studies of the nineties. Winston was never taught anything about bombs or hand grenades. These weapons were known to be long obsolete, gone out of use in the eighteenth century, and the military mind could not conceive that they could be useful in modern war.

While he was still at Sandhurst young Winston made his maiden speech in a public, if not exactly a political, cause. He and his fellow cadets were in the habit, when in London on leave, of visiting the old Empire Theatre in Leicester Square. At that time a purity campaign was being conducted against the music halls, and in particular the promenade of the Empire, by a Mrs. Ormiston Chant, member of the London County Council.

The defenders of the liberties of the music hall had the powerful backing of the *Daily Telegraph,* which ran a "Prudes on the Prowl" campaign. An Entertainments Protection League was formed, of which Winston became a member, and he pawned his gold watch to aid the league's finances. Mrs. Chant, though she did not carry everything before her, was successful in getting a light canvas screen erected between the offending bars at the Empire and the promenade.

On the first Saturday after its appearance, Churchill and his friends visited the theater. Many sympathizers were present. Comment led to action and a crowd of some 200 to 300 persons stormed the barricades and tore them down.

At this moment of triumph young Churchill made his maiden speech. Mounting the debris, he harangued the throng and pointed to the moral of the occasion. "You have seen us tear down these barricades tonight: see that you pull down those responsible for them at the next election."

These words, we are assured, were received with rapturous applause.

Churchill's career at Sandhurst ended in 1894. He graduated eighth in his class of 150. In March of the following year he was appointed to the Fourth Hussars.

CHAPTER TWO

LITTLE WARS

1895–1898

A MAN OF ACTION is subject to an implacable and unceasing urge to fulfill his life's purpose. Always he must act, and for Winston Churchill, subaltern in His Majesty's Hussars, action meant fighting.

In the nineties it was not so easy to find scope for indulging one's taste for battle. The nineteenth century and the Victorian age were drawing peacefully to a close: it looked as if war was about to become extinct. Somehow, somewhere, the young Hussar must find the means to gratify his longing.

In the mess a young man who could say he had been in action would have an advantage over his fellows, none of whom had gained so coveted a distinction in the piping years of peace. He would have an advantage when it came to promotion. So Lieutenant Churchill bent all his energies to the single purpose of getting under fire; and when the Churchillian energies were devoted to a single purpose the walls of Jericho invariably fell. He was to spend five years soldiering and in those five years he contrived to push himself into five campaigns. Agamemnon could not have done more.

The revolt of the guerrillas in Cuba first brought him under fire. He graduated with the Malakand Field Force under General

Sir Bindon Blood. He forced himself into Kitchener's force in the Sudan and was just in time to take part in the charge of the 21st Lancers at Omdurman. And he was the hero of an episode or two in the Boer War. Such was the record he could look back on when he left soldiering for politics at the age of twenty-six, all unconscious that ahead of him lay active service in a far greater war than those.

They were magnificent, these carefree, swashbuckling days of life lived to the full as Winston swept through one war and so on to the next.

The opening affair in Cuba was a small thing as wars are reckoned now—a few thousand men on either side, and none of the complicated paraphernalia of the modern army. But the essentials of war are the same from age to age. It has always been the greatest gamble of all whether waged with flint axes or the atom bomb. And the price of failure has always been the same: whether death from bow and arrow or from a rifle bullet, it is no less inexorably final.

Churchill's approach to war was always that of the eager amateur. "Did you enjoy it?" he asked a sergeant after they had emerged from the charge at Omdurman. Of the private on the Western Front twenty years later he inquired, "Don't you like it?" Churchill liked it and played his part with rare zest.

The first taste of war in Cuba came after seven months with the Hussars on his first spell of long leave. It was not, as I said, much of a war, but it was all that offered. So Churchill soon pushed through the formalities of getting himself attached to the army of General Campos. For this he was indebted to the good offices of his father's old friend and colleague in the Fourth Party, Sir Henry Drummond Wolff, then ambassador in Madrid.

There was not much difficulty about it for General Campos felt flattered that the British Army in the person of two of its subalterns—Churchill was accompanied by a fellow officer—should be interested in his tactics against the guerrillas. One other arrangement Churchill had to make before setting off. His subaltern's allowance of £500 a year did not permit trips to Cuba. So, following the example of Lord Randolph, who was commissioned by the *Daily Graphic* to write about his tour in South Africa, he obtained a commission for a series of articles from Cuba.

Like another Long John Silver seeing Treasure Island for the first time, Churchill landed on the lovely isle of Cuba and joined a mobile column advancing in pursuit of an elusive enemy with whom contact was rarely to be made in the Cuban jungle.

They marched for several days and then, at last, came the adventure for which Churchill had traveled halfway across the world. There was a volley from the forest and all was scurry and commotion; bullets whistled through the air and a horse was hit.

Churchill had been under fire. His reactions he analyzed in the record he gives of his early life.[1]

> Meanwhile I had been meditating upon the wounded horse. The bullet had struck between his ribs, the blood dripped on the ground, and there was a circle of dark red on his bright-chestnut coat about a foot wide. Evidently he was going to die, for his saddle and bridle were soon taken off him. As I watched I could not help reflecting that the bullet had certainly passed within a foot of my head. So at any rate I had been "under fire." That was something. Nevertheless, I began to take a more thoughtful view of our enterprise than I had hitherto done.

A few days later there was a more formal engagement between the troops and the guerrillas. There was heavy firing on both sides; the air was full of whizzings and there were dull thuds as bullets found a billet in the trees. To Churchill, the observer, it seemed very dangerous indeed and he was astounded to note how few people were hit amid all the clatter.

Churchill came home to find his regiment preparing for India, and in India there was trouble among the restless tribesmen who live nearly on the top of the world on the North-West frontier. A field force was sent to deal with the disturbance of the Empire's peace but, alas, Churchill's regiment was not part of it.

Happily, however, the O.C. was Sir Bindon Blood, who had already promised, if the opportunity came his way, to give Winston the chance of active service. A telegram reminding Sir Bindon of the pledge drew the response that there were no vacancies in the Command but that Churchill could come along as officer correspondent if some paper would commission him.

Those were still the easy days when officers of the Army were permitted to serve Fleet Street as well as their country. Churchill was soon armed with the commissions of the *Pioneer* of Allahabad and the *Daily Telegraph* of London, the latter journal being prepared to pay £5 per column for the privilege of publishing his dispatches.

Leave granted from his own regiment, Churchill was shortly presenting himself at the headquarters of the Malakand Field Force engaged in some tight places in the Himalayan passes.

Here were no elusive Cuban rebels, but Pathan tribesmen, untamed by civilization, among the best fighters in the world.

The British force made their advance through rocky passes, gorges 5,000 feet high. On either side the rocks might shelter enemy riflemen. The Pathans are a fighting race, trained from infancy in their tribal feuds.

In the action of September 16, 1896, the British troops were not wisely commanded and extricated themselves, with considerable losses, only by reason of the pluck and determination of the junior officers and men. It was hand-to-hand fighting in the Mahmund Valley that day and Winston was in the thick of it. You can judge the sort of thing it was from his own inimitable account. The advance party had been forced to retreat down a rocky space, harassed by the enemy.

> The Adjutant had been shot. Four of his soldiers were carrying him. He was a heavy man, and they all clutched at him. Out from the edge of the houses rushed half a dozen Pathan swordsmen. The bearers of the poor Adjutant let him fall and fled at their approach.
>
> The leading tribesman rushed upon the prostrate figure and slashed at it three or four times with his sword. I forgot everything else at this moment except a desire to kill this man. I wore my long cavalry sword well sharpened. After all, I had won the Public Schools Fencing Medal. I resolved on personal combat *à l'arme blanche*.
>
> The savage saw me coming. I was not more than twenty yards away. He picked up a big stone and hurled it at me with his left hand, and then awaited me, brandishing his sword. There were others waiting not far behind.
>
> I changed my mind about the cold steel. I pulled out my revolver, took, as I thought, most careful aim, and fired. No result. I fired again. No result. I fired again. Whether I hit him or not

I cannot tell. At any rate he ran back two or three yards and plumped down behind a rock.

The fusillade was continuous. I looked around. I was all alone with the enemy. Not a friend was to be seen. I ran as fast as I could. There were bullets everywhere. I got to the first knoll. Hurrah, there were the Sikhs holding the lower one! They made vehement gestures, and in a few moments I was among them.

Churchill gained a mention in dispatches, Sir Bindon Blood praising "the courage and resolution of Lieut. W. L. S. Churchill, 4th Hussars, the correspondent of the *Pioneer* newspaper, who made himself useful at a critical moment."

A few days later, owing to losses in action, he was appointed officer in the 38th Dogras—the first time a British cavalry officer had been attached to a native cavalry regiment. The men liked their new officer and he warmed to them. There was only one real drawback, the barrier of language. He could only boast of three words in the native vernacular—*chalo*, meaning "get on"; *maro*, meaning "kill"; and *tallyho*, which means the same the world over.

They were good days, and I do not know who enjoyed himself the more—Lieutenant Churchill of the Hussars, or Mr. Churchill, correspondent of the *Pioneer*, Allahabad, and the *Daily Telegraph*, London. His newspaper work was as good as his soldiering, and in his double role he would have been content to go on getting in and out of tight corners in the mountains until the last tribe in the last valley had been subdued. But he was attached only unofficially to the expedition while on leave, and at length he could no longer delay returning to his own regiment at Bangalore.

It was time to exchange the real thing on the frontier for the imitation of maneuvers. But the leisure of regimental life gave Churchill the opportunity to present to the world his account of the frontier war in *The Malakand Field Force*.[2]

The book was an immediate success and the author found solace amidst the tedium of regimental life in savoring the fame of a best seller. There was praise on all sides, from the reviewers to the Prince of Wales, who sent a kind note of congratulation assuring the author that everyone was reading his book, which was spoken of "only with praise."

The latter statement was true enough for the general reader, but it did not tell all the story; for in the highest military circles there was indignation that the young lieutenant should so far have departed from the professional proprieties as to criticize the operations of his superior officers. *The Malakand Field Force*, indeed, was a lively piece of military criticism in which the mistakes of the commanders were exposed by a man who had been on the spot. It was good fun for the reader, and the wits renamed the book *A Subaltern's Hints to Generals*.

The descendant of Marlborough had given the first illustration of his quality. Then, as thereafter, in engagements ashore or afloat, he had the conviction that he knew, when admirals and generals might not, how the fight should be fought. The book was a financial as well as a literary success and it set the author thinking. If, he reflected, books were as easy as that to write—and there were plenty more where that one came from—and if they paid so well, then a man on subaltern's pay must really consider whether his future lay in the Army.

Again there was the chance of action among the wild passes of the Himalayas. Again it was a spur to Churchill's ambitions. Authority was resolved to deal with the Afridis, and an expedition was organized against them in their rocky homes in the Tirah Maidan. Churchill watched from afar with wistful eyes. He caused wires to be pulled, but without avail. Resolved to take part in this new adventure, he went to apply in person to join the expedition. Refusal would have involved the offense of overstaying his leave, but he won his way—and a junior post on the staff. He was delighted, but not for long. Hardly had he put on the red tabs of a staff officer, than authority changed its mind.

The Tirah expedition was recalled and Churchill had disconsolately to return once more to regimental routine. But once again he saw his chance. After Cuba and India came the Sudan.

There had been trouble in the Sudan for long enough. Under the Mahdi of famous memory—Mohammed Ahmed—the Sudanese had expelled the Turks and Egyptians in 1885, killing General Gordon in the process. The Mahdi had been succeeded by the bloody tyranny of the Khalifa. At last, after long preparation, General Kitchener was sent south to settle the account with the Mahdists.

It was a favorable moment for Lieutenant Churchill, who was

on home leave. But though the time might be propitious, the authorities were unkind. The subaltern who had had the hardihood to teach the generals their job in public print was not *persona grata* in military circles.

Application was made to Kitchener, as Commander in Chief of the Anglo-Egyptian Army. He replied with an uncompromising negative.

Winston Churchill's star seemed always to have been in the ascendant when circumstances were least favorable. Kitchener might oppose, but what matter if the fates were favorable? And the fates decreed that at that juncture Lord Salisbury, the Prime Minister, should read the story of *The Malakand Field Force.*

Salisbury was Conservative Prime Minister, but he had a mind that was not fettered by orthodoxy. He read the Churchill book with relish and invited the author to call on him. The interview was cordial and Churchill made use of the occasion to enlist the Prime Minister's aid on his behalf. So Lord Salisbury himself cabled to Egypt; still Kitchener was uncompromisingly negative in his reply.

The young man who could find a champion in a prime minister was not to be gainsaid. Lady Randolph pleaded her son's cause with the Adjutant General, Sir Evelyn Wood. A mother's charm and a prime minister's support were conclusive. Sir Evelyn decreed that, Kitchener or no Kitchener, young Churchill should have his way. Kitchener's authority did not run to the 21st Lancers, so Lieutenant Churchill could have a commission so long as it was unpaid. It was also a condition that if he were wounded or killed there would be no charge on Army funds.

Next and equally important was a commission from Fleet Street. The author of *The Malakand Field Force* had no difficulty there. The *Morning Post* was glad to appoint him correspondent, and the rate was now advanced to £15 a column.

So, in the summer of 1898, the young subaltern left for the wars again, his fourth campaign and in a third continent. In August he was at Cairo; a month later he had reached the battle front just in time to take part in the charge of the 21st Lancers at the battle of Omdurman.

They still talk of the affair in Army circles—the last of the classic charges of cavalry. It was not as desperate a thing as that of

the Light Brigade at Balaclava, but it was hot enough while it
lasted. Many who galloped over the sands of the desert that day
were missing from the mess that night. Lieutenant Churchill came
through the hazards of the ride. He gained the distinction among
Hussars of publishing in print a description of the charge in
which he rode. As a piece of writing it is up to the quality of the
charge, tense, fast-moving, dramatic.

There had been several breath-taking moments in the opening
moves of the British forces. Young Churchill had been sent out
on patrol, ahead of the advance, to reconnoiter a rocky ridge.
They set off in the dim light before dawn. There were 60,000
fanatical, well-armed Dervishes ahead. How far away? It was his
job to find out and to report. He, with six men and a corporal,
rode up the ridge towards the unknown.

Dawn broke as they reached the summit. It was clear of the enemy. As the sun lighted up the desert, thousands of glittering
flashes showed the polished steel of the enemy at no great distance
away across the sands. Lieutenant Churchill sent word to his command. Back came the reply "Remain and report." So he stayed,
delighted beyond measure to have this view.

The batteries opened fire. Shells went shrieking through the air
to fall on the dark mass of the tribesmen. The enemy were advancing. The observer remained enthralled by the spectacle before
him, heedless of his own increasing danger, not merely from foe,
but from friend.

There was a sudden order "Come back at once, infantry about
to open fire." The patrol withdrew in haste.

When the enemy's rush had been stayed, Kitchener gave the
order to advance toward Omdurman, the Dervish capital. The
21st Lancers led the way up the slopes of Jebel Surgham. Lieutenant Churchill rode in command of one of the sixteen troops,
the second from the rear. From the top of Jebel Surgham, the
eye could see across the sandy plain with the Dervishes in the
foreground. In the distance was Omdurman, crowned by its domes
and minarets. There was little time for admiring the view.

"Trot," came the order and the long column began to move
quickly down the slope. Another order followed: "Right wheel
into line." The Lancers had been committed to the assault. The

trot became a gallop. The line of horsemen, 300 strong, were charging 3,000 of the enemy.

Ahead was the bluish mass from which arose puffs of smoke. In the clatter of the charge the bullets could not be heard as they shrieked by, but there were gaps now in the Lancers' line. Horsemen and tribesmen met in a melee.

Lieutenant Churchill, on his grey Arab pony, had sheathed his sword, too heavy for use with a dislocated shoulder. Instead he was armed with a Mauser automatic. As he reached the enemy, a Dervish threw himself to the ground with his sword ready for an upward cut. Churchill swerved his pony and fired.

Ahead was another Dervish. He fired again. The range was so close that the pistol itself struck the target as well as the bullet. The swordsman dropped. There was an Arab horseman in chain-mail. Again the pistol spoke. The Arab turned aside.

Churchill was through. He reined his horse and looked about him. To his left there was a mass of thrusting, stabbing tribesmen, so closely grouped that in places the Lancers had been held back by the wall of human bodies. Many had been torn from their horses and hacked to death. Along the line Lancers and Dervishes were fighting it out.

Ahead, enemy riflemen made him their target. It seemed to Lieutenant Churchill that he was cut off, alone, isolated in the midst of battle. He felt a sudden spasm of fear. Three hundred yards off, the men of his troop were reforming. Crouching over his pony he galloped towards them.

A solitary Dervish rose from the sand. The troopers thrust at him with their lances. Several times he was wounded but he came on with brandished spear. The revolver crashed again. The Dervish fell dead on the sand. It was the last bullet in the Mauser. It was, for Churchill, the last incident in the charge.

He had come through unscathed. Five of his fellow officers and sixty-five men had been killed or wounded. The 21st had lost a quarter of their strength. Lieutenant Churchill's luck had held.

The Battle of Omdurman settled the war. The Sudan was shortly recovered from the Mahdists. But before that, Lieutenant Churchill, with the Lancers, had left for home. Thereafter, he fought the battle over again in print in his book—*The River War*.

The two volumes again made a stir for they were highly critical of the Commander in Chief. Kitchener was a popular figure with the public and the attacks made upon him by the lancer-journalist were not everywhere relished.

Churchill's most stringent criticisms concerned Kitchener for his treatment of the enemy. At home the cry of "Avenge Gordon" had been raised, and the Dervishes were spoken of as the scum of the earth. This may have had its influence on the attitude of the British force. Anyway, Churchill asserted that the impression was general that the "fewer the prisoners taken the greater would be the satisfaction of the Commander."

He also uttered strong condemnation of the manner in which the Mahdi's tomb was destroyed and the body of the Mahdi was flung into the Nile by the Sirdar's order. This destruction, he declared, of what was sacred and holy to the natives, was an "act of which a true Christian must express abhorrence." It should be said that these passages were expunged by the author from later editions of the book.

The River War enhanced the reputation Churchill had won with *The Malakand Field Force*. Very shortly he was to become a national figure as the result of his activities in the Boer War. But between the Sudan and South Africa a political interlude intervened.

CHAPTER THREE

INTERLUDE IN POLITICS

1898

RETURNING HOME from the Nile campaign in the autumn of
1898, Winston Churchill resigned his commission in the
army and announced that he proposed to follow his father's example in a political career.

The Adjutant General, his friend Sir Evelyn Wood, attempted
to dissuade him, but his mind was made up, and though we may
wager that Churchill would have won through to the highest positions in the Army, we cannot say that he was wrong in leaving
soldiering for politics. For a man of his restless ambition and
varied interests, the Army offered too limited a scope.

Besides, Churchill was bound to have found himself a marked
man with the War Office chiefs who have no partiality for subalterns bursting into print with criticisms of their superiors. Already there was displeasure in Service circles. He had to make up
his mind between soldiering and journalism. Journalism won the
day, with the opportunities it offered for entering the political
field.

So, in November, he made application to Conservative Party
headquarters to be supplied with a constituency. He did not make
much progress for there was the bar of finance. The party man-
ager asked him bluntly how much he could contribute to local

party funds, explaining that the safer the seat, the greater the contribution expected from the prospective member. Churchill had to confess that he could offer little more than his personality and his election expenses.

This obstacle of financial contribution continued to deprive young men of talent but limited means from entering Parliament as Conservatives and the result was that the party representation in Parliament was in the past largely made up of third-rate, elderly men, with the means to impress local associations. This experience weighed with Churchill when in 1941, as leader of the party he took steps to see that the Central Office (Conservative Party headquarters) should have power to call in question financial arrangements between local organizations and candidates.

Churchill's interview, though it failed in its main objective of a seat, at least provided him with a platform. There was difficulty over accepting him as a candidate, but as a speaker, he learned, he would be welcomed.

So a fortnight later Churchill delivered the first of the speeches which were to be the foundation of his political fortunes. It would not be correct to say that he created a political sensation, but, thanks to his connection with the *Morning Post,* he was accorded greater publicity than is usually given to utterances of budding politicians.

The occasion was a garden party in the city of Bath. With the promise of a special reporter to inspire him he polished his periods and when the appointed day came he delivered them to the faithful Conservatives of Bath. To his surprise his observations were well received. His audience cheered at all the appointed places and at one or two others that he had not foreseen. What was more important, the special reporter was appreciative and the following morning a short leader in the *Morning Post* introduced Lord Randolph's son to the world as a new figure upon the political scene.

The following month he was introduced to an immensely greater public by the *Daily Mail,* then conducting a series of articles on prominent young men of the time. Churchill was presented as the "Youngest Man in Europe," and it says much for the discernment of the anonymous author (later revealed as G. W. Steevens, the eminent war correspondent) that he could prophesy with uncanny accuracy that at the rate Churchill was going, "there will scarcely be room for him in Parliament at 30 or in Europe at 40." The pen picture deserves quotation:

> In years he is a boy; in temperament he is also a boy; but in intention, in deliberate plan, adaptation of means to ends, he is already a man. In any other generation but this he would be a child. Any other than he, being a junior subaltern of Hussars, would be a boisterous, simple, full-hearted, empty-headed boy. But Mr. Churchill is a man, with ambitions fixed, with the steps towards their attainment clearly defined, with a precocious, almost uncanny judgment as to the efficacy of the means to the end.
>
> He is what he is by breeding. From his father he derives the hereditary aptitude for affairs, the grand style of entering upon them, which are not the less hereditary in British noble families because they skip nine generations out of ten. Winston Spencer Churchill can hardly have seen much of Government and Parliament and forensic politics at twenty-three, but he moves in and out among their deviations with the ease, if not with the knowledge, of a veteran statesman. But that inheritance alone would not give him his grip and facility at twenty-three; with us hereditary statesmen and party leaders ripen later. From his American strain he adds to this a keenness, a shrewdness, a half-cynical, personal ambition, a natural aptitude for advertisement, and, happily, a sense of humour.
>
> He may or may not possess the qualities which make a great general, but the question is of no sort of importance. In any case they will never be developed, for, if they exist, they are overshadowed by qualities which might make him, almost at will, a great popular leader, a great journalist, or the founder of a great advertising business.

A month or two later Churchill stood on the hustings for the first time to seek the votes of the electors of Oldham in industrial Lancashire, one of the largest constituencies in the country. Oldham, according to Asquith who once went there to advise the Corporation on legal niceties of sewerage, is one of the most dismal of manufacturing towns in the country, peopled by wan-faced, grimy, tired artisans, who "have never known life in its real sense and never will know it to their dying day." But to the young politician Oldham appeared as one of the most romantic places on earth, peopled by men of enlightenment and discernment who would appreciate the qualities of the "youngest man in Europe."

Churchill's chance to contest the seat was not due to the party managers at Conservative headquarters, but to the whim of a Mr. Robert Ascroft, the senior Conservative member and legal adviser to one of the cotton workers' unions. Oldham was a two-member constituency, and Ascroft was on the lookout for someone to stand with him, as his fellow Conservative was ailing. Why his choice fell on Churchill is not explained, but so it was.

Before Churchill had addressed his first meeting, however, Ascroft died suddenly. Oldham Conservatives honored his choice and, the second member retiring, Churchill contested the election in association with a working-man candidate, James Mawdsley, secretary of a local trade union.

They were an ill-assorted pair, the grandson of a duke and the Tory Socialist, and they had to face two strong opponents, champions of Liberalism. The senior of these was a Mr. Emmott, a wealthy local employer already prominent in Oldham politics, who rose to be Deputy Speaker in the House of Commons; the other, Mr. Walter Runciman, son of the noted shipowner, who was destined to hold a Cabinet office under four Prime Ministers.

Churchill conducted his first campaign with more vigor than discretion. At his adoption meeting he startled one of his most influential supporters with a blunt disclaimer: "I disagree with you."

Party headquarters he defied. They expected him to champion the Government's Tithes Bill; but he pledged himself to oppose it, thereby drawing rebuke from the great Arthur Balfour who said bitingly: "I thought he was a young man of promise, but it appears he is only a young man of promises."

"Winnie," as he was soon named by the electors, gave early evidence of his quality in dealing with opponents. Mr. Runciman, who had been beaten in a previous byelection at Gravesend, had the temerity to boast that he had not been a "swashbuckler round the world."

The opening was too good to be missed. "Is this," Churchill asked Oldham, "the sort of welcome you will give the Lancashire Fusiliers when they come home from Omdurman? Mr. Runciman has not had the experience of the Lancashire Fusiliers—his contests have been more pacific, and while they were fighting at Omdurman for their country he was fighting at Gravesend for himself; while they were gaining a victory, Mr. Runciman at Gravesend was being defeated."

Mr. Runciman did not have the last word but he had the last laugh. When the votes were counted, the champions of Liberalism headed the poll; the Tory Democrat and the Tory Socialist were over a thousand votes behind.

"I don't think that the world has seen the last of either of us," was Walter Runciman's comment to young Churchill after the declaration. This at least was an observation from which the youngest man in Europe did not dissent.

CHAPTER FOUR

PRISONER OF THE BOERS

1899

IN THE MONTH of October, 1899, Winston Churchill sailed for South Africa to report the Boer War as special correspondent of the *Morning Post*. He was not yet twenty-five, but it was his fifth campaign and it was to place him in a position of unparalleled popularity with the British public as the hero of the day.

Churchill, indeed, could find cause for satisfaction in the fact that within a fortnight of his arrival at the Cape, he was taken prisoner by the Boers. The circumstances and the escape that followed won him renown he could not have gained in a dozen years of politics.

He set out for the Cape well satisfied with himself that he had been commissioned as war correspondent for the princely salary of £250 a month, and all expenses paid. He was privileged to be a fellow passenger of the commander of the British forces, Sir Redvers Buller.

On the voyage out, he, like the subalterns aboard, was fearful lest the show should be over, and victory for the British gained before he got there. There need have been no anxiety on that score, for before the Boers had been beaten, the war had lasted three years and involved the use of 448,725 men.

When the *Dunnottar Castle* landed its distinguished passengers, the situation was very different from what they, in their contempt for the Boers, had expected. Far from a British victory, there had been British defeats. At Nicholson's Nek 1,200 British infantry had been forced to surrender. The remnant of the force had retired to Ladysmith, which, with Mafeking and Kimberley, lay besieged.

Churchill made his way to the front at Estcourt, where his former schoolmate, later Cabinet colleague, Leo Amery, had preceded him as correspondent of *The Times*. From Estcourt, on November 14, an armored train steamed out early in the morning bearing a company of Dublin Fusiliers and another of the Durban Light Infantry (under the command of Captain Haldane), a six-pounder naval gun and Winston Churchill. The force was instructed to reconnoiter.

The Boers were reconnoitering that day, too, and the armored train came under heavy fire. There were puffs of white smoke, a pause, and then the spluttering of a rain of bullets on the armor of the trucks. It was shrapnel which Churchill experienced for the first time and, for him, all but the last, for his head was above the armor when the first volley was fired.

The Boers would tear up the track and the train would be cut off. The order was given to reverse. The engine clattered into mounting speed. They were traveling at 40 miles an hour, with high hopes of escaping, when the crash came. The leading truck was derailed. In every coach there was a scramble of humanity shuffled suddenly on to the floor. Bullets began to patter on the plating. The naval six-pounder gave answering fire.

Was the track destroyed? Could the train be made to go again? Churchill set out to discover, running with the shelter of the trucks to protect him from the marksmen on the hill. The engine, amidships the train, was on the rails, but the three leading trucks were not. Many of the troops were badly hurt and some had been killed. But the track was intact.

What was to be done? They were at the foot of a high cutting. The enemy were finely placed on the hill above, keeping up a steady fire. If the engine could be made to push aside the obstructing coaches, they could drive off.

The driver, with a wound in the face, was panicky. Churchill rallied him. No man, he said, was hit twice the same day. The driver returned to his cab.

For an hour they toiled, hauling and pushing, bullets spattering like hail. Under Churchill's direction the trucks were bumped aside. There was a new obstruction and another hour of hauling and tugging. The enemy fire grew hotter. At last the engine was across all obstacles.

It was decided to place the wounded in the engine and as many troops as could be should march on the leeside protected from the Boer fire. They drove off, with Churchill in charge, and traveled too fast for the marching troops. Halting the engine, Churchill jumped down, bade the driver go on to safety, and himself ran back along the track to rejoin Captain Haldane and his men.

As he ran two riflemen appeared a hundred yards ahead. They were Boers. They aimed and fired. Near misses. He was in a cutting, without cover. On either side the banks rose six feet high. The marksmen were aiming again. He sprang aside. Again the bullets missed. He jumped for the top of the bank. The earth quivered behind him. He was over the top and lay safe for a moment in a dip in the ground.

Not far away was the Blue Krantz River. There was shelter, there in the gorge. He would run for it. As he rose a horseman came galloping up. Churchill felt for his Mauser—as a war correspondent he had no right to be armed, but he had had his pistol with him in the morning. Now it was missing, fallen from his belt during his labors in the locomotive.

There was a breathless moment. The horseman raised his rifle. He was no more than forty yards off. Churchill stood, undecided. Should he risk it and run? The river was not far away. The Boer looked along his sights. The chances for the unarmed man were slight. He raised his arms in token of surrender. He had been captured by the Boer leader who was to become famous as General Botha.

He was escorted back along the railway track. Captain Haldane and his company were not in sight. They, too, had been made prisoners. They were at Boer headquarters when he was marched in. When he made to join them he was ordered to stand apart. What was to be his fate? As a non-combatant, a civilian who had taken a prominent part in the fighting, he was liable, he knew, to drumhead court martial and to be shot.

After a quarter of an hour his anxieties were relieved. He was to be made prisoner with the others. "We don't catch the son of a lord every day," said one of his captors, almost apologizing for the necessity of retaining him in custody. They had had no thought of executing him. The Boers, he found, when not engaged in the business of fighting, were kind-hearted fellows.

Even with their benevolence, however, they were not disposed to set Churchill free. They lodged him in prison in Pretoria, with sixty British officers. He demanded to be released as a war correspondent. They declined, and very properly, to treat him as anything but a prisoner of war.

For three weeks he was confined in the buildings of a school that had been turned into a prison. It was pleasant enough, with books to read, cigarettes to smoke, chess, cards and rounders, a game not unlike baseball, to pass away the time. He was not prepared to stay tamely a prisoner till the fighting was over. He planned to escape.

There was a wildcat scheme for an organized outbreak by all the 2,000 prisoners in Pretoria. They dreamed of holding the entire town against the Boers. Plans were drawn up, debated and, fortunately, abandoned without putting them to the test. Instead Churchill resolved on an individual bid for freedom.

The prison walls were not difficult to scale. But within and around them were the patroling sentries armed with rifle and revolver. At night the wall was brightly lighted.

After some nice calculation a spot was found where the lighting was bad. For a moment, on each beat, it would be out of sight of the patrol. One night in December the chance came. Two others were to have joined with him. They did not fancy their chances. He stood ready at the chosen spot.

The sentries obligingly turned their backs. He scrambled for the top of the wall. He was over. For a moment he was caught by his clothes and hung suspended, in plain view of the patrol had they chanced to look. Their backs remained towards him. He freed himself and dropped to the gardens below. He had not been seen.

He waited in the shadows for his companions. No one followed him over the wall. He heard voices on the other side, bits of Latin and some nonsense. He coughed to show he was listening. The news was given him. His companions had called it off.

There was another patrol to pass. He walked boldly across the garden, through the outer gate and by the sentry. He was unchallenged and walked on. He reached the distant streets. He was at large in Pretoria. He was free. But safety was far off—300 miles away to be precise—300 miles of enemy country.

He had slabs of chocolate in his pocket and £75 in cash, but beyond this nothing except the Churchill audacity. There was neither map nor compass to guide him. He began the long trek to Delagoa Bay in Portuguese East Africa. He was in the highest spirits.

By dawn his escape would be known and he would be a hunted man. By then he must be miles away. There was only one possibility—he must find the railway to Delagoa Bay and hide himself somehow in one of the carriages. He was clear of the town at last. The road crossed a railway track. Was it the right line?

There was the rattle of an approaching train. The engine went clattering by. It was a freight train traveling at a fair speed. He made a jump for it, missed his hold and clutched again. He hauled himself up and found a seat on the couplings. He scrambled into the car. It was filled with empty coal bags. They were excellent cover. He buried himself beneath them. The train clattered on into the night. He slept.

When he awoke the stars were still shining. He must leave the train while the cover of the darkness held. Once more he was seated on the couplings and then he sprang. He rolled into a ditch and was unhurt beyond bruising.

Throughout the day he lay concealed. From time to time trains went by traveling, he noted, to the point where the sun had risen —to the East, that is, and Delagoa Bay. His course was clear. He would travel again by train at night, lie up during the day and by stages would be borne to safety.

When the stars came out he took his place beside the track. Time passed but trains did not. For six hours he waited and, in despair, began to trudge on. There were guards on the bridges and when he made detours he fell into swamps and bogs. He was chilled with the wet and cold, hungry, exhausted and miserable.

Lights twinkled in the distance. As he gazed at them his spirits lifted. He would make for them. Perhaps it was a kraal, but whatever the habitation might be he had confidence it would be a refuge. So it proved. A couple of hours' walking brought him to the place. It was no Kaffir dwelling, but a mine. He had, by providence, been brought to the doors of an Englishman, and the only friends within twenty miles.

John Howard might be a friend, but there was danger on every hand, Dutch servants and Kaffir employees. The patrol had been round that afternoon raising the hue-and-cry. As a citizen of the Transvaal, Howard would be liable to be shot for helping the escape of the prisoner.

Churchill offered to leave forthwith. His host would not hear of it. Producing food and drink he went off to arrange for a hiding-place. His assistants were let into the secret. Churchill was taken down into the pit and he lay concealed throughout the day in one of the distant workings.

For some days he had to remain concealed. Below, in the mine, rats, white rats with pink eyes, were his attendants. Above, the Boers were scouring the countryside. A reward was offered in printed notices—£25 for the person of Churchill, alive or dead. The description of the wanted man was not a flattering portrait. He was thus described:

> Englishman, 25 years old, about 5 ft. 8 in. tall, indifferent build, walks with a forward stoop, pale appearance, red-brownish hair, small and hardly noticeable moustache, talks through his nose and cannot pronounce the letter "s" properly.

Meanwhile, Mr. Howard was making plans. A consignment of wool was to be sent to Delagoa Bay. The owner, a Dutchman, was well disposed. He agreed to come into the plot. As the bales were loaded on the freight cars, a space would be left, a hide-out in the wool. The train would do the rest.

The night came. Churchill stepped into a gap between the bales. It was a tunnel leading into a space large enough to sit up in. More bales were lowered overhead. The tarpaulin was fixed. The train began to move. In 16 hours, all being well, he would emerge outside enemy territory. They were the most anxious hours he had spent. The perils of his wanderings at night were preferable to the long-drawn-out suspense of waiting. Sometimes the train would stop and Dutch voices were to be heard. Would there be a search?

The train jolted on. He had ample food and drink and was comfortable enough on the wool—too comfortable, in fact, for an overwhelming drowsiness came over him. But if he slept he might begin to snore and betray himself. Despite his fears he slept; he could not keep his eyes open.

When he awakened his ordeal had neared its end. The train rolled across the frontier. The porters were talking Portuguese. He had reached safety. He fired his pistol to express his joy.

At Durban, Churchill was received with acclamation, and he learned for the first time that his exploits had made him famous on two continents. Indeed, in the full flow of tribute, the popular press at home had turned on a torrent of gush, and this produced a secondary stream of defamation from those sections of press and populace that can never bear to see merit praised. One paper wanted to know by what unwarrantable liberty he got on to the armored train. Another accused him in escaping of having broken his parole. It was Churchill's first experience as a target for the mudslingers.

Balancing praise against calumny left him, however, a credit definitely on the right side. And, anyway, Churchill did not care very much for either. What was much more important, his exploits had commended him to the notice of the British commander.

Like the father of the fairy princess whose life has been saved by the deserving young man, Sir Redvers Buller asked Churchill: "Is there anything I can do for you?" to which Winston replied: "Give me a commission."

Now this was a difficult matter, for the correspondent of the *Morning Post* insisted that he must continue to report the war, and the War Office authorities, largely because of the writings in previous campaigns of this same officer-reporter, had put a peremptory stop on officers holding press appointments. However, Sir Redvers was ready to get around the obstacle by agreeing to a commission in one of the irregular volunteer corps—"Bungo's Regiment," commanded by Colonel Byng, who is known to history as Lord Byng of Vimy.

"You will," said Sir Redvers, "do what you can for both jobs, but you will be unpaid for ours."

So for a space Churchill returned to the Army as lieutenant in the South African Light Horse—the Cockyolibirds.

He was present at the relief of Ladysmith, and then got himself transferred to the main British army under Lord Roberts. He followed the campaigns in the Orange Free State and the Transvaal. He cantered into Pretoria at the side of his cousin, the young Duke of Marlborough, and he made a point of being among the first to release his former fellow-prisoners of war. Then, after taking part in the action of Diamond Hill, he decided to return home to new operations in the political field.

BOOK TWO

FIGHTING THE TORIES

Just his conceptions, natural and great;
His feelings strong, his words enforced with weight . . .
View the whole scene, with critic judgment scan,
And then deny him merit if you can.
Where he falls short, 'tis Nature's fault alone;
Where he succeeds, the merit's all his own.
—CHARLES CHURCHILL, The Rosciad

CHAPTER ONE

CONSERVATIVE M.P.

1900–1901

W HEN THE TIDE of war began to change in South Africa with
the fall of Johannesburg and Pretoria and the relief of Ladysmith and Mafeking, the Government at home decided to gain
what electoral benefit they could from the improving situation.
Young Winston Churchill, on returning to the country in the
late summer of the year 1900, found a general election in progress,
the famous "Khaki Election," a title marking the fact that the Boer
War was the first major war in which British soldiers were clad in
khaki. Without loss of time he plunged himself into the campaign.

The Parliament that was about to be elected, the first of the
twentieth century, was also the last of that venerable sovereign,
Queen Victoria, whose long life was drawing to its close.

The Prime Minister and Conservative leader was the Queen's
ancient servitor, the Marquess of Salisbury, the last of the great
landed proprietors to hold office as the first Minister of the Crown.
He had succeeded Disraeli in the Conservative party leadership
and except for a break from 1892-95 had been Prime Minister
since 1885, conducting affairs with the assistance of his nephews
of the House of Cecil. Of these the principal was Arthur James
Balfour, his uncle's chief lieutenant in the lower house.

It was the same Lord Salisbury with whom Lord Randolph

Churchill had had his fateful quarrel. And it was the same Arthur Balfour who had been Lord Randolph's collaborator in the brilliant days of the Fourth Party.

Lord Salisbury and Mr. Balfour were the hereditary leaders of conservatism, but the most powerful force in the Government ranks was Joseph Chamberlain, Birmingham businessman and father of the two statesmen of later days—Sir Austen, Chancellor of the Exchequer and Foreign Secretary, and Neville, Chancellor of the Exchequer and Prime Minister.

"Old Joe," though he failed to reach the position gained by his younger son, was a greater political personality than either of his sons. For all their attainments they did not succeed in dominating the political scene in the manner of their father, whose ascendancy was derived from elemental force of character.

In Gladstone's day "Radical Joe" had split the Liberal Party over Home Rule. In his last phase he joined forces with the Tories and, a radical turned imperialist, sat on the Treasury bench * as Colonial Secretary. The office was considered to be a reward for second-rate politicians, but Joseph Chamberlain brought a new importance to it. He was recognized as the most prominent member of the Conservative administration to which he contributed in equal measure a feeling of strength and insecurity—strength from the force of his support, insecurity from the uncertainty as to where his incalculable inspiration might lead the party.

When the war in South Africa opened and the despised Boers inflicted the series of reverses traditional for British troops, the utmost anxiety prevailed in England. Discontent was general with leadership in the field and in the Government. The Liberals, had they been in a position to exploit the situation, might have inflicted a decisive defeat on the Salisbury administration, but they were in no wise able to take advantage of the opponent's weakness. But they were at the height of one of their periodic indulgences in party schism. Weakened by the disruption over Home Rule, they had been riven again by the feuds that had followed the resignation of the aged Gladstone.

---

* Members of the House of Commons are provided with benches for their seats. A long table, with the Speaker at its head, separates the rival parties. To the right of the Speaker sit the Government supporters; their leaders, the Ministers, occupying the front bench known as the Treasury Bench.

In the Khaki Election of 1900 the Conservative electoral tactics were of utmost simplicity. The Government appealed to the country for a mandate to bring the war to a successful conclusion. They classed their political opponents of every description under the all-embracing title of Pro-Boer. In the effective slogan of Joseph Chamberlain, "Every seat lost by the Government is a seat lost to the Boers."

Returning to England from the front, Churchill found the election under way and himself the man of the hour. Eleven constituencies solicited the honor of his candidature, but though Oldham had been the scene of his discomfiture, and though the prospects of victory were by no means assured, he resolved to give Oldham a chance to rectify its previous error.

It would be difficult to imagine a greater contrast in political fortunes than between the circumstances of the young candidate at his first attempt in 1899 and at his second in 1900. Then he was an unknown young man of aristocrat connections with nothing much more to commend him. Now he was one of the best known and most popular men in England. His exploits in the war in South Africa had been well publicized. In young Winston the people could find an object on which to expend their will to hero worship.

Winston entered Oldham to the tune of "The Conquering Hero" with the bands playing, flags flying and crowds cheering. He drove through the street in an open carriage, proclaimed in the slogan of one electoral banner as "England's Noblest Hero." Such was the laudation showered upon the young man that a liberal newspaper could write: "Oldham appears to be in some doubt whether it was Lord Roberts, Mr. Winston Churchill or Bill Adams that took Pretoria."

The Lancanshire Liberals were not daunted by the magic of his personality, and made him fight every inch of the way. It was a campaign which a young man of action could relish to the full. One advantage was his—he had himself participated in the war which was the chief subject of contention between the parties. His political position was clear-cut.

"I was nearly," he said, "a peace-at-any-price man up to the time of the declaration of the war. After that I was a victory at-any-price man."

His opponents, whom he had met the year before, **Mr. Emmott** and Mr. Runciman, were Liberal Imperialists, and offered an easy target. The contest, Mr. Churchill declared, was between "the turtle soup of Tory Imperialism and the mock-turtle soup of Liberal Imperialism."

Mr. Emmott and Mr. Runciman agreed that the war was a just war. They denounced Kruger, the Boer president, and disclaimed all connection with the Pro-Boers. In that event, Mr. Churchill inquired, why were they opposing the Government?

"The Liberals," he said, "have no policy of their own and find no fault with our policy except that they would like to carry it out."

The great Joseph Chamberlain came to Oldham to speak in support of the young candidate, and the name of Joseph Chamberlain was one to conjure with among the Conservative working classes.

Churchill was fortunate that he could count upon such support, and he received a commendation that at once pleased him, and impressed the citizens of Oldham. "I think," declared Mr. Chamberlain, "that Lord Randolph's son has inherited some of the great qualities of his father—his originality and his courage."

Courage—you might have thought that a man with young Churchill's record behind him would not have needed a commendation on that score; but in the heat of the Khaki Election, wild charges were made, and even his courage was called into question. He was accused of personal cowardice, of having left his fellow-prisoners in the lurch at Pretoria.

One of the fellow prisoners at once came forward to expose that particular lie, and to state emphatically that there was no truth in the accusation. Churchill was also able to produce the testimony of Sir Evelyn Wood, the Adjutant General, who wrote, "The officer who was in command of the train which was captured by the Boers with all its occupants, reported highly on the decision and marked courage which you showed on that occasion when, at his request, you assumed temporarily the position of an officer."

It was a hard fight for Oldham and victory was hardly won. When the result of this two-member seat was declared, it was found that Mr. Emmott was again at the top of the poll and

Churchill was second, leading Mr. Runciman by the slender margin of 222 votes.

The young member's delight was unbounded. Congratulations showered upon him. He was the most sought-after man of the moment.

In those days polling in a general election did not take place throughout the country on the same day, but was spread over a number of days. The first results to be declared had a considerable influence on the polls which were still to take place. The first successes, indicating the way in which the tide was flowing, served to accentuate the flow of the tide, for there is a certain satisfaction to the wavering voter to find himself on the winning side.

Oldham was almost the first constituency to poll and the victorious young Conservative received summonses from all parts of the country to speak for fellow Conservatists at their final meetings. He hurried off to Birmingham to return the support he had received from Mr. Chamberlain. On the way an appeal reached him to speak at Manchester on behalf of Mr. Balfour, the leader of the party in the House of Commons. There, indeed, was a tribute to delight the young M.P.—the two chief figures in the party soliciting the favor of his support.

The eloquence of the young member for Oldham contributed no little to his party's success. The Khaki Election firmly established the Conservatives in office for another term, and before going to Westminster to take his seat, Churchill went off on a lecturing tour in Britain, and then across the Atlantic to the United States and Canada. His fame preceded him, and the tour enhanced his reputation. It had the further advantage of setting his finances on a firm footing, and he had the comfortable feeling to be derived from a sum of £10,000 safely invested.

In the new year, Churchill had to make his debut in the House as the junior member for Oldham. Even accomplished orators of experience confess to a certain nervousness before rising to address an assembly that has the reputation of being the most critical in the world.

Nervousness was never a Churchillian characteristic, but nervous he was when the time came to deliver his maiden speech. His concern was the greater as he had a reputation to live up to, but this did not deter him from speaking at the first chance that was offered.

The session, which opened on January 23, 1901, was only four days old when he was seeking the eye of the Speaker of the House. South Africa and the war was the subject of debate, and no member knew more of South Africa and the war from first-hand experience.

His speech had to be prepared in advance, for in those days he could only deliver himself of orations that he had prepared and learned by memory. It is a style not well suited to the cut and thrust of debate, but it was a sheer impossibility for him to address the House in any other way. All he could hope for was to improvise an introductory sentence or two by which to introduce his carefully prepared eloquence.

The fateful night arrived. Encouraged by friends, who said that now was his chance, and not dissuaded by others who urged that it was too soon, Churchill took his seat behind the Conservative front bench, next to that Parliamentary veteran, Gibson Bowles, and waited for his turn to rise.

It had been arranged that he should follow the member for Carnarvon Boroughs, that young Welshman Lloyd George, who had already laid the foundations of a Parliamentary career, but whose promise scarcely betokened the brilliance that was yet to come.

Lloyd George had tabled an amendment, which seemed to provide Churchill with an easy approach for his speech, but for some reason he did not choose to move it. So Churchill saw his opening spoiled.

As Lloyd George spoke, the member for Oldham could have been seen hurriedly drafting alternative exordiums, but each in turn became unsuitable as the Welshman's speech proceeded. Then with the words that he knew the House would wish him to be brief, because it was waiting to hear the new member who was to follow, Lloyd George sat down.

Mr. Speaker called on the member for Oldham. Churchill must rise, though he had not yet found the initial sentence without which the speech he had prepared could not be launched.

He rose and stood for a moment tongue-tied, his difficulty unsolved. The course of his career, even of history itself, might have been changed, had not that veteran of debate been sitting at his side. In a whisper, Gibson Bowles suggested, "You might say—instead of making his violent speech, without moving his moderate amendment, the member for Carnarvon had better have moved his moderate amendment without making his violent speech."

Churchill accepted the improvisation. It was just the phrase needed to start him on his way. The failure which had threatened to overwhelm him a moment before was averted. The magic formula delivered, he could safely entrust himself to his memory and his prepared passages.

The debate had turned on the treatment of the Boers, with whom Liberal members had expressed sympathy because of the manner in which their farms had been burned. Churchill began by saying that he did not think the Boers were likely to overvalue those expressions of sympathy—no people had received so much verbal sympathy, and so little practical support.

"From what I saw of the war in South Africa, and I saw something of it," Churchill went on, "I believe that as compared with other wars, especially those in which a civil population took part, it has been on the whole conducted with unusual humanity and generosity. The immediate policy of the Government should be to make it easy and honorable for the Boers to surrender and painful and perilous for them to continue in the field."

There was a note of sympathy in the speech which raised it above the level of the ultrapatriotic declamations of the platform. The Boers he termed "brave and unhappy men." They should, he urged, be beaten in the field, and made to recognize that their smaller independence must be merged in the larger liberties of the British Empire. Then there should be a full guarantee for the security of their religion and property, an assurance of equal rights, promise of representative institutions and last of all, but not least of all, what the British Army would most readily accord to a brave and enduring foe—all the honors of war.

The war ended, what then? "I have," said Churchill, "traveled a great deal about South Africa during the last ten months, and I should like to lay before you some of the considerations which have been forcibly borne upon me during that period." He argued that an administrator such as Alfred Milner should be set at the head of the civil administration during the interim period before representative rights were granted. The speech concluded with a reference to the speaker's father.

"I cannot sit down without saying how grateful I am for the kindness and patience with which the House has heard me. It has been extended to me, I well know, not on my own account, but because of a splendid memory which many old members still preserve."

So Churchill ended to the sound of applause from all quarters of the House. He had done well. He heard praise from the next speaker, a Liberal, Sir Robert Reid, afterward to sit on the woolsack * as Lord Loreburn, who said, "I am sure the House is glad to recognize that the honorable Member who has just sat down possesses the same courage which so distinguished Lord Randolph Churchill during his short and brilliant career in this House. I have listened with great pleasure to the honorable gentleman."

From his own side of the House, Churchill received the tribute of Joseph Chamberlain, who found in the admirable speech an indication "that we may see the father repeated in the son." That Mr. Chamberlain should have particular praise for the son of a famous man was to be expected, for had not he a father's pride? There was his own son Austen, who was to fill all posts except the very highest, and Neville, who was to reach the highest post of all, that Joseph Chamberlain coveted, but never attained.

On the following day the voice of Asquith, future Prime Minister, was heard from the Liberal benches praising the interesting speech, which "we must all hope and believe and especially those of us who, like myself, enjoyed the friendship of his illustrious father, is the first speech in a Parliamentary career of the highest distinction."

The tributes were an encouragement to the young M.P. He was launched on his political career. He gained the acquaintance of the Welshman to whom he was introduced. The meeting of Churchill and Lloyd George began an association that persisted through the vicissitudes of forty years of political life.

* The wool cushion on which the Lord Chancellor sits in the House of Lords.

CHAPTER TWO

THE TATTERED FLAG

1901–1902

WITH HIS MAIDEN SPEECH creditably delivered, Winston Churchill could afford to sit back to study the strategic position and the way to fame.

The aspirant to honors in the House has two courses open to him. The easiest way to ministerial office is the safe game of follow-the-party-leaders and obedience to the party whips. Having voted with his leaders for the qualifying period of years, the M.P. becomes known as a safe party man. If he can show the necessary modicum of talent, promotion to junior office will at last reward his political devotion.

Winston Churchill gave early indication that the safe way was not going to be his. The subaltern who had lectured the generals was now the junior M.P. who was ready to state a policy for ministers. South Africa was the subject of his first demonstration of independence.

Ministers had expected that with the fall of Ladysmith and Pretoria the collapse of the Boers would quickly follow, but in this they underrated the tenacity of the enemy. The war in South Africa dragged on. As a means of inducing the Boers to cease resistance, the Government issued a proclamation that every Boer leader who did not surrender within a month would be banished for life. This brought Winston into open revolt. "I do not think," he declared, "that this is either a very wise move or one that is likely materially to improve the chances of victory and peace in South Africa."

More vigor in the field was his demand. He called for the dispatch of an overwhelming force to South Africa, better equipped and of greater mobility. They were demands that might have proceeded from the Opposition front bench had not the occupants been paralyzed by their own divisions.

In his second year as member, young Churchill openly allied himself with an Opposition motion. A Mr. Cartwright, editor of a South African newspaper, had been sent to prison a year previously for publishing a seditious libel—that Kitchener had issued secret instructions to the troops to take no prisoners. On the conclusion of his year's sentence he proposed to return to England, but the military authorities refused to permit him to leave South Africa.

Liberals regarded this as unwarrantably harsh treatment of a man who had already been punished for his offense, and dangerous tampering with the principles of personal liberty.

The junior member for Oldham rose to support the Liberals in a speech in which he protested against the violation of the liberty of the subject and of the constitution.

It was, he said, monstrous that the military authorities should dictate who should be free and what opinions should be expressed in England. There were some on that side of the House who were not prepared to see a great constitutional principle violated, not perhaps with deliberate intent but simply because those who administered the law had got used to an over-exercise of power.

Churchill's speech did not commend him to the party whips. It was not playing the party game for a Conservative member to support a Liberal motion.

Over South Africa, Winston showed his prentice hand. Army reform enabled him to give a clearer indication of the metal of which he was made. It enabled him, too, to raise his father's tattered flag and to avenge his father's memory.

Army reform was the province of the Secretary for War, Mr. St. John Brodrick, who is better remembered under the title of Lord Midleton.

In the light of deficiencies disclosed in South Africa, Mr. Brodrick wanted to reorganize and extend the Army by constituting
six Army corps on the continental model, of which three corps of
120,000 men would be ready for foreign service at immediate notice. It was a vast project as military preparations were still regarded in Britain in the opening years of the century, before the
menace of world war had made men think of armies on an altogether more stupendous scale.

The proposals, outlined by Mr. Brodrick in a speech which only
temporarily concealed the vagueness of the measures, were viewed
with doubt even by his own party. When Churchill had finished
dissecting them, doubts had developed into dissent. St. John Brodrick's deficiencies were exposed by a dissector who recalled the
method of Lord Randolph and his Fourth Party.

To appreciate the situation you must go back for a moment
into Parliamentary history. Thirty years before, that is to say in
the early seventies, Lord Randolph was the *enfant terrible* of the
Conservative Party. The Tory leaders in those days were venerable and sedate men. As the son of a duke, Lord Randolph might
have been expected to qualify as one of the same august circle,
but an excess of spirits and original sin caused him to attack and
ridicule those ponderous respectabilities—bearding the goats was
the name he gave to the diversion.

Three other Conservatives joined him in the game of attacking
Gladstone and the Liberals and imparting some vigor to their
own party—Arthur J. Balfour, Sir Henry Drummond Wolff and
Sir John Gorst. This quartette formed the Fourth Party, and their
attacks were carried out with such brilliance that they are still remembered at Westminster though it is almost ninety years since
they cooperated to enliven the dullness of debate.

Lord Randolph may have begun in jest but he continued in
earnest with the avowed aim of making the Conservative program more liberal and popular, one that would appeal to the
masses, more of whom, Parliament by Parliament, were being
given the right to vote. In the eighties he was the champion of
Tory Democracy, acknowledged leader of the Conservative working man.

I cannot, here, tell the story of how he came to capture the
party organization from its leader—it is divertingly told in the

son's biography. "Randy" forced himself into the Cabinet and Lord Salisbury ultimately appointed him Chancellor of the Exchequer. It looked as if Lord Randolph must in due course become Prime Minister.

Promotion to high office did not tame him as it does many of those who start out as firebrands and reformers and end their days as pillars of the party and the state. Inside the Cabinet he continued to strive for social reform.

To obtain the finances necessary to that end he advocated economies in other directions and demanded that the estimates of expenditure for the Army and the Navy should be considerably reduced. When the Cabinet overruled him, he flung his resignation at Lord Salisbury's head, imagining himself to be indispensable as chancellor to a government that was not rich in talent. It was a political miscalculation; he had forgotten Goschen. Lord Salisbury accepted the resignation and appointed Goschen to the Treasury. Randy had to go. It was the end of his career. Not long afterwards his health broke down, and in his final days in the House the man who had delighted members by his shafts of wit was unable to complete his sentences.

Winston held his father's memory dear. He conceived it his duty at once to carry on his father's work and to avenge his father's fall. The Brodrick Army reform proposals gave him the opportunity.

Two months were allowed for the discussion of the Brodrick scheme. The first challenge came from Winston Churchill, who gave notice of an amendment:

> That this House, while fully recognizing the necessity of providing adequately for Imperial defence and the plain need for extensive reforms in the organization and system of the Army, nevertheless cannot view without grave apprehension the continual growth of purely military expenditure, which diverts the energies of the country from their natural commercial and naval development; and having regard to the extraordinary pressure under which all connected with the War Office are now working, desires to postpone final decision on future military policy until calmer times.

The inspiration of the amendment was clear. As one old Parliamentary hand observed: "It is as if Lord Randolph has risen from his grave and answered with his own voice, for this is the identical issue which wrecked his career." It was an act of political insubordination that was not pleasing to the party.

The Times, recognizing the inspiration of the father, disowned the son. "Mr. Winston Churchill," the newspaper pronounced, "repeats again the most disastrous mistake of his father's career."

The son heeded not, but proceeded with his attack. His amendment had to give way to official motion of the Opposition moved by the Liberal leader, Sir Henry Campbell-Bannerman, but it was the speech of the young Conservative rebel that was the principal feature of the debate. It may still be read with interest for its phrases and its well-presented argument, as well as for the light it shows on the development of its author as a public speaker. Already he had matured in style, though not in delivery.

The observations he addressed to the House on May 12, 1901, would have in no way disgraced the Prime Minister forty years later. He was then only twenty-six and had been a member of the House of Commons for less than a year. He spoke with the assurance and authority of a Parliamentary veteran, though with proper deprecation he confessed himself to be a very young man.

The Brodrick scheme of Army reorganization was judged by appeal to the highest principles. Churchill invited the House to take a wider view of Army reform than was possible from the windows of the War Office, and to consider Army expenditure in the light of national economy; Army strength in the light of Continental army strengths; and the place of the Army in imperial defense in the light of British naval power.

At the outset Winston identified himself with his father's arguments. It was an astute and effective device. The House was propitiated by the mark of filial respect and the young speaker gained the added advantage that the words of Winston the son became invested with something of the posthumous authority of Lord Randolph the father.

> If, [he said] I might be allowed to revive a half-forgotten episode—it is half-forgotten because it has passed into that period of twilight which intervenes between the bright glare of newspaper controversy and the calm light of history—I would recall that once upon a time a Conservative and Unionist Administration came

into power supported by a majority, nearly as powerful, and much more cohesive, than that which now supports His Majesty's Government. When the time came round to consider the Estimates, what used to be the annual struggle took place between the great spending Departments and the Treasury.

The Government of the day threw their weight on the side of the great spending Departments, and the Chancellor of the Exchequer resigned. The controversy was bitter, the struggle uncertain, but in the end the Government triumphed, and the Chancellor of the Exchequer went down for ever, and with him, as it now seems, there fell also the cause of retrenchment and economy, so that the very memory thereof seems to have perished, and the words themselves have a curiously old-fashioned ring about them. I suppose that was a lesson which Chancellors of the Exchequer are not likely to forget in a hurry.

I am very glad the House has allowed me, after an interval of fifteen years, to lift again the tattered flag I found lying on a stricken field. . . .

I stand here to plead the cause of economy. I think it is time that a voice was heard from this side of the House pleading that unpopular cause; that some one not on the benches opposite, but a Conservative by tradition, whose fortunes are strongly linked to the Tory party, who knows something of the majesty and power of Britain beyond the seas, upon whom rests no taint of cosmopolitanism, should stand forward and say what he can to protest against the policy of daily increasing the public burdens. If such a one is to stand forward in such a cause, then, I say it humbly, but with, I hope, becoming pride, no one has a better right than I have, for this is a cause I have inherited, and a cause for which the late Lord Randolph Churchill made the greatest sacrifice of any Minister of modern times.

Having thus placed himself before the House as the heir to his father's politics, Winston indulged himself by flinging a few oratorical brickbats at Mr. Brodrick. The Secretary for War was told that he held an office whose occupant does not usually direct or even powerfully influence the policy of a government. His scheme, he was assured, which had looked so attractive at its conception had been sadly knocked about. It had been crushed in the press, exploded in the magazines, and had excited nothing but doubt in the country. As to what the soldiers thought about it—Churchill did not feel equal to voicing their expressions on the floor of the House but he would be "delighted to inform any honorable member desiring information privately."

Three Army corps to be kept ready for expeditionary purposes? No! The proposed three should be reduced to two on the ground that "one is quite enough to fight savages and three are not enough to begin to fight Europeans."

By way of this telling phrase Churchill passed on to warn the House of the magnitude of the scale of modern war. His words within a few years were proved to be fatally prophetic. Today we are, alas, but too conscious of what Continental warfare means for the nations that are involved. At the beginning of the twentieth century our fathers lived in happy ignorance of the devastating consequences. The Boer War was fought in the comfortable remoteness of South Africa. Though many a family suffered bereavement, the operations provided no indication of the way in which war between peoples involves every phase of national existence.

Churchill, the young man of twenty-six, had the gift of prophetic insight. His words in that debate in the year 1901 showed how instinctive was his knowledge of war. The passage is worthy of full quotation:

> The enormous and varied frontiers of the Empire, and our many points of contact with barbarous peoples, will surely in the future, as in the past, draw us into frequent little wars. Our military system must therefore be adapted for dealing with these minor emergencies, smoothly and conveniently. But we must not expect to meet the great civilized Powers in this easy fashion. We must not regard war with a modern Power as a kind of game in which we may take a hand, and with good luck and good management may play adroitly for an evening and come safe home with our winnings. It is not that, and I rejoice that it cannot be that.
>
> A European war cannot be anything but a cruel, heartrending struggle, which, if we are ever to enjoy the bitter fruits of victory, must demand, perhaps for several years, the whole manhood of the nation, the entire suspension of peaceful industries, and the concentrating to one end of every vital energy in the community.
>
> I have frequently been astonished since I have been in this House to hear with what composure and how glibly Members, and even Ministers, talk of a European War. I will not expatiate on the horrors of war, but there has been a great change which the

House should not omit to notice. In former days, when wars arose from individual causes, from the policy of a Minister or the passion of a King, when they were fought by small regular armies of professional soldiers, and when their course was retarded by the difficulties of communication and supply, and often suspended by the winter season, it was possible to limit the liabilities of the combatants. But now, when mighty populations are impelled against each other, each individual severally embittered and inflamed—when the resources of science and civilization sweep away everything that might mitigate their fury, a European war can only end in the ruin of the vanquished and the scarcely less fatal commercial dislocation and exhaustion of the conquerors. Democracy is more vindictive than Cabinets. The wars of peoples will be more terrible than those of kings.

"Why then," it may be said, "surely we must neglect nothing to make ourselves secure. Let us vote this thirty millions without more ado."

Sir, if this vast expenditure on the Army were going to make us absolutely secure—much though I hate unproductive expenditure—I would not complain. But it will do no such thing. The Secretary for War knows—none better than he—that it will not make us secure, and that if we went to war with any great Power his three army corps would scarcely serve as a vanguard. If we are hated, they will not make us loved. If we are in danger, they will not make us safe. They are enough to irritate; they are not enough to overawe. Yet, while they cannot make us invulnerable, they may very likely make us venturesome.

Next Churchill dealt with the role of the Navy in imperial defense. Again the words were prophetic. Here in his second speech to the House he was emphasizing the role the Navy would play in the defense of the Empire—a role that was to be prepared and undertaken under his direction.

The honor and security of the British Empire, he declared, did not depend and could never depend on the British Army. The Admiralty was the only office strong enough to insure the British Empire, and it could only be strong enough to do so because it had hitherto enjoyed the preferential monopoly of the sea. He continued:

The only weapon with which we can expect to cope with the great nations is the Navy. This is what the Chief Secretary to the

Lord Lieutenant [Mr. Wyndham] calls the "trust to luck and the Navy" policy. I confess I do trust the Navy. This new distrust of the Navy, this kind of shrinking from our natural element, the blue water on which we have ruled so long, is the most painful symptom of the military hydrophobia with which we are afflicted. Without a supreme Navy, whatever military arrangements we may make, whether for foreign expeditions or home defence, must be utterly vain and futile. With such a Navy we may hold any antagonist at arm's length and feed ourselves in the meantime, until, if we find it necessary, we can turn every city in the country into an arsenal, and the whole male population into an army.

Sir, the superiority of the Navy is vital to our national existence. That has been said before. No one will deny that or thank me for repeating the obvious. Yet this tremendous Army expenditure directly challenges the principle, and those who advocate it are false to the principle they so loudly proclaim. For the main reason that enables us to maintain the finest Navy in the world is that whereas every European Power has to support a vast Army first of all, we in this fortunate, happy island, relieved by our insular position of a double burden, may turn our undivided efforts and attention to the Fleet.

Why should we sacrifice a game in which we are sure to win to play a game in which we are bound to lose? For the same rule most certainly has a converse application; and just as foreign Powers by reason of their pressing land responsibilities must be inferior to us at sea, so we, whatever our effort, whatever our expenditure, by reason of our paramount sea responsibilities, must be inferior to them on land. And surely to adopt the double policy of equal effort both on Army and Navy, of spending thirty millions a year on each, is to combine the disadvantages and dangers of all courses without the advantages or security of any, and to run the risk of crashing to the ground between two stools, with a Navy dangerously weak and an Army dangerously strong.

From that passage I would ask you to look again at the forecast: "With such a Navy we may hold any antagonist at arm's length and feed ourselves in the meantime, until, if we find it necessary, we can turn every city in the country into an arsenal, and the whole male population into an army." The prophecy was delivered and twice in a score of years he was destined to see it fulfilled, to see himself at the head of a Navy discharging its vital function of keeping the antagonist at bay while every city in the country was turned into an arsenal and the entire male population into an army. How many M.P.s aged twenty-six and with less than a year's membership in the House have been gifted with such prophetic insight? But, then, how many M.P.s have by nature been men of war?

In an eloquent peroration Churchill made his final protest against the scheme of Mr. Brodrick and proclaimed his faith in what he termed the moral force of the British people:

> From the highest sentimental reasons, not less than from the most ordinary practical considerations, we must avoid a servile imitation of the clanking military empires of the European continent, by which we can never obtain the military predominance and security which is desired, but may only impair and vitiate the natural sources of our strength and vigour.
>
> There is a higher reason still. There is a moral force which, as the human race advances, will more and more strengthen and protect those nations who enjoy it; which would have protected the Boers better than all their cannon and their brave commandos, if, instead of being ignorant, aggressive, and corrupt, they had enjoyed that high moral reputation which protected us in the dark days of the war from European interference—for, in spite of every calumny and lie uttered or printed, the truth comes to the top; and it is known, alike by peoples and rulers, that upon the whole, and it is upon the whole that we must judge these things, British influence is a healthy and kindly influence, and makes for the general happiness and welfare of mankind. And we shall make a fatal bargain if we allow the moral force which this country has so long exerted to become diminished, or perhaps destroyed, for the sake of the costly, trumpery, dangerous military playthings on which the Secretary of State for War has set his heart.

Such was the first considerable speech which Winston Churchill addressed to the House of Commons. I have quoted from it at length to show the quality of the speaker revealed at the very outset of his Parliamentary career. There was an immediate outcry from the Conservative ranks at the temerity of the young rebel from Oldham. Criticism was not soothed by the prediction in a liberal paper that the critic of Mr. Brodrick would one day be Liberal Prime Minister of England.

When the debate continued the following day, Mr. Brodrick's critic received as much attention as Mr. Brodrick's scheme.

Churchill was rebuked by Mr. Arthur Lee (later Lord Lee of Fareham), who thought that this was not the time to parade or pursue family traditions. Mr. Dillon, the Irish Nationalist, considered that Lord Randolph never did a better thing than his son had done the previous night—"and I have never seen a young Member of the House spring so suddenly and decisively to the front of debate."

Mr. Brodrick himself descended upon the member for Oldham with ponderous rebuke. "I hope," he said, "in fact, I confidently expect, that Parliament, which was not afraid to part company with a brilliant statesman in 1886, will not be the less severe because of the financial heroics of my honorable friend. Those of us who disagree with him can only hope that the time will come when his judgment will grow up to his ability."

Mr. Brodrick might utter his rebukes, but his opponent emerged the victor. For two years the Brodrick scheme was under debate and for two years Churchill heaped his criticisms upon it with vigor and resource.

I cannot refrain from giving yet one more illustration of Winston's Parliamentary style when he was still in his novitiate as politician. He enjoyed himself hugely as the critic and tormentor of the unfortunate Mr. Brodrick and it is a pity that the wit with which his attacks were enlivened should be entirely forgotten in the limbo of the Parliamentary debates.

In his address to the electors of Wallsend in February 1903, he dealt with the progress, or lack of progress, in transforming the Brodrick scheme from blueprints to practice. His main charge was that though the taxpayers were paying for the whole of the six Army corps which were to form the new divisions, the greater part of the strength of the corps had not yet got beyond the paper stage. He stated:

> While the Fourth Army Corps has got its general, the General has not yet got his Army Corps—though I observe from the papers that he is to take up his command on the first of April. As for the two remaining Army Corps, they are still in the air, organized, apparently, on the Marconi system.
>
> Now I come to what is in some ways an even more serious charge. It is what is called "throwing dust in the eyes of the public," and because it is such an expensive process I will call it

throwing gold dust in the eyes of the public. Nearly four months ago you might have read in the newspapers an official *communiqué* from the War Office to this effect: "General Bruce Hamilton is appointed to command the Third Division of the First Army Corps." "Ah," says "the Man in the Street" when he reads this, "what did I tell you? There is Mr. Brodrick persevering, in spite of so much criticism, with his great Army Corps scheme. Here is a popular South African General appointed to one of the most important commands."

But what the public do not see—unless it is pointed out for them by inconvenient and tiresome people like me—is that this same General has no division to command at all, because there is no Third Division of the First Army Corps yet formed. Nor is there likely to be one for a long time to come, and General Bruce Hamilton, instead of being at the head of eighteen guns and 10,000 infantry, may go away and amuse himself on leave with the satisfaction of knowing that his name is being exploited for a purely political purpose, namely, to make believe that Mr. Brodrick's scheme is much further advanced than it really is or is likely to be. I do not hesitate to say that there are numerous cases of officers, particularly popular officers, being appointed to commands which either do not exist or only partially exist, and I characterize these methods as wasteful and uncandid, and as throwing gold dust in the eyes of the public.

I dare say some of you have read a book called *The Phantom Millions,* or the story of the great French fraud. It describes in very eloquent language how a number of people in France were induced to lend huge sums of money on the security of a safe which was supposed to contain millions of pounds. For a long time they were kept quiet by all kinds of paper promises and all kinds of legal dodges; but at last the end came. The farce could not be kept up any longer. The safe was opened by the indignant creditors, and inside they found—nothing but a few brass buttons and a few worthless bits of paper.

No doubt when you read that story you could not help feeling that these French people must have been very simple and even silly to be taken in like that; and with that sense of superiority which it is one of our national characteristics often to feel, you felt inclined to say, "That may be all very well in France, but it could never happen over here in England. We are much too shrewd." Do not be too sure about that.

Sometimes lately when I have watched the proceedings of the

War Office, their desperate attempts to increase the paper strength of the Army by any means, whether by enlisting immature boys or "specials," or "flatfoots" who cannot march, or by creation of phantom Army Corps—just about as real as the Humbert millions, or by the appointments of distinguished South African generals whose names will go down well with the public, to command brigades and divisions which do not exist, I have felt convinced that the great French fraud at which we have been so amused, is merely a poor, wretched, private concern compared to the great English fraud which the War Office is perpetrating every day.

What do you think you will find in the War Office safe on the day when it is opened? You have advanced vast sums of money on it—thirty millions a year—ten millions a year more than you ever paid before. Some of that money is raised by the taxation of very poor people. You believe that the safe contains an efficient and economical Army, suited to your needs, proportioned to your resources, and what will you find? You will find a few brass buttons —made in Germany—and a few worthless bits of paper on which are written the names of the brigades and the divisions which make up Mr. Brodrick's *papier mâché* Army scheme.

At last the grandiose Brodrick scheme for Army reform perished. Reform had to wait until Haldane became War Minister. Mr. Brodrick retreated from the War Office to the comparative safety of the affairs of India.

Lord Randolph was indeed avenged.

Churchill in those days was always reminding the House of Randy. When he was speaking he could be observed to be fingering the plain gold signet ring which Lord Randolph had worn. Those who had known the father were startled by the re-incarnation of his mannerisms and attitudes in the son. There was the same stoop, the same gait, the same lurching movement in his walk. When he spoke he grasped the lapels of his coat just as his father had done. Even in frock coat and large bow tie and even down to the shape of the collar there was a resemblance.

Churchill was now passing through his Hughlighan days.

The Hughlighans were the discontented members of the Conservative Party, young, liberal-minded and progressive. We should call them now a "ginger group," this party within a party, but they were styled Hughlighans from their distinguished member Lord Hugh Cecil (later Lord Quickswood), who was later to repent of the error of challenging authority and become concerned with securing the respect that is authority's due as Provost of Eton College. They were less scintillating, perhaps, than the Fourth Party, these Hughlighans, but they carried heavier guns. Faithful Tories burst into print with indignation to denounce these disloyalists of the party. Never had they known an attack upon a government organized and pressed with so much bitterness and apparent determination by members elected to support it. And of all the Hughlighans, Winston Churchill was the most forceful in sniping at Arthur Balfour, languid philosopher on the Treasury bench.

CHAPTER THREE

IN REVOLT

1903–1905

IN THE DEBATE on Army reform Winston Churchill had gone a long way on the road of political independence. He had established himself as a Parliamentary franc-tireur. But though he would not accept the lead of his party in all things, he was still within the party fold. The next turn of the political wheel brought him to the parting of the ways.

When the year 1903 opened, the political barometer seemed to be set moderately fair. The Boer War was over. The Irish were comparatively quiescent. There were still rumblings of discontent over religious education in schools.

No great national issue for the moment divided the parties. It was the lull before the storm—the last lull before a succession of bitter controversies that continued without a break and were in progress when the greater tempest of World War I broke in 1914.

The storm of 1903 was produced by Joseph Chamberlain. Returning from a visit to South Africa he loosed upon the country a political bombshell, product of his ruminations on the veldt. Addressing his Birmingham constituents in May, he declared himself to be in favor of a system of imperial preference designed to assist the producers of the Empire in meeting the competition of foreign production. This involved a radical change in England's fiscal system and the abandonment of the principle of free trade, which had been her traditional policy since protection was abandoned sixty years before by Sir Robert Peel.

Joe Chamberlain advocated a complete break with the free-trade past, calling not merely for taxes on imported food but for the employment of tariffs as a bargaining weapon with protectionist states. The speech produced an entire transformation in the political scene. The attack on free trade served to bring immediate unity to the Liberals. Old feuds forgotten, they seized on the occasion which brought them together to fight for a cause on which all Liberals were agreed.

For the Conservatives, the Chamberlain bombshell had precisely the contrary effect. As the Liberals coalesced so the Conservative Party disintegrated.

Balfour was principally occupied, for the remaining two years of his premiership, in trying to find some means of compromise by which the party could be saved from the split that threatened to rend it. To neither protectionist nor free-trade wing would he commit himself, but always he searched for a magic formula that would enable the dissentient wings to continue to support the administration. Never was there a more brilliant exhibition of walking the political tightrope, but the alternative attacks from the rival flanks placed him in a series of predicaments.

Here was an ideal field for the Parliamentary franc-tireur. Winston Churchill, richer from the experience of two sessions of Parliament, exploited the situation to the full. He was in no doubt about the evil of tariffs. To tamper with free trade was to trifle with political sin. Free trade, he declared, was to England not merely a right and logical policy but a bread-and-butter policy. To say that protection meant a greater development of wealth was an economic absurdity and to say that it meant a fairer distribution of wealth was a downright lie.

"This move," he said, "means a change not only in historic English parties but in conditions of our public life. The old Conservative Party with its religious convictions and constitutional principles will disappear, and a new party will arise—rigid, materialistic and secular—whose opinions will turn on tariffs and who will cause the lobbies to be crowded with the touts of protected industries.

The Liberal leaders leapt to denounce what one of them termed "the reckless criminal escapade of old Joe's." But the Liberals were not more outspoken and persistent in their attacks than was the junior member for Oldham. Joseph Chamberlain stumped up and down the country in his raging, tearing campaign advocating imperial preference. Winston Churchill stumped up and down the country after him, pressing the case for free trade.

As soon as Birmingham had spoken Oldham replied, and Winston carried the fight even to the Birmingham citadel. The Birmingham crowd might threaten the opponents of their political idol. Kruger's followers had been more threatening than old Joe's. The crowd that came to mob the member for Oldham remained to cheer.

Old Joe made tariffs the sole issue of the hour. He also made Winston Churchill a national figure in politics. The elder man might be a political giant, the younger was a not ineffective David. His oratorical stones were not fatal, but they were sorely troublesome.

His ability as a speaker grew with practice. So did his aptitude for dealing with opponents, and the shafts of his ridicule became more pointed.

Mr. Brodrick, in his phrase, was a sufferer from German measles; Arthur Balfour became a "Sheffield Shuffler"; Arnold Forster was dubbed a "Jack in Office." Chamberlain's patriotism was measured by the "imperial pint" and the Tariff Reform League was that "disreputable body" whose support was as fatal as prussic acid to candidates for Parliament.

A certain Colonel Kenyon-Slaney ventured to make a personal attack upon him. Winston's reply was coruscating:

> I notice that Colonel Kenyon-Slaney says that I and my honourable friend are renegades and traitors. I have often noticed that when political controversy becomes excited, persons of choleric disposition and limited intelligence are apt to become rude. Ladies and gentlemen, if I am a traitor, at any rate I was fighting the Boers in South Africa when Colonel Kenyon-Slaney was slandering them at home. My honourable friend and I had the honour of

serving in the field for our country, while this gallant, fire-eating colonel was content to kill Kruger with his mouth in the comfortable security of England.

Arthur Balfour missed an opportunity to retain Winston Churchill in the Conservative Party. Out and out Free Traders resigned their posts as ministers. It was a chance to have brought Churchill in, thereby silencing a damaging critic and attaching this rising young man to the party. He made no such offer. Chamberlain recognized the blunder, even if Balfour did not. "Winston," he said to Mrs. Asquith, otherwise Margot, the diarist, "is the cleverest of all the young men and the mistake Arthur made was to let him go."

For a while Churchill maintained his formal connection with the party, but the final break could not be long delayed when he called upon Free Traders of all parties to form one line of battle against the common foe. When, in a public speech, he thanked God for the existence of the Liberal Party, Oldham Conservatives formally disowned him. But they dared not call upon him to resign; they feared the verdict of the electors more than did he.

In the House, Conservative members no longer cheered the member for Oldham—indeed, there was one occasion, celebrated in the annals of Westminster, when they declined even to listen to him. Winston rose to indulge his favorite pastime of baiting the Conservative leaders, still nominally his own. He had not finished his opening sentence before a number of M.P.s left their seats and walked out. As he proceeded, so did the exodus. Members who had passed through the doors could be seen through the glass panels beckoning to the men who remained. Gradually the audience dwindled and before he reached his peroration Winston Churchill was standing alone midst empty benches on his side of the chamber.

This marked the end of his connection with the Conservative Party. A few evenings later he was discovered in a new seat—the corner of the front Opposition bench below the gangway. He had crossed the floor. The seat he had chosen was the one from which twenty years before his father had made his own.

There were angry taunts from the young Conservatives seated around Joseph Chamberlain as Churchill rose to speak. With hands on hips and head thrust forward in characteristic attitude of defiance, he flung his taunts at the aggressors. In this form of Parliamentary hostilities he could easily hold his own, but the contest soon reached the stage where brute power of lung outmatched felicity in repartee. There was no hearing the member for Oldham above the din.

A new Labour member, Mr. Shackleton, protested. "Mr. Speaker," he said, "for the last ten minutes I have been endeavoring to listen to the speech of the honorable member and I have been unable to follow him. I think it is one of the privileges every honorable member is entitled to that he should be heard."

The Speaker replied that it was impossible for him to compel every member to keep silence, but he trusted that the rules of the House would be observed.

Churchill made another attempt to deliver himself of his speech, but his remarks were lost amid what the official report described by the remarkable understatement of "continued interruptions." Churchill was heard to observe that he saw the Prime Minister was in his place: was it to be supposed that he was a consenting party to the uproar? At this, babel was renewed.

In a calmer moment Churchill appealed to the good sense of the House to say whether he was receiving fair treatment. Was this carefully organized attack on the liberties of debate, in which the right honorable member for West Birmingham—designating Joseph Chamberlain—was an accomplice and consenting party . . .

The question was not completed. There were shouts of "Order" and "Withdraw." Old Joe sprang to his feet. "Mr. Speaker," he protested in his turn. "I rise on a point of order."

There were interruptions here from the Opposition benches. "I merely wish to know," he went on amid shouts and countershouts, "whether it is in order for the junior member for Oldham to say that there is a conspiracy against him in which I am an accomplice—a statement which is absolutely untrue." This disclaimer was received with cries of "Oh! Oh!" and "Order! Order!"

The Speaker, thus appealed to, pronounced that the honorable member for Oldham should not make such charges.

"Withdraw," bawled the Conservatives.

Churchill made a nicely phrased withdrawal. "Mr. Speaker," he said, carefully choosing his words, "if I have said anything which passes in any degree the limitation of the order of debate I completely withdraw it. I have made my protest which I venture to commit to the good sense and calmer consideration of the House."

Churchill, in opposition, was separated by the floor from his Hughlighan associates, but he had soon taken his place in a first-rate team of Liberal parliamentarians. Lloyd George was the unofficial leader of a band of Liberals, so we are assured by old Parliamentary hands, who improved on "Fourth Party" methods, and were the authors of the most virile opposition that the House had witnessed in living memory.

Snap divisions which, catching the ministerial supporters at a numerical disadvantage, might involve the Government in the discomfiture of a defeat, became a popular pastime, so that the Chief Government Whip, Acland Hood, the hunting squire, became the hardest-worked man in London. On one occasion Churchill and his friends made a night of it on one of the budget debates. Hour after hour they kept the discussion going and forced the Government back-benchers to tramp wearily through the lobbies.*

All the honors of the night did not go to Churchill. Between six and seven o'clock in the morning Claude Lowther, one of the younger Conservatives, called the attention of the House to a report that the disease of beriberi had broken out among the Chinese laborers in South Africa. He suggested that the member for Oldham was suffering from this malady. From the Chair, Claude Lowther was reminded that these observations had no bearing on the motion under discussion, at which he commented, "I bow entirely to your ruling, sir, but I made that remark because I have heard that the most marked characteristic symptom of the disease is a terrific swelling of head."

It was twenty minutes to four in the afternoon before the Government completed its appointed business. Churchill and his friends had kept the House in being for twenty-five hours.

Throughout the sessions of 1904 and 1905, Arthur Balfour continued his dexterous exhibition of sitting on the fiscal fence. In the country, tariffs or free trade was the question of the hour.

---

* Voting in the House of Commons is accomplished by members passing through one or other of two "division" lobbies, or passages. When a division is called, the "ayes" and the "noes" file through the pertaining lobby to be counted by tellers. "Snap divisions" are engineered to catch opponents off their guard.

All attempts to raise the matter in Parliament were skillfully evaded. The House of Commons, as the veteran Gibson Bowles remarked, was "the only place on God's earth" where the matter could not be discussed.

Churchill neglected no opportunity to add to the embarrassments of his ex-leader. One evening when he was speaking, Balfour rose from his place and passed along the front bench toward the door. In a flash came the gibe from Churchill, "The right honorable gentleman need not go out. I am not going to talk about free trade."

On another occasion, when a lengthy fiscal debate was taking place, Balfour absented himself. Said Churchill, "To keep in office for a few more weeks and months there is no principle which the Government are not prepared to abandon, no friend or colleague they are not prepared to betray, and no quantity of dust and filth they are not prepared to eat."

Only by evading the issue could Balfour prevent his Cabinet from breaking up. Ministers made little attempt to hide their differences. As Churchill said, "Cabinet Ministers abuse, contradict and disavow each other. Members of the Government and of the Conservative Party fight over the Prime Minister as dogs worry over a bone."

At length, even the patience of Arthur Balfour broke under the continued strain of attempting to reconcile the irreconcilables in his party and he resigned office. Campbell-Bannerman formed a Liberal ministry and Winston Churchill found a place in it as Parliamentary Secretary for the Colonies. His political apprenticeship was ended. At the age of thirty-one, the youngest man in Europe had become a junior minister of the Crown.

In fact, Campbell-Bannerman had proposed that Winston should take the office of Financial Secretary to the Treasury. This is the foremost of the junior ministerial posts and its occupant may count on reaching the Cabinet at the first reshuffle in the ministry. At that time, too, the salary was £500 a year more than that of an under-secretary. Churchill, on declining this offer and asking to go to the Colonies, was wise, for on the affairs of South Africa he could speak with the authority of knowledge gained at first hand—and South Africa was going to be one of the principal matters of debate.

When he crossed the floor of the House, his action was criticized by old Parliamentary hands. Churchill, they suggested, would now suffer the handicap of arousing the aversion that is always incurred by the man who turns his coat. He would also, in running for the prize of office, be brought into competition with many able men of his own age who, having been Liberals throughout their careers, would resent being set aside in favor of a later comer. There was jealousy among the younger members of the party, but by the elders Churchill was accepted as a valued colleague. By several he was received as a close friend, in particular by John Morley, biographer of Gladstone, and by Asquith, the coming man, already indicated as the next Prime Minister.

CHAPTER FOUR

MINISTER OF THE CROWN

1905–1908

IT WAS SHEER ZEST for conflict that made Winston Churchill choose North-West Manchester as his next constituency. There were plenty of safe Liberal seats which would have considered it a privilege to be represented in Parliament by the young Under-Secretary for the Colonies. Manchester North-West was a Tory stronghold, but for Churchill it had the attraction that a victory there would be the more resounding.

The former member, Sir William Houldsworth, had retired from politics and the Conservatives had chosen as their nominee an unknown man—a busy young solicitor, Joynson Hicks by name, afterwards Viscount Brentford, or more affectionately, "Jix." He was of the plodding efficient type of politician, who form the mainstay of their parties. The Home Secretaryship ultimately rewarded his services, and his single indiscretion in a life of Parliamentary rectitude was to have the effect of giving "flappers" the vote.

When chosen by the Conservatives of Manchester North-West, his experience had been limited to the small affairs that provide work for county court judges. He had been concerned with pirate omnibuses and glanders in horses, rather than with the complexities of commerce on which the prosperity of Manchester rests.

He lacked nothing in assurance, however, and it was he who pronounced Churchill excommunicate from the Conservative Party for his free-trade heresies. "Let not Mr. Churchill think that he can return to the Unionists," Joynson Hicks declared. "There is between him and our party a gulf fixed by himself, which authorizes me to declare in your name, that while there is seed-time and harvest, summer and winter, we will never have him back."

The prophet lived to see his prophecy confounded—not merely to see the return of the excommunicate to the party, but to sit with him in the same Conservative Cabinet.

Joynson Hicks thought that his opponent offered an easy target as a deserter from his former party, and he had devoted much energy and research to drawing up a pamphlet, recalling what Churchill had said as a Conservative and contrasting it with his later statements. In the Tory camp they set great store by this exposure of the Conservative now turned Liberal.

For a less ready speaker than Churchill, it might have proved embarrassing, but he was equal to the occasion. In a single phrase he destroyed the effect of the carefully prepared attack. The pamphlet had been circulated throughout the constituency and some Conservative hecklers came along to one of the opponent's meetings; they saw to it that Churchill was given a copy of the leaflet, and they asked him what answer he had to this chronicle of his inconsistency—"Answer it," they shouted.

Churchill replied that when he was a Conservative he had said a number of stupid things. He had left the stupid party because he no longer wished to go on saying stupid things. Thereupon he tore the pamphlet in pieces and flung it from him with a gesture of contempt. It was an effective reply, and he was not troubled further with the famous pamphlet.

Thereafter the hecklers contented themselves with the simple accusation of "turncoat." Whereupon the Liberal supporters retorted with "What about Joe?" Joseph Chamberlain was a more conspicuous example even than Churchill of political desertion. That great imperialist, pillar of Toryism, had started in politics as a Radical and republican.

In addition to the Conservative hecklers, Churchill had to face the interruptions of the Suffragettes, then a rising force in the country. Christabel Pankhurst, the suffragette leader, declared that in the person of Winston Churchill the Liberal Government was to receive the weight of the women's opposition. The method decided on was to wreck his meetings and scarcely a night passed at which the "henpeckers" did not break in upon his eloquence. Joynson Hicks, who was not so embarrassed by their attentions, endeavored to appeal for fair play on behalf of his opponent, only to be informed that suffragette tactics "will be determined without reference to the works of yourself or of your opponent."

Sylvia Pankhurst, sister of Christabel, and the leader of the campaign, was delighted when she could sting Churchill into an angry retort. On one occasion she was invited to mount the platform to submit her questions. She was forced to remain there to hear the candidate's answers. When she rose to interrupt he told her that she was bringing disgrace upon an honored name, and he added: "Nothing would induce me to vote for giving women the franchise. I am not going to be henpecked into a question of such importance."

In her history of the women's movement,[1] Sylvia gives a lively account of the result:

> I would have gone then, but in a scuffle . . . I was pushed into a side room. I was left there, the door being locked on the outside, but not before I had opened the window and called to the people in the street to witness the conduct of one enthusiastic Liberal who was jumping about like a madman and threatening to scratch my face. It appeared that I was a prisoner, for the windows were barred, but the people who had gathered outside called to me that a window at the other end of the room had a couple of bars missing. They helped me out and called for a speech. When the night's speaking was done, I gave my story to the newspapers. It appeared with big headlines the next day, producing innumerable jokes at the candidate's expense. There was no more kidnapping.

All the country watched the fight at Manchester North-West.

The prosperity of this great industrial city was based on the export market and the citizens were in no doubt where their interests lay. Free trade was synonymous with prosperity for Manchester, and when the day of the poll came, Free Traders were returned for all six seats, five of which at the Khaki Election had sent Conservatives to Westminster. Balfour was one of the victims on the stricken field. Churchill, the Liberal, was returned by the comfortable majority of 1,241 votes. Once again his return helped to swell the tide of victory for his party. The triumph at Manchester was the precursor of a Liberal landslide throughout the country. The Conservatives suffered their worst defeat since the days of the Reform Bill * eighty years before.

Of Churchill's part in the Liberal victory that shrewd political observer, Lord Mottistone, wrote in his reminiscences:

> Winston Churchill at Manchester conducted a really wonderful Free Trade campaign. Of course Manchester was the home of Free Trade, but making all the allowances for the fact it was nevertheless true that Churchill's achievement at this election in winning votes for Free Trade not only in Manchester but throughout the country was one of the most remarkable electoral performances of our time.

And Churchill, mark you, was a young man of thirty-one, fighting his third election. He returned to Westminster, to the dignity and responsibilities of the front bench. He was a junior member of a ministry which contained as brilliant men as have been included in any administration. At the Exchequer, as right-hand man to Campbell-Bannerman, was Herbert Asquith. Sir Edward Grey, who has his place among the great Foreign Secretaries, was at the Foreign Office. At the Board of Trade Lloyd George was beginning his rise to the highest place. John Morley, philosopher in chief of the Liberals, was at the India Office, and at the War Office was Haldane, one of the subtlest intellects of his day.

It was a complete education for a young man starting on his ministerial career to be associated with such redoubtable Parliamentarians. It is also an indication of Churchill's native ability that though he had not had the benefit of their longer experience in affairs, he could take his place among them without suffering by comparison.

He was particularly attracted by the personality of John Morley. The association of this young man of action and the elderly contemplative philosopher, can be explained only by the principle of the attraction of opposites. The younger man learned much

---

* A landmark in British political history, the Reform Bill of 1832 came near to producing a revolution. Its purpose was to extend the right to vote and it was strenuously opposed by the Tories. It was carried after a bitter struggle, enfranchising the middle classes and its authors, the Whigs (Liberals), were abundantly rewarded by the new electors.

from "Honest John," whose influence could be seen twenty years later, when Churchill was leading the opposition to the great India Reform Bill.

As Under-Secretary for the Colonies, Churchill was not holding a post usually associated with prominence in the political scene. But he was never a man to languish unnoticed and he lost no time in establishing himself as the most conspicuous of the junior members of the Ministry.

The late Conservative administration had conducted the war in South Africa to a successful conclusion. The new Liberal Government had to provide for South Africa's future. The minister principally concerned, the Colonial Secretary, was the Earl of Elgin, newly returned from India, where he had filled the office of Viceroy. His place was in the House of Lords. Churchill as his understudy in the Commons found himself in charge of the measure, the principal piece of Government legislation of the session and the most controversial.

It was a fine opportunity for winning ministerial spurs and Churchill made full use of it. His knowledge of South Africa and its people gave him an advantage in debate that few members enjoyed. For his old enemies, the Boers, he had always had sympathy and no little admiration, and he was able to put his heart as well as his brains into his speeches for the bill.

Campbell-Bannerman, during the war, had denounced the "methods of barbarism" with which the Boers were treated, and the South African Constitution Bill was the measure of a liberal and enlightened policy. It carried out the pledge in the treaty of peace that "as soon as circumstances permit representative institutions leading to self-government will be introduced."

The Conservatives, who considered that they had a special interest in South African affairs, seeing that it had been their war, objected that the time had not arrived for the conferment of self-government. Lord Milner, Lord Lansdowne, and Arthur Balfour expressed their fears over the outcome of the policy in speeches of gloomy foreboding. Twenty years or so later Churchill was to express the same sort of fears about granting self-government to India. In 1906 he felt no such alarm over South Africa. Then he spoke of the blessings of self-government and it was Tory opponents who murmured their apprehensions. To his critics he replied:

> We do not ask honourable gentlemen opposite to share our responsibility. If by any chance our counsels of reconciliation should come to nothing, if our policy should end in mocking disaster, then the resulting evil would not be confined to South Africa. Our unfortunate experience would be trumpeted forth all over the world wherever despotism wanted a good argument for bayonets, wherever an arbitrary government wished to deny or curtail the liberties of imprisoned nationalities.
>
> But if, on the other hand, as we hope and profoundly believe, better days are in store for South Africa, if the long lane it has been travelling has reached its turning at last, if the near future should unfold to our eyes a tranquil, prosperous, consolidated Afrikander nation under the protecting ægis of the British Crown, then, I say, the good, as well as the evil, will not be confined to South Africa; then, I say, the cause of the poor and the weak all over the world will have been sustained, and everywhere small peoples will get more room to breathe, and everywhere great empires will be encouraged by our example to step forward—and it only needs a step—into the sunshine of a more gentle and a more generous age.

Winston and his ministerial chief formed by no means a happy combination. You can imagine that the earl, who had just ceased to occupy the position of Viceroy of India, the most exalted post to be filled by a subject of the Crown, might well have expected more deference than he was likely to receive from the junior minister. Sir Austen Chamberlain, in his recollections, recounts a story which mirrors their uneasy relationship. Winston, on one occasion, submitted to his chief a long memorandum on a matter of colonial administration. He concluded his paper with the observation "These are my views." "But not mine," was the comment added in Lord Elgin's own hand.

Dr. Jameson, leader of the famous raid, who had business at the Colonial Office about this time, asserted that for the most part State papers were not shown to Winston by Elgin, who was "scarcely fitted to govern the Colonies."

Churchill, nevertheless, had the satisfaction of contributing to the achievement of a settlement in South Africa. Lord Mottistone once sought to apportion the praise due to those who set relations with South Africa on a friendly footing. At the top of the list he placed "the courage of Campbell-Bannerman and Churchill in taking the first step by giving Home Rule to the Transvaal."

The policy of conciliation found its justification when in 1914 and again in 1939 the Union of South Africa rallied to the aid of the Crown to play no mean a part in the struggle against a despotism which in Churchill's phrase wished to "deny the liberties of imprisoned nationalities."

It was during the discussions on South Africa that he coined a phrase that still has its use as a euphemism for inaccuracy of statement. There was much concern in those days about the employment in South African mines of Chinese labor under a system of indentures which gave rise to cries of protest against Chinese slavery. The Colonial Under-Secretary was called upon to answer a question on the subject of this labor contract and in his reply he made use of the phrase "terminological inexactitude," which is still current as a coin of speech though the occasion of its minting be forgotten. Let the words appear in their full context:

"The contract," said Churchill, "may not be a desirable contract, but it cannot be in the view of His Majesty's Government classified as 'slavery' on the extreme acceptance of the word without some risk of terminological inexactitude."

So the years of ministerial apprenticeship passed until Campbell-Bannerman, stricken with illness, resigned, and was succeeded by Asquith. The Government was reconstructed and Churchill, already a Privy Councilor,* became a member of the Cabinet as President of the Board of Trade.

He was only thirty-four years of age and could congratulate himself on political advancement, gained by sheer merit and ability, of a rapidity with which few could compare. He had sat in Parliament only seven years and had belonged to the Liberal Party for a little less than four years. He was already recognized as one of the ablest speakers in the country—one of the leading assets possessed by the Liberal Party.

It was from the heights that Churchill surveyed the world in

* At one time the body through which the Sovereign governed the land, the Privy Council has been superseded by the modern Cabinet. Privy Councilor is a title of honor conferred, on his appointment, on a Minister of the Crown and is occasionally bestowed in recognition of political service. Privy Councilors meet on the occasion of the succession of a new Sovereign.

the spring of the year 1908. And then Fortune changed her smiling face for a moment.

Under a Parliamentary procedure, which has since been changed, it was necessary that the new President of the Board of Trade should submit himself to the verdict of his constituents. So amidst the first cares of high office he had to engage in the ordeal of a hard-fought election campaign. Joynson Hicks was again his opponent.

Winston Churchill did not fail to extract what advantage he could from the constitutional necessity that required him to fight for election, just because he had moved up from the second eleven to the first eleven in the Liberal team. Having pointed out that the office to which he had been promoted was not wholly unsuited to the representation of Manchester North-West, he proceeded:

> To oppose the election of a Minister once elected as the Member of Government is, to say the least, unusual. To delay and hamper the work of a great department, charged with important legislation of a purely non-party character, betokens a keener zest for factional than for national interest. Yet, anomalous as is the technicality which renders a contest possible, mischievous as is such opposition which makes it necessary, I welcome this opportunity of dealing with the taunts and challenges, so cheaply uttered during the eighteen months by politicians still smarting from their last defeats.

Joynson Hicks, in his address to the electors, used vigorous language to attack the Liberal Ministry. He declared that it was the first opportunity North-West Manchester had had of proclaiming its opinion of a Government, which in the short space of two years had alienated the Colonies, weakened the navy, increased taxation, flouted religious convictions, and let loose chaos and bloodshed in Ireland—which, all things considered, is a pretty generous measure of liability.

There was a Socialist in the field, Dan Irving, standing in the name of the extreme left wing of the Labour movement, but neither of the members of the senior parties gave much heed to this intervener. The contest was a lively one, and the ambulance had to be summoned on more than one occasion when the partisans did not limit themselves to the arbitrament of words.

Despite the unwritten law against the participation of Cabinet

Sir Winston Churchill's grandfather, John Winston Spencer-
Churchill (1822-1883), seventh
Duke of Marlborough, was a
Conservative statesman who for
four years served as Lord Lieutenant of Ireland

Bettman

Lord Randolph Spencer-Churchill (1849-1895), Sir Winston's
father, was a progressive Conservative Member of Parliament for
many years, was Secretary of State
for India, Chancellor of the
Exchequer, and Leader of the
House of Commons

Bettman

Sir Winston was born in Blenheim Palace, Woodstock, Oxford-shire, the home of his ancestors. The room, (below) originally allotted by the first Duke of Marlborough to his domestic chaplain, Dean Jones, is where Sir Winston was born, November 30, 1874.

Sir Winston's American grandmother, Mrs. Leonard Jerome

Brown Brothers

Lady Randolph Churchill, before her marriage Miss Jennie Jerome,
with her two sons—Winston (right) and his only brother, John, who
died in February, 1947, at the age of 67. At the time this photo was
taken, Winston was a student in a preparatory school.

FPG

Two years old: 1876

FPG

Hussars lieutenant: 1895

Brown Brothers

At Harrow: 1889

Brown Brothers

South Africa: 1899

Brown Brothers

M.P.: 1900

Brown Brothers

Wedding day: 1908

Brown Brothers

First Lord: 1914

Combine

Sailor: 1912

Combine

World War I major: 1916

Combine

Honorary degree: 1925

Combine

Campaigning: 1924

Combine

"Railroad engineer": 1937

Fox

Wide World

The young war correspondent
for *The Morning Post* after
he was taken prisoner-of-war
by the Boers, November 15,
1899 (shown at right)

Only a month after his capture, Churchill escaped and
was welcomed as a hero at
Durban where he is shown addressing an outdoor meeting

Bettman

Newly appointed as President of the Board of Trade, Churchill—a Liberal—sought re-election in Manchester, April, 1908, but was defeated by the Conservative candidate, Joynson Hicks

In 1909, Churchill attended maneuvers of the German Army and is shown here shaking hands with Kaiser Wilhelm II, German Emperor

A detective follows the Churchills' baby nurse as she takes daughter Diana for a stroll in 1910. It had been reported that the Suffragettes, who frequently made Churchill the "target" of their attacks, had threatened to kidnap the Churchill baby and hold her as a "hostage."

ministers in a by-election, Lloyd George appeared at Manchester to speak on behalf of his colleague. The influence of his oratory was heightened for local patriots by the fact that the member for Carnarvon was Lancastrian by birth, and had in fact first seen the light of day not a mile from the constituency. His participation gave a target for his opponents, and A. J. Balfour, writing from a sickbed in Scotland to urge support for Joynson Hicks, remarked: "That a President of the Board of Trade should find his powers insufficient to defend his own seat, and that a Chancellor of the Exchequer, new to his office, with his Budget immediately pending, should be driven to come to his assistance, is a tribute to your own eloquence and to the enthusiasm of the Party which any Cabinet might envy." With this message A.J. sent a characteristic personal note to Joynson Hicks, saying that his remoteness had left him out of touch with the situation and adding, "If there are any alterations which you desire, please wire them to me."

The Suffragettes again made Churchill the particular object of their attentions.

On this occasion Christabel Pankhurst favored Manchester with her presence to lead the women's fight against the Liberal minister. By this time the women's cause had gained supporters and Winston declared himself to be less opposed to their enfranchisement. "Trust me, ladies," he said. "I am your friend and will be your friend in the Cabinet. I will do my best as and when occasion offers, because I do think sincerely that women have always had a logical case and that they have now got behind them a great, popular demand amongst women." Nothing, however, short of a pledge on behalf of the Government for the passing of an enfranchisement bill could satisfy Christabel Pankhurst, and the "henpeckers' " offensive was in no way relaxed. Many prominent women Liberals were induced to withdraw their support from the Liberal candidate.

The last speech delivered, the electors gave their verdict and Churchill found himself defeated by the narrow margin of 492 votes in a poll of over 10,000. He could derive some satisfaction from the howl of exultation that went up from the Unionists ranks—the fall of the Government itself could scarcely have inspired such an outburst of delight. Even the staid *Daily Telegraph* was moved into a sudden insobriety of language, declaring:

"Churchill out—language fails us just when it is most needed. We have all been yearning for this to happen, with a yearning beyond utterance. Figures—oh, yes, there are figures, but who cares for figures to-day. Winston Churchill is out, OUT, OUT!"

Why was the victor of 1906, the man who in Lord Mottistone's phrase had then achieved "one of the most remarkable electoral performances of our time" rejected by Manchester? His record in the House was good, his Liberalism appeared sound enough, he was not a waverer on free trade and he had held junior office with distinction. What was the explanation?

His colleague, John Morley, provided an explanation:

> The belief among competent observers is that the resounding defeat of Winston at Manchester was due to wrath at rather too naked tactics of making deals with this and that and the other groups without too severe a scrutiny in his own political conscience of the terms that they were exacting from him. In other words Winston has no principles. It is believed that he lost 300-400 of these honourably fastidious electors.

To this judgment Morley added another:

> I have a great liking for Winston for his vitality, his indefatigable industry and attention to business, his remarkable gift of language and skill in argument and his curious flair for all sorts of political cases as they arise though even he now and then mistakes a pretty bubble for a great wave. All the same as I so often tell him in a paternal way a successful politician in this country *needs* a good deal more computation of other people's opinions without anxiety about his own.

An interesting pendant to this opinion is provided by Morley's contrast—it was made some years later—between Winston Churchill and Lloyd George: "Whereas Winston knows his own mind, Lloyd George is always more concerned to know the minds of other people."

The break in the Churchillian fortunes was only temporary. The very evening of his defeat, he received an invitation from the Scottish Liberals of Dundee, and hurried north. The campaign was in the main a repetition of that at Manchester North-West, but the result was very different. The President of the Board of Trade polled over 7,000 votes, far ahead of the Conservative and

Socialist nominees, who only just exceeded that total between them.

Winston Churchill was able to go back to the front bench and his work at the Board of Trade. He held that office for two years, two years of hard work, and had the satisfaction of putting upon the Statute Book measures that produced decisive changes in national life. It was his bill that established the labor exchanges, now a national institution. He also set in operation boards for the prevention of sweated labor and put through the bill for the constitution of the Port of London Authority.

In 1908, at thirty-three, Churchill took one of the decisive steps in his life by marrying Miss Clementine Hozier, daughter of Colonel Hozier and Lady Blanche Hozier, and granddaughter of the Earl of Airlie. The wedding at St. Margaret's was one of the social events of the year, and Lord Hugh Cecil, confederate of his Hughlighan days, acted as his best man. It was one of the happiest marriages of the century. According to Lord Rosebery, an authority on the affairs of Prime Ministers, the wives of statesmen are not invariably successful though they are generally devoted. Mrs. Churchill was as successful as she was devoted, a partner in the enterprise of life who was a comfort and support for her husband. Unaffected by the vagaries of his restless brilliance, she provided the domestic base for his operations, a refuge stable and serene from the storms of public life. Whatever the strains and stresses, her balance was preserved and she remained calm and collected.

In the enduring romance of his marriage, Churchill repeated the good fortune of the great Duke, for whom Sarah, his Duchess, was the true love of his life. And it was this Duchess who paid to her husband the tremendous compliment, in her widowhood, when she was asked in marriage, "If I were young and handsome as I was, instead of old and faded, and you could lay an empire at my feet, you should never shade the heart and hand that once belonged to John, Duke of Marlborough." Winston Churchill showed that he shared the secret of inspiring the same devotion. Four children grew up in the privileged circle of this home. The son, Randolph—the name was an inevitable choice for a parent who hero-worshipped his father—continued the political tradition of the Churchill family into a further generation.

CHAPTER FIVE

THE RADICAL PHASE

1909–1911

WINSTON CHURCHILL was now a radical of radicals. With the impetuosity of his fervent nature, his change of party had carried him to the farthest pole of liberalism.

At Cabinet councils, his seat was beside that of John Morley, to whose captivating charm he surrendered himself. It was an association between a man of action and a man of philosophy which could not have been foreseen. Here on the one hand was a young man who had fought in the Boer War; there on the other was a man thirty-five years his senior, who had denounced it as: "A hateful war, and a war insensate and infatuated, a war of uncompensated mischief, of irreparable wrong." Morley was not an easy colleague, but between him and the young President of the Board of Trade there developed a relationship which bordered on the affectionate. On Churchill, he once said, "I looked with paternal benignity."

Churchill's other close companion was Lloyd George. The acquaintance begun on the night of the maiden speech had developed into friendship, and when Churchill crossed the floor, Lloyd George was the first to welcome him. In Cabinet they sat together and acted in concert.

It was another unexpected association for the young man who

fought in the Boer War to have formed, for in opposition to that war Lloyd George had gone even farther than John Morley. Lloyd George and Morley were the recognized pacifist leaders of the party. Churchill worked closely with them but, though he might pass as a lover of peace, never could he be classified as a pacifist.

It was under the inspiration of Lloyd George that Churchill turned social reformer. This was not a role that would have been foreseen for a man who reached the world through the magnificent portals of a ducal mansion and who had first looked out on the spacious vistas of Blenheim park. Nor had his early years brought him into contact with the toiling workers, the deserving and the undeserving poor. With Lloyd George it was different. He knew at first hand how harshly life could press upon lower classes, families who were often hungry and were mostly ill-fed. He had seen the reversals of fortune that brought misery in their train—illness, the death of the breadwinner, prolonged unemployment when "everything they possessed was sucked relentlessly into the voracious maw of the pawn shop, and the inexorable portals of the workhouse gaped for them at the end of the road." [1] The cause of destitute humanity fired Lloyd George with the enduring purpose of his political career. With unwavering constancy he devoted himself to bringing relief to lowly lives and giving them, in the phrase perpetuated by Franklin Delano Roosevelt, "freedom from want." Churchill was fired by the Welshman's crusading zeal.

The spirit of reform was abroad. The country was ripe for a step forward. The conscience of the nation was beginning to be outraged by the contrasts between the two ends of the social scale. After twenty years out of office, the Liberals were eager to carry through measures of reform. The foundations of the welfare state were laid in those days, but the reformers were met by the unyielding opposition of the reactionaries of the Conservative Party, who in the easy affluence of their privileged position were set against any tampering with the established order. Through the House of Lords the Tories had the controlling power over legislation. The Liberals could pass their measures through the House of Commons and the Tories in the House of Lords would throw them out. For long enough had the Liberals suffered from this legislative stranglehold. The radical wing denounced the peers. The Lords, said Lloyd George, had ceased to be the watchdog of the constitution and had become Mr. Balfour's poodle. Their lordships were unmoved and continued in their course of saving the country (as they conceived it) from the consequences of ill-conceived and revolutionary reform.

Lloyd George, with Churchill as his coadjutor, took up the Tory challenge. The House of Lords must be deprived of this power of veto. To this end the peers must be maneuvered into a position in which they would by their own obstinacy be placed patently before the country as legislative wrong-doers, willful ob-structionists of the people's rights.

As Chancellor of the Exechequer, Lloyd George saw the budget as the instrument of his opponents' discomfiture. Over money bills the power of the peers was limited. For half a century it had been accepted that the Lords could neither amend nor repeal the budget. Lloyd George baited the budget so that it would arouse the utmost hostility from the Tories. Income tax was advanced to the then stupendous height of one shilling and nine pence for every Pound Sterling—almost nine per cent—to finance old-age pensions, provision for which were incorporated into the Finance Bill. It was the "people's budget" and it realized its author's hopes. With obliging readiness (and unsuspected political ineptitude) the Tories worked up opposition to "pillage" and "brigandage." Men of large fortunes professed to see profligacy in a scheme to provide five-shilling-a-week pensions for the over-seventies. Stimu-lated by the taunts of the radicals, the Tory peers threw out the budget.

Immediately there was a political uproar. Asquith, the Prime Minister, rolled his stately sentences of reprobation against the breakers of the constitution. Lloyd George and Churchill pushed on to attack on lower and more personal levels. The nephew of the Welsh cobbler and the grandson of the English duke made common cause against the privileged and the aristocrats. The name of duke was made a term of reproach. The peers were de-nounced for defending themselves and their "vulgar, joyless luxury." The august House of Cecil was reproached for sending its sons to sit in the House of Commons, their hands "dripping with the fat of sacrilege."

Lloyd George and Churchill were delighted at the turn of events. The rejection of the "people's budget" had given them and their party the target they had hoped for. A general election was ordered. The country echoed with the cries of the people versus the peers. The electors, curiously enough, did not identify themselves with the people's champions as completely as those self-styled champions had expected. The Liberals were returned to power but their majority was reduced. A bill to limit the powers of the House of Lords was immediately hurried through the Commons. It was thrown out by the Lords. A second election was held. It confirmed the verdict of the first. Again the veto bill was sent up to the Lords. Asquith let it be known that if the Tories persisted in rejecting it, the King would create a sufficient number of new peerages for Liberal supporters to outvote the Tories and carry the bill. The Tory extremists wanted to "die in the last ditch," but wiser heads favored compromise. The Parliament Bill was passed and the Lords were deprived of their power of absolute veto.

In the political hubbub of these years (1909-10) Winston Churchill was conspicuous. Lloyd George, for his extravagant language, might incur the displeasure of King Edward VII. Churchill was unfaltering in his support. His speeches, indeed, aroused the apprehensions of his Sovereign, whose name he introduced into politics. Instructions were given that the young minister was to be told that "it has been most distasteful to the King to find speeches attributing various opinions to His Majesty." Asquith defended his minister against criticism, writing to the King's private secretary: "I hope you have noticed the moderation of tone and the absence of personalities and bad taste—as well as the conspicuous ability—which have characterized Winston Churchill's campaign in Lancashire."

By then Churchill was one of the foremost foemen in the Liberal ranks, more popular as a public speaker with massed audiences than the stately Asquith. In the House of Commons, he and F. E. Smith were winning fame for their personal combat. F.E., rising star of the Tories, was to crown his career as politician and advocate by becoming, as Lord Birkenhead, the youngest Lord Chancellor in history. Churchill and Smith sought to surpass each other in the acrimony and brilliance of debate. The scope of their inventiveness alone placed a limit on the taunts they would hurl at each other across the floor of the House, or from their rival platforms. Yet in private life they were the firmest of friends, even despite F.E.'s taunt, once made in the Commons, that Winston Churchill had "devoted the best years of his life to the preparation of his impromptu speeches." In his liking for the Liberal minister, F.E. stood in contrast with other Conservatives.

At that time Churchill was the most hated politician in the country. In the House the personal animosity which he had aroused among the Conservatives when he crossed the floor was maintained by his conduct in office. Of all the members of the Liberal Ministry, he was the one most disliked by the Opposition. He kept alive the hostility of his former associates by the pungency of his repartees.

Nor did he go out of his way to conciliate the back-benchers in the Liberal Party. He made his way among men at the top but, of rare capacity himself, he had not the art of attracting the admiration and support of men of lesser talents. Showing sometimes little consideration for mediocrity, he hurt the feelings of some of the more sensitive members of his party.

His unpopularity did not, however, prevent his advancement. As he gained in reputation, so he rose in the ranks of the Ministry. In 1910 Asquith offered him the Irish Secretaryship, grave of many a political reputation. Churchill declined it and took instead the Home Office.

Before dealing with his conduct as Home Secretary, I must here refer to another occasion in which Winston played his father's role of economist, this time as a result of his collaboration with the Chancellor of the Exchequer.

One of the consequences of the Lloyd George projects for social reform and improving the lot of the poor was that economies were necessary on defense expenditure. Churchill supported the Chancellor and had as his opponent Reginald McKenna, the First Lord of the Admiralty, who afterward left politics for finance to preside over the affairs of one of the great London banks. In 1909 McKenna sought an increase of £3,000,000 for the naval estimates, which provided for the construction of six dreadnoughts.

Politics takes men up many strange streets. There was never a stranger street in which to find Winston Churchill than the one called Naval Economy.

McKenna wanted six dreadnoughts. Churchill and Lloyd George were ready to accord only four. There was heated debate in the Cabinet and Asquith had to use all his powers of conciliation to avert a split.

At one point, the Cabinet had definitely decided not to authorize the building that Admiral Fisher (then First Sea Lord) and the Board of Admiralty recommended, and the resignation of McKenna seemed to be inevitable. Then the Admiralty received support from an unexpected quarter. Sir Edward Grey, pausing from his concentration on affairs at the Foreign Office, acquainted himself with the Admiralty claims and recommended that they should be reconsidered. Grey recognized that a strong Navy was an urgent necessity in view of the expansionist policy of Germany.

Ultimately a compromise was reached which Churchill termed a "curious and characteristic solution." The Admiralty wanted six dreadnoughts. The Cabinet agreed to the laying down of eight, though spread over a period of time.

Admiral Fisher in several vigorously phrased letters reproached Churchill for the part he then played as the advocate of economy. "I never," he wrote, "expected you to turn against the Navy after all you had said in public and private. (Et tu, Brute) . . . It's too sad and deplorable. The Apostle is right. The tongue is the very devil. (N.B.—Yours is strong amidships and wags at both ends.)"

Churchill might be amused and not ill-pleased over the conclusion of the fight, his first considerable tussle in the Cabinet, but the Asquith Government suffered in prestige. There had been no keeping the Cabinet split secret and the unedifying spectacle of the Little Navy men and the Big Navy men wrangling and threatening resignation was as gratifying to the Tories as it was embarrassing to the Liberals. An entry in Sir Austen Chamberlain's recollections indicated how the Tories gloated over the difficulties of the Cabinet:

And so Lloyd George's Budget was to be approved. The Little Navy men were to be told it was a programme of only four ships and the Big Navy men were to be assured it was really eight. And now as the result of all this manœuvring the whole country wants eight and will not be happy with less. Asquith jumps about like a parched pea in a frying-pan and doesn't know which way to face, the Liberal Party is divided and all sections of it dissatisfied and uneasy.

As Home Secretary one of Churchill's major problems was the maintenance of order during the prolonged and bitter ill feeling of the miners' strike of 1910. In Wales there was a succession of ugly incidents and he decided to call upon the military to come to the aid of the civil police who, being unarmed, might not have the strength to cope with the serious disorders. It was a decision fraught with unlimited possibilities for evil unless the utmost discretion were observed by the officers in command of the troops. Winston made the wise decision to press for the appointment of a senior Army officer to take charge.

Choice for this responsible post fell upon General Sir Nevil Macready, then Director of Personal Services at the War Office, who was requested to place himself under the Home Secretary. There were 600 Welsh police, 500 of the Metropolitan force and two squadrons of the Hussars, and Winston gave Macready authority to control both police and military in the event of disorder occurring. They made a successful job of a delicate operation and Macready, on terminating three months' stay in the valleys of South Wales, paid tribute to the Home Secretary: [2]

> It was entirely due to Mr. Churchill's foresight in sending a strong force of Metropolitan police directly he was aware of the state of affairs in the valleys that bloodshed was avoided. . . . I was in daily communication with the Home Office and during the first few days after arriving in the district noticed an inclination to interfere from Whitehall in details which could only be appreciated by the man on the spot. This, however, very soon wore off, and from that time up to the time I left South Wales nothing could exceed the support given me by Mr. Churchill or the entire absence of any interference in measures I judged necessary to cope with the situation.

Miners' strikes, railwaymen's strikes, labor troubles in London, in Manchester—it was a harassing time. Macready was called upon to render continued assistance, to the neglect of his duties as Director of Personal Services. He gives an amusing picture of a sorely tried Winston:

The night was very hot, and about 11 p.m. Mr. Lloyd George appeared in a white alpaca or silk motor coat, beaming with good humour, and evidently in a hurry to get away. Winston, at the moment, was deadly serious, pacing up and down the room within the circle of serious-looking officials, and holding forth in regard to the measures that were to be taken. Mr. Lloyd George made straight across the room to the fire-place, where John Burns was standing, and began to tell him what was evidently, to judge by their laughter, a really good story.

I do not think I have ever seen anybody look more angry than Winston did as he stopped in front of the table, and called Lloyd George to order. For a moment I thought he would hurl one of the official red books on the table at the future Prime Minister, who continued to be amused either at his own story or at Winston and explained that he wanted to get off on his drive to Brighton.

It was in the Session of 1910 that Churchill made clear his position on the question of woman's suffrage. The Suffragettes, as I have already said, had made him one of the principal objects of their unwelcome attentions during a succession of elections.

A bill to give the Parliamentary vote to women who were already entitled to vote in municipal contests was introduced by David Shackleton from the Labour benches. The discussion that followed was enlivened by a speech from F. E. Smith, one of the wittiest that even he made. Moving an amendment against the bill, he expressed his belief that true womanhood would be menaced by the intrusion of women into politics. He did not decry the claim of women to intellectual distinction but added, "I venture to say that the sum total of human happiness, knowledge and achievement would have been almost unaffected if Sappho had never sung, if Joan of Arc had never fought, if Siddons had never played and if George Eliot had never written."

Churchill had been expected to support the measure and it was in an expectant House that he rose and said: "Sir, I cannot support this bill." His reasons, however, were diametrically opposed to those of F.E.—he could not support the bill because it did not go far enough.

Although the second reading of this measure was carried, women had to wait till 1918 to gain the vote. Both Churchill and F.E. were members of the Government that enfranchised them.

Shortly after this debate, Churchill was threatened by a suffragette enthusiast with a horsewhip. He was traveling back to London by train from a Bradford meeting, when a young man, Hugh Franklin by name, forced his way into the compartment brandishing a whip. He was prevented from carrying out his intention of using the whip.

Early in 1911 Winston Churchill was brought into the limelight in the Sidney Street affair when, to the delight of the popular press, he directed the operations of troops gathered in a street in the East End of London to deal with a couple of gunmen who styled themselves anarchists.

The siege of Sidney Street took place nearly fifty years ago, but its memory still lives in the picture of the top-hatted Home Secretary, with a force of police behind him and a squad of riflemen before, peering round the corner of a gateway which offered very inadequate shelter from a gunman's bullet.

It was about ten o'clock in the morning of January 3, and the Home Secretary was in his bath, when there came an urgent knocking at the door. He was informed that a gang of anarchists led by Peter the Painter, responsible for recent murders of the police at Houndsditch, had taken refuge in a room at 100 Sidney Street. They had plenty of arms and ammunition and even home-made bombs.

The gunmen had been traced the night before and as they were expected to stop at nothing to avoid capture, the police had taken the precaution of ordering all the other occupants out of the house. The men were then called upon to surrender. They replied with their guns and a detective-inspector was wounded. More shots came from the house and the police returned fire.

As no progress was being made, the police sought the Home Secretary's sanction to send troops to the scene. Permission was at once given.

Churchill was dripping wet and had no more than a towel about him when he went to the telephone to learn of the drama in Sidney Street. Within twenty minutes he was at the Home Office receiving the latest information from the front. The dispatches were obscure, as dispatches customarily are while operations are still in progress. No one could say precisely what number of gunmen had to be dealt with or what measures might be necessary.

Churchill conceived it to be his duty to investigate on the spot, though he was afterward frank enough to admit that "convictions of duty were supported by a strong sense of curiosity."

The siege had started at three o'clock in the morning and firing was still brisk when he reached Houndsditch. There were metropolitan police armed with guns hastily procured from the nearest gunsmith—since British police, traditionally, go unarmed—and Scots Guardsmen with rifles. From shotgun and rifle a fusillade was poured into 100 Sidney Street. The answering whine of bullets through the air and the splintering of bricks and woodwork showed that the gangsters were still in a condition to reply.

Law-abiding London could not remember a comparable occasion. For some hours the desultory sniping continued. Soldiers and police surrounded the house and a contingent of men were posted in a brewery opposite to fire across the street into the enemy's quarters.

The Home Secretary watched the operations from the shelter of a warehouse doorway where he was joined by Lord Knutsford, Chairman of London Hospital. Among the besiegers differences of opinion developed as to the better method of dealing with the gunmen. Some, wanting an immediate decision, were for storming the house, though it might result in casualties. Others, more cautious in their methods, advocated delay.

While this controversy was developing, the Home Secretary became conscious of the embarrassing situation into which his curiosity had led him. It was really no part of his duty to give executive decisions. That was the responsibility of the man in charge on the spot. From his desk in the Home Office it would have been proper for him to have sent an order, but being there himself it was scarcely proper for him to meddle. On the other hand, his position of paramount authority was not to be gainsaid. It was an unfortunate dilemma and the Home Secretary, as he stood, top-hatted in that East End street, with Lord Knutsford beside him, and the bullets spluttering round, found it in his heart to regret that his curiosity had led him into so delicate and difficult a position, from which he could scarcely drive away. Far better had he been less precipitate and remained in his departmental chair.

At length the controversy was settled and the men of action

were to have their way. It was resolved to storm the house from several points at once. Here the experience of the man of war was of value. He suggested that a few steel or iron plates were needed so that each member of the storming party could carry one before him as a shield against enemy bullets. Search, accordingly, was made in metal works in the neighborhood.

While this was proceeding a new development occurred. Smoke was seen to come from the besieged house and it was soon evident that the place was on fire. This would put an end to the siege, for the gunmen would be driven either to bolt from their refuge or perish in the smoke and flames.

The matter did not prove to be as simple as that. A fire had been reported and soon men of the fire brigade were on the scene, ready to discharge their duties. Gunmen? What were gunmen to them? There was a fire: it was their duty to put it out; and their duty would be done as laid down by regulations which knew nothing of gangsters or gunmen. The police protested that lives would be lost if the firemen went within range of the bullets that were still spluttering every now and then across the street. The fire brigade officer could not allow bullets to divert him from his duty and made ready to get to work.

At this point Churchill intervened. On his authority as Home Secretary, he gave orders that 100 Sidney Street was to be allowed to burn; only if the surrounding property were to be seriously endangered were the brigade to run the risk of intervening. The necessity never arose.

By then the flames had gained a hold on the building. No shot had been fired for some time and it seemed that the gangsters were no longer in a condition to use their guns. A police inspector strode across the street. The Home Secretary followed him. A sergeant of police marched behind with a double-barreled shotgun.

The inspector kicked open the door. Nothing was to be seen save smoke and flames. No bullet came from within. The siege was over. At last the firemen could be permitted to discharge their duties as laid down in their regulations.

Later in the day two charred bodies were found in the ruins. It was established that one had been shot by a bullet of the attackers.

No trace of wound was found on the other, who apparently had succumbed to suffocation.

There was a debate in the House, and Balfour, as leader of the Opposition, made what capital he could out of Churchill's appearance on the field of battle.

"We are concerned to observe," he said, "photographs in the illustrated papers of the Home Secretary in the danger zone. I understand what the photographer was doing but not the Home Secretary."

It was not to be the last occasion that Winston Churchill was to be criticized for leaving his departmental desk to appear on the field of action.

The siege of Sidney Street was a nine days' wonder and the publicity was of the kind not to benefit the Home Secretary in the eyes of the sober and sedate members of the public. There had always been a tendency to accuse Winston of flamboyance in his methods, and his critics now declared that he had made the operations unnecessarily complicated by calling out troops and artillery. He retorted that, although he was present, he did not take charge of the siege, nor did he send for the troops. What he did do was to restrain the firemen from risking their lives on the burning building.

CHAPTER SIX

FIRST LORD OF THE ADMIRALTY

1911–1913

IN THE MONTH of August, 1911, the German Government dispatched the gunboat *Panther* to the harbor of Agadir in Morocco. It was a typical instance of Teuton aggressiveness. It caused an immediate crisis throughout Europe; and it sent Winston Churchill to the Admiralty to begin the most important ministerial work of his career.

The Agadir crisis was the prelude to the War of 1914. It brought home, for the first time, to many of those holding responsible positions, the gravity of the German menace to world peace.

In those days, the powers were concerned about spheres of influence in Africa. France had been assigned the zone of Morocco in the Treaty of Algeciras in 1904, and found it necessary to dispatch an expedition to Fez. The Germans concluded that France would try to annex her zone of influence and considered that they should be given corresponding compensation.

As a preliminary to staking their claims, they sent the gunboat *Panther* to Agadir. It was no more than a gesture made in the Teutonic fashion. It provided an occasion for a test of international opinion, and of military preparedness.

It had the immediate effect of drawing Great Britain and

France closer together. In the Cabinet, it made the radical and pacifist wing, of which Lloyd George and Morley were principal members, conscious as they had not previously been of the extent of German aggressiveness. Lloyd George, in a speech to the bankers in the City of London, delivered himself of a warning to Germany that won its place in history. "If," he said, "a situation were to be forced upon us in which peace can only be preserved by the surrender of the great and beneficent position Britain has won by centuries of heroism and achievement, by allowing Britain to be treated where her interests were vitally affected as if she were of no account in the cabinet of nations; then I say emphatically that peace at that price would be a humiliation intolerable for a great country like ours to endure."

This speech came as something of a shock to the leaders of Germany, who had always reckoned that the pacifism of Lloyd George and the radicals would keep Britain out of any war in which Germany might engage.

The crisis and the speech also produced a remarkable change in Churchill's outlook. His receptive mind responded instantly to the shock of events. Hitherto he had been concerned as Home Secretary with home affairs and his vision had not been extended to any great degree to events across the Channel. In common with other departmental chiefs in the Government he had been so immersed in the affairs of his own department that he had showed no particular concern in foreign policy and the development of the Entente with the French. This was the special sphere of Asquith as Prime Minister, Sir Edward Grey as Foreign Secretary, of Lord Haldane at the War Office and of McKenna at the Admiralty.

The Agadir crisis caused Churchill to inquire into these things. With characteristic enthusiasm, the subject of international affairs, which he had hitherto neglected, now became his principal preoccupation. That Britain should be in a state of preparedness for the contingency of war became his immediate concern.

As Home Secretary, military preparedness did not come within the scope of his departmental responsibilities. His scope of action was limited. But there were the nation's reserves of cordite. By chance, he found that the Home Office was responsible for safeguarding this stock, a duty discharged by a few constables. This did not seem sufficient for the Home Secretary, in the light of his sudden awareness of international danger. So there and then he rang up the Admiralty and asked that some marines be sent to guard the magazines. The admiral to whom he spoke did not respond to Churchill's alarm, seemed indeed almost to resent the intrusion of the Home Secretary in the affairs of the Navy. He flatly refused to send marines.

Churchill was not in the mood to be balked by an admiral. Straightway he telephoned to the War Office and found Haldane, the minister, more sympathetic. In a few hours troops had been sent to reinforce the constables and Churchill could sleep untroubled in his bed. The nation's cordite resources were safe.

The Agadir crisis, menacing as it seemed for a while, passed and the peace of Europe was not then disturbed. But such was the alarm it caused that, in August, Haldane persuaded the Prime Minister to summon a special meeting of the Committee of Imperial Defense, to consider what action Britain should take were France to be attacked by Germany. It disclosed vital differences between the Admiralty and the War Office.

Haldane, in five years at the War Office, had carried out a thorough reform of the Army. His purpose had been to create an expeditionary force which could give aid to the French. In conjunction with French staff officers, plans were drawn up so that a British expeditionary force should be shipped across the English Channel to serve in a position on the French left wing as speedily as possible.

In contrast with the War Office, the Admiralty had no plans for the placing of a British force at the side of the French. The War Office scheme had been completed in minutest detail, but in a departmental water-tight compartment. The War Office had arranged for trains on land—it was even fixed where the troops were to stop for coffee—but not for vessels for the crossing. The Admiralty had not been consulted and the crisis showed that the Navy was not in a position to supply transports as and when the Army should need them.

It is easy enough to understand the lack of Admiralty interest. Their strategy had not been worked out in conjunction with the French. The Admiralty was, in fact, antagonistic to the idea of sending a small British Army to northern France. It was Fisher's dictum that the Army was "too little for a big war." Fisher was no longer First Sea Lord, but his successor, Sir Arthur Wilson, was a Fisher man; indeed, Fisher had antedated his own retirement from office by a few months to ensure that Wilson should succeed him.

At the meeting of the Committee of Imperial Defense, Sir Arthur opposed the sending of an expeditionary force to the Continent at all. He submitted that the Army should be used in conjunction with the Navy to make raids on the German coast.

Haldane was dismayed to find that if an emergency were to arise, his well-thought-out plans would be frustrated for lack of naval cooperation. He wrote to the Prime Minister to protest against the Admiralty policy and Admiralty methods, and to urge that there should be established at the Admiralty a scientifically trained war staff, similar to that which had been created at the War Office. He backed up his demands with the threat of resignation:

> I have, after mature consideration come to the conclusion that this, in the existing state of Europe, is the gravest problem which confronts the Government to-day; and that unless it is tackled resolutely, I cannot remain in office. Five years' experience of the War Office has taught me how to handle the Generals and how to get the best out of them; and I believe that the experience makes me the best person to go to the Admiralty and carry through as thorough a reorganization there as I have carried out at the War Office. In any event, I am determined that things at the Admiralty shall not remain any longer as they are.

Asquith was persuaded of the need for a change at the Admiralty, where Reginald McKenna was in charge. The Prime Minister was for a time undecided whether to send Haldane to the Admiralty, or whether Churchill should succeed as First Lord.

Haldane was one of Asquith's closest associates. He was an outstanding intellectual force in the Liberal Government. His mind was remarkable alike for its breadth of vision and its subtlety. He had reformed the Army; he was concerned with reforms in the educational system, and in the intricate laws which govern the holding and transfer of property. In spite of the heavy weight of his duties, he was always ready to preside over this or that investigation into problems of social welfare. Churchill, then only thirty-seven, was a comparatively new recruit to the Liberal Party of which Haldane had been for many years an ornament. He lacked Haldane's long and wide experience of affairs, but he had two qualities which recommended him—his vigor as a speaker only surpassed in the party by Lloyd George, and his energy and ability to get things done.

Asquith had gone on holiday to Scotland. He invited both Churchill and Haldane to meet him there to discuss what should be decided—whether to send Haldane to the Admiralty and let Churchill succeed at the War Office, or to make one change alone and appoint Churchill First Lord. Of this meeting, Haldane wrote to his close friend, Edward Grey:

> Asquith asked me to see him first alone, and then with Winston. I did so without mincing matters. Winston was very good, reasoned that if he went there [the Admiralty] he would work closely with me at the War Office, in the spirit of his father, who had always said that there ought to be a common administration. I felt, however, that, full of energy as he is, he does not know his problem or the vast field of thought that has to be covered. Moreover, though I did not say this to him, I feel that it was only a year since he had been doing his best to cut down mechanized armies, and that the Admiralty would receive the news of his advent with dismay; for they would think, wrongly or rightly, that as soon as the financial pinch begins to come eighteen months from now, he would want to cut down. He is too apt to act first and think afterwards, though of his energy and courage one cannot speak too highly.

Thereafter Asquith went to Balmoral to talk the matter over with the King. He then concluded that to send Haldane from the War Office would look too much like a snub for the Admiralty.

It was in this manner that Winston Churchill was installed at the Admiralty, and given the specific commission to put the Fleet into "a state of instant and constant readiness for war in case we are attacked by Germany." For this task, he felt that life had been preparing him.

Before passing on it should be remarked that Haldane came to renounce the criticism of Churchill he had made in advance, and was writing a few weeks later to his mother to say:

> Winston and Ll. G. dined with me last night and we had a very useful talk. This is now a very harmonious Cabinet. It is odd to

think that three years ago I had to fight these two for every penny for my Army Reforms. Winston is full of enthusiasm about the Admiralty, and just as keen as I am on the war staff. It is delightful to work with him. Ll. G. too has quite changed his attitude, and is now very friendly to your bear, whom he used to call the 'Minister for Civil Slaughter.'

Churchill's first principal task, as is apparent from the record of events that led to his appointment, was the creation of a Naval Staff. This innovation was the cause of much naval heartburning and he came in for unjustifiable criticism because of it. The critics' point of view was expressed by Admiral Sir Reginald Bacon, who, in his life of Lord Fisher, published twenty years later, wrote:

When Mr. Churchill came to the Admiralty knowing nothing at all about the Navy and not appreciating that the Navy both in peace and war is fundamentally a different machine from the Army, he was determined to introduce a War Staff at the Admiralty, modelled on the one at the War Office. . . .

Mr. McKenna, the finest First Lord of the Admiralty we have seen in modern times, was superseded by Mr. Winston Churchill, who at once began to bring in a scheme for a Naval War Staff. His ideas were not agreed to by Lord Fisher or by Admiral of the Fleet Sir Arthur Wilson. These two Admirals had far more general experience of the Navy than any other officers, and both were strongly against the creation of Chief of Staff other than First Sea Lord. This arbitrary act of over-riding the experience and advice of the two greatest Admirals of modern times brought retribution to Mr. Churchill later on in the early days of the war.

There the picture is clear-cut. You are presented with the inexperienced, masterful Churchill, devising the scheme of a Naval War Staff out of the maliciousness of his own fertile brain, resolved to carry it out in the face of the advice of the highest technical experts, the greatest admirals of modern times.

Of the wisdom or unwisdom of the establishment of a Naval War Staff much may be written. It is, however, irrelevant to the major point—that the decision to create such an authority was not made by Churchill after being appointed First Lord. It was a decision which originated in the first place with Haldane, and for which Asquith, as Prime Minister, was primarily responsible.

Asquith decided that McKenna should be replaced at the Admiralty so that the reorganization might be carried out, and he appointed Winston Churchill as First Lord with this specific object in view.

The criticism of Churchill falls plainly to the ground. Nor can it be agreed that he "at once began to bring in" his scheme. In his record of events in his *World Crisis* he described how, knowing that Sir Arthur Wilson was opposed to it, he delayed setting up the naval staff until Sir Arthur's period of office had expired.

One of his earliest decisions as First Lord was to enlist the services of Fisher as his unofficial adviser. The veteran admiral, creator of the modern battleship and the modern navy, was then living in honored retirement as Baron Fisher of Kilverstone. The partnership between the young First Lord and the veteran sea dog bore good fruit, and was to have a fateful influence on the course of their lives.

Fisher, as First Sea Lord, from 1904 to 1910, had revolutionized the Navy. His reforming zeal and methods of turbulence had involved him in a feud with Lord Charles Beresford and reactionaries of the naval service. The Navy was in danger of being split into Fisher's men and Beresford's men. The operations in this battle of the admirals spread beyond the service. The politicians discussed it in the Parliamentary lobbies and the hostesses of Mayfair argued about it over their teacups.

Finally an inquiry was ordered by the Cabinet. Fisher did not consider that the findings were sufficiently in his favor, though Beresford was declared to have been guilty of indiscipline toward the Admiralty. When he went into retirement in 1910 Fisher left the country disgusted with the ways of politics and politicians. For some time he remained aloof doing, as he said, "a little of Achilles sulking in the tent," but the fit did not last for long. Winston fetched him out of his tent, "to carry on, as unofficial adviser, his work of securing the fighting efficiency of the Fleet and its instant readiness for war."

When Churchill first made advances, Fisher hung back out of loyalty to his old chief, McKenna. It is pleasant to be able to write that McKenna himself urged the Admiral to place the invaluable aid of his wisdom and experience at Churchill's disposal for the good of the Navy and the country.

One result of this collaboration was the advancement of Sir John Jellicoe, so that it was this naval strategist who was in command of the Fleet when war came. This was a matter on which Fisher placed the greatest store. He regarded Jellicoe as a seaman with "all the attributes of Nelson." Churchill was converted to his view and arranged the succession accordingly. In a letter dated November, 1911, Fisher gloated over the success he had achieved. He wrote:

> My two private visits to Winston were fruitful. I'll tell you the whole secrets of the changes—to get Jellicoe Commander-in-Chief of the Home Fleet prior to October 1914, which is the date of the battle of Armageddon. He will succeed Callaghan automatically in two years from December 19, 1911, so will have all well in hand by the before-mentioned date! Nunc Dimittis. Everything revolved round Jellicoe.

October 1914—the date of the war he foresaw—a shrewd forecast.

Within the Admiralty the First Lord selected as his private secretary the youngest flag officer in the Fleet—David Beatty, who was destined to take over the command of the Battle Cruiser Squadron and finally to succeed Jellicoe. Churchill had first met Beatty after the charge of the Lancers at Omdurman, and later events confirmed his first impressions of Beatty's character and abilities, a favorable view that was not shared by many of Beatty's brother officers.

The harmonious collaboration between Churchill and Fisher was interrupted when, in 1912, the First Lord appointed to important commands admirals who did not enjoy Fisher's respect. The old sea dog sent in an indignant protest: "I fear," he wrote, "this must be my last communication with you on any matter at all. I am sorry for it but I consider you have betrayed the Navy in these three appointments, and what the pressure could have been to induce you to betray your trust is beyond my comprehension."

Fisher then left for Naples and *dolce far niente*. Churchill had been warned. Fisher while he had his own way was the finest fellow in the world. Fisher thwarted was insufferable.

Churchill did not leave Achilles to sulk for long on this occasion although the temperamental sea-dog required careful wooing before he could be brought back from his Mediterranean refuge.

Winston addressed numerous appeals to him and requests for advice. The appeals were backed by letters from Lord Esher, Sir John Jellicoe and Captain (later Lord) Hankey, Secretary of the Committee of Imperial Defense. It was balm to the heart of the exile.

Finally the First Lord and the Prime Minister himself, traveling in the Admiralty yacht, came to Naples to beg him to return. They found him "reluctant to give up his freedom" but that Sunday he heard an eloquent sermon in the course of which the preacher, appearing to fix his eyes on the retired admiral, declared, "No man possessing all his powers and full of vitality has any right to say 'I am now going to rest as I have had a hard life,' for he owes a duty to his country and fellow men."

Fisher's biographer makes the comment on this remarkably inspired apropos-ism—"Had the circumstances been reversed and Lord Fisher and Mr. Churchill changed places, we should have had little doubt that the clergyman had been primed by Lord Fisher to persuade a member of his congregation. It is exactly the class of foresight, preconception and action which was characteristic of Lord Fisher."

Personally I feel there is ground for suspecting that Winston Churchill's "foresight, preconception and action" on this occasion were in actuality equal to those attributed to Lord Fisher. Whatever the inspiration of the preacher's words, Fisher returned to England.

One decision of far-reaching consequences followed the healing of the breach—the ensuring for the Navy of the vast resources of the oil fields in Persia. Like all innovations in the services, the use of oil as propelling power for warships gave rise to acute controversy. Its employment was opposed by stick-to-the-old-methods men, just as the use of steam in a former age was decried by the seamen who had been trained to sail.

Fisher, a pioneer in the use of oil, had neglected no occasion to advocate the development of sources of supply independent of foreign control. On his advent to the Admiralty Churchill was equally quick to appreciate the importance of oil and the necessity for ensuring supplies. To obtain an authoritative opinion as a basis for action, he decided on the appointment of a powerful

Royal Commission, and over this body Lord Fisher, on his return from Naples, presided. The proceedings were conducted in secrecy: the findings of the commission were not made public. But the results were to be seen in the conclusion of a long-term contract between the British Government and the Persian Oil Company.

In his life of Fisher, Sir Reginald Bacon included a memorandum on the oil position from the authoritative pen of Lord Greenway, who was president of the Anglo-Persian Oil Company, which indicated the debt owed to Churchill. Having set out the part Fisher took in the development of oil for the Navy ("Oil Maniac," was the title given to him), Lord Greenway dealt with the setting up of the Royal Commission, and proceeded:

> One outcome was that the potentialities of the Persian oilfields as great producers of oil were revealed, and eventually, in July, 1914, after an examination of the fields by an expert Committee (under the leadership of Admiral Slade), which was sent out by Mr. Churchill, the British Government entered into a long contract with the Anglo-Persian Oil Company, by which it secured for the Navy a large proportion of its peace-time requirements of oil fuel and the whole call on its production at times of war. At the same time an agreement was concluded whereby the Government, by investing £2,000,000 to be expended on further developments (the programme for which has since been far exceeded), secured a controlling interest in the Company.
>
> Mr. Churchill, when giving, in the first volume of his book "The World Crisis," an estimate of the financial result of this investment, showed that the then return was £40,000,000. To-day (1928) at the much enhanced value of the shares held by the Government, a further £20,000,000 can be added to these figures—a colossal gain on an investment which was embarked upon, in the face of great opposition, merely as a measure of national defence! The only measure of defence (with the exception of the purchase of the Suez Canal shares) ever entered upon by the British Government which, instead of costing taxpayers a large sum of money, has given them an enormous profit!
>
> The credit of carrying through these extraordinarily favourable contracts is, of course, entirely due to Mr. Churchill, and, more particularly, to the able and forceful manner in which he dealt with the consequent Money Bill in the House of Commons in the

teeth of the strongest possible opposition. From the point of view of the Navy it was a great feat of statesmanship for which the country should always be grateful.

There was a period of three months short of three years between the October day in 1911 when Churchill first entered the Admiralty as First Lord and the fateful Tuesday in August 1914 when Britain and Germany were at war. They were for him years of the most strenuous endeavor. He quickly put his political past aside once more and became the champion of naval expansion. He developed himself and inculcated in his staff around him a sense of ever growing menace inspired by the activities of the power on the other side of the North Sea. He was determined to raise the British Navy to the greatest possible strength in the shortest possible time.

No First Lord ever succeeded in identifying himself more closely with the service. Such time as he was not at Admiralty headquarters in Whitehall he passed afloat with men of the Navy —in warship, submarine or seaplane, or in the Admiralty yacht, *Enchantress.*

And all the while, across the North Sea, the Germans were striving to come to terms of equality in naval strength. In a speech on Clydeside in 1912, Churchill warned them that Britain would not yield the mastery of the seas:

> The purposes of British naval power are essentially defensive. We have no thoughts, and we have never had any thoughts, of aggression; we attribute no such thoughts to other great Powers. There is, however, this difference, between the British naval power and the naval power of the great and friendly empire—I trust it may long remain a great and friendly empire—of Germany. The British Navy is to us a necessity, and from some points of view the German Navy is to them more in the nature of a luxury. Our naval power involves British existence. It is existence to us; it is expansion to them.

"The nature of a luxury"—the phrase was quickly taken up in Germany. *Luxusflotte*—why should their navy be thus described? The big navy men of Germany were furious and ranted extravagantly at the First Lord's temerity.

There was by now no disguising the naval race between Great Britain and Germany. The First Lord in the following year made the offer of a naval holiday but no response came from across the North Sea. Germany was not interested in introducing, as he suggested, a blank page into the book of misunderstanding. The Germany of 1913 and the Germany of 1939 displayed the same spirit and the same purpose. There was no avoiding the fatal end.

During the last months before the Germany of the Kaiser opened the gates of destruction on Europe, Ireland came to occupy the principal place of political controversy in Britain. For long years the Irish had been struggling to regain their older independence. Gladstone carried a Home Rule Bill through the Commons, but the Tory Lords had rejected it. Now the Asquith government were pledged to carry Home Rule despite their Tory opponents and the men of Ulster. The northern province of Ireland, peopled by emigrants from the United Kingdom, did not share Irish aspirations. The Irish are Roman Catholics; the men of Ulster, Protestant and puritan. The Irish were not prepared to relinquish the richest province of their country. The Ulstermen were prepared to fight rather than be separated from the United Kingdom. They were led by Edward Carson who gave up his lucrative profession of advocate to devote himself to their cause. Carson had as his able lieutenant F. E. Smith, "Galloper Smith" as he was called.

In the folly of their extravagance, the rival political leaders brought the country to the verge of civil war rather than yield ground to their opponents. Bonar Law, head of the Conservative party and leader of the opposition, was prepared to encourage officers of the British Army to disobey orders if the armed forces were brought in to coerce Ulster.

Churchill supported the Government, though his father, as Bonar Law reminded him, had coined the slogan, "Ulster will fight and Ulster will be right." This view, despite its parental origin, Churchill repudiated as one from which "every street bully with a brickbat and every crazy fanatic fumbling with a pistol may draw inspiration." He denounced Bonar Law as "a public danger seeking to terrorize the Government." He condemned Carson for taking part in a "treasonable conspiracy."

Ireland, through a succession of crises, took up much of the time that the First Lord was not called upon to devote to the affairs of the Navy. Leading members of a government are never allowed to devote themselves exclusively to the work of their departments. Each has to accept individual responsibility for their collective decisions, and must give his support to them. It was on Churchill and Lloyd George that Asquith had chiefly to rely for the presentation of the Government's case to the House and to the country.

Winston Churchill found by experience the truth of Mr. Balfour's complaint that "Democracy threatens to kill its servants by the work it requires of them—but what is play to it, is death to us." He was called upon to move the second reading of the 1912 Home Rule Bill, a duty he performed, for once, without any great credit to himself. Scarcely a week passed in the next two years but he had to support by public speech the latest Government proposal on Ireland or to answer the latest criticism of the Opposition. His opponents found his speeches "fiery," but then Winston "does not exactly walk about with an oil-can," as one of his colleagues once told King Edward VII.

During the height of one of the Parliamentary storms over Ireland, Churchill was the recipient of a more than usually ponderous argument against Home Rule. The debate, even for an Irish debate, had been extremely stormy. At one stage Sir William Bull was ordered out of the chamber. At another, the Speaker suspended the sitting for an hour for tempers to cool. When the House resumed the Attorney-General, Sir Rufus Isaacs (later Lord Reading), was howled down. It was obviously useless to continue and the Speaker adjourned the House to the next day.

As Churchill and his friend, Colonel Seely (Lord Mottistone), Secretary for War, who also had broken with the Conservatives on the tariff issue, left the front bench, Conservative M.P.s opposite raised a chorus of "Rats." Churchill waved his acknowledgment of the greeting. His smile did nothing to placate the demonstrators. One of them, Ronald M'Neill, in the heat of the moment seized a book from the table and flung it at the First Lord. By an ironic coincidence it was a manual of rules and advice for the observance of good order in Parliamentary proceedings. It was well-aimed and caught Churchill a glancing blow on the face.

For a moment it looked as if the blow would be returned. Supporters came hurrying to the side of the contestants when Will Crooks, with his ready Cockney wit, shouted cheerily, "Should auld acquaintance be forgot." The interjection was so quaint that it raised a laugh and the crisis passed.

The aggressor hurried after the aggrieved to express his regrets but was unable to find the First Lord. When the House met the following day he made a handsome apology. It was handsomely accepted. Said Churchill, "I can assure the honorable member that I have not, nor have I had at any time, any personal feeling in the matter, and if I had any personal feelings the observations he has thought proper to address to the House would have effectually removed them."

During another debate Churchill was involved in a passage at arms with Bonar Law. There had been threats by Ulstermen to appeal abroad for protection, following the precedent of Protestants of another generation who sought the aid of William of Orange, the Dutch Protestant, against the Roman Catholic king, James II. The name of the Emperor of Germany had been mentioned as one whom Ulster might approach rather than submit to being governed by the Irish in Dublin.

Bonar Law, to indicate the strength of feeling in Ulster, remarked: "These people in Northeast Ireland, from old prejudices perhaps more than from anything else, from the whole of their past history, would prefer, I believe, to accept the government of a foreign country rather than submit to be governed by honorable gentlemen below the gangway [the Irish Nationalists]."

Churchill seized upon this passage as an indiscretion to be exploited. "I refer," he said, "to the statement which he quoted with approval that the Loyalists of Ulster would rather be annexed to a foreign country . . ."

"Than under moonlighters," interjected Sir Edward Carson.

The First Lord sought to continue but there was much interruption. When he could make himself heard he went on, "Ulster would rather be annexed to a foreign country than continue in her allegiance to the Crown . . ."

"Withdraw" and "Scandalous" shouted Conservative M.P.s.

Churchill waited again till the uproar was spent and added, "This then is the latest Tory threat—Ulster will secede to Germany."

The storm broke out afresh at this. "Germany? Who said Germany?" shouted Conservatives above the general clamor.

One Tory M.P., Lord Winterton appealed to the Speaker. Was not the reference the First Lord had made to Germany deliberately provocative and calculated to cause ill feeling between this country and Berlin?

Churchill retorted that he had felt bound to draw the attention of the House to the statement as indicating what the Leader of the Opposition considered to be proper conduct for Ulster loyalists.

Bonar Law rose to explain. He did not, as the House had expected, disavow the reference to Germany. Churchill had accused him of quoting the statement as to the Ulster people's intentions "with approval." This was inaccurate. He had stated what he believed to be a fact, but neither with approval nor disapproval.

During these months Churchill was playing the double role of fiery partisan and pacificator—firebrand in public, pacificator behind the scenes. He had come to the conclusion that a coalition government was the best means of reducing the political tension and finding the way to solve the acute problem which the warfare of parties made more difficult. Late in 1913 Sir Austen Chamberlain wrote: "This autumn I was engaged with others in an attempt to find a compromise on the Irish question which both parties could accept. Mr. Churchill was the prime mover in this overture and again suggested a coalition to make a national settlement of some of the great problems of the day."

There was a meeting between Austen and Churchill aboard the Admiralty yacht *Enchantress* in November 1913. A frank if discursive discussion took place. Austen thought that Churchill "orated" overmuch, but he was genuinely impressed by the sincerity of his desire for a settlement.

This good impression was somewhat dissipated by a speech that Asquith made the following day. Austen was too much engaged in the heat of the struggle to see things as clearly as the Conservative Leader in the Lords, the venerable Lord Lansdowne, to whom Austen communicated both his account of the meeting in the *Enchantress* and his criticisms of Asquith. Lansdowne sagely replied: "Your comments on Asquith's speech were perfectly justified but I am inclined to think that Asquith probably believed himself to be doing exactly what Churchill apparently thinks the leaders of both parties ought to do, viz.: to make speeches full of party claptrap and No Surrender with a few sentences on the end for wise and discerning people to see and ponder."

Claptrap and sayings for the wise in a judicious amalgam—it is the recipe for the greater number of political speeches of the partisan type.

The conversations Churchill and Austen had begun led to exchanges between Asquith and Bonar Law, but they came to naught. The Liberal Government proceeded with their plans to enforce Home Rule for Ireland; Carson, Galloper Smith and the Tory extremists completed their arrangements to safeguard Ulster if necessary by fighting. Tension became more acute than ever.

"Carson's Army" now had some 100,000 members, with large supplies of rifles and machine guns pouring into the country. In March 1914 came the affair at Curragh Camp, in southern Ireland, where the officers were asked whether they would undertake active service in Ulster or resign from the Army. All resigned. Churchill had no official concern in the incident, but his friend, Colonel Seely, who ordered the question to be put to the officers, was compelled to resign from the War Ministry.

A military coup by Ulster Volunteers followed a month after the Curragh affair. The ports of Larne and Donaghadee on the northeast coast were seized, and large supplies of munitions were landed and dispatched by car all over the northeast of Ireland.

Churchill, as First Lord of the Admiralty, ordered a cruiser squadron to the Scottish coast opposite Ulster in readiness to land a force of Royal Marines in the event of serious disorders. This drew down on him a storm of denunciation in the House of Commons. He replied with characteristic vigor by describing the Opposition motion as "a vote of censure by the criminal classes upon the police." He also suggested the opening of fresh discussions with Carson.

The Buckingham Palace Conference was the result, a conference that ended in failure just eleven days before Great Britain declared war on Germany. In Churchill's own phrase, "The discussion had reached its conclusive end and the Cabinet was about to separate when the quiet grave tones of Sir Edward Grey's voice were heard reading a document which had just been brought to him from the Foreign Office." It was the Austrian note to Serbia containing the demand that precipitated the war. "The parishes of Tyrone and Fermanagh faded back into the mists and squalls of Ireland, and a strange light began immediately, but by imperceptible gradations, to fall and grow upon the map of Europe."

BOOK THREE

FIGHTING THE KAISER

God give us men! A time like this demands
Strong minds, great hearts, true faith and ready hands!
Men whom the lust of office does not kill,
Men whom the spoils of office cannot buy,
Men who possess opinions and a will,
Men who love honour, men who cannot lie.

—J. G. HOLLAND

CHAPTER ONE

THE FLEET WAS READY

1914

AGADIR was the rehearsal; Sarajevo raised the curtain on war. It was on June 28, 1914, that the Archduke Franz Ferdinand of Austria, with his wife, was assassinated at the Bosnian capital of Sarajevo by Slav nationalists who thereby struck the fatal spark to send Europe up in explosion. Five weeks intervened before Britain entered the war.

It was not until those fateful weeks had nearly run their course that the British Cabinet as a whole regarded the European situation as their chief problem. Ireland was their principal preoccupation and as late as July 25, and even July 28, Ireland was reviewed at Cabinet councils before the menacing state of affairs on the Continent was considered.

At the Admiralty, however, there was of necessity a different evaluation of the importance of the pressing questions of the hour.

As the threat of war spread, and Russia, Germany and France became involved in the original dispute between Austria and Serbia, Winston Churchill at the Admiralty, like Sir Edward Grey at the Foreign Office, became more and more concerned with the march of events. Grey labored to preserve the peace. Churchill speeded up strategic precautions lest the peace efforts should fail.

He was determined that the diplomatic situation should not get ahead of naval preparations.

In those days Churchill had two duties to perform. He had to marshal the fleets and he had also to lead the section of the Cabinet which was in favor of a strong policy and the fulfillment of British obligations to France should the occasion arise. The first of these two responsibilities was the lighter.

The First Lord, in his wisdom, had decided to hold no naval maneuvers in the summer of the year 1914. Instead he had arranged for a test mobilization of the Navy in which the men and ships of the 2nd and 3rd Reserve Fleets were put on a war footing. As the climax to this test, a Naval review was held, bringing together the most formidable assembly of warships that the world had witnessed to that time.

It so chanced that the massing of the ships at Spithead on July 17 and 18 coincided with the worsening of the situation in Europe. The fleets dispersed to return to port, but Churchill and the First Sea Lord, Prince Louis of Battenberg (afterward Lord Milford Haven), decided, in view of the gravity of the hour, not to allow the dispersal to be completed. On the following Monday morning, the press contained the announcement:

> Orders have been given to the First Fleet, which is concentrated at Portland, not to disperse for naval leave for the present. All vessels of the Second Fleet are remaining at their home ports in proximity to their balance crews.

Steps such as these, grave as was the responsibility involved, were carrying out matters of mere routine in accordance with plans long formulated. On the political front, however, there was no such simplicity. Opinion among ministers was hopelessly divided. The majority of the Cabinet were pacifist.

The peace-at-any-price men were for a declaration of neutrality without imposing any conditions on Germany. Lord Morley was the chief of this group, and associated with him were John Burns, Sir John Simon, then Attorney-General (later Viscount Simon and Lord Chancellor), Earl Beauchamp and Mr. Hobhouse. Allied with these, but a shade less pacific in their opinions, were Lloyd George and Lord Harcourt.

A center body of opinion was not committed to any definite

decision. The Marquis of Crewe, Mr. Reginald McKenna and Sir Herbert (later Viscount) Samuel were the principals of this center front. Grey and Churchill were solid for intervention.

Asquith himself was of the same opinion, but as Prime Minister he did not allow himself the same freedom to express his views. His was the task of striving to reconcile the irreconcilables and avert the threatened disintegration of the Ministry. We have it on his authority that Churchill, during that final week, was "very bellicose, demanding instant mobilization." His mind was brimming with ideas and he was in what Asquith almost censoriously described as "tearing spirits" at the prospect of war.

So that fateful week, the last week of peace, passed. Debates in the Cabinet were followed by conferences outside. Talks between perplexed ministers lasted to midnight and beyond.

On Tuesday, Churchill, on his own initiative, and without Cabinet sanction, dispatched the Fleet to its war station. During the hours of darkness, the battleships and their attendant flotillas steamed from Portland up Channel, through the Straits of Dover out into the spaces of the North Sea, on the way to the appointed base at Scapa Flow.

There were still the complete reserves to be mobilized. On the Saturday, the first day of August, Winston sent out a warning at the Admiralty to have everything in readiness for this step. "It seems certain," he wrote, "that the order to mobilize will be issued after the Cabinet this morning." The Cabinet, however, would not give their assent for this to be done.

On Sunday the Foreign Office boxes conveyed to the ministers the information that Germany had declared war on Russia. Churchill, on receipt of this information, went immediately to Number 10. To the Prime Minister, who was conferring with Grey, Haldane and Crewe, he announced his intention to complete mobilization forthwith, notwithstanding the Cabinet decision to the contrary.

"I will take full personal responsibility," he declared, "to the Cabinet tomorrow morning."

Asquith did not demur. And so, with no legal authority to back him, and without the royal proclamation that should have been signed, Churchill sent out the orders to mobilize.

Twenty-four hours later the Cabinet gave its formal assent to these wholly justified but strictly unconstitutional actions. By then there was no resisting the pressure of events. Only a few hours remained before Britain, too, was at war.

In those last hours the First Lord was busily engaged in sending out final directions to the commands of the Navy, warning them to be prepared to meet surprise attacks, to cooperate with the French, to respect the neutrality of Italy. There was the German cruiser *Goeben* in the Mediterranean. Orders were given that she was to be shadowed by two battle cruisers, but she got away.

Churchill, during the nerve-racking final hours, was a monument of calm, clear-headed steadiness. His dispositions had been made, his preparations were complete, he could await the event with confidence.

He was in his place in the House on the Monday afternoon when Sir Edward Grey made his historic declaration to the world that Great Britain would stand loyally shoulder to shoulder with the French against German aggression. As Grey made his speech, we are told, tears were seen to trickle down Churchill's cheek. Why those tears? Tears of sadness at the thought of the tragedy to come? Or tears of relief that the peace-at-any-price men had been foiled? We do not know.

Carson, who had been ranged against Churchill over Ireland, saw those tears. The champion of Ulster, who knew that the first Lord had never faltered over Britain's duty in the greater crisis, went up to him. As they passed behind the Speaker's chair, they shook hands in silence.

The British ultimatum to Germany expired at midnight in Berlin—eleven o'clock in London.

The ultimatum was a communication to which no reply was expected. As the sands ran out Asquith sat waiting in the Cabinet Room at Number 10. Sir Edward Grey was there to certify the silence of Berlin.

The hour struck. Britain was at war.

In another room at Whitehall, the First Lord was waiting. The notes of Big Ben came reverberating through the open windows. It was the signal for the dispatch to British ships and naval establishments throughout the world of the terse instruction: *"Commence hostilities against Germany."*

On land the enemy had had the advantage of the initiative.

They chose the place and hour for the first tremendous stroke. At sea, thanks to Winston Churchill, the advantage was with the British Navy. Von Tirpitz was unable to take the Fleet at a disadvantage by a surprise attack. "Great Britain," says the German official naval historian, "had received extensive military advantage by her test mobilization and her subsequent measures which Germany could not counter or overtake."

CHAPTER TWO

DUNKIRK AND ANTWERP

AUGUST–OCTOBER, 1914

SURVEYING THE COURSE of his long career of service to the country, Winston Churchill could do so with justifiable pride in
his work of ensuring that the Navy was fully prepared in 1914.

The Allies then were faced with a German Navy of considerable
force. It was not on a parity with the Royal Navy, but its line of
battleships made it much more formidable than the navy of
pocket battleships with which Hitler entered the war in 1939.

In 1914, had the Germans been able to catch the Grand Fleet
at a disadvantage, they might have inflicted severe losses upon it.
The warships were in a position to do untold harm to British
merchant shipping. Yet, such was the pinnacle of preparation to
which the Navy had been brought under Churchill's care that
England had command of the seas from the onset; she had chased
enemy raiders off the oceans of the world in a comparatively short
space, and for the rest of the war, except for a few minor excursions—Jutland was the chief—the German fleet dared not put out
from its harbors of refuge.

The first role of the British Navy was to safeguard the transport
of the British Expeditionary Force to France. The Grand Fleet in
full majesty patrolled the North Sea not far from the German
coast, challenging the enemy to come out and try to reach the

troopships plying to and fro across the English Channel. Not a German ship appeared. The transportation of the BEF was accomplished without the remotest attempt at interference. Not a man of its entire company was drowned.

Before the end of August the Battle of Heligoland Bight had brought havoc to the enemy light cruisers three of which were crippled and three sunk, without loss to the British Fleet. It was a lesson that made the Germans hug the safety of their shores more assiduously than ever.

With the war at sea so auspiciously begun, the First Lord could allow his mental vision to range over other fields. As a spare-time occupation he undertook, at Lord Kitchener's request, the responsibility for the aerial defense of Britain, there being no aerial force available for the purpose except the planes with which the Admiralty had provided itself to guard dockyards and ports.

Here I must break in upon the narrative to touch briefly on the part that Churchill played in the development of the Air Force as the third defense service. It gives yet another instance of his vision in estimating the possibilities of a new invention. Oil for ships, tanks to beat trenches, and airplanes—he took a hand in the development of these three ideas and their application to the national purpose.

It was only in the years immediately before the catastrophe of 1914 that the airplane had proved itself. Bleriot flew the Channel in 1909. In 1911 a Bleriot monoplane traveled at 81 miles an hour; in 1912 a French pilot exceeded 100 miles. With these advances made, the more open minds began to explore the possibilities of the plane as a weapon of war. The mass of conservative opinion in the services was not impressed.

It was fortunate that the political heads of both Navy and Army were receptive to new ideas. Winston at the Admiralty was no less impressed than Jack Seely at the War Office. They took up the exploitation of the air in a spirit of happy rivalry, like schoolboys with a new toy. Each strove to go ahead of the other—which was of benefit to the new arm, though there was inevitably some overlapping of activities. Under this eminent patronage military aviation made progress. By 1912 the new service had won sufficient recognition to be accorded the dignity of an establishment of its own.

The Royal Flying Corps came into being. Its parentage was attested by its dual structure—a naval wing and a military wing, bound together somewhat loosely by an Air Committee on which there were representatives of the two services, men of science and the political heads of the departments.

In 1913, Churchill and Seely announced to a startled public that they had made a deal over airships. It was an unparalleled piece of interdepartmental barter and each minister complimented himself that he had got the better of the other. Seely gained for the Army a credit of £25,000 from the Admiralty budget and for this sum Churchill obtained a fleet of airships for the Admiralty. There was an outcry from the Army service chiefs. The Military Aeronautics Directorate invoked the heavens against the politicians. The General Staff rocked with fury—but the deal had been done and the public service benefited. The airships proved their worth in coast reconnaissance and submarine hunting.

Churchill, when the war began, lent his powerful support to the movement for creating an independent ministry to control and develop the new corps, but at that time the resources in men and machines were hopelessly inadequate. Not until two years afterward was an Air Board established under Lord Curzon.

Two Air Forces controlled by two ministers led to some anomalous situations in the early months of the war. While some of Churchill's planes were allocated to the defense of the home front, others were dispatched to collaborate with the armies in northeastern France. It was not an ideal arrangement, but at least it produced action. A racy description of the situation was given in the memoirs of Air Vice Marshal Sir Sefton Brancker, Director of Civil Aviation, who perished in the R. 101 Airship disaster near Beauvais in October 1930.

Brancker viewed events from the Army standpoint of Deputy Director of Military Aeronautics and was thus less sympathetic to aerial activities directed from the opposite side of Whitehall at the Admiralty. He wrote: [1]

> Immediately after mobilization I went over to the Admiralty and had a talk with my opposite number, Murray Sueter, about the allocation of available contractors, aircraft and engines. He was prepared to draw up as clear a line of delimitation as possible

between the trade activities of the two Departments. We divided available contractors to suit this policy.

I endeavoured to co-operate thoroughly with him and I think that he was anxious to meet the wishes of the War Office in every way possible: but he was not his own master, for the vigorous and enthusiastic personality of Mr. Winston Churchill had come into play. He believed in aviation. Even at that time he had realized the enormous possibilities of the attack on hostile territory by an independent air force, and had grasped the necessity of some central control over all aeronautical matters. But the Admiralty conceived that this control should be vested in the Admiralty, with the independent force part and parcel of the Navy, his particular responsibility at the moment; and to this end he worked assiduously during the last months of 1914.

The first sign of this policy was his sudden announcement that the Naval Wing of the Royal Flying Corps had become the Royal Naval Air Service—this without any reason or warning being given to the War Office.

The second step was of interest and of considerable importance. Responsibility for Aerial Home Defence lay with the War Office, and I had already had some difficulty in persuading Lord Kitchener at that time that it was utter waste of our small available resources to keep good pilots and aircraft pottering about the coast on the chance of meeting a Zeppelin. I constantly urged that as matters stood every available pilot and aeroplane should either be at the Front or busy training new pilots at home. This apparent neglect of Home Defence led to considerable outside criticism, and Winston Churchill began to use it as a whip with which to chastise the War Office.

Shortly afterwards, at a Cabinet meeting, Kitchener asked Winston to take over the responsibility of Aerial Home Defence. Lord Kitchener realized that offence was the truest form of defence, that every available military aeroplane would be required with the Army on the Western Front for some time to come, and that aerial home defence by aircraft had not developed sufficiently to be worth talking about. The creation of the first Anti-Aircraft Corps for the Defence of London was then placed in the hands of Commodore Murray Sueter.

The demands of the Expeditionary Force were so great that it was obvious that every new military pilot and aeroplane would be fully and most usefully employed from the moment of their creation. In the Naval Air Service matters were quite different. Senior

Naval Officers had not been educated to the use of aviation and had no experience of aircraft; the Grand Fleet was not immediately employed in active operations, and the seaplane was not nearly so far developed as the landplane. The result was that the Navy made no real demand on the Royal Naval Air Service at all, and their magnificent personnel and material were practically unemployed so far as the Fleet was concerned. Neglected by the Navy and rejected by the Army, the Royal Naval Air Service, backed by Winston Churchill's vitality, naturally had to find some scope for their activities. On August 27, 1914, Commander Samson with a R.N.A.S. Squadron of aeroplanes landed at Dunkirk, and from that date the R.N.A.S. undertook many duties which were far more nearly akin to the land than to the sea.

Commander Samson's operations on the left of the Army might almost form the subject of an epic by themselves. With a handful of men, a few nondescript aeroplanes, and some commandeered cars with improvised armour, he was here, there and everywhere, terrorizing marauding Uhlans and inspiring French Territorials. I remember a most enterprising telegram from Commander Samson addressed to Lord French personally, which in the existing state of our communications had to come through the War Office; he briefly reported that he was operating on the Field Marshal's left and would be glad of information regarding the movements of the British Army as he wished to co-operate!

The Naval Air Service undertook a most remarkable series of air raids on German airship sheds at Cologne and Friedrichshafen, deeds of daring which were in accordance with the finest traditions of the Navy, but which, unfortunately, were rather loudly boomed in the Press. Before this I had always rather believed in the popular myth that the Navy was really the "Silent Service." The comparative success and glamour of these enterprises led the First Lord to undertake a big programme of air operations overland. The R.N.A.S. efforts at Dunkirk in bomb attacks on the submarine bases near Zeebrugge and the observation of the fire of the monitors were sound and quite justified; but there were other enterprises which, although on the surface they appeared harmless and even useful, actually led to a very evil competition between the Army and Navy in the purchase of aeroplanes and engines; this deprived the Expeditionary Force of aeroplanes which were frittered away on side issues, although the Army in the Field constituted the decisive factor in all the operations in progress at the time.

Even the Naval Air Service did not exhaust Churchill's capacity for spare-time occupations. He found time to give directions for the construction of an armored car, which showed a mind groping toward the invention of the tank. In the Admiralty records you can find the instructions the First Lord issued on the subject. He called for the construction of armored motor cars that would be provided with the means of crossing trenches. "An arrangement of planks capable of bridging a ten or twelve-feet span quickly and easily should be carried with every ten or twelve machines," the instructions ran.

The first resultant tank in embryo, designed by Admiral Bacon, carried a portable bridge forward, which it dropped down on reaching a trench and raised automatically on passing.

Next, the fertile mind of the First Lord was engaged in the organization of the Dunkirk Circus.

Dunkirk was to become the scene in World War II of the miracle of deliverance of the British armies which had been cut off by the Germans in 1940. In September 1914, this vital Channel port lay back from the route along which the German hordes were pouring into France. Their lines of communication, those sensitive arteries which are essential to an army's existence, ran from east to west, not far away. Joffre, then French Commander in Chief, suggested that a British force should make a landing at Dunkirk, held by the French, and make a demonstration with the object of causing the Germans anxiety over their communications and the diversion of some of their troops to deal with the menace.

Kitchener appealed to Churchill to carry the thing through with marines—again the Navy had the only forces available. So under the First Lord's inspiration the Circus came into being.

"Circus" is a word not ill-suited to describe the force of marines and yeomanry that trooped in and out of Belgian villages in a fleet of motor buses. In contrast with an army that seeks to do much by stealth, the Circus was intended to do little and parade much, so as to ensure that its well-advertised movements caused as great concern as possible to the enemy. In this it was successful.

Churchill was highly delighted with the activities of his force and he made frequent visits of inspection to see how the fun was going.

According to the accounts Lord Beaverbrook has given, the Circus had an influence on Churchill's fortunes, causing Asquith to have for the first time a sense of misgiving about the judgment of the First Lord. The Prime Minister had been as amused as Winston himself when the Circus opened, but while the First Lord's relish increased, Asquith's waned. There was something undignified in the affair which could not have appealed to the sedate Asquithian mind for long. His irritation grew when he had to take charge of the Admiralty in the First Lord's absence.

In the end Asquith had the Circus wound up. Yet, these promenaders had caused a serious disturbance of the German plans. Reports of the presence of British marines in Belgium worked upon the enemy's concern. Anxieties stimulated the German imagination into the belief that their flank was threatened by 40,000 men. Coming at a moment of crisis, the reports accentuated a German retreat and contributed to the salvation of the Allied armies.

Another and more serious intervention by the First Lord in the operations on land was made in October, when he figured in the episode of the expedition to Antwerp. This was one of the decisive events in the opening phases of the war. Its results were of the highest importance to the Allies, yet Churchill emerged from it with a damaged reputation. His enemies distorted the facts to injure him politically and undermine his position.

In the month of October, though the decisive battle of the Marne had been won, the French were still in retreat. The Germans were pouring through Belgium. Up in the North the fortress of Antwerp still held out—though Liège and Namur had fallen—protecting the Allied left flank and the Channel ports.

Orders were given to the German commanders that Antwerp must be taken at all costs. The Belgians could not continue their resistance, and sent urgent appeals for aid to Paris and London. They announced that on the day following they would fall back, thereby causing consternation to the Allies, whose left flank would have been fatally exposed, as it was by a similar defection in World War II.

On the night of October 2, Churchill was traveling from London to Dover by special train on his way to Dunkirk. The journey to the coast was half completed when the train was stopped and hurriedly sent back to London. The First Lord had been recalled at Lord Kitchener's request, to undertake at midnight an immediate journey to Antwerp. British reinforcements were to be sent over to aid the Belgians, but they could not reach the city for some days and Churchill must somehow induce the defenders to hold out.

Asquith was out of town and heard of the matter the following day. He made the following entry in his diary:

> I was away but Grey, Kitchener and Winston held a late meeting and, I fancy with Grey's rather reluctant consent, the intrepid Winston set off at midnight and ought to have reached Antwerp about nine o'clock. He will straight away see the Belgian Ministers. Sir J. French is making preparations to send assistance by way of Lille. I had a talk with K. this morning and we are both anxiously awaiting Winston's report. I do not know how fluent his French is, but if he is able to do justice to himself in a foreign tongue the Belges will have to listen to a discourse the like of which they have never heard before. I cannot but think that he will stiffen them up.

Churchill went duly impressed with the importance of his mission, and resolved to fulfill it. His arrival in the picturesque uniform of Elder Brother of Trinity House at the Belgian headquarters was in the highest degree spectacular. An American newspaper correspondent has preserved the scene:

> At one o'clock that afternoon a big, drab-coloured touring-car, filled with British naval officers, drove down the Place de Mer, its horn sounding a hoarse warning, took the turn into the March-aux-Souliers on two wheels, and drew up in front of the hotel. Before the car had fairly come to a stop the door of the tonneau was thrown violently open and out jumped a smooth-faced, sandy-haired, stoop-shouldered, youthful-looking man in undress Trinity House uniform. . . .
>
> As he charged into the crowded lobby he flung his arms out, in a nervous characteristic gesture, as though pushing his way through a crowd. It was a most spectacular entrance, and reminded me for all the world of a scene in a melodrama where the hero dashes up bare-headed on a foam-flecked horse, and saves the heroine, or the old homestead, or the family fortune, as the case may be.

Critics at home might scoff. The arrival impressed the Belgians. They were inspired into fighting on.

Next the First Lord appealed to the Prime Minister in London to be appointed to command the Allied forces to be sent to Antwerp's relief. He wrote:

If it is thought by H. M. Government that I can be of service here, I am willing to resign my office and undertake command of relieving and defensive forces assigned to Antwerp in conjunction with Belgian Army, provided that I am given necessary military rank and authority, and full powers of a commander of a detached force in the field. I feel it my duty to offer my services, because I am sure this arrangement will afford the best prospects of a victorious result to an enterprise in which I am deeply involved. I should require complete staff proportionate to the force employed, as I have had to use all the officers now here in positions of urgency. I wait your reply. Runciman would do Admiralty well.

Lord Kitchener was prepared to give Churchill the job. "I will make him a major general," he said, "if you will give him the command." The Government, however, was not prepared to make the appointment.

Again there are interesting entries in Asquith's diary:

October 5. I found when I arrived here this morning a telegram from Winston who proposes to resign his office to take command in the field of this great military force. Of course, without consulting anybody I at once telegraphed to him warm appreciation of his mission and his offer, with a most decided negative saying that we could not spare him at the Admiralty. I had not meant to read it at the Cabinet but, as everybody, including K., began to ask how soon he was going to return, I was at last obliged to do so. Winston is an ex-Lieutenant of Hussars and would, if his proposal had been accepted, have been in command of two distinguished Major-Generals not to mention Brigadiers, Colonels, etc., while the Navy are only contributing their Light Brigade.

October 6. Winston persists in remaining there, which leaves the Admiralty here without a head and I have had to tell them to submit decisions to me. I think that Winston ought to return now that a capable General is arriving. He has done good service.

Churchill remained to assist in the operations, in which some 8,000 men of the Royal Naval Division took part. Sir Ian Hamilton paid tribute to the manner in which the First Lord took charge of them. "Churchill," he wrote, "handled them as if he were Napoleon and they were the Old Guard, flinging them right into the enemy's opening jaws."

Lord Mottistone, who was sent by Sir John French to find out what was being done at Antwerp, gives another picture of Winston in command.

"From the moment I arrived, it was apparent that the whole business was in Winston's hands. He dominated the whole place— the King, ministers, soldiers, sailors. So great was his influence that I am convinced that with 20,000 British troops he could have held Antwerp against almost any onslaught."

Antwerp could not be held, but the Belgians, heartened by the presence of Winston and the marines, delayed the enemy for the space of five invaluable days. And what is more, the Belgian Army made a valiant recovery and got away intact. By this means the Belgian coast and the Channel ports were saved.

In the fighting some 900 men of the Naval Brigade were taken prisoners, 50 were killed, 130 or so were wounded, and a couple of battalions that inadvertently crossed the Dutch frontier were interned. These circumstances and the fact that Antwerp was not held were made the subject of attacks on the First Lord.

His control of affairs at the Admiralty had already given rise to much criticism in Conservative circles, where they called him the "amateur Commander in Chief of the Navy." The manner of his departure for Belgium provided new scope for the inventions of the malicious. Stories were put abroad of Churchill talking Kitchener into sending him to Antwerp and then willfully acting in excess of his instructions. The charge of involving "a pitiful loss of brave men's lives" was laid at his door.

It is to be regretted that Asquith did not deal with some of the critics and speak in defense and praise of the First Lord's efforts, of which he should have had a more just appreciation than their political opponents. From entries in the diary you can see that Asquith was not one of the staunchest supporters of the First Lord. He was not one of those large-minded men among whom Lord Mottistone has placed Churchill—men who have "the rare and engaging quality not only of supporting you when you are right, but also of supporting you when you are wrong."

On October 11, Asquith's soldier son, Brigadier General Arthur

Asquith, who was himself at Antwerp, visited him, and the Prime Minister noted in his diary:

> I had a long talk after midnight, in the course of which he gave me a full and vivid account of the expedition to Antwerp and the retirement. Marines, of course, are splendid troops and can go anywhere and do anything but Winston ought never to have sent the two Naval Brigades. I was assured that all the recruits were being left behind and that the main body at any rate consisted of seasoned naval reserve men. As a matter of fact, only about a quarter were Reservists and the rest were a callow crowd of the most raw recruits most of whom had never fired off a rifle while none of them had ever even handled an entrenching tool.

Later in October Churchill sought an interview with the Prime Minister who, in his diary, painted a satirical picture of the First Lord.

> I have had a long call from Winston who, after dilating in great detail on the actual situation, became suddenly very confidential.
>
> Having, as he says, tasted blood these last few days he is beginning like a tiger to raven for more and begs that sooner or later, and the sooner the better, he may be relieved of his present office and put in some kind of military command. I told him that he could not be spared from the Admiralty. He scoffed at that, alleging that the naval part of the business is practically over as our superiority will grow greater and greater every month.
>
> His mouth waters at the thought of Kitchener's Armies. Are these glittering commands to be entrusted to dug-out trash, bred on the obsolete tactics of twenty-five years ago, mediocrities who have led a sheltered life, mouldering in military routine?
>
> For about an hour he poured forth a ceaseless invective and appeal and I much regretted that there was no shorthand writer within hearing as some of his unpremeditated phrases were quite priceless. He was, however, three parts serious and declared that a political career was nothing to him in comparison with military glory.

These entries of the Prime Ministerial diarist show clearly enough why he did not lend the authority of his name to the defense of Churchill's reputation. For all the superiority of his brain Asquith—it is plain to see in the all-revealing diary—was lacking in elevation of character. He indulged the cynical amusement of the spectator of life's little ironies, but lacked the strength and compassion of the noblest minds.

History, when history came to be written, with greater appreciation gave Antwerp its place as one of the key points when the war was won and lost.

Winston Churchill's achievement in prolonging the resistance at Antwerp was shown to be one of the principal successes in his career. Here is the impartial verdict of the British official history of the war:

> The British effort to save Antwerp had failed. Nevertheless it had a lasting influence on the operations. Until Antwerp had fallen, the troops of the investing force were not available to move forward on Ypres and the coast; and though, when they did, they secured Zeebrugge and Ostend without a struggle, they were too late to secure Nieuport and Dunkirk and turn the northern flank of the Allies, as was intended. Further, the whole general movement of the German forces in the north was affected. The advantages of a day, nay, even a few hours, in the advance of the Germans on Ypres or an equal delay in the arrival of the French and British reinforcements might have tipped the scale to the enemy's side. Had events turned out more favourably for the main Allied armies in the first week of October, the defence of Antwerp might have proved decisive.

The catastrophe of the loss of the Channel ports in the Battle of France in World War II underlines the value of Winston Churchill's services at Antwerp.

CHAPTER THREE

RECALL OF FISHER

NOVEMBER, 1914–1915

IN NOVEMBER 1914 Winston Churchill, taking his political life in his hands, recalled Lord Fisher to his old place as First Sea Lord. Thus destiny brought together the greatest naval administrator of his time and the greatest sailor since Nelson in a combination which was to have a decisive effect on their careers and on the fortunes of the Asquith Government.

It was a venturesome step for Churchill to take: for the dynamic Admiral, intense in his likes and hatreds, had in his day been the chief figure in the controversy that had split the Navy into two rival camps—Fisher's adherents and those of Lord Charles Beresford, Commander in Chief of the Channel Fleet. Politicians were involved as well. The old animosities had died down but there was no guarantee that the flames might not break out afresh.

Churchill considered that the risk was worth running to get Fisher back as service head of the Navy. In this the First Lord was guided not only by his estimate of the work that the old admiral could do for the nation. There were younger admirals who might have been expected to do as well, but they had not the reputation in the country and, however good they might be, they would not serve to the same degree to provide a substantial prop for Churchill's administration. And of some such prop he was in need.

The fact was that by November his star no longer burned with quite the same luster as when the war began. For this there were a variety of reasons. The failure of the Antwerp expedition was pre-eminent.

Then there was the sinking of three cruisers which made him the target for renewed attacks. Their loss was laid at his door and he was accused of having sent them to their doom by acting against the advice of the Sea Lords. One writer, in what the First Lord described as a venomous brochure, committed himself to this statement:

> The loss of the *Aboukir, Cressy* and *Hogue* with 1,459 officers and men killed, occurred because, despite the warnings of Admirals, Commodores and Captains, Mr. Churchill refused until it was too late to recall them from patrol so carried on as to make them certain to fall victims to the torpedoes of our active enemy.

In point of fact, Churchill, before the disaster occurred, had given instructions to terminate the very patrol system that caused these ships to be lost. Unknown to him, delay in carrying out his orders had occurred. These facts would have been a complete answer to the allegations inspired by malicious minds, but it was against the national interest for the facts to be publicly stated.

Looking back, nearly half a century later, you may find it difficult to understand either that such disgraceful things should have been said or that, being said, they should have found listeners to credit them. It is only by taking into account the bitterness of party politics in the years before the war that you can see events in their proper setting.

Home Rule for Ireland had been the principal subject of debate for a generation. It had brought the country to the verge of civil war. Disputes over tariffs, Lloyd George budgets and House of Lords reform had accentuated party bitterness. In all these controversies Winston Churchill had played a leading part. Deserting from the ranks of the Tories to the political enemy, he had become with Lloyd George the principal attacking force in the ranks of the Liberals. He had baited the Tories, taunted them, smitten them hip and thigh—and always, hardest to forget, he had emerged from the conflicts on the winning side.

When the war came, Churchill, laboring devotedly at the Admiralty, forgot in a flash the animosities of party politics. All his energies were bent in an instant on winning the war, all his thoughts were concentrated on that single purpose.

For the Tories there was not the same pressure of affairs. The cares and labors of office were not driving the thoughts of past feuds from their minds. They looked upon the First Lord with no kindly eyes, and at each loss of ships at sea found new cause for alarm until they conceived that the continuance of Winston at the Admiralty to be a menace to the Allied cause.

In the opening months of the war, Prince Louis of Battenberg was First Sea Lord. Because of his German origin, Prince Louis became a target for perfervid patriots who were unaware of the valuable work he was doing. For a while no heed was paid to this clamor—a circumstance that caused some damage, politically, to Churchill—but at length Prince Louis came to the conclusion that it was impairing his usefulness on the Admiralty Board and he tendered his resignation.

It was then that Churchill brought Lord Fisher back from retirement. For three years Fisher had been Churchill's unofficial mentor and there was an affectionate friendship between the young Sea Lord and the old sea dog, now a veteran of seventy-four. But despite his years, Fisher had given sufficient indication that his volcanic powers were largely unimpaired. He leaped at the opportunity to take charge of the Navy that was largely the product of his inspired creation.

"He was," wrote Churchill in his account of affairs, "strongly inspired with the sense of a message to deliver and a mission to perform."

A mission to perform—there, if you come to think of it, was a situation fraught with explosive possibilities, for Fisher was not the only man holding that view of himself. The old admiral might regard himself as the creator of the Navy, but Churchill, too, had had a hand in events. He had seen that Navy prepared against the day and he had, in defiance of Cabinet orders, mobilized the Fleet in the hour of crisis. Winston no less than Fisher could reckon himself to be a man with a mission.

Forceful characters both, Fisher and Churchill had in common a tenacity of purpose and determination not easily to be turned. While the two forces were working in harmony, the cooperation would be splendid. But if ever were discord to arise the collision would be shattering.

In the first flush of exultation at returning to duty, Fisher could not sufficiently accommodate himself to his political chief. They made an agreement by which neither would take any action without informing the other. Under another arrangement they made, one or other was on duty on the Admiralty quarter-deck almost around the clock. Fisher was an early riser whose mental vigor slackened by the evening. Churchill altered his routine so that he could be on duty into the early hours while Fisher slept.

So First Lord and First Sea Lord began their cooperation in complete harmony and with beneficial results for the Allied cause upon the high seas.

The first fruits of Fisher's return to duty were seen in the Battle of the Falkland Islands, in which von Spee's squadron, consisting of the *Gneisenau* and *Scharnhorst* and a couple of smaller cruisers, was annihilated. It was Fisher's dynamic methods that got the two British cruisers *Inflexible* and *Invincible* out of port in time to deal with von Spee.

The two cruisers arrived for coaling at Devonport on November 8, and Fisher gave orders that they were to leave on November 11. The dockyard officials declared it to be impossible; they wanted a week to get the ships ready. The First Sea Lord would have none of it: three days and no more. The dockyard officials replied that brickwork on the boilers of the *Inflexible* could not be finished in time. Fisher replied that the necessary material should be put aboard the *Inflexible* and if the work were not done, then the workmen should sail with her.

The cruiser sailed and sailed on time.

The drive of the septuagenarian sea dog was irresistible. His "Rush"-labeled orders were not to be ignored. Their effect was shown by a marked speeding up in shipbuilding output.

Fisher extended the building program which had been authorized before he took office, and ordered a number of special ships needed for the carrying out of his pet idea—a combined Navy and Army operation for the landing of troops in the Baltic to cause confusion behind the German lines. Russian troops, he suggested, could be put ashore on the Pomeranian coast; that is within one hundred miles of Berlin.

This was Fisher's pet plan and knowing his character you may imagine that he believed in it with all the concentrated faith of his forceful nature. For him the Baltic was, potentially, the decisive theater of war; its neglect, a calamitous strategic blunder responsible for most of the disasters that befell the Allied armies.

Writing in 1918, shortly before the war ended, he bewailed the German conquests which gave them control of dominions "greater than the Roman Empire ever possessed at its utmost period of expansion," and added: "All this terrible calamity directly results from our not going to the *Baltic as the decisive theater of war* when we could so easily have done so."

This belief in the Baltic plan had an important psychological effect on Fisher's judgment. Always it was in the background of his mind coloring his views on Allied strategy. When it was a question of "What plan shall we adopt now?" or "Is this operation practicable?" Fisher's opinion was inescapably affected by his predilections for the Baltic scheme.

It was with this psychological handicap that he was called upon to give his advice on the operations at the Dardanelles and Gallipoli.

CHAPTER FOUR

THE DARDANELLES

MARCH, 1915

THE DARDANELLES and Gallipoli—what incredible heroism and what incredible human folly are betokened by those two names. For men of the Army and the Navy the Dardanelles and Gallipoli mean deeds of renown as imperishable as any in Britain's annals. For the statesmen who then formed the War Council they are words of reproach for muddle and delay that cost good men's lives. For Winston Churchill they are names that recall the greatest personal misfortune in his career.

At the time, and for some years afterward, Churchill was made the chief target for censure over the failure of the Dardanelles and Gallipoli. A royal commission cleared his reputation, but some of the mud stuck. In the twenties you could frequently hear it said that "Churchill landed us in the mess of Gallipoli." Even during World War II, men who should have known better, could be heard to say: "We don't want Winston to land us in another Gallipoli."

The genesis of the Dardanelles operations and the Gallipoli campaign—it is important to differentiate between the two—can be simply explained.

On October 31, 1914, Turkey declared war on the side of Germany. On November 25 the Dardanelles first came up before the

War Council in Downing Street. The possibility of an attack was discussed but the question was shelved on the advice of Lord Kitchener, Secretary for War, then at the height of his reputation. He thought that the moment was not yet ripe. By the mere raising of the question ministers became conscious of the fruits of a successful attack, which would open the way to Constantinople. It was only necessary to look at the map to realize the importance of Constantinople, at once the London and Berlin of the Near East. Its capture would be likely to have a vital effect on the future policy of the Balkan states, Bulgaria, Greece and Romania, or on Italy, still neutral at that date but inclined to join the Allies.

Just over a month later, on January 2, 1915, an urgent appeal was received from Russia. Grand Duke Nicholas reported that the Russian troops in the Caucasus were being hard pressed and he asked the Allies to undertake some military demonstration against the Turks as a means of relieving Turkish pressure on the Russians.

This brought to a head a controversy among the ministers which had been developing. In the autumn, when deadlock was reached on the Western Front, various members of the Government cast their minds about to find the means of winning the war elsewhere. Lloyd George was for the Balkans. Fisher preferred his pet plan for amphibious operations in the Baltic. Churchill advocated a naval-cum-military attack on Constantinople. A memorandum from the Secretary to the War Council, Lieutenant Colonel Hankey, stated the case for operations against Turkey.

Each project had its secondary supporters and a tripartite tug-of-war developed. It was rendered the more inconclusive by the resolve of Sir John French, Commander in Chief on the Western front, not to release a single man or a rifle of his command for any adventure elsewhere. Kitchener backed Sir John.

Such was the division among the politicians at home when Russia's SOS was received. The appeal was one that could not be ignored. At the time when the Anglo-French forces were in the greatest peril at Mons, the Russians had invaded East Prussia as a means of drawing off German divisions from the Western Front. Now in the time of their own need the Russians must be given relief. To this even Kitchener agreed. He replied to the Grand

Duke that something would be done against the Turks and he sent a memorandum to the First Lord of the Admiralty pointing to the Dardanelles as offering the best chance. Kitchener wrote:

I do not see that we can do anything that will seriously help the Russians in the Caucasus. The Turks have evidently withdrawn most of their troops from Adrianople, and are using them to reinforce their forces against Russia, probably sending them across the Black Sea. We have no troops to land anywhere. The only place where a demonstration might have some effect on stopping reinforcements going East would be the Dardanelles. We shall not be ready for anything big for some months.

The following day Fisher, who had been informed of the various tentative schemes and of the Russian appeal, wrote to the First Lord recommending military operations against Turkey on a grandiose scale. As they involved the cooperation of Greece and Bulgaria and the dispatch of 75,000 troops it was not within the range of possibilities; for the Bulgars were not prepared to fight, the Russians themselves objected to Greek participation and there were no troops to be found anyhow.

As part of his operations Fisher also envisaged a naval attack to force the Straits, an operation which he proposed should be assigned to Admiral Sturdee with ships that were becoming obsolete. In the Fisher scheme this was only one part of the vast, combined operations. But when the other parts fell to the ground, attention became directed to this alone.

Churchill, hitherto, had looked upon the capture of the Straits as a matter for the Army, but the suggestion made by the First Sea Lord attracted him at once. The prize to be won was rich enough to warrant great risks. Could the Navy, unaided by the Army, undertake the task? At least it was worthy of investigation.

With Fisher's full concurrence he telegraphed to Admiral Carden, commanding British naval forces at the Dardanelles: "Do you consider the forcing of the Straits by ships alone a practicable operation? It is assumed that older battleships fitted with mine-bumpers would be used. Importance of result would justify severe loss."

Two days later Carden replied that though the Straits could not be rushed they might be forced by extended operations. The Admiral was then invited to submit a detailed plan. He outlined the possible operations under four heads:

1. Destruction of the defenses at the entrance to the Straits.
2. Action inside the Straits to clear up defenses.
3. Destruction of the defenses of the narrows.
4. Sweeping a clear passage through the minefield and advance through the narrows, followed by a reduction of the forts further up.

The novelty of the proposition outlined by the Admiral consisted in the abandonment of any attempt to rush the Dardanelles and the substitution in its place of a scheme by which the forts would be methodically attacked and destroyed one by one. It squared with the impression produced by the German successes in reducing strong forts on land by their heavy artillery.

On January 13 the War Council met again and Churchill presented details of the expert reports he had received. Kitchener gave the naval operations his blessing. Thereafter the Council unanimously decided that the Dardanelles project should be prepared, the actual decision being recorded as follows:

> The Admiralty should prepare for a naval expedition in February to bombard and take the Gallipoli peninsula with Constantinople as its objective.

It was a curiously worded decision. To force the Straits was possibly within the competence of the Navy. To take a peninsula was a strange task for a fleet. To this confusion the ministers added another. The majority of those present believed that they had given their final approval to the launching of the attack; others, the Prime Minister among them, imagined they had done no more than to sanction provisional plans. A few—Lord Fisher and Admiral Sir Arthur Wilson included—left the meeting before Asquith read out the terms of the decision and were not aware that anything had been settled at all.

The First Lord knew that the governing word was "prepare" and proceeded with the preparations. A fortnight later the Council met again. In that interval Fisher developed doubts. He came to two conclusions—first, that the Dardanelles scheme was unsound; second, that he did not wish to attend any further meetings of the Council. The second conclusion did not arise out of the first, was indeed unconnected with it. It did not even spring from his contempt—he made little attempt to disguise it—for what he termed the "Aulic Council," finding some special stigma of reprobation in the courts of the Holy Roman Empire. His opposition arose from promptings of jealousy caused by the disparity in power and prestige between his own position and that of Lord Kitchener.

These two were the Nelson and Wellington of their day—Kitchener's reputation being then comparatively undamaged by revelation of his limitations. Kitchener, the leading military authority, was political head of the War Office and thus at meetings of the War Council spoke in his own right for the Army. His views were received with the respect due to oracular pronouncements.

When the war began the ministers knew nothing about war and he, they thought, knew everything. Their attitude of humility was enhanced by the disdain with which he treated them. As he did not trust the discretion of their tongues—and still less their wives —he imparted few secrets to their keeping, and the appearance of his strength was heightened by his silence.

Fisher, on the other hand, was no more than the service head of the Navy; he could only advise his political chief and leave it to him to represent his views to the Council—or not represent them, as the case might be, for the First Lord did not consider himself necessarily bound to echo or even report the First Sea Lord's opinions. Fisher was only one—though he might be the leading—member of the board, and the First Lord was entitled to form his estimate of the sum of opinions expressed by his naval advisers.

This position of inferiority was intensely galling to Fisher. He was loyal to his chief but in his mind he brooded enviously over the discrimination which placed the greatest living sailor so far inferior to the greatest living soldier.

The result was that he informed the Prime Minister that he did not wish to attend further meetings of the War Council, whereupon Asquith summoned the First Lord and First Sea Lord to meet him. At this conference, held in the Prime Minister's private room on January 28, Fisher opposed the Dardanelles plan, representing that it interfered with his own projects for amphibious operations against the Germans on coasts nearer home. Asquith expressed himself in agreement with Churchill. Fisher's disagreement was not overcome but he withdrew his objection to taking part in ministerial consultations.

A full meeting of the Council followed shortly afterward. The members, with a celerity unusual for them, prepared to sanction the launching of the Dardanelles naval attack. Many of them gave the scheme their blessing.

Kitchener's opinion was that the naval attack was "vitally important." Balfour, although a Tory and not a member of the Government, was brought in as a member of the War Council—found it difficult to imagine a more helpful operation. Edward Grey was impressed by the diplomatic possibilities—it might finally check Bulgaria from throwing in her lot with the Germans and it would influence the whole of the Balkans.

Fisher was disconcerted. He had not been prepared for so prompt a decision by the "Aulic Council." But his mind was made up—rather than be associated with the Dardanelles plan he would resign his office. He rose from the table and made to retire both from the room there and then, and from office immediately thereafter.

Kitchener noticed his action and surmised his intention. The greatest soldier acted promptly, induced the greatest sailor not to pass from the room and drew him aside into the window recess. There in hushed tones, rendered less inarticulate than usual by the urgency of the moment, he appealed to him not to carry his objections to the Dardanelles plan to the point of resignation. After all, he argued, Fisher was the only one present who disagreed with the proposed operation; and even if he thought the scheme unsound, there were overwhelming political reasons why it should at least be attempted.

Fisher reluctantly gave in to Kitchener's entreaty and resumed his seat. He agreed to carry on though the Dardanelles attack was to proceed, but I should not imagine that any member of the Council was under any misapprehension about his continued and unabated opposition to what they were determined on. No one, however, thought it necessary to ask him to state the reasons for his opposition, and Fisher himself did not consider that he was entitled, unasked, to express his views.

There is no need here to retell in detail the tale of the Navy's operations. Sufficient to indicate that the first bombardment took place on February 19; the results were not decisive, but fairly satisfactory. By the beginning of March the outer defenses of the Dardanelles had been destroyed. The first phase had been successfully accomplished. The intermediate and inner defenses remained. The first attempts to reduce these failed and it was not until March 18 that an onslaught could be made by the whole of the available Allied fleet. In the interval Admiral Carden had been prevented by ill health from continuing to direct the operations and he was succeeded by his second in command, Admiral de Robeck.

The great attack opened auspiciously, and then at the moment when Fate seemed to smile there was a sudden change. A row of mines which had escaped the attentions of Britain's sweepers took toll of her ships. In a short space of time three battleships had been lost and three others had been badly damaged. De Robeck decided to break off the engagement for the day. He wished only for time to readjust his plans before resuming. Churchill consulted with his naval experts and reported to the War Council. The continuance of the operations was authorized and hopes still ran high.

Before another week had run its course, however, there came telegrams from the Dardanelles which transformed the situation. General Sir Ian Hamilton had been sent out to report on the operations from the standpoint of the Army; and having consulted with him, Admiral de Robeck recommended postponing the resumption of the naval offensive until the Army could cooperate.

Churchill received this message with consternation. The Admiral's advice ran counter to all his opinions and to all his hopes. Why break off when the prize was already partly won? Why give the enemy the benefit of delay? Better by far go ahead.

He convened a meeting of the Admiralty War Group. He placed before them a telegram for dispatch to the Dardanelles to instruct de Robeck to renew the attack at the first available opportunity. The telegram was never sent. The Chief of the Staff (Admiral Oliver) concurred in the sending of the instructions, but it was opposed by Lord Fisher, by Admiral Wilson, and by Admiral Jackson. They would not overrule the man on the spot.

Winston was not able to move them from their decision. He expostulated, but in vain. He consulted the Prime Minister. Asquith agreed with his views, but that made no difference. In Winston's phrase "The 'No' principle had become established in men's minds and nothing could ever eradicate it."

The admiral on the spot said "No" to going on. The Board of Admiralty said "No" to overruling the admiral. And the Prime Minister said "No" to overruling the board. No became never. The Fleet waited in vain for the opportunity to resume the attack in the narrows.

Churchill was later reproached for having sought to bring about that one more attempt. To Fisher's biographer, Admiral Sir Reginald Bacon, it was a mark of the gambler's recklessness—"the 'fatal once more' is the seductive will-o'-the-wisp of the gambler—it is the vain hope which is the cause of his ultimate ruin."

But the gambler in all probability would have been justified in his faith had the operations been resumed. The abandonment of the attack caused no more surprise to the First Lord in London than it did to the enemy and enemy's high command. So little ammunition had the Turkish gunners left that on that March 18 they reckoned defeat to be inevitable. The medium howitzers and minefield batteries had fired off half their supply. The long-range heavy explosive shells were nearly all used up—and only the H.E. shell was effective against the armor of warships.

A gambler's throw? Take the verdict of the British official history [1] on the situation of the Turks:

> On the evening of the 18th of March the Turkish command at the Dardanelles was weighed down by the premonition of defeat. More than half the ammunition had been expended, and it could not be replaced. The antiquated means of fire control had been seriously interrupted. The Turkish gun crews were demoralized and even the German officers present had, apparently, little hope of successful resistance if the Fleet attacked next day. Of the nine rows of mines, many had been in position for six months, and a large proportion of these were believed either to have been carried away by the current, or to have sunk to such a depth that ships would not have touched them. For the rest, many were of old pattern, and not too trustworthy, and, owing to the shortage of numbers, they were, on an average, 90 yards apart, more than three times the beam of a ship. A German journalist describes the

great astonishment of the defenders of the coast forts when the attack suddenly ceased. He records that the German naval gunners who were manning the batteries at Chanak told him later that they had made up their minds that the Fleet would win, and that they themselves could not have held out much longer.

Turning to the military measures for the defence of the capital, Liman von Sanders, head of the German Military Mission, roundly asserts that the orders issued by Turkish G.H.Q. between the 20th February and 1st March entailed the worst defensive dispositions imaginable, and placed the Dardanelles at the mercy of a hostile landing. "If the orders given at that moment had been carried out," he writes, "the course of the world war would have changed after the spring of 1915, and Germany and Austria would have been constrained to continue the fight alone."

Such was the perilous position of the Turks when the naval operations against them were halted; such was the narrowness of their escape; such the effect of those twenty unspotted mines.

Thereafter there was an interval in the British attack. The purely naval phase was ended. And the Army was to be involved in an attempt to pull the Navy's chestnuts out of the fire.

Before proceeding to consider Churchill's responsibility for the Gallipoli landing we must consider events at home where a political storm was about to break.

CHAPTER FIVE

FISHER'S MUTINY

MAY, 1915

BY MID-MAY of the year 1915, events were moving to a crisis—
moving indeed to a concentration of crises. Things had not
been going well in France; Sir John French, British Commander
in Chief, was complaining about the shortage of shells, which was
producing a crisis. Things had not been going well in Gallipoli.
Gallipoli was producing a crisis. Things were not going well at
the Admiralty. Tension between First Lord and First Sea Lord
was mounting. A Fisher crisis was imminent.

Within the Government there was disquiet. Among the Opposition ranks there was dissatisfaction. Disquiet and dissatisfaction
were mirrored in the press and echoed in the country. A wartime
truce prevailed in politics, but the back-bench members of the
Opposition were more than restive; they pressed for the chance
to speak out in Parliament and accuse the Government of gross
mismanagement. Bonar Law, the Glasgow ironfounder who had
succeeded Arthur Balfour as Tory leader, was with difficulty keeping his wilder men in check.

Churchill was a principal target for Tory criticisms. When anything went wrong at sea, they blamed Churchill. When a warship
fell victim to a U-boat's torpedo, they blamed Churchill. When
the Antwerp expedition failed, they blamed Churchill. And now

that Gallipoli looked like adding to the list of non-successes, they blamed Churchill more than ever.

For some of their criticisms of the First Lord they were provided with material by the First Sea Lord. Fisher had always had his contacts in the political world since the days of the *affaire* Beresford. Now, in his growing irritation at Churchill's managing ways at the Admiralty, he was resorting more and more to his political confidants to ease his burden of resentment. He found ready listeners who conceived that if Churchill was the man who was imperiling the Navy, then Fisher was its salvation. Fisher could scarcely demur to that.

Churchill was scarcely aware of the extent of the mistrust which his administration at the Admiralty inspired. He did not frequent the House in these days. His time was taken up by conduct of naval affairs, the pressing problems of Gallipoli and the delicate task of managing Fisher. In his devotion to his tasks he had practically isolated himself from the larger political world. His concentration was magnificent, but it was a political mistake. Ministers of the Crown derive their strength from Parliament to whom they are responsible. If a minister has the confidence of the House he can afford to ignore the assaults of his enemies. But if that confidence is lacking, he lies open to attack. By his conduct Churchill showed himself to be a better public servant than politician.

Operations at Gallipoli, since the naval assault on the Dardanelles had been succeeded by the attack on land, held out no promise of immediate success. The troops, landed on April 25, had a precarious footing on the Gallipoli peninsula but the Turks —forewarned by the naval attacks—had improvised trench and barbed wire defenses. Reports were received at the Admiralty of the presence of enemy submarines in Mediterranean waters.

Fisher became concerned for the safety of the newest battleship, the *Queen Elizabeth,* which had been sent to test her guns on the Dardanelles defenses. He demanded the withdrawal of the battleship. To this Kitchener objected, looking on it as the first sign that the Navy was about to desert the Army. Fisher insisted, with the threat of resignation and, supported by Churchill, gained his point. The *Queen Elizabeth* was withdrawn, and it should be added that within a fortnight a dummy of the battleship which was rigged up was torpedoed by a German submarine.

This dispute over one vessel was the herald to a more sustained controversy. Fisher's objections to the Navy's part in the operations and to the diversion of forces there which he wanted to be employed on his own schemes were no longer to be contained. He had not thought it his duty in April to state his views before the War Council, but in May he wrote to the Prime Minister protesting against the gradual draining of the naval resources from the decisive theater of war. The admiral had founded his original objections to the Dardanelles project on Nelson's dictum that "any sailor who attacked a fort was a fool." His criticism was continued although there was not the same basis for it, since the Army was attacking Gallipoli and the Navy's role was the subsidiary one of safeguarding the Army.

Churchill did his best to placate Fisher and succeeded in coming to terms with him once again, but within a few hours all was undone. The following day Fisher launched a new protest to Asquith because he had heard Churchill remark to Kitchener, "In the event of the Army's failure the Fleet would endeavor to force its way through."

> I desire to convey to you [Fisher wrote] that I honestly feel that I cannot remain where I am much longer, as there is an inevitable drain *daily* (almost hourly) on the resources in the decisive theatre of the war.
>
> But that is not the worst. Instead of the whole time of the whole of the Admiralty being concentrated on the daily increasing submarine menace in home waters, we are all diverted to the Dardanelles, and the unceasing activities of the First Lord, both day and night, are engaged in ceaseless *prodding* of everyone in every department afloat and ashore in the interest of the Dardanelles Fleet, with the result of the huge Armada now there, whose size is sufficiently indicated by their having as many battleships out there as in the German High Seas Fleet! Therefore this purely private and personal letter, intended for your eye alone and not to be quoted, as there is no use threatening without acting, is to mention to the one person who I feel *ought* to know *that I feel that my time is short.*

Fisher continued his offensive the next day (May 14) at a meeting of the War Council. Kitchener brought up the withdrawal of the *Queen Elizabeth* and protested against the ordering away of the battleship at a time when the soldiers were fighting on the peninsula with their back to the sea. Fisher interrupted to declare that he had been opposed to the operations from the start and that both Kitchener and the Prime Minister knew this to be the case.

The Council received the interjection without comment—a fair enough indication that Fisher's attitude was well-known before then. Members proceeded with their discussions. Churchill did not consider he could leave the matter there. The meeting over, he sent the following to the Prime Minister:

> I must ask you, to take note of Fisher's statement to-day that he was against the Dardanelles, and had been all along, or words to that effect. The First Sea Lord has agreed in writing to every executive telegram on which the operations have been conducted, and had they been immediately successful the credit would have been his. But I make no complaint of that.
>
> I am attached to the Old Boy and it is a great pleasure to me to work with him. I think he reciprocates these feelings. My point is that a moment will arise in these operations when the Admiral and General on the spot will wish and require to run a risk with the Fleet for a great and decisive effort. If I agree with them, I shall sanction it; and I cannot consent to be paralysed by the veto of a friend who, whatever the result, will say, "I was always against the Dardanelles."
>
> But I wish to make it clear to you that a man who says, "I disclaim responsibility for failure," cannot be the final arbiter of the measures which may be found vital to success.
>
> This requires no answer, and I am quite contented with the course of affairs.

Later that evening Churchill went to Fisher's room at the Admiralty to continue his role of pacificator. There was a long talk and at its close First Lord and First Sea Lord parted amicably, Churchill saying as he left, "Good night, Fisher. We have settled everything and you must go home and have a good night's rest. Things will look better in the morning and we'll pull the thing through together."

So Churchill went off to his night's work on the Navy's affairs with the comforting feeling that he had staved off trouble once again. Fisher summoned his naval assistant to tell him that, after all, he "need not pack up just yet."

The following morning, Saturday, Churchill was walking across the Horse Guards, returning to the Admiralty from a Foreign Office conference, when his private secretary came running up to him, anxiety plain to see upon his face.

"Fisher," he said, "has resigned, and I think he means it this time."

Fisher, indeed, had not merely resigned, but had quitted his post and was not to be found.

Churchill that fateful Friday night had been engaged on Admiralty work until the small hours. After midnight he received an appeal from the Italian Naval Attaché for the dispatch of four light cruisers to reinforce the Italian Fleet in the Adriatic. If these ships were to arrive forthwith, it might have a decisive influence on bringing Italy into the war on the side of the Allies.

Fisher had already concurred in the agreement with Italy under which these ships were asked for, and had initialed the instructions for four vessels to be detailed for this service. All that was now required was to accelerate their departure by forty-eight hours. Rather than call Fisher from his rest, Churchill decided to authorize the matter himself. He marked the file "First Sea Lord to see after action."

It appears, however, that this unhappily worded comment did no more than strengthen the decision Fisher had already made to resign. That Friday night four memoranda were sent from the First Lord to the First Sea Lord, the fourth of which dealt with the sending to the Dardanelles of monitors to release battleships for home waters and two more submarines. There was a brief accompanying letter informing Fisher that the memorandum was sent to him before being circulated so as to give an opportunity for discussion if he considered it necessary.

Captain Crease, Fisher's naval assistant, gave the following account of the proceedings:

> I was working in my room at the Admiralty on the night of the 14th May, when towards midnight Masterton Smith [the First Lord's private secretary, later Sir J. E. Masterton Smith], came in with the minute [No. 4] and covering letter, and said that the First Lord wished the First Sea Lord to have them in the morning.

Masterton Smith asked me to read them through, and I did so. He was evidently uneasy about the minute and asked me "how I thought the old man would take it." Knowing well Lord Fisher's frame of mind during the past few days and his letter to the Prime Minister of the day before, and reading that submarines were now included in the proposed reinforcements, in addition to various other ships and materials that Lord Fisher had not mentioned a few hours earlier, I had no hesitation about my reply. I said at once, that I had no doubt whatever Lord Fisher would resign instantly if he received the minute; for these new proposals, coming at that moment, would be the last straw. . . .

After some discussion Masterton Smith said he would tell the First Lord my opinion before definitely handing me the minute to pass on. After some delay he came back with the dispatch-box and said it must be sent on, for the First Lord was certain that Lord Fisher would not object to the proposals; but the First Lord had also added that, in any case, it was necessary that they should be made. I repeated my warning as to the consequences, and then arranged for the dispatch-box to be delivered early in the morning to Lord Fisher.

In the early morning Fisher opened the dispatch box. A first glance at the contents aroused his resentment. Churchill had gone back on the pledge he had given the night before. Fisher took up his pen and dashed off a letter of resignation. This had already left his hand when the instruction to send cruisers to Italy was placed before him. The accompanying minute served to confirm him in his view that it was impossible to continue to serve under Winston.

His decision was made known in letters to the Prime Minister and First Lord. To Asquith he wrote:

MY DEAR PRIME MINISTER,

As I find it increasingly difficult to adjust myself to the increasing policy of the First Lord in regard to the Dardanelles, I have been reluctantly compelled to inform him this day that I am unable to remain as his colleague, and I am leaving at once for Scotland, so as not to be embarrassed, or embarrass you, by any explanations with anyone.

Your admiring Master at Balliol said "Never explain," but I am sure you will understand my position.

Yours truly,

FISHER

The letter to Churchill was in pretty much the same terms, the quotation of Jowett's, "Never explain," included.

There was a flurry in Government circles that Saturday—hurried consultations between Prime Minister, First Lord, and Chancellor of the Exchequer. At first Asquith was inclined to treat the matter lightly. "Fisher," he said, "is always resigning. This is nothing new." Lloyd George, however, was not so sanguine, and his information was good for it was to the Chancellor of the Exchequer that the First Sea Lord had gone to unburden himself of his sense of wrongs early that morning. Lloyd George was on the point of leaving Downing Street for the week-end when the veteran admiral arrived.

"I want to speak to you," he said, and then, in the hearing of the messengers, blurted out, "I have resigned. I can stand it no longer. Our ships are being sunk, while we have a fleet in the Dardanelles which is bigger than the German Navy. Both our Army and Navy are being bled for the benefit of the Dardanelles."

Fisher took refuge in his official residence adjoining the Admiralty and declined to receive any member of the Government. McKenna was sent for, McKenna who had earned Fisher's respect and gratitude for backing him in the days of the Beresford feud. There were drawn blinds in the Admiral's house, but from behind one of them McKenna caught sight of Fisher peering out at him.[1] He insisted on being let in.

There was a painful interview. McKenna used every conceivable argument to induce the First Sea Lord to change his course. Fisher was obdurate. He had struck his colors and he was not going to hoist them again. He did not, however, take the train to Scotland but remained on the scene, though declining to deal with any of the routine work of First Sea Lord. If there was any advantage to be gained from the political crisis he had caused, he would be at hand to gain it.

The other Sea Lords added the weight of their counsel to the advice Fisher had received to go back to duty. They drew up a joint memorandum supporting him in his dissatisfaction at the method of directing the distribution of the Fleet and the conduct of the war "by which orders for controlling movements and supplies appear to be largely taken out of the hands of the First Sea Lord." But they urged that to prevent a national disaster the step of resignation must be averted. Differences of opinion, they advised, should be capable of adjustment by "mutual discussion and concession."

It was not advice that Fisher needed. It would have given him greater satisfaction had they backed up his resignation by tendering their own. He thought that in the moment of crisis they failed in loyalty to him as a colleague. He replied tersely:

"My dear friends, I am obliged by your memorandum. If you knew as much as I did I am sure you would not wish me to remain—but my motto is: 'Never explain' (and always has been)."

To his private secretary he remarked: "I grieve they [the Sea Lords] allowed themselves to be made use of to send me advice which I did not require and which was exceedingly bad advice."

Churchill, even when matters had reached this pass, did not despair of inducing his old friend to change his mind. He wrote persuasively—Fisher would not meet him face to face—pressing him to remain.

> In order to bring you back to the Admiralty I took my political life in my hands—as you well know. You then promised to stand by me and see me through. If you now go at this bad moment and therefore let loose on me the spite and malice of those who are your enemies even more than they are mine, it will be a melancholy ending to our six months of successful war and administration. The discussions that will arise will strike a cruel blow at the fortunes of the Army now struggling on the Gallipoli Peninsula and cannot fail to invest with an air of disaster a mighty enterprise which with patience can, and will, certainly be carried to success.
>
> Many of the anxieties of the winter are past. The harbours are protected, the great flow of new construction is arriving. We are far stronger at home than we have ever been, and the great reinforcement is now at hand.
>
> I hope you will come and see me to-morrow afternoon. I have a proposition to make to you, with the assent of the Prime Minister, which may remove some of the anxieties and difficulties which you feel about the measures necessary to support the Army at the Dardanelles.
>
> Though I stand at my post until relieved, it will be a very great grief to me to part from you; and our rupture will be profoundly injurious to every public interest.

Fisher would not respond to the appeal. He replied at length to Winston, the gist of his letter being contained in the two following paragraphs:

> You are bent on forcing the Dardanelles and nothing will turn you from it—Nothing. I know you so well. I could give you no better proof of my desire to stand by you than my having remained by you in this Dardanelles business up to the last moment against the strongest conviction of my life.
>
> You will remain and I shall go—it is better so. Your splendid stand on my behalf I can never forget when you took your political life in your hands, and I have really worked very hard for you in return—*my utmost;* but here is a question beyond all personal obligations. I assure you it is only painful to have further conversations. I have told the Prime Minister I will not remain. I have absolutely decided to stick to that decision. Nothing will turn me from it. You say with much feeling that *it will be a very great grief to you to part from me*—I am certain that you know in your heart no one has ever been more faithful to you than I have since I joined you last October. *I have worked my very hardest.*

On Sunday, Churchill wrote again in terms of extreme conciliation. The method of concession recommended by the Sea Lords could not have been pressed further. Admiral Bacon himself remarked of the proposals submitted in this letter: "He goes on to meet Lord Fisher's views in every way as regards the reinforcements for the Dardanelles, nothing could have been more completely in accord with Lord Fisher's views had it not come too late."

"Your letter is most persuasive," Fisher wrote in his reply, but he would not be turned from his purpose. "Please don't wish to see me. I could say nothing as I have determined not to. I know I am doing right."

There was nothing for Churchill to do but acquiesce. That Sunday he dined with the Prime Minister in the country, spending a "pleasant evening" despite the trouble of the time. He had, it appeared, Asquith's support and on Monday he went down to the House with a list in his pocket for the constitution of a new Board of Admiralty, with Sir Arthur Wilson to fill the vacant place of First Sea Lord. The appointments, however, were not destined to be announced. The Tories had intervened.

CHAPTER SIX

A TORY ULTIMATUM

MAY, 1915

MEMBERS OF THE GOVERNMENT were not the only persons who had been concerned that week-end in considering the problem of Fisher's resignation. While the Dardanelles dispute had been proceeding, various Opposition members in the House of Commons had received letters from Fisher, worded in the Admiral's customary explosive phrases, denouncing the operations. The Conservatives, to whom the name of Winston Churchill was anathema, instinctively concluded that the Admiral was right and the Minister wrong. They were disposed to agree when in conversation Fisher suggested that "Churchill should go and I ought to succeed as First Lord." [1]

Bonar Law, though he did not endorse Fisher's methods, was aware of his followers' views and indeed shared to the full the mistrust of Churchill. Only a month before the Conservative leader had attempted to convey to the First Lord some indication of his party's feelings but the intended caution was not diplomatically conveyed. Bonar Law and Churchill were temperamentally incapable of appreciating each other's merits. To Lord Beaverbrook (Bonar Law's intimate friend) Churchill complained that Bonar had lectured him on his conduct at the Admiralty, "rating me like an angry Prime Minister rebuking an unruly subordinate."

During that week-end of crisis Bonar Law received by post a curious, anonymous communication. In an envelope, without any accompanying letter, was a cutting from a London evening newspaper stating: "Lord Fisher was received in audience by the King and remained about half an hour." [2]

The envelope gave the clue to the mystery—it was addressed in the unmistakable handwriting of Lord Fisher. Bonar Law had no knowledge of the events that had taken place that Saturday but he placed the correct interpretation on this communication—that Fisher had resigned and wished the fact to be known to the Conservative leader.

Now why should it have been of any consequence to Fisher that Bonar Law—and thus the Conservative Party—should be informed of his resignation? If he was simply withdrawing from office and taking refuge in Scotland, as he had at first informed both Churchill and Asquith, it was of no concern to him what the Opposition leaders might think or do. The surreptitiously conveyed communication was an all-revealing indication of Fisher's intention—a bid for political support. The resignation, dramatically and violently executed, was not that of a man who was concerned over naval strategy and that alone. It was, as Lord Beaverbrook, with his knowledge of the circumstance, put it, "directed against the Government as a whole and the subordinate position he occupied under it. A new Government was to make him First Lord to right the Navy's wrongs."

Bonar Law was no party to any Fisher intrigue. But he was concerned over the wider issues raised by the Fisher-Churchill clash. He immediately consulted with Lord Lansdowne, the Tory leader in the Lords, on the steps to be taken. Other leaders of the party were informed. So, at the very time Winston was making arrangements for replacing Fisher, the Conservative leaders were resolving that his own tenure of the Admiralty must be terminated.

Following up his anonymous communication, Fisher sent Bonar Law a properly signed letter of attack on Churchill: "He is leading us to ruin, he is a bigger danger than the Germans." Bonar Law's alarm grew. He wrote to the Prime Minister and also arranged an interview with Lloyd George. On receiving confirmation from the Chancellor of the Exchequer that Fisher had resigned, Bonar remarked: "Then the situation is impossible." He explained that his followers would not tolerate the departure of Fisher if Churchill were to stay. Were such an announcement to be made in the House, then the Conservatives would feel it their duty to break the political truce and denounce the developments at the Admiralty.

Discussion between the two statesmen developed beyond the crisis at the Admiralty, the primary purpose of the interview. In a space it was not merely Churchill's future but the fate of the Liberal Ministry that was in the balance. The inclusion of Conservatives in the Government was raised, the word Coalition was spoken, and the entire political outlook had been transformed. Lloyd George became immediately converted to the idea of an all-party Government. "We must have a coalition," he said, "the alternative is impossible."

It was a matter beyond the competence of the Chancellor alone. The Prime Minister had become involved. Asquith at once acquiesced in the idea for a coalition, bowing to the inevitable, unpalatable as it was. Bonar Law left to convey the tidings to other Conservative leaders. They met at Lansdowne House early on the Monday and at the close of their deliberations Bonar Law sent the following letter to the Prime Minister:

LANSDOWNE HOUSE,
17th May, 1915.

DEAR MR. ASQUITH,

Lord Lansdowne and I have learnt with dismay that Lord Fisher has resigned, and we have come to the conclusion that we cannot allow the House to adjourn until this fact has been made known and discussed.

We think the time has come when we ought to have a clear statement from you as to the policy which the Government intends to pursue. In our opinion things cannot go on as they are, and some change in the constitution of the Government seems to us inevitable if it is to retain a sufficient measure of public confidence to conduct the war to a successful conclusion.

The situation in Italy makes it particularly undesirable to have anything in the nature of a controversial discussion in the House of Commons at present, and if you are prepared to take the necessary steps to secure the object which I have indicated, if Lord Fisher's resignation is in the meantime postponed, we shall be ready to keep silence now. Otherwise, I must to-day ask you whether Lord Fisher has resigned, and press for a day to discuss the situation arising out of his resignation.

Yours, etc.,

A. Bonar Law

Of these developments Churchill was in entire ignorance when he arrived at the House of Commons that Monday afternoon prepared to announce his new Board of Admiralty. He was told that no such announcement could be made, as the Liberal Ministry was on the point of dissolution. Hurrying to the Prime Minister's room, he was met with the announcement that a coalition was being set up and another man would have charge of the Admiralty.

"What," asked Asquith, "can we do for you?"

Lloyd George had a suggestion. "Send him to the Colonial Office; there is great work to be done there."

At this moment there came an urgent call for Churchill from the Admiralty.

The German High Seas Fleet had put to sea. Churchill, as he hurried back to the Admiralty War Room, would have been less than human had he not reflected on the changes in his fortunes the next few hours might bring. He was left in sole charge of the Admiralty. If the German Fleet should be engaged by the Navy and Jellicoe should win the victory of a second Trafalgar, then all the miserable tangle of the Dardanelles would be forgotten and the First Lord would be the hero of the hour, his position at the Admiralty unassailable.

Back in the War Room he received confirmation of the report. The entire German Fleet was coming out from its refuge—battle squadrons, scouts, and destroyers.

There was no First Sea Lord for the emergency. Churchill was adequate to the occasion. In a little while messages were on their way to units of the Fleet ordering them to prepare for sea at once and immediate action—to the Home Fleet, the 1st Battle Squadron, the Battle Cruiser Fleet, the 3rd Battle Squadron, and to the commanders of all the lesser units. The enemy would find all of Britain's naval power ready to meet him.

These orders given, the First Lord, in compliance with the request he received, had to place his resignation in the Prime Minister's hands. That done, he went to bed early, to await the morrow—a day that might bring such a victory at sea that the letter of resignation would be rendered out of date.

In his house next to the Admiralty, Fisher, too, was waiting for the morrow. He, also, had been told that the enemy squadrons had put out to sea. Churchill had sent a message requesting him, as he was still First Sea Lord (his resignation not having been accepted), to take his customary place in the War Room. It was a generous gesture, for in the event of victory Fisher would have had his share in the credit. He declined, however, to enter the Admiralty building. His biographer says he was convinced that the Germans had no intention of making a fight of it, but were merely seeking to learn if the British, by some means, had knowledge of the secret ciphers they were using to direct the operations of their ships. It may be so, but all the same, even on this occasion, he would not return to his duty.

The morrow came, but it did not bring the hoped-for victory. The German Fleet was out at sea at seven A.M., but by half past ten it was apparent that it was on its way back to port. The clash between the navies was not to take place. The British squadrons returned to the monotony of eternal watchfulness and Winston to the unpalatable realities of the political crisis.

For him the crisis was soon over. The Conservatives were unrelenting in their opposition to his retention at the Admiralty. There was precious little support for him from any source. Asquith seems to have made little effort to retain him; his fellow Liberals were more concerned over their own fate than his.

He induced his friend Balfour to plead his cause with the other Tory leaders, but the appeal was coldly received. Balfour, indeed, was criticized for having made it.

One advocate on the Conservative side made a strong intervention on Churchill's behalf. This was Max Aitken, later Lord Beaverbrook, proprietor of the *Daily Express*. For some years the two men had been on friendly terms and Beaverbrook had formed a high opinion of Churchill's merits and capabilities. In his account of the affair he wrote:

> My sympathies were entirely with Churchill, for I had heard his speeches and read some of Lord Fisher's letters, and I was more impressed by the lucidity of the speeches than by the volubility of the letters.

I pressed Bonar Law very strongly to retain Churchill at the Admiralty on account of the immense abilities he had already displayed there. Bonar Law replied that it was useless to argue; that the Tory Party had definitely made up its mind not to have him there—and that, in fact, any attempt to retain Churchill at the Admiralty would result in the complete and sudden collapse of the substructure of the new Coalition Government.

Here was an unexpected, if unsuccessful, championship for which Churchill, in his dark hour, was grateful. His gratitude, indeed, endured over the years.

Churchill himself wrote a letter of appeal to Bonar Law, but it brought him only the briefest of acknowledgments, and a reiteration that his departure from the Admiralty was inevitable. It had been a superfluous act of humiliation. The letter set forth in such cogent language the record of his administration at the Admiralty that I cannot forbear giving it.

ADMIRALTY,

WHITEHALL,

21.5.15.

MY DEAR BONAR LAW,

The rule to follow is what is best calculated to beat the enemy and not what is most likely to please the newspapers. The question of the Dardanelles operations and my differences with Fisher ought to be settled by people who know the facts and not by those who cannot know them. Now you and your friends, except Mr. Balfour, do not know the facts. On our side *only* the Prime Minister knows them. The policy and conduct of the Dardanelles operations should be reviewed by the new Cabinet. Every fact should be laid before them. They should decide and on their decision the composition of the Board of Admiralty should depend.

It is not in justice to myself that I am asking for this; but primarily because of the great operation which is in progress, and for which I bear a tremendous responsibility. With Sir Arthur Wilson's professional aid I am sure I can discharge that responsibility fully. In view of his statement to the Prime Minister and to the naval Lords that he will serve as First Sea Lord under me, and under no one else, I feel entitled to say that no other personal combination will give so good a chance.

If this view of mine should prove to be true it affects the safety of an Army now battling its way forward under many difficulties, and the success of an operation of the utmost consequence for which more than 30,000 men have already shed their blood; and I suggest to you that it is your duty to refuse to judge so grave an issue until you know the facts.

My lips are sealed in public, but in a few days all the facts can be placed before you and your friends under official secrecy. I am sure those with whom I hope to work as colleagues and comrades in this great struggle will not allow a newspaper campaign—necessarily conducted in ignorance and not untinged with prejudice—to be the deciding factor in matters of such terrible import.

Personal interests and sympathies ought to be strictly subordinated. It does not matter whether a Minister receives exact and meticulous justice. But what is vital is that from the outset of this new effort we are to make together we should be fearless of outside influences and straight with each other. We are coming together not to work on public opinion but to wage war: and by waging successful war we shall dominate public opinion.

I would like you to bring this letter to the notice of those with whom I expect soon to act: and I wish to add the following:

I was sent to the Admiralty 4 years ago. I have always been supported by high professional advice; but partly through circumstances and partly no doubt through my own methods and inclinations, an exceptional burden has been borne by me. I had to procure the money, the men, the ships and ammunition; to recast with expert advice the war plans; to complete in every detail that could be foreseen the organisation of the Navy.

Supported by the Prime Minister, I had last year for 4 continuous months of Cabinet meetings to beat down the formidable attack of the Chancellor of the Exchequer backed by ¾ths of the Cabinet upon the necessary naval estimates. On the approach of war I had to act far in excess of my authority to make the vital arrangements for the safety of the country. I had to mobilise the Fleet without legal sanction and contrary to a Cabinet decision. I have had to face 9 months of war under conditions no man has known, and which were in the early months infinitely more anxious than those which confront us now.

Many Sea Lords have come and gone, but during all these 4 years (nearly) I have been according to my patent "solely responsible to Crown and Parliament" and have borne the blame for every failure: and now I present to you an absolutely secure naval position; a Fleet constantly and rapidly growing in strength, and abundantly supplied with munitions of every kind, an organisation working with perfect smoothness and efficiency, and the seas upon which no enemy's flag is flown.

Therefore I ask to be judged justly, deliberately and with knowledge. I do not ask for anything else.

Yours very sincerely,

WINSTON S. CHURCHILL

It was the crowning irony of Churchill's fall that the man who brought it about in no way profited from it. On hearing that his friends in the Conservative Party were to join the Ministry, Fisher thought that his hour of triumph was at hand. He actually issued tentative instructions for the operations he would order, drawing up a memorandum for his naval assistant, beginning, "Prospective —get all below cut and dried ready for instant orders being given." It was a clear indication of what he imagined his mutiny was to yield him—indication, too, of the personal reasons that had prompted the mutineer. The first and last measures on the list concerned the evacuation of the troops from Gallipoli and the ordering home of the naval vessels.

While he was thus preparing for taking over the Admiralty, unpleasant tidings reached him. Asquith, it appeared, was not after all going to make him First Lord, was indeed proposing to appoint Balfour to succeed, and Balfour next to Churchill was to be reckoned chief advocate of the Dardanelles policy. Fisher's chagrin may be imagined. Was he, after all, to be deprived of the position that was his due? Was he still to be inferior in status to Kitchener? He took up his pen and launched an ultimatum to the Prime Minister, demanding to be placed in complete control of the war at sea. He demanded, too, the exclusion of Churchill and Balfour from the Cabinet. Even Sir Arthur Wilson was on the exclusion list—he had been ready to take over as First Sea Lord and for that must be dismissed from the Admiralty. Only a mind distraught by jealousy could have conceived such a letter as suitable for dispatch to a Prime Minister. The actual terms, in the brusqueness of their arrogance, are:

If the following six conditions are agreed to, I can guarantee the successful termination of the war, and the total abolition of the submarine menace.

I also wish to add that since Lord Ripon wished, in 1885, to make me a Lord of the Admiralty, but at my request made me Director of Naval Ordnance and Torpedoes instead, I have served under nine First Lords and seventeen years at the Admiralty, so I ought to know something about it.

(1) That Mr. Winston Churchill is not in the Cabinet to be always circumventing me. Nor will I serve under Mr. Balfour.

(2) That Sir A. K. Wilson leaves the Admiralty, and the Committee of Imperial Defence, and the War Council, as my time will be occupied in resisting the bombardment of Heligoland and other such wild projects. Also his policy is totally opposed to mine, and he accepted the position of First Sea Lord in succession to me, thereby adopting a policy diametrically opposed to my views.

(3) That there shall be an entire new Board of Admiralty as regards the Sea Lords and the Financial Secretary (who is utterly useless). *New measures demand New Men.*

(4) That I should have complete professional charge of the war at sea, together with the sole disposition of the Fleet and the appointment of all officers of all ranks whatsoever.

(5) That the First Lord of the Admiralty should be absolutely restricted to Policy and Parliamentary Procedure, and should occupy the same position towards me as Mr. Tennant, M.P., does to Lord Kitchener *(and very well he does it).*

(6) That I should have the sole absolute authority for all new construction and all dockyard work of whatever sort whatsoever, and complete control over the whole of the Civil Establishments of the Navy

[Initialed] F.

19.5.15.

PS. The 60 per cent of my time and energy which I have exhausted on nine First Lords *in the past* I wish *in the future* to devote to the successful prosecution of the war. That is the sole reason for these six conditions. These six conditions must be published verbatim, so that the Fleet may know my position.

It seems scarcely necessary to add that Lord Fisher did not remain at the Admiralty. The Prime Minister's reply was of unsurpassable brevity.

DEAR LORD FISHER,

I am commanded by the King to accept your tendered resignation of the office of First Sea Lord of the Admiralty.

Yours faithfully,

H. H. ASQUITH

The Churchill-Fisher clash had as its main consequence the installation in office of the first of the Coalition Governments. It also deprived the country of the full benefit of the services of these two outstanding men of ability in the arts of war. To whom is to be ascribed the blame? It is easy enough to be the partisan and declare that Fisher was temperamental or that Winston was meddlesome. The fault seems to lie further back than that. Arthur Balfour, who was not taken in by the partisan appearances of things, gave his judgment on the affair a few years later—and Balfour was in a position to know the facts from both sides. Writing [3] in September 1917 to his kinsman Robert Cecil (later Viscount Cecil of Chelwood) he delivered himself of the following pronouncement:

> You mention the case of the Dardanelles and draw from it the moral—a very good moral in its way—that civilians ought not to ask soldiers and sailors to carry out operations in which they disbelieve. But there is another moral to be drawn. In the Dardanelles affair the principal actors at home were a soldier [Kitchener] without strategical genius who controlled the military machine; a sailor [Fisher] equally without strategical genius who ought to have controlled but didn't the naval machine, and a brilliant amateur [Churchill] who attempted but failed to dominate both. If ever there were two men between whom hearty co-operation was impossible it was Kitchener and Winston.
>
> There was the opportunity for the Prime Minister to do what a Prime Minister alone can do, which is to compel subordinate departments to work together. Asquith did nothing. He never seriously attempted to co-ordinate in one homogeneous whole the effort of soldiers, sailors and diplomatists. The result was disaster.

CHAPTER SEVEN

GALLIPOLI—AND RESIGNATION

JUNE–NOVEMBER, 1913

IN WINSTON CHURCHILL's hour of adversity two personal tributes were paid him that were the more acceptable because they were unexpected.

The first was a declaration from Sir Arthur Wilson, declining to serve as First Sea Lord under any other First Lord but Churchill. Sir Arthur made his views known in a letter to the Prime Minister, and Churchill was profoundly moved on learning of this expert and impartial testimony to the work he had accomplished. It did not affect the result, but it provided balm for a lacerated mind.

The second act of solace was a visit of state paid to him by the Secretary for War. Kitchener and Churchill had not always been in agreement and the Field Marshal had often been the object of Churchill's criticism. But he came now to express his sympathy and good wishes for the future. The final word of leave-taking was a tribute that Churchill was never to forget—"Well, there is one thing at any rate they cannot take from you—the Fleet was ready."

Lord Riddell, calling at the Admiralty, found a worn-out and harassed Winston, dejected and disconsolate. "I am," he said, "the victim of a political intrigue. I am finished."

"Not finished at forty," objected Riddell, "with your remarkable powers."

"Yes," he said, "finished in respect of all I care for—the waging of the war, the defeat of the Germans."

Churchill went on to talk of his future. "I have had a high position offered to me," he confided, "a position which has been occupied by many distinguished men. But that all goes for nothing. This"—with a wave of the arm to indicate his room, with the charts on the walls, so plainly betokening the war—"this is what I live for."

To his visitor he gave a copy of the statement he had prepared defending his administration. He admitted with regret that the foreign situation did not permit him to make use of this apologia to silence his traducers.

They talked of the conduct of the war in general. Riddell sought Churchill's opinion of Asquith. "Do you think," he asked, "the Prime Minister has been weak?"

To this Churchill replied: "Terribly weak—supinely weak. His weakness will be the death of him."

It was a hard judgment but events were to prove its justness. Asquith was weak in not making a stouter defense of his First Lord. By sacrificing him to the Tory lions he lost, in the hour of his own need, the support of a loyal colleague and friend, whose aid might have averted his own fall.

At that very time Asquith was providing another illustration of his weakness, sacrificing yet an older friend, Haldane, the Lord Chancellor. Haldane was hated by the Tories only a whit less intensely than Churchill. He was called pro-German because of his sympathy with the German philosophers and his remark, "My spiritual home is Germany." With Edward Grey he was Asquith's oldest political associate. Now, under Conservative pressure, Asquith let him go—without a word of regret, an interview or a letter. It was, I suppose, a sign of grace that he could not face a meeting with the friend he was deserting.

It is not without reason that the cynic hath said there is no honor in politics and at the top there are no friendships.

Churchill himself, though reduced in rank, survived in office. Lloyd George, more loyal than Asquith, put up a fight for his friend, tried to install him at the India Office, or to get him sent to India as Viceroy. But Lloyd George could not induce Asquith to stand up to the Tories, so that when Churchill next took his seat on the Treasury bench, he was holding the subordinate office of Chancellor of the Duchy of Lancaster. A post without special duties attaching to it, it sets the holder free to concentrate on a special task. Churchill's task was Gallipoli.

At the Admiralty he was succeeded by A. J. Balfour, whose appointment he had recommended when he realized that his own departure was inevitable. This did not work out well, for Balfour's subtle mind did not find its best scope in the administration of the Navy. But Churchill preferred that it should be Balfour, as they had seen eye to eye on naval questions. Now they were to work together on Gallipoli.

In the War Council—renamed the Dardanelles Committee—the new members were Lansdowne, Curzon, and Bonar Law. For the benefit of the new men, the pros and cons of the best course at Gallipoli had to be restated—and reargued.

I must now briefly indicate the course events had taken. It must be borne in mind that the Gallipoli offensive was launched before the political crises chronicled in the last chapters, and it is for the purposes of clarity that I have refrained from confusing the issues of the Dardanelles and the Churchill-Fisher dispute with the history of the Gallipoli operations, although the earlier stages of Gallipoli were contemporaneous with the events already narrated.

The Navy's operations at the Dardanelles were Churchill's special responsibility. The Army's attack at Gallipoli was not as much his concern as Kitchener's. Churchill gave it the powerful aid of his advocacy. His belief was intense and unwavering in the ability to achieve success and in the vast benefits which success would produce.

On one important issue Churchill was critical of the Secretary for War; that was the manner in which Kitchener had produced troops after his initial, uncompromising refusal to do so. First he had said no men at all, then some men, and later more men. The decision to let the Navy, singlehanded, attempt to force the Dardanelles was taken only because, as Kitchener stated, no troops could be found. Churchill, Fisher, and all the experts were agreed that joint naval and military operations offered a greater chance of success. To permit the Navy to have undertaken operations alone in the first place and thus give the enemy a warning to get his defenses in order, was unsurpassable folly if, eventually, troops were going to be employed.

Churchill after the event could only make his unavailing protest and tell the War Council that had he known an army of 80,-000 to 100,000 men would be ultimately available for the attack, then the assault by the Navy singlehanded would never have been ordered.

Kitchener's declaration against the dispatch of troops was made in January in the light of the situation on the Western Front, where a German onslaught was then believed to be imminent. By mid-February anxiety at GHQ in France had been somewhat relieved and the 29th Division became free for employment in the Near East. Salonika, rather than Gallipoli, was the contemplated sphere of action, Salonika being favored by Lloyd George.

On February 16 the War Council decided to send the 29th Division to Lemnos to be ready for use as occasion might require. There was no definite determination to use it against the Turks—but it was from this decision to send the division across the Mediterranean that the enterprise against the Gallipoli peninsula sprang.

Transports were collected for the conveyance of the division to the East, but at the last moment Kitchener changed his mind and countermanded the orders. The news from GHQ in France was not so good. The division could not go.

Again the French barometer rose. The division might after all sail. But by then the transports had been dispersed. There was further delay until they had been reassembled.

These decisions and counterdecisions by the Secretary for War occasioned anxious discussions by the War Council in February. It was during the course of them that Kitchener delivered himself of the statement that if the Fleet, unaided, could not get through the Straits, then the Army ought to see the business through. British prestige would be at stake, the effect of a defeat serious. With this view Grey concurred; failure at the Dardanelles would be equivalent in its effect on opinion of neutral states to a great defeat on land.

Though holding this opinion, Kitchener neglected to take the essential first steps of preparation for immediate action should action be decided on. One obvious preliminary was the drawing up of a plan of operations and of landing. No such plan had been worked out at the War Office. Even so elementary precaution as the securing of maps was neglected.

On March 12 General Sir Ian Hamilton was appointed to command the Mediterranean expeditionary force. He left London to take up his Command with the utmost haste on March 13. The only information which he was able to obtain before leaving consisted of the official handbooks, the outline of a plan which had been worked out by the Greek General Staff for an attack on the Dardanelles, and a statement by Lord Kitchener that the Kilid Bahr plateau had been entrenched and would be sufficiently held by the Turks, and that south of Achi Baba the point of the peninsula would be so swept by the guns of the Fleet that no enemy position would be encountered in that quarter. This last statement was made on the authority of a map which afterward proved inaccurate, and of little use. No really good maps were available until some were taken from Turkish prisoners.

It was bad staff work—no staff work at all. And the general lack of direction was to be seen in the haphazard manner of the embarkation of troops and stores.

When the transports for the 29th Division arrived at Avonmouth, it was found that some of them had already been partially loaded at another port with fodder for horses, and it was accordingly impossible to stow on them all the wagons forming the first-line transport for the units on board. The wagons were therefore sent in three freighters, which arrived ten days later than the transports. In addition to this some of the ships were not well or conveniently loaded.

Nor were the units of the Royal Naval Division embarked complete. Personnel was placed in one ship, wagons in another, and horses in a third, with the result that no transport was self-contained. Stores could not be properly packed as they did not arrive until a few hours before the vessels sailed.

It was suggested that the transports which were bringing out the 29th Division could be restowed at Malta, but the accommodation in the harbor did not permit. The transports were, therefore, sent to Alexandria, and further delay was caused by the fact that they had to await the arrival of the slower ships which had essential things on board. A great deal of transport useless for the actual expedition was taken—a much larger number of horses than was necessary, and the customary mechanical transport. The Quartermaster General's department at the War Office pointed out that the latter would not be needed, but it was sent by the direct order of the Secretary for War. When the objectives of the expedition became more clearly defined, this was discontinued.

Had the transports been loaded efficiently, the men could have gone into action within a few days of arrival. At that date the Turks had not sent large reinforcements to the peninsula. By the time the ships had reloaded at Alexandria, the Turkish reinforcements were in position.

For these matters no responsibility attached to Churchill, who throughout this period (February, March and April) was concerned with the Navy's undertaking at the Dardanelles. He had, however, noted some of the omissions at the War Office and became increasingly anxious that some breakdown would occur.

He was determined "not to be involved in responsibility for actions far more momentous than any which the Admiralty was taking, but over which I had absolutely no control." He arranged therefore to have an interview with Kitchener in the presence of the Prime Minister.

This took place early in March and he put the question formally and in plain terms to Kitchener: Did he assume responsibility for any military operations that might arise and in particular for the adequacy of the forces to achieve success?

Kitchener replied that he did assume such responsibility.

On this assurance the Admiralty transferred the Royal Naval Division to his command.

When the naval attacks at the Dardanelles were halted, the operations against Gallipoli developed. Ian Hamilton launched his offensive on April 25 and the landing of the force of 29,000 men was successfully accomplished. Heavy casualties were, however, suffered, and by May 9 it was apparent that nothing could be achieved unless reinforcements were sent.

When the War Council met after the change of government, the first matter for decision was the future of the operations at Gallipoli. Should losses be cut by withdrawal, or should reinforcements be sent to Ian Hamilton and a new assault ordered? Kitchener pronounced for going on, in no uncertain language.

He would not, he said, remain in his office, responsible for the conduct of the war, if it were decided to abandon the Gallipoli venture.

It was accordingly decided to dispatch reinforcements—no fewer than three divisions, thus contemplating action on a far larger scale than had hitherto been envisaged. The Council also resolved to reinforce with various naval units the fleet under de Robeck. These were slightly stronger than had been proposed by Winston in his minute of May 14 which caused the flurry of Fisher's resignation.

Ian Hamilton had appealed for further aid on May 17; it was not until June 9 that the Cabinet agreed to send the men. The delay caused by the change in the ministry was of fateful consequence. The attack was renewed, but again Ian Hamilton's resources were inadequate. Reinforcements were always too small and too late. As Winston regretfully phrased it: "A week lost was about the same as a division. Three divisions could have occupied Gallipoli in February with little fighting; seven were insufficient in April, but nine might just have done it; eleven might have sufficed in July; fourteen were to prove insufficient in August."

Throughout summer and autumn, Churchill strove to impart a spirit of resolution to the War Council in its conduct of the Gallipoli enterprise. By autumn Gallipoli was almost past striving for. A new general was sent out to replace Ian Hamilton, and with a cursory examination of the situation he recommended evacuation. Kitchener exploded violently and went East himself to investigate. After some further delays—the War Council of 1915 could achieve nothing without delay—it was definitely decided to withdraw. Gallipoli ended with the melancholy success of a brilliantly executed evacuation.

For Churchill the time he spent in 1915 as Chancellor of the Duchy were months of frustration and growing despair. He had full knowledge of events and little power to influence them. He had to watch others halfheartedly pushing measures in which he wholeheartedly believed. He was forever mortified by the sight of great opportunities cast away.

From the strenuous labors of the Admiralty he passed suddenly to the comparative leisure of his sinecure office. He took to painting as a solace, and with brush and palette found some partial means of relieving the tedium of the days, of providing an outlet for his superabundant vitality. A few experiments with a child's box of colors in the country one Sunday gave him the idea. A full set of colors, easel and canvas soon followed.

With the evacuation of Gallipoli, the fall of the final curtain on the scene of his greatest hopes, he could no longer tolerate his subordinate role in the Cabinet. His thoughts turned to the field of battle. The trenches called. Demanding a command in the field he resigned from his office.

On November 15 he took his seat in the House of Commons on the bench behind the ministers. For the first time in ten years he rose to speak as a private member free from the responsibilities and restraints of office. He was free at last to answer his critics—at least partially free, for overriding national necessities prevented him from making a full disclosure, at the height of the war, of all the facts of his administration.

He was able, however, to present an impressive case. His speech of resignation was not well received at the time. That was, I think, because it was so complete an answer to his critics. Opinion had been aroused against him. He had been the victim of a sustained whispering campaign, and the whispering campaigns of Whitehall omit nothing that virulence and venom can inspire. The slanders had created such prejudice that the very effectiveness of the reply militated against acceptance. Men who suspected the worst could not be persuaded that on all the counts Churchill was in the right and his critics wrong. Reading the speech in the complete knowledge of the facts that later became available, it was possible to appreciate the completeness of his answer.

Dealing first with his mission to Antwerp, he described in detail what transpired at the midnight conference on October 2, 1914, between Kitchener, Grey, the Foreign Secretary, the First Sea Lord, Prince Louis of Battenberg, and himself, when the decision of the Belgian Government practically to abandon the defense of the city was discussed, and he agreed to go to Antwerp at once and see what he could do to prolong the defense. He crossed the Channel that night.

Next day, having consulted with the Belgian Government and with the British Staff officers who were in Antwerp watching the progress of operations, he made a report to London by telegram.

In reply he received instructions to do what he could to maintain the defense pending the arrival of a relieving force. This he did "without regard to consequences in any direction." History has endorsed the view he expressed in his resignation speech, when he said:

I believe that military history will hold that the consequences conduced extremely to the advantage of the Allies in the West. The great battle which began on the Aisne was spreading day by day more and more towards the sea, and everything was in flux. Sir John French's Army was coming into line, and beginning the operations of the battle of Armentières, which developed into the great battle of Ypres, and everything was in flux. The prolongation of the resistance of Antwerp, even by only two or three days, detained the German forces in the vicinity of the forts.

The sudden and audacious arrival of a fresh British Division, and a British Cavalry Division at Ghent and elsewhere, baffled the cautious German staff, and led them to apprehend that a large Army was arriving from the sea. At any rate, their advance proceeded in a halting manner, although opposed by weak forces; and I believe it will be demonstrated in history—and certainly it is the opinion of many highly competent military officers at the present time—that the whole of this enterprise and moving of those British troops, and the French troops who were in association with them, although it did not save Antwerp, had the effect of causing the great battle to be fought on the line of the Yser, instead of 20 or 30 miles further south. If that is so, the losses which were incurred by our Naval Division, not very heavy in life, will certainly have been well expended in the general interest.

Of course, it is true that these operations were begun too late. But that is not my fault. On 6 September, nearly a month before, I drew the attention of the Prime Minister, the Secretary for War, and the Secretary for Foreign Affairs to the dangerous situation which was developing at Antwerp, and to the grave consequences to the Admiralty interests which would be entailed in the loss of that fortress, I suggested that a Territorial Division should be sent to stimulate the defence, and made other proposals of which I will say that the difficulty of adopting them was certainly not less than the need to adopt them. But no action was taken upon that, and the situation of 2 October supervened, as I have described.

That is all I wish to say on this point, except in regard to the

Naval Brigade. The decision to send the Naval Brigade was actually taken over here by the Government, at my desire; but the decision was actually taken here. I had no authority from Antwerp, where I was, but the quality of these brigades was known only to me. If there is any blame for putting troops of that character into a business of this kind, that blame falls on me, and on me alone. Let us see whether there was any blame.

The situation was desperate, and the need bitter. I knew that Lord Kitchener would not send a Territorial Division. I knew it would be wrong to lock up a Regular Division in a mere fortress line. These were the only men who were available. They were the nearest. They were at Deal; they had a few hours' march into Dover, where the transports were lying. They were the only ones that could get there in time.

It is quite true that the Naval Division was only made up out of what the Navy could spare and leave behind after the mobilization took place. They had good non-commissioned officers, and a sprinkling of trained professional officers, and they had rifles, and plenty of ammunition. They had been together for a couple of months or six weeks. They had acquitted themselves elsewhere on terms which would not do any discredit to the finest troops of the Regular Army. They were undoubtedly unfit to manœuvre in the field, but that was not what they were for. They were going into trenches alongside of exhausted Belgian troops and townsfolk, who had received far less training than they had, and who were far less well equipped.

Under all the circumstances they were, I may mention, in exactly the same position as the Division of Fusiliers and Marines who were sent by the French at the same time, and fought in a most gallant manner in all these operations. Therefore, I say, there being nothing else in view, I was justified in proposing to the Government to use those troops, in spite of their want of training. Of course, all these matters can only be judged fairly in relation to the great emergency in which we stood. That is all I say about Antwerp.

Churchill then turned to the Dardanelles enterprise which he described as profoundly, maturely and elaborately considered and framed and supported by expert and technical minds. All at the Admiralty recognized that in a joint amphibious *coup de main* lay the best hope of a successful attack, but Kitchener's verdict that no arms were available invalidated such a plan. At the same time the need for action in the Eastern Mediterranean was constantly pressed on the War Council from many quarters.

As a result of all those representations and discussions [Winston continued], I telegraphed on 3 January to Admiral Carden, who was our admiral blockading the Dardanelles, and who had been there since the Turkish declaration of war, and I put to him this specific question—of course these are not the actual words; it is a paraphrase—"Do you consider the forcing of the Dardanelles by ships alone a practicable operation?" The admiral replied to the effect that the Dardanelles could not be rushed, but could be reduced by a regular and sustained naval bombardment. I put the same question simultaneously to Sir Henry Jackson, the present First Sea Lord of the Admiralty, and I received from him an almost similar answer. The coincidence of opinion between those two officers, both of the highest attainments and so differently circumstanced—one man on the spot, and the other the expert at the Admiralty, who was studying the Eastern theatre with the War Staff—the coincidence of opinion between those two made a profound impression on my mind.

Admiral Carden was asked to formulate his plans and state his requirements, which he did on January 11. The Admiralty was in a position to meet the very large requirements which he put forward and his plan was then examined by the Admiralty War Staff.

Sir Henry Jackson expressed his full concurrence in it, and advised in writing an attack on the outer forts being made as early as possible. Lord Fisher, of course, knew everything that was passing, and he never expressed any opinion against this specific operation, nor indeed against the operations at all at this stage. He was very much impressed with the proposal of the Admiralty War Staff to add the *Queen Elizabeth* to the bombarding Fleet. We had seen— it was fresh in everybody's mind—great fortresses, reputed the strongest in Europe, collapsing, fort by fort, under five or ten shells from 15-inch howitzers; and here was the *Queen Elizabeth* going through her gunnery at Gibraltar with eight 15-inch guns on the broadside.

Lord Fisher was also strongly in favour of action in Turkish waters, and wrote to me repeatedly on the subject, especially of a joint operation of the Fleet and Army at the Dardanelles. His scheme involved the co-operation of Powers which were neutral, and of an Army which was not available; but they all led up to the central points of the forcing of the Dardanelles with old ships of the "Majestic" and the "Canopus" class. Sir Arthur Wilson was in favour of attacking the outer forts, but felt that the future progress must depend on the amount of Turkish resistance. I state all these points, not in order to shield myself from responsibility, but to let the House know that the business of the Admiralty had been properly conducted.

After these preliminary discussions, I brought Admiral Carden's plan before the War Council on the 13th January. This meeting was attended by the principal Members of the Cabinet, by various high military officers, by the First Sea Lord, and by Sir Arthur Wilson. The War Council was immensely impressed with the political advantages of the plan if it could be carried out, and pressed the Admiralty to find a way to carry it out. No one spoke against the methods proposed. No expert adviser indicated any dissent.

On the 25th January Lord Fisher gave me a memorandum on naval policy. This memorandum did not question the feasibility of the particular operation which was being studied, but it deprecated reducing our margins in Home waters, or using fighting ships for bombarding purposes except in conjunction with military operations. It was a memorandum directed not only against the Dardanelles operation, but against others which were being very strongly pressed forward at the time. I sent the memorandum to the Prime Minister, with an analysis, which I drew up myself, of the naval margins available at the time. I think on that point I may claim that my view has been vindicated by events, because, not only did Lord Fisher himself at a later date consent to the naval operation, but the new Board of Admiralty sent to the Eastern Mediterranean all the ships which were then under consideration and a great many more; and, so far from any misadventure occurring in Home waters, it is well known that our position has become all the time increasingly safe.

On the 19th February the attack on the outer forts began. The first phase of the operations was successful beyond all our hopes. The outer forts were destroyed; the Fleet were able to enter the Straits, and attack the forts at the Narrows. Up to the time that this happened, we had always kept in view the possibility that if this operation, which necessarily depended for its success upon a number of incalculable factors, did not develop as we hoped, and if the obstacles were found to be much greater than had been foreseen, we could convert it into a demonstration, and turn our attention to some other part of the Mediterranean theatre. We had kept in view, and had prepared, an amphibious operation which would serve as an alternative in case we wished to withdraw, so as to safeguard our prestige. But the success which we had achieved at the outer forts produced an electrical effect throughout the Balkans. Its repercussion was evident from the first moment in Italy. We had touched the great strategic nerve centre of the world war of 1915, of this year's campaign.

Within a fortnight the Turks were forced to move back to Adrianople, and to develop their defences against Bulgaria. A panic was created in Constantinople. Everyone supposed that the enterprise was going to succeed. Day by day I held Staff meetings at the Admiralty, at which I received the appreciation of the greatest authorities, who were unanimous that the movement was progressing in the most favourable manner—more favourable even than we had anticipated, though we quite recognized that the greatest difficulties were yet to come. It was not now desired by anyone to go back, or to ride off on any alternative operation. The eyes of the whole world were riveted on the Dardanelles. Every interest, military, naval, political, and economic, urged the prosecution of the enterprise.

Churchill's speech, having thus put on record in the House the success of the initial operations, now took on a different note:

Across the prospect of the operations a shadow began to pass at the end of the first week in March. The difficulties of sweeping up the minefields increased, and although great success was obtained by the guns of the ships in silencing the forts, they were not able at that stage to inflict decisive permanent damage. The mobile armament of the enemy began to develop, and to become increasingly annoying. It was, therefore, decided that the gradual advance must be replaced by more vigorous measures. Admiral Carden was invited to press hard for a decision, and not to be deterred by the inevitable loss.

The Admiralty telegrams gave to the officer on the spot, and were intended to give to him, the feeling that whatever he felt inclined to do in the direction of vigorous measures he could do with the certainty of being supported. These Admiralty telegrams were the result of close consultation between the First Sea Lord and myself, and, like every other order of importance which has emanated from the Admiralty during my tenure in peace or war, bear the written authority of the First Sea Lord. I wish to make that point quite clear. I may extend it, and say there is no important act of policy, no scheme of fleet distribution, of movements of ships, or of plans of war which have been acted on during my tenure at the Admiralty in which the First Sea Lord has not concurred in writing.

The Admiral on the spot, Admiral Carden, expressed himself in entire agreement with the spirit of the Admiralty telegrams, and announced his intention to press forward in his attack on lines which had been agreed upon, and with which he said he was in exact accord. The date of the attack was fixed for 17 March, weather permitting.

On the 16th Admiral Carden was stricken down with illness, and was invalided by medical authority. On the advice of the First Sea Lord, who fully concurred, I appointed Admiral de Robeck, the second in command, who had been very active in the operations, to succeed him. I thought it indispensable, on the eve of this difficult attack, to find out whether the new Admiral shared the opinions of his predecessor. Admiral de Robeck replied that he was in full agreement with the Admiralty telegrams, which expressed his views entirely. He would attack, he said, on the 18th.

The House is fully acquainted with what followed. I should like to point out that the total British casualties in this formidable adventure scarcely exceeded 100. The French, it is true, had the misfortune to be unable to save the crew of the *Bouvet*, who perished. We lost two old vessels, of a class of which we had about thirty, and which, if they had not been employed at the Dardanelles, would have been rusting uselessly in our southern ports. Therefore I do not think in making this attack—on which so much depended, and the results of which, if successful, would have been so far-reaching—we risked or lost any vital stake.

Meanwhile, time was passing. The Army, which earlier in the year we had been told would not be available, was gradually assembling, and Sir Ian Hamilton had arrived with the leading Divisions of his Force. The Admiral, on coming out of the attack on the 18th, determined to renew it at the first opportunity, and telegraphed accordingly. After, however, consultation with the General, it was decided to substitute, for the purely naval operation, a joint naval and military attack. I regretted this at the time, and I endeavoured to persuade the First Sea Lord to send a telegram ordering a resumption of the naval attack. But we could not reach an agreement, and, in view of the consensus of opinion of the naval and military authorities on the spot, I submitted to the alternative, but I submitted with great anxiety.

Every day the danger of the German submarines arriving—a danger which we greatly exaggerated in our minds—seemed to become more imminent. Every day the possibility of a renewed German attack on Serbia—I think already it has almost succeeded —seemed to draw nearer. Every day I knew the Turks were digging. I knew they were drawing reinforcements from all parts of their Empire; and I can assure the House that the month which apparently had to be consumed between the cessation of the naval attack on 18 March and the commencement of the military attack on 20 April was one of the least pleasant I ever experienced. I have gone through this story in detail in order to show and to convince the House that the naval attack on the Dardanelles was a naval plan, made by naval authorities on the spot, approved by naval experts in the Admiralty, assented to by the First Sea Lord, and executed on the spot by Admirals who at every stage believed in the operations. I am bound—not only in justice to myself, but in justice to the Fleet, who require to know that the orders sent to them from the Admiralty are those which always carry the highest responsible professional authority—I am bound to make that clear. I will not have it said that this was a civilian plan, foisted by a political amateur upon reluctant officers and experts.

So much for the naval operations. For these Churchill willingly, and confidently, accepted responsibility. The military operations were another matter. For these he took no responsibility except that which was implied by his having remained a member of the Government. And he went on:

The naval attack finished on the evening of 18 March. The military attack did not begin until the 25th of April. If in that period we had known what we now know of the course of the military operations, I cannot conceive that anyone would have hesitated to face the loss of prestige in breaking off the attack on the Dardanelles.

I do not consider the naval operations, begun as they were, necessarily involved the military operations, begun as they were. That was a separate decision, which did not rest with me or the Admiralty either in principle or in method; but I wish to make it quite clear that I was very glad that the War Office authorities were willing to prosecute the enterprise by military means, and I certainly did my best to induce them to do so, and to support them in doing so.

There are, however, two observations which I wish to make of a general character upon the military operations. First, the essence of an attack upon the Gallipoli Peninsula was speed and vigour. We could reinforce from the sea more quickly than the Turks could reinforce by land, and we could, therefore, afford to renew our attacks until a decision was obtained. To go slow, on the other hand—to leave long intervals between the attacks, so as to enable the Turks to draw reinforcements from their whole Empire, and to refresh and replace their troops again and again—was a great danger.

Secondly, on the Gallipoli Peninsula, our Army stood all the summer within a few miles of a decisive victory. There was no other point on any of the war fronts, extending over hundreds of miles, where an equal advance would have produced an equal, or even a comparable, strategic result. It has been proved in this War that good troops, properly supported by artillery, can make a direct advance of two or three miles in the face of any defence. The advance, for instance, which took Neuve Chapelle, or Loos, or Souchez, if it had been made on the Gallipoli Peninsula would have settled the fate of the Turkish Army on the promontory, would probably have decided the whole operations, might have determined the attitude of the Balkans, might have cut Germany from the East, and might have saved Serbia.

Churchill concluded his speech with a word on the general situation, and I take the liberty of quoting this as a striking example of his continuity of thought and outlook through the years. This passage, spoken in the middle of November, 1915, was as applicable in World War II as it was then:

There is no reason to be discouraged about the progress of the War. We are passing through a bad time now, and it will probably be worse before it is better, but that it will be better, if we only endure and persevere, I have no doubt whatever. Sir, the old wars were decided by their episodes rather than by their tendencies. In this War the tendencies are far more important than the episodes. Without winning any sensational victories, we may win this War. We may win it even during a continuance of extremely disappointing and vexatious events.

It is not necessary for us to win the War to push the German lines back over all the territory they have absorbed, or to pierce them. While the German lines extend far beyond their frontiers, while their flag flies over conquered capitals and subjugated provinces, while all the appearances of military successes attend their arms, Germany may be defeated more fatally in the second or third year of the War than if the Allied Armies had entered Berlin in the first.

The record of history has endorsed the case that Winston Churchill placed before the House in his resignation speech on that November afternoon.

When he sat down Asquith rose and paid what appeared to be a graceful tribute to the "brilliant colleague" whose services he was losing. It looked so fair—the Asquithian phrase, the Asquithian manner, the perfect expression for the Parliamentary occasion. Examining its terms, however, in the light of our knowledge of affairs—knowledge that was hidden from the majority of the members he was addressing—Asquith's speech appears to be more noteworthy for its omissions, despite its tribute to "brilliant colleague" and "faithful friend." The speech consisted of only three hundred words and I ask you to consider them:

> There is no question before the House, and it would be entirely out of order for me to deal with any of the topics which have been so ably and eloquently dealt with in the very moving speech to which we have just listened from my right hon. Friend. The House is always accustomed, and properly accustomed, to give great latitude, and even to expect great latitude, to explanations from a Minister of the Crown who has resigned his office, and my right hon. Friend has taken advantage of that privilege in a manner which, I think, will be generally appreciated and admired. I only wish to say two things. I think my right hon. Friend has dealt with a very delicate situation not only with ability and eloquence, but also with loyalty and discretion. He has said one or two things which I tell him frankly I had rather he had not said, but, on the other hand, he has necessarily and naturally left unsaid some things which, when the complete estimate of all these transactions has to be taken, will have to be said. But that does not affect his personal position at all, and I desire to say to him and of him, having been associated with him now for ten years in close and daily intimacy, in positions of great responsibility and in situations varied and of extreme difficulty and delicacy, I have always found

him a wise counsellor, a brilliant colleague, and a faithful friend. I am certain, sir, he takes with him to the new duties which he is going to assume, having with great insistency abdicated those he has hitherto discharged, the universal good will, hopes, and confident expectations of this House and of all his colleagues.

Is that the speech that Asquith ought to have made on the occasion of the resignation of his "faithful friend"? Was it the speech of a man faithful to his friend? Supposing that the roles had been reversed. Would Churchill, had he played Asquith's part, have let Asquith go with a specious tribute to brilliance and loyalty? For every decision taken over the Dardanelles—and it applies also to Gallipoli—Asquith was responsible even as Churchill was responsible, in fact with the greater responsibility of the Prime Minister. He had Churchill's knowledge, he knew of Fisher's objections. His biographers explicitly stated: [1] "Asquith too was captured by the idea [of the Dardanelles and Gallipoli] and he never for a moment threw back any of his responsibility on to Mr. Churchill. Whenever the curtain is lifted he is seen urging both military and naval authorities to persevere and begging them to consider and consider again whether more effort could not be made and more troops spared."

Even that admission brings its challenge. "Did not throw back any of the responsibility"—by explicit word perhaps not, but not by implication? Where in that tribute to his "faithful friend" is there any admission of his own liability? Why did he not frankly and boldly say—'Churchill's responsibility is my responsibility: if he was wrong then I was wrong: but I claim that I was right and he was right too"?

You can imagine the speech that Churchill, the Prime Minister, would have made on such an occasion. Look at his speeches on the evacuations of Greece and of Crete. He did not throw a colleague to the lions and pay the mockery of a tribute to a "faithful friend."

It is fitting here to record what followed, for though the incident belongs to the sequence of events chronicled in the next chapter, it provides the best comment on the sincerity of that Asquithian tribute. I quote once again from Lord Beaverbrook's reminiscences.[2]

Churchill went to France and was offered by French, who was then nearly at his last gasp as Commander-in-Chief, an A.D.C.'s post at G.H.Q., or, in the alternative, a Brigade. Churchill chose the Brigade, but insisted on first obtaining some practical experience of trench warfare. For this purpose he served a month with the Grenadier Guards. After that Churchill was actually given a brigade in Bridges' Division. But the very day after this was apparently settled French happened to go home to London and told Asquith what he was doing. The Premier was apparently frightened and urged French, who was in no position to insist on having his way, to give Churchill no more than a Battalion.

This really was rough. A Premier may have to throw a colleague overboard sometimes to save the ship, but surely he should not jerk from under him the hen-coop on which the victim is trying to sustain himself on the stormy ocean.

Even an aging politician perplexed by the problems of the war that beset him, might have shown greater respect than that for the claims of faithful friendship.

CHAPTER EIGHT

MALBROUK

NOVEMBER, 1915–1916

FIFTEEN YEARS had passed since Winston Churchill had been a'soldiering. During those years he had devoted himself to the career of politics and the service of the State. Now for a time his political mantle was changed for an Army uniform. He gave himself to a soldier's life with the zest of his ardent nature. He got ready for the trenches inspired by a determination to gain new laurels in a military career now that politics seemed closed to him.

On the eve of his departure, his household was upside down as he completed his preparations. Downstairs his faithful secretary, Eddie (later Sir Edward) Marsh, was in tears; upstairs Lady Randolph was in despair at the thought of her brilliant son leaving for the trenches, their discomforts and their danger. Mrs. Churchill alone remained calm.

Arrived in France, Churchill went to the headquarters of Sir John French, then nearing the end of his service as Commander-in-Chief of the BEF. Commander in Chief and ex-First Lord met as old friends. "What would you like to do?" asked Sir John, to which Winston replied that he left the matter to French's decision. The command of a brigade was offered, at which Churchill suggested that he would like a month's experience in the line to qualify for the command. He chose the Guards as the best school and so it was agreed.

A few days later Major Churchill reported at headquarters of a Grenadier battalion.

It was a dull November afternoon. The weather cold. A drizzle was falling. The battalion was taking over in the line. Churchill and the Colonel in charge followed in the rear of the troops. For half an hour neither spoke. Only the distant sound of the guns broke the stillness of that somber afternoon. Then the Colonel observed: "I think I ought to tell you that we were not consulted at all on the matter of your coming to join us." It was a chilling welcome.

For some days the weather remained cold and so did the Colonel. Churchill was amused at the pains that were taken to impress him that his previous eminence counted for nothing with the Grenadiers. He was in no way disconcerted and when the battalion went out of the line for a rest period, there was a distinct thawing of the atmosphere. A little later and he was able to report that personal prejudice had been overcome and he was accepted as a regular officer. When the second in command went on leave, the Colonel invited him to take over the duties. Churchill was delighted. It was one of the greatest honors ever done him. At the end of his period of instruction, he secured an impressive report from his Colonel testifying that he had gained exceptional knowledge of trench warfare in all its forms and was fully competent for a command.

So Churchill went back to French's GHQ to claim the promised brigade, only to be disappointed because of the ban imposed by Asquith, as recorded in the previous chapter. It was at this time that French was recalled from Flanders and Sir Douglas Haig was made Commander in Chief. Churchill was not on the same terms of friendship with Haig and as a brigade was no longer offered to him, he had, perforce, to accept a battalion. Never was he so disappointed and hurt. His actual command had been nominated and he had spent his spare time evolving his plans, devising in his fertile brain new methods for encompassing the downfall of the enemy. His mortification was extreme, but it was soon forgotten when he took over his battalion—the 6th Royal Scots Fusiliers.

It was not a crack battalion, but Churchill, now promoted to lieutenant colonel, was as proud as if he had succeeded to the command of the Old Guard.

With characteristic thoroughness and efficiency he announced his intention of making the unit "the smartest in the army," and here his experience in previous campaigns stood him in good stead. He was at pains to establish close personal relations with both officers and men, and his concern for cookhouse and sanitary squad efficiency impressed them as much as his demand for a high standard of rifle drill and musketry.

From the moment that the battalion took over trenches at Ploegsteert, near Hazebrouck, his popularity among the men steadily increased. He was continually among them both day and night, frequently stopping on rounds of inspection to share the vigil of the sentry or to discuss the situation—and a whole host of other things besides—with the platoon sergeant. So he gained the fullest confidence of the rank and file, who keenly appreciated the concern he displayed for their welfare.

Craving for action he sought to relieve the tedium of life in the trenches by private wars on the Germans opposite, usually at night. He would order his men to put up bursts of rifle and machine-gun fire until the enemy replied. Then he would telephone to the artillery demanding support, and more than once the nocturnal hate of the 6th Royal Scots Fusiliers led to a general flare-up in the sector.

Adjacent units who preferred quiet nights did not hold Colonel Churchill and his battalion in high favor. There is no doubt that he was one of the comparatively few who enjoyed active hostilities. His attitude toward the serious business of war in the trenches found expression in the exclamation, "This is great, isn't it?" with which on one occasion he sought to dispel the nervousness of some young recruits during one of his private strafes.

While his concern was marked for the safety of his men his own disregard of danger was often embarrassing to those close to him. He was no stranger to "Plugstreet's" daily peril from enemy shells.

One day, working on a confidential memorandum on the employment of the tank, he was seated before the window at his "rest" headquarters, a convent building only a thousand yards from the enemy, when a bombardment began. Shells fell closer and closer. After a 4.2 had burst less than fifty yards away he decided that greater protection was needed than a glass window could afford. He left his office at a pace he termed "dignified yet decided." The protection of the cellars he despised and he put a couple of walls between himself and the enemy gunners by entering the battalion office in the adjoining building.

After an hour or so the blitz died away and he left his refuge for his headquarters. He found that the room in which he had been working was wrecked and shattered. A 30-lb. shell had struck the convent and after smashing through the office had crashed through the brickwork of the cellar and fallen, unexploded, on the floor. Providence had watched over Colonel Churchill.

While in the trenches he maintained his political contacts. Many distinguished visitors made their way to "Plugstreet," among them his old friend F.E. Smith, then holding the post of Attorney-General.

It was while visiting Colonel Churchill that F.E. suffered the indignity of arrest for being at large in France without a permit. The Attorney General's discomfiture was received with delight by his friends, and the incident lost nothing in retelling. It seems fitting to give the correct facts of the affair as stated by Sir Nevil Macready, who was himself concerned as Adjutant General. Sir Nevil wrote: [1]

> Late in January, 1916, some Cabinet Ministers attended a conference in Paris, and applications came through for passes for certain of them to visit St. Omer from Boulogne. On the morning of the 30th January information was received that Sir F. E. Smith, intended to come through to visit Lieut.-Col. Winston Churchill, then in the trenches near Ploegsteert Wood. No pass had been applied for by the gentleman, and therefore the Provost-Marshal automatically warned all road posts to look out. Whether the information reached the Provost-Marshal too late, or whether one of the posts neglected his duty is not known, but it was discovered that Sir F. E. Smith, who was dressed in uniform, obtained a car without authority from the Mechanical Transport Depot at St. Omer, and went on. When this was known late in the afternoon word was sent by telephone to the 2nd Army to arrange for his return to G.H.Q.
>
> At 10 p.m. Sir Frederick was discovered in Lieut.-Col. Church-

ill's dug-out, and was conducted to G.H.Q. by the Assistant Provost-Marshal of the 2nd Corps, not arriving, however, until 4 a.m., owing to an unfortunate breakdown of the car. An officer of the Provost branch at G.H.Q. who had arranged accommodation for Sir Frederick at the local inn was waiting for his arrival, and at the inn asked for his assurance that he would not disturb the Commander-in-Chief, or the Cabinet Ministers then in St. Omer, until he had seen the Adjutant-General in the morning. There was some little difficulty over this, which, however, was overcome, and at 9 a.m. the next morning I saw Sir Frederick. He was annoyed, perhaps naturally, that he had been technically 'arrested,' a step that was not intended, the original order from G.H.Q. being that he should be escorted back to G.H.Q.

It was, I think, the fear of ridicule more than anything else that disturbed the equilibrium of the Attorney-General, but, as I pointed out to him, the Commander-in-Chief's order in regard to passes had evidently not been unwittingly evaded, because the other members of his party had arranged for the necessary permits, and further, in view of the fact that he himself had been on the Staff of the Indian Corps earlier in the war, it was a matter of greater surprise that he should have placed himself in such a position. In addition, I explained that had an application been made for him to visit Lieut.-Col. Winston Churchill, I should have been glad to arrange it with the 2nd Army. . . .

Churchill was indignant over the treatment F.E. had received. He got in touch with politicians at the front and sent the following letter to Bonar Law:

PLOEGSTEERT,

January, 1916.

MY DEAR BONAR,

The arrest of F. E. in the present circumstances seems to me to be a very serious event. I received him here in virtue of a telegram from the A.D.C. to the C. in C. transmitted to me through the H.Q. of the LXth Division in which I am serving. Of this I enclose a copy. The act of placing the Cabinet Minister charged with the ultimate appeal in all Court Martial cases in arrest and removing him in conditions of indignity is one which cannot and will not end here in France. It will become public knowledge and will draw with it many other things. I am of course resolved to take any steps which the law allows. And I rely upon you to give the subject your most earnest and immediate attention as his colleague and friend. You should show this to Lloyd George.

Yours very sincerely,

WINSTON S. C.

Bonar Law lost no time in interviewing Haig and so prevented His Majesty's Attorney from the further indignity of being sent under escort to Boulogne and deported. Haig sent his private secretary with an invitation to lunch at Headquarters where the incident was brought to a close in a manner befitting the occasion.

Churchill's months of service in the trenches form the least-known period, though not the least eventful, of his career. Happily, they did not pass unrecorded. I was fortunate enough to come across a small volume, *With Winston Churchill at the Front,* of which the authorship was concealed by the *nom de plume* of "Captain X." On inspection it proved to contain a diverting account of the Colonel's service and I am privileged to reproduce the high lights of it here with the consent of its author who, under a title less romantic than Captain X, instructed the youth of Glasgow in the mysteries of the law as Professor Dewar Gibb. Captain X wrote:

Winston arrived at noon at Battalion H.Q. and in the most businesslike way at once set about knowing his officers. He summoned them all to the orderly-room at 2.30 p.m.

First of all the Company Commanders were called in and were introduced formally by the retiring Colonel. Then the rest of the officers were presented. After each officer had come up and saluted and shaken hands, Winston relapsed into his chair and scrutinized him, silently and intently, from head to foot. It was not easy to know how to parry this unconventional attack on one's composure. It was necessary to stand at attention, of course, so that no relief could be sought in the diversion of a mere social and friendly observation. I found myself forced to stare hard back at him and trust to time to bring this, like all other trials, to an end. So I stared, but I admit the experience was distasteful to me.

That was orderly-room No. 1, which terminated after we had all been "vetted" in this novel fashion, but orderly-room No. 2, held the next day, was all bustle and business.

"War is declared, gentlemen," observed Winston to an audience thoroughly aroused to attention, "on the lice." With these words did the great scion of the house of Marlborough first address his Scottish captains assembled in council. And with these words was inaugurated such a discourse on *pulex Europaeus,* its origin, growth, and nature, its habitat and its importance as a factor in wars ancient and modern, as left one agape with wonder at the erudition and force of its author.

When Winston's masterly biography of the louse was completed, and in order that we might not abandon all hope, he called upon the Doctor, hitherto a silent but not unmoved listener, to suggest remedies and make proposals, and thereafter he created a committee of Company Commanders to concert measures for the utter extermination of all the lice in the battalion. I may here say that it was done, and done well, after three or four days spent in toil as unsavoury as any I have ever devoted myself to. I remember the Corps Commander passing the billet when we were busy with our hot irons, extruding the lice from trousers and shirts.

From day to day the C.O. introduced particular little innovations which he liked and by the end of ten days he had produced a manifest smartening up on every side. Ritchie indeed sarcastically observed that he had only come "to teach us to click our heels and polish our guns and to turn us into a first-class eye-wash battalion," but that was too sweeping a statement, and it is only just to admit that he improved us greatly. Meantime he improved *on* us. All the Company Commanders were invited to dine in the H.Q. mess and there learnt a little of the charm and courtesy of the man as distinct from the Colonel. No doubt he sought to win us, but for that he is only to be admired, and his capacity for coaxing and charming the best even out of the most boorish is a gift which I never ceased to wonder at. He materially altered the feeling of the officers towards him by this kindliness and by the first insight we thus gained into the wonderful genius of the man. And so he began a conquest which when he left us was complete—a complete conquest achieved in two or three short months and over men of a race not easily moved and won over.

The men meanwhile seemed to be delighted with their new Colonel. Obviously each man thought that he himself was the person whom Winston's coming was especially designed to honour. Many of them did not know even his name correctly: he was Lord Churchill, Viscount Churchill, Sir Winston Churchill, even the Duke of Churchill, but whatever his name was, his being there was a feather in their caps. For a week their letters told of nothing else.

On the second day of Winston's tenure of office he gave orders that all the companies should parade in a certain slushy meadow, when he intended personally to inspect the work of each company and meet the officers and men in their official capacity. I had command of our company that day and we were bidden to come forth first and display our prowess. I was given a free hand, so I chose company-drill, which I knew, and which I thought Winston as a cavalryman was as little likely to know as anything. And the company-drill went off to my own entire satisfaction. Then we paused, while the Colonel went along each platoon and spoke to the men. They loved that. They always do love a chance of spreading themselves to one of the "high heid yins" as they call them.

"What is your age?" asked the Colonel, of His Royal Beeriness No. 6 in the rear rank.

"41, sir," was the reply.

"41? An excellent age: it's my own."

He was very nice to them all, and as I have said they responded well, but I didn't like some of the buttons I saw and I had no eye for the humour of the situation; I felt there was more to come. There was. There was bayonet-drill to come.

"Mr. X., will you put your company through a few bayonet exercises?"

I parried that and summoned the Company-Sergeant-Major. He played up like a man and had begun to bellow orders at the men before the C.O. saw what had happened.

"No, no, I want *you* to do it," he then said to me. So I took up the tale. As I had never been interested in bayonet fighting and held decidedly unorthodox views on it, I can honestly say I felt most uncomfortable. I summoned up to my aid all the mystic phrases which I had heard in the past and which I imagined might convey something to my willing company, but all the time I felt sure that I should have been better understood by a company of British soldiers in front of Sevastopol in 1854 than here in Flanders in 1916.

"I want you to take a rifle and bayonet yourself and demonstrate, Mr. X., demonstrate."

Officious hands thrust the necessary implements into mine, and I began to indulge in a wild series of warlike gestures. I felt that it all bore no possible resemblance to bayonet exercises as "laid down," but I had to do something, and so I went on lunging and parrying and thrusting, all the while wondering if Winston would have me reduced to the ranks afterwards for such an exhibition of buffoonery. And matters were *not* helped out by the fact that the other companies and their officers were standing around, and at ease, to witness this amusing spectacle, and that I had already heard one hastily stifled cackle from Ramsey, whom I knew to be even more ignorant of the whole subject than I was.

I cannot say that after this I read with much enthusiasm in orders that on the following day the battalion would parade at 9.30 a.m., and that the Company Commanders would be mounted. At all times a C.O.'s parade is an utter abomination, and not one of us could contemplate with calm the prospect of seeing added to the horror of it the spectacle of the four Company Commanders on their horses. It may be imagined that this would only affect the four wretches principally concerned, but it is not so, for an uncontrolled and fiery infantry charger in a small field together with a great many men armed with rifles forms a source of danger, alarm and panic. Fortunately, our company beast, which I always thought resembled a large trench rat (and which was called "Eagle"), was pretty steady, so I made up my mind to bolt from the *mêlée* which I felt sure was inevitable.

The scene of operations was a field about 2½ acres in extent with trees scattered about in it at intervals the least convenient. Underfoot it was wet, it was nowhere level, and in short it was at all points in perfect contrast to what a parade ground ought to be.

The horses were in a remarkable state of calm, which I feared must presage a storm. Nothing and nobody else was in a state of calm. Some, ordinarily more or less stolid, were fussing about, fastening straps here, covering dirty buttons with other straps there, pushing and pulling, dressing up, dressing back and behaving generally in a panic-stricken and utterly unsoldierlike fashion.

Then Sinclair,* the Second-in-Command, arrived. The high spirit of his horse communicated itself to the horses of the Company Commanders, unspeakably increasing the misery of those officers. After he had called the battalion to attention he was followed quickly by the C.O., who was at once saluted with the remarkable announcement, "D Company absent, Sir," which might have daunted a lesser man on first assuming command of a battalion.

We stood, and waited and after mistaking the transport, a milk-cart and a gang of red-throated staff for the company, it at last marched on with the piper gaily playing "The Barren Rocks"

* Sir Archibald Sinclair, member of the Churchill Cabinet in World War II as His Majesty's Secretary for Air.

and Ramsey looking well-fed and happy. Nothing was said then, but Ramsey was later called on for explanations.

Then we presented arms. We presented arms quite a number of times, Winston returning the compliment by touching his hat to us. The ponies, too, did not let the feat of arms pass unnoticed. Foulkes's took him for a short stroll to a muck-pond. Mine fortunately did no more than lose its dressing. Harvey's and Ramsey's turned about and glowered at their companies.

Having done with handling arms, we were put in motion. Now Winston was a cavalryman and his commands might legitimately have been expected to lack all the precision of phrase that is expected of an infantry Colonel. They lacked that, it's true, but that was the least of it. We set off in column of fours and an early fence made it necessary to wheel, which emergency was met by the command:

"Head of the column three-quarters left wheel."

Unhappily the head of the column was at the disposal of poor Foulkes, already too much occupied in curbing the forwardness of his horse to be able to spare a moment for translating such a command into the language of "Infantry Training." Imploringly he turned round, and his horrid beast, encouraged by this, made a straight line for the Colonel in mid-field. Meantime the company was up against the fence and with the resource of men determined, as British soldiers are said always to do, to think for themselves, it started to "mark time in front."

At last Foulkes was borne back to them, and having gleaned the Colonel's wishes during his short escapade, he wheeled them to the left and relieved a tense situation. It is rumoured that during this impasse the Colonel turned to Sinclair and whispered, "Shouldn't they gallop, Archie?" This is probably untrue, as it came from MacDavid, still smarting under a rebuke by the C.O. for the unauthorized addition to his uniform of a yellow bandana handkerchief, three-quarters of which flaunted bravely from his left sleeve.

The horses only became unmanageable, when we began to march in column of companies, constantly turning about and wheeling and forming. Sometimes I was beside my company, sometimes in front, sometimes behind. Never, save by accident, was I where I should have been, and the other equestrian performers on the field were in no better case. The companies lurched forward, the subalterns swore, the horses rammed the companies from behind and before, the commands ground out unceasingly, as one or other fence of the wretched enclosure was encountered and the upshot of the whole matter was a *mêlée* of blasphemous humanity and outraged horseflesh. It was all rather astonishing to us, for we had come to have a real regard for Winston's sense of propriety and decorum and orderliness in matters of duty.

At last the time drew nigh for our return to the trenches, a prospect at no time exhilarating, but now one calculated to give rise to the greatest uneasiness. I myself recollected some remarks of Winston's when he said:

"We will go easy at first: a little digging and feeling our way, and then perhaps later on we may attempt a deed."

It was just such "deeds" that were becoming unpleasantly popular at this epoch.

On a cold raw day in January the Colonel and the Company Commanders with a few other important officers of the battalion moved out of the billeting area in a motor omnibus, bound for the neighbourhood of Armentières and Plugstreet.

Winston by this time had donned the French helmet which we were all to become so familiar with and was in great fettle.

"Here we are," he said, turning to me, "here we are, torn away from the Senate and the Forum to fight in the battle-fields of France."

"Yes," I replied. I often said merely "yes" on these occasions, as I felt that the time was quite inappropriate for me to enlarge on his observations.

The line we were to take over was being held by the 8th Border Regiment, and we were shown all the beauty spots by them in the most approved fashion. Winston was in his element. Very few of the people seemed to recognize him, but on the way down from the trenches my guide said to me:

"Excuse me, sir, but your commanding officer is very like Mr. Winston Churchill."

I agreed and said that the resemblance had often been remarked. It was the blue tin-hat which prevented people from recognizing him with certainty.

Winston certainly got some work out of his battalion. Early and late he was in the line. On an average he went round three times a day, which was no mean task in itself, as he had plenty of other work to do. At least one of these visits was after dark, usually about 1 a.m. In wet weather he would appear in a complete outfit of waterproof stuff, including trousers, or overalls, and with his French light-blue helmet he presented a remarkable and unusual

figure. He was always in the closest touch with every piece of
work that was going on, and, while at times his demands were a
little extravagant, his kindliness and the humour that never failed
to flash out made everybody only too keen to get on with the work,
whether the ideal he pointed out to them was an unatainable one
or not.

To see Winston giving a dissertation on the laying of sand-
bags, with practical illustrations, was to come inevitably to the
conclusion that his life-study had been purely of poliorketics and
the corresponding counter-measures. You felt sure from his grasp
of practice that he must have served apprentice to a bricklayer and
a master-mason, while his theoretical knowledge rendered you certain that Wren would have been proud to sit at his feet, or even
such a master of the subject as Uncle Toby Shandy.

And yet sometimes Winston was wrong about those sand-bags
and 2nd Lieut. Stickinthemud was right. In fact while professing a
great admiration for the Colonel's zeal and enthusiasm as regards
building of parapets and traverses and parados, I must confess that
he did not seem to be able to get into touch with the actual practical handling of these accursed sand-sacks. It was a case of the "last
infirmity of noble minds."

It was always a matter of especial interest to watch our Colonel
in his relationships with his superior officers, those men who while
a thousand times smaller in all essentials were yet by the accident
of the time in a position to issue orders to him. Such of us as expected to see sparks flying were disappointed. The Colonel's bearing was studiously respectful, but no General whom I ever saw
with him was ever rash enough to be very critical or very severe.
During his command of the battalion, we had to deal with two
Brigade Commanders. The former of these two shall remain name-
less. The battalion disliked him and into the Colonel's feelings I
was not permitted to see. What was to Winston an occasional
cause for stumbling, namely, the setting of too hard a task, was
General X's constant failing.

I remember a visit of his on one occasion to Battalion Headquarters at Lawrence Farm just after that stronghold had been
considerably knocked about by shelling and various protective
works destroyed. He sent for the Colonel, who arrived promptly
and greeted him in debonair fashion. The General at once opened
out about the defective condition of those same protective works.

"Look here, Churchill," he fussed, "this won't do, you know.
There's no protection at all here for men. You ought to get some-

thing done—build something to make it safe. Men cannot go on living here: look at that sentry there—it's dangerous, you know, it's positively dangerous."

The Colonel was pardonably nettled.

"Yes, sir," he replied, "but, you know, this is a very dangerous war."

And with that let us leave General X.

Going round the line on a beautiful morning about one or two o'clock the Colonel would see perhaps a man or men brought in badly wounded on patrol. This sight brought with it apparently a desire to get some of his own back. I remember well one evening in particular, when we had two men seriously wounded and one killed, Winston's coming into the dug-out in the front-line where my Company Commander was sitting, just returned from leave, and recounting his experiences, exciting and highly discreditable, to an enraptured audience. The blue helmet appeared round the door and we heard a voice say: "Come on, war is declared," and we were bidden all to turn out and superintend the rapid-fire of our half-waking platoons.

We found that Winston had arranged for almost all the guns of the Division to support our little alarum, and as soon as the rifle-fire began there was a perfect blaze of artillery behind us and the Hun very soon became alarmed and fired off rockets "of every colour in the summer solstice," as Ramsey put it. Unfortunately he did not confine himself to firing off rockets, but fired off a multitude of whizzbangs and other unpleasant projectiles as well. Just as the enemy field guns began, the Colonel came along to our trench and suggested a view over the parapet. As we stood up on the fire-step we felt the wind and swish of several whizzbangs flying past our heads, which, as it always did, horrified me. Then I heard Winston say in a dreamy, far-away voice: "Do you like War?"

The only thing to do was to pretend not to hear him. At that moment I profoundly hated war. But at that and every moment I believe Winston Churchill revelled in it. There was no such thing as fear in him.

These little intervals did good in very dull times, but they were not invariably popular. Especially were they unpopular with Gibb, the Adjutant. The position for him was an invidious one. He remained of course at Battalion Headquarters and it was his pleasant task to keep in touch with the Colonel and the artillery. It was all very well when we were getting support purely from our own covering battery, though even then the battery officers didn't like being asked to fire off their cannon in the middle of the night, merely to get the wind up. But the C.O. was a great friend of General Tudor, who commanded the Divisional artillery, and he did not hesitate therefore to call for more efficient support than could be rendered by a mere 18-pounder battery.

The purely administrative side of his command, what is known as "A" work by the Staff, and the countless and somewhat formal "G" reports, the Colonel left as a rule to the Adjutant. He used, however, to see the companies' reports each morning, usually laconic and unenlightening save when Ramsey broke the monotony by introducing—well, conversational epithets into his "wind" or "operations" reports, which had in consequence to be bowdlerized by the Adjutant, before submission to the C.O. Once, however, in the interests of literary form the Colonel did interfere and issue a manifesto directing that "in company reports a blind shell should be referred to as such and not as a 'dud'."

Not long before we left Plugstreet there was a dinner-party in the line such as cannot have had many parallels during the war. The guests included the Divisional General, the Brigadier-General on the General Staff of the Corps, two very distinguished flying-officers, and the Divisional General's A.D.C.

These people, in addition to the usual members of the Mess, made a pretty tight fit, but all went well and the mess-waiters managed to spill the minimum of soup on the General's lap, and the sulphurous parleyings in the outer darkness between the various functionaries interested were for once conducted in an undertone. But Winston was too good a host to give his guests merely a good dinner and leave it at that. There must be entertainment beyond the merely gastric. And so with his blandest manner he turned to the General and said:

"I'm sure you'd like to see my trenches, General."

"Yes," said the General.

"Very well: you'd like to come, too?" to another General.

"Oh yes, rather," said he, not to be outdone.

"We'll all go up then," said Winston, "it's a lovely night, though very quiet. We might go out in front."

The scene in front I did not witness, but I can imagine it. Winston in his element, pointing out the sights—the warm effect of the Very lights upon the unwonted red and gold—the polite "after you's" of the visitors—the hugging of mother earth and proximity to the cooling swamp—and over all, the savour wafted softly on the breeze from the age-old carcass of the loyal cow, killed in front of Burnt-out Farm.

The battalion was delighted with this performance. I think the invitation to go forth was made in all good faith by the Colonel, but it was a first-rate joke to the jaded infantry to see them all out there tearing breeches and thumbs on the wire; wallowing in mud and cursing over clothes that had never been grovelled in before.

I am firmly convinced that no more popular officer ever commanded troops. As a soldier he was hard-working, persevering and thorough. The expected fireworks never came off. He was out to work hard at tiresome but indispensable detail and to make his unit efficient in the very highest possible degree. I say nothing of his tactical and strategic ability—these were not tested in our time, but I cannot conceive that exceptionally creative and fertile brain failing in any sphere of human activity to which it was applied. And, moreover, he loved soldiering: it lay very near his heart and I think he could have been a very great soldier. How often have we heard him say by way of encouragement in difficult circumstances, "War is a game to be played with a smiling face." And never was precept more consistently practised than this.

CHAPTER NINE

BACK TO OFFICE

1916–1917

IN THE AUTUMN of 1916 Winston Churchill was back in the House of Commons, his last period of active service completed, his career as politician resumed. His return to Westminster was the result of military as well as political circumstances. First and foremost there was the disappearance of his command. Authority decided that the 6th Royal Scots Fusiliers, under strength, should be amalgamated with another battalion. Churchill, as the junior of the two C.O.'s concerned, would have to forfeit his command. He would have been able to secure another battalion without much delay, but his displacement coincided with the pressure of his judgment and his friends to return to the political scene.

It had been represented to him by several visitors to "Plugstreet" that a man of his brain and genius had no right to waste on a small command abilities that were needed at home. Tidings of disquiet about the lack of direction in the running of the war were brought to him. Despite the high value which he placed on his work in the trenches, with its risk and honor, Churchill was persuaded that he had not the right to remain. The war situation was grave and the feeling grew within him that he had the knowledge and the power to help to mend matters.

His inclination was fortified by appeals in letters he received from home. Edward Carson wrote to him—and Carson at that time was the Government's chief critic; the energies Sir Edward had devoted in the past to Ulster were now concentrated, under the impulse of the highest patriotism, on the task of prodding the Ministry into a state of greater efficiency and resolution. Sir Arthur Markham, also a member of the patriotic Opposition, added his appeal to Carson's. C. P. Scott, the eminent Liberal who edited the *Manchester Guardian,* was another who wrote to Churchill indicating the proper sphere for his activities.

So Malbrouk packed up his kit and returned from the wars, at which we can indulge in a sigh of heartfelt relief. A chance bullet from a German rifle might have changed the course of history when Churchill was in "Plugstreet."

Once during his period of service he had made a hurried journey to Westminster to take part in a debate. He rose to advise Arthur Balfour, his successor at the Admiralty, to make available adequate means to cope with a renewal of the German U-boat campaign against merchant shipping. During the speech he startled the House by urging the recall of Fisher. It was a suggestion prompted by the best of intentions, a gesture intended to let the world know that he harbored nothing but good-will for the veteran admiral. As political tactics it was a mistake. It made Fisher's return impossible and it did not improve Churchill's own position.

Some time elapsed before Churchill was restored to ministerial office. The old prejudices against him still existed, though among the Conservative leaders to whom office had brought knowledge of the facts of the Gallipoli situation there was a fairer appraisal of his case. Bonar Law, at the time of the resignation speech, had conceded that Winston had the defects of his qualities and that as his qualities were large the shadow they threw was fairly large also.

To this equivocal tribute Bonar Law added: "I entered the Cabinet with, to put it mildly, no prejudice in his favor. I have now been his colleague for five months. I say deliberately that in mental power and vital force he is one of the foremost men in the country." Bonar Law told a friend afterward that he thought too much blame had been attached to Churchill over Gallipoli and that the failure was really due to the inefficiency at the War Office.

When he resumed his Parliamentary work, Churchill set about the task of clearing his reputation. This could be done by the revelation of the facts. National interests in wartime provided the Government with the best of reasons against permitting this. Winston's reputation could be made good only by damaging others. He was entitled to take the view that the fact that the nation was at war was not a compelling reason why injustice should be done to individuals, particularly when he was one of them.

Churchill pressed for the publication of the papers, but Asquith would not agree. Churchill grew dejected. It was hard that he should have to remain under a stigma that was a bar to office. The war was going badly, he had the conviction that he could do as much as any man to put things right, but he was powerless, his boundless energy denied the scope of employment. "My life," he complained again, "is finished. I am banished from the scene of action."

Lloyd George wanted Churchill to take over at the Ministry of Munitions. He pressed the Prime Minister to make the appointment. Asquith would not hear of it. Gallipoli—one word to blast a man's fame.

Churchill did not disguise his feeling that Asquith had treated him badly. "He has not defended me as he should have done," he told Lord Riddell. "He shared all the responsibility for all that was done. But beyond a general statement that he accepted responsibility—a statement which was calculated to show how magnanimous he is—he never made any case in my favor. When the documents are published my position in the country will be very different. I have demanded publication and the Government have promised that the documents shall be published. But publication is delayed and I am beginning to doubt if the pledge will be kept."

Riddell asked him what he proposed to do.

"Earn my living and go on painting," he replied. "Painting has been a great solace. It helped me to tide over the horrible time after the Admiralty. Look at this."

Here Churchill exhibited with an artist's excusable pride one of his canvases.

"What I want," he went on, "is some position in which I can be of service—in which I can utilize my knowledge and experience. Asquith could readily have given me such a post. I might have taken over the Air. Had I done so twelve months ago you would not have had the scandals that have exercised the public mind."

Riddell was impressed by Churchill's accuracy, his methodicalness, and his knowledge of his subjects down to the last detail. Despite his mass of papers and documents he could produce any particular document and knew precisely what every one contained.

The Gallipoli papers never were published. Asquith finally evaded Churchill by appointing a commission to investigate. There were ten commissioners under the chairmanship of Lord Cromer and they were given a roving commission—to inquire "into the origin, inception, and conduct of operations of war in the Dardanelles and Gallipoli including the supply of drafts, reinforcements, ammunition, and equipment to the troops and Fleet, the provision for the sick and wounded and the responsibility of those departments of the Government whose duty it has been to minister to the wants of the Forces employed in the theatre of war."

This clearly was an investigation into much besides Winston Churchill's part in the operations. Not Churchill alone was on trial, but the Government of which he had been a member and in particular Asquith as head of that Government. The inquiry was a prolonged one. The subject matter was involved, the witnesses to be heard many. The commission held twenty sittings and published an interim report; held a further sixty-six sessions and produced a further report.

Before the labors of investigation were completed Lord Cromer was dead; two other commissioners had found a place in the Government; Lord Kitchener had passed from the scene (he was not available as a witness), losing his life in the sinking of the cruiser *Hampshire;* and Asquith had been succeeded by Lloyd George as Prime Minister.

Throughout the autumn of 1916, when Churchill was cooperating with the patriotic Opposition, the position of the Asquith Coalition was one of increasing difficulty. It was assailed from without and riven within by dissatisfaction and intrigue. It is difficult to pronounce which attacks were the more damaging— those of the outsiders who, without knowledge, denounced it because things were going wrong; or those of the insiders who spoke with knowledge of its shortcomings. Of the outsiders, the principal was Carson who threatened to split the Conservative Party and force Bonar Law to resign. Of the insiders the leading dissentient was Lloyd George, who sought to wrest the conduct of the war from the hands of a Prime Minister he had come to look upon as weak and irresolute.

In the events that led to the final clash between Asquith and Lloyd George in the month of December, Churchill took only a minor part. He associated himself with both forms of the attack on the Ministry. He supported Carson in his general criticisms of the Government and he also agreed with Lloyd George.

There was a meeting between Churchill and Bonar Law at Lord Beaverbrook's home in mid-November and through the eyes of their host we are privileged to see the clash that developed between the two men. Beaverbrook described it as follows: [1]

> The contrast between the temperamental attitude of the two men was remarkable. Churchill frequently showed at the outset of the discussion a really conciliatory and friendly attitude towards Bonar Law. In fact, he more than once behaved as if he had no rancour towards the older man. Bonar Law, on the other hand, was, from start to finish, rigid, harsh, and repelling to Churchill. His opponent might give an opening for better relations. Bonar Law kept his doors closed and his window blinds drawn.

> Then Churchill began to deliver an allocution denouncing the Government as though he were addressing not a single individual, but a public meeting—or at least a secret session of the House in war-time. He arraigned the Government on every kind of count as though he were marshalling all the various sections in the Commons to come out together and overthrow the Ministry.

> The only times Churchill ever bores his friends are when he talks to them as if they were a large audience. I saw the effect this style of address was having on Bonar Law, and I several times tried to break into the oration and bring the argument down to a conversational tone. In vain—Churchill swept on unheeding.

At last Bonar Law said, "Very well, if that's what the critics of the Government think of it—we will have a General Election." Churchill was absolutely staggered by this remark.

The meeting had no influence on the course events were to take within the month, events that removed Asquith from the control of affairs and installed Lloyd George in his stead as Prime Minister. Churchill had no part in the sorry drama of the passing of Asquith. Nor was he included in the new administration. Lloyd George wished to have the benefit of his cooperation, but the Tories would not admit him—"not at any price. Had I insisted the new Ministry would have been wrecked."

Churchill had to wait. The Dardanelles commissioners were still striving with their task. March (1917) had nearly arrived before the interim report was presented. Its conclusions may be summarized as:

Mr. Churchill appears to have advocated the attack by ships alone, before the War Council, on a certain amount of half-hearted and hesitating expert opinion.

We think that there was an obligation first on the First Lord, secondly on the Prime Minister and thirdly on the other members of the War Council to see that the Naval Advisers should have expressed their views to the Council, whether asked or not, if they considered that the project which the Council was about to adopt was impracticable from a naval point of view.

On the 20th February Lord Kitchener decided that the 29th Division, part of the troops which by the decision of February 16th were to have been sent to the East, should not be sent at that time, and Colonel Fitzgerald by his order instructed the Director of Naval Transports that the transport for that division and the rest of the Expeditionary Force would not be required. This was done without informing the First Lord, and the despatch of the troops was thus delayed for three weeks. This delay gravely compromised the probability of success of the original attack made by the land forces, and materially increased the difficulties encountered in the final attack some months later.

There was no meeting of the War Council between March 19th and May 14th. Meanwhile important land operations were undertaken. We think that before such operations were commenced the War Council should have carefully reconsidered the whole position. In our opinion the Prime Minister ought to have summoned a meeting of the War Council, should have pressed for a meeting. We think this was a serious omission.

We are unable to concur in the view set forth by Lord Fisher that it was his duty, if he differed from the Chief of his Department, to maintain silence at the Council or to resign. We think that the adoption of any such principle generally would impair the efficiency of the public service.

We are of opinion that Lord Kitchener did not sufficiently avail himself of the services of his General Staff, with the result that more work was undertaken by him than was possible for one man to do, and confusion and want of efficiency resulted.

We think that, although the main object was not attained, certain important political advantages, upon the nature of which we have already dwelt, were secured by the Dardanelles expedition. Whether those advantages were worth the loss of life and treasure involved is, and must always remain, a matter of opinion.

The disclosures in the report were not pleasant reading, but there was nothing to cause Churchill disquiet. Publication of the findings removed the stigma that had lain upon him. He had come out of it well, but the same could not be said of Asquith or Kitchener. Asquith, indeed, made efforts to prevent publication and wrote to Lloyd George urging that the report should not be issued without the evidence—which, as he knew, was not possible, containing as it did secret matter that could not be disclosed during the war. Lloyd George did not agree. He told his confidant, Riddell, that he suspected Mr. A., whom he had known for years, of playing a deep game and that "at the right moment he will endeavor to strike and regain his office." [2]

With the publication of the commissioners' report, Churchill made a good recovery in the House and clinched his position with a speech in May 1917, delivered at a secret session that was held principally as a result of his demands. His criticisms were based on a memorandum on the Somme battle which he had prepared and which F. E. Smith had circulated to the Cabinet. In this he accused General Headquarters in France of dissipating the strength and energies of the Army by using up division after division in a war of attrition.

"So long as an army possesses a strong offensive power," he said, "it rivets its adversary's attention. But when the kick is out of it, when the long-saved-up effort has been expended the enemy's anxiety is relieved and he recovers his freedom of movement. This is the danger into which we are now drifting."

The secret session provided him with an opportunity to develop this argument and to advocate concentration on the anti-U-boat campaign. He urged the maintenance of an active defense on the Western Front until the United States, by that time a fighting partner, had thrown her millions of men into the scale, to permit the conservation of French and British lives and the perfection of an organization for the decisive effort later.

The speech made a great impression on the House and it was plain that Churchill's return to office could not be long delayed. On July 16, 1917, he was appointed Minister of Munitions, despite lingering opposition among the backwoodsmen of the Conservative Party.

He justified his choice by a triumph of organization. When he took over, the department had a staff of 12,000 civil servants working in more than fifty groups or sub-departments. He reduced the number of groups to a dozen and to ensure complete liaison established an advisory committee with some of the best brains of the country, including ordnance and explosives experts and industrial chiefs. The groups were referred to by initials in the Admiralty fashion, thus G for guns and P for projectiles; and to the advisory committee Churchill gave the expressive title of "Clamping Committee."

The system worked with amazing efficiency, as he wrote: "Instead of struggling through the jungle on foot I rode comfortably on an elephant whose trunk could pick up a pin or uproot a tree with equal ease, and from whose back a wide view of the scene lay open."

That wide scene embraced the entire battlefields of France and Flanders to which he paid frequent visits as the guest of Sir Douglas Haig at GHQ. Thus he obtained first-hand knowledge of the requirements of the Army as they arose and saw to it that they were speedily supplied. He was with General Tudor, the commander of the 9th Division, when the Germans broke through in 1918 and was able to ensure that the urgent demand for replacements was met.

His activities in France were not confined to the work and requirements of the British Expeditionary Force. He accompanied Clemenceau, the French Premier, on a visit to the front, saw Foch and other French commanders and discussed with them plans of action. The French Government placed the Château of Verchoq at his disposal. On many occasions, after attending to work at the Ministry in the morning, he flew from Hendon to France, followed at close quarters the operations on the battlefronts and returned for an evening's duty at his Ministry.

From the time he became Minister of Munitions he saw every important engagement in France, often from a British warplane flying over the lines.

The range of his departmental activities was widely extended. From his reserve supplies he made good the Italian losses in munitions in the Caporetto disaster. He was entrusted with the task of equipping the whole of the American armies as they arrived in France. His initial contract was one of £100,000,000 to supply medium guns, the transaction being arranged on a "no profit" basis. The vast business was carried out with the utmost satisfaction to both sides despite the fact that Churchill and his opposite number in the United States, Bernard Baruch,* had never met.

When labor troubles threatened to affect the efficiency of his immense supply machine Winston adopted a strong line. Faced with a series of strikes he secured the backing of Lloyd George and threatened that the immunity of the strikers from military service would be withdrawn unless they returned to work, and he announced that the ringleaders would be prosecuted with the full rigor of the law. The strikes collapsed and the work of the department went on unhampered.

He was spectacularly engaged with his old colleagues from the Admiralty in a battle for steel. Churchill wanted steel plates for his huge tank program; the Admiralty required them for naval building. Churchill had the advantage of controlling the supplies of steel plates. So with great wiliness he suddenly let loose a deluge on the Admiralty to satiate them temporarily, and then appropriated the remaining supplies for his tanks.

To his success at the Ministry of Munitions let his friend, the

---

* Baruch served as an adviser on national defense under President Wilson and was Chairman of the War Industries Board during 1918 and 1919.

late Lord Birkenhead, testify: "Here Winston was in his element, and the immense value of the public services he rendered, though well known to Sir Douglas Haig and his staff, has never been sufficiently appreciated at home. The War Office still preserves a comparative chart illustrating the output of destructive agencies when he went to the Munitions Office and when he left it. Had he done no other work in the war he would have deserved well of the nation."

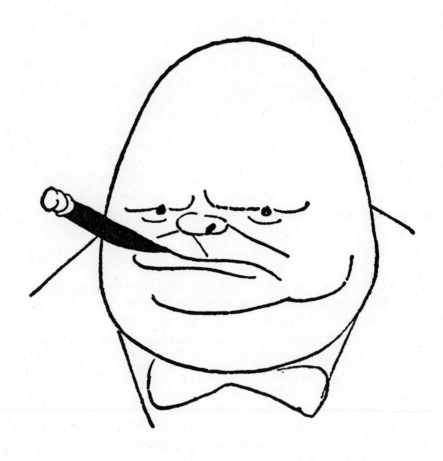

CHAPTER TEN

WINSTON'S FOLLY

1918

THROUGHOUT THE CLOSING months of the war, tanks were an obsession with the Minister of Munitions. He had a double interest. Plans were ready to launch in the Spring of 1919 a vast and overwhelming tank offensive of a strength to extinguish German resistance. Winston Churchill was responsible for producing the new weapon of assault in the number required. As creator he had a concern almost parental in the fortunes of the tank.

There had been a time when "Winston's Folly" was laughed at by the skeptics. The tank in embryo had not impressed its merits upon the onlooker. By 1918 it was a different tale. The folly was seen to apply to the skeptics, not to Churchill. The tank had proved itself on the battlefield and Generals were clamoring for the caterpillar contrivance that climbed in and out of trenches, untroubled by the machine-gun. The tank was cracking the enemy's crumbling morale.

In the Autumn of 1918, when the Germans were driven to defeat, Churchill was stepping up tank production for the Spring assault. The Ford Motor Company alone was given a contract for 10,000 tanks. To provide the personnel required, Churchill urged the creation of a Tank Corps of 100,000 men.

The German collapse and the Armistice in November, 1918,

made this blitzkrieg superfluous. It was left to another war and an enemy attack to demonstrate what the tank could achieve when employed on a vast scale. It was ironic that Churchill's inventive genius should have contributed to the fall of France in 1940.

Too many persons played their part in its evolution for Churchill to be termed the "Father of the Tank," but without his intervention there would in all probability have been no such machine in the 1914–18 war. He did not invent the tank, but it was the result of his foresight that the search was begun for an appliance to beat the trench. It was because of his encouragement that the disheartening process of experiment was pressed forward until the tank came into being. His exact contribution was determined by the Royal Commission which, after the war, adjudicated on the claims of inventors.

> In the first place the Commission desire to record their view that it was primarily due to the receptivity, courage and driving force of the Rt. Hon. Winston Spencer Churchill that the general idea of the use of such an instrument of warfare as the tank was converted into a practical shape, but Mr. Churchill has very properly taken the view that all his thought and time belonged to the State and that he was not entitled to make any claim for an award, even if he had liked to do so. But it seems proper that the above view should be recorded by way of tribute to Mr. Winston Churchill.

The tank later became the major weapon of land warfare. For its genesis the soldier is largely indebted to a politician who was First Lord of the Admiralty, to funds which were voted for Admiralty work, and to men who were officers in the Royal Navy. To complete the picture it should be added that these officers of the Navy were engaged on the work of the Royal Naval Air Service. Other minds at a later stage contributed to the invention, but—*ce n'est que le premier pas qui coûte.*

The dispatch of a squadron of the Royal Naval Air Service to Ostend in August 1914 was the initial move. Planes of the squadron came down behind the German lines and parties set out to rescue the airmen. For this purpose fast-moving vehicles were needed, protected against enemy fire, and the need produced the armored car. When the Germans began to dig themselves in, there was a further demand on inventive genius—an armored car that would climb trenches. As I have already stated Churchill, then First Lord, gave instructions for the production of a car provided with a portable bridge, but this was not successful. It did, however, have the effect of setting the mental yeast fermenting. When the stalemate of trench warfare developed in France in the autumn of 1914, Churchill's fertile brain was directed to the problem of circumventing the trench. In a letter to Asquith he put forward the idea that machines on caterpillar wheels should be employed:

> It is extraordinary that the Army in the field and the War Office should have allowed nearly three months of warfare to progress without addressing their minds to its special problems.
>
> The present war has revolutionized all military theories about the field of fire. The power of the rifle is so great that 100 yards is held sufficient to stop any rush, and in order to avoid the severity of the artillery fire, trenches are often dug on the reverse slope of positions, or a short distance in the rear of villages, woods, or other obstacles. The consequence is that war has become a short-range instead of a long-range war as was expected, and opposing trenches get ever closer together, for mutual safety from each other's artillery fire.
>
> The question to be solved is not, therefore, the long attack over a carefully prepared glacis of former times, but the actual getting across 100 or 200 yards of open space and wire entanglements. All this was apparent more than two months ago, but no steps have been taken and no preparations made.
>
> It would be quite easy in a short time to fit up a number of steam tractors with small armoured shelters, in which men and machine-guns could be placed, which would be bullet-proof. Used at night, they would not be affected by artillery fire to any extent. The caterpillar system would enable trenches to be crossed quite easily, and the weight of the machine would destroy all wire entanglements.
>
> Forty or fifty of these engines, prepared secretly and brought into positions at nightfall, could advance quite certainly into the enemy's trenches, smashing away all the obstructions, and sweeping the trenches with their machine-gun fire, and with grenades thrown out of the top. They would then make so many *points d'appui* for the British supporting infantry to rush forward and rally on them. They could then move forward to attack the second line of trenches.

The cost would be small. If the experiment did not answer, what harm would be done? An obvious measure of prudence would have been to have started something like this two months ago. It should certainly be done now.

The caterpillar-traction vehicle clearly foreshadows the tank. But, strangely enough, Winston was diverted to another idea—instead of crossing the trenches, why not demolish them? Experiments in producing armored cars were already in progress at Wormwood Scrubbs under the vigorous direction of Commodore Murray Sueter (later Rear Admiral Sir Murray Sueter, M.P.), Director of Air Department. To him Churchill delivered an enthusiastic harangue. Striding up and down his room he dictated a minute directing trials to be held. Between sentences he would interject: "We must crush the trenches, D.A.D.: it is the only way; it must be done."

Murray Sueter left to carry out a steam-roller test for which Churchill's directions were:

> I wish the following experiment made at once. Two ordinary steam-rollers are to be fastened together side by side with very strong steel connections, so they are to all intents and purposes one roller covering a breadth of at least twelve to fourteen feet. If convenient, one of the back inside wheels might be removed and the other axle joined up to it. Some trenches are to be dug on the latest principles somewhere handy near London in lengths of at least a hundred yards, the earth taken out of the trenches being thrown on each side, as is done in France. The roller is to be driven along these trenches, one outer rolling wheel on each side and the inner rolling wheel just clear of the trench itself. The object is to ascertain what amount of weight is necessary in the roller to smash the trench in. For this purpose as much as they can possibly draw should be piled on the steam-rollers and on the framework buckling them together.
>
> The ultimate object is to run along a line of trenches, crushing them all flat and burying the people in them. If the experiment is successful with the steam-rollers fastened together on this improved system, stronger and larger machines can be made with bigger driving wheels and proper protection for the complements, and the rollers of these machines will be furnished with wedge-shaped ribs, or studs, which can be advanced beyond the ordinary surface of the wheel when required, in order to break the soil

on each side of the trench and accentuate the rolling process. The matter is extremely urgent, and should be pressed to the utmost. Really the only difficulty you have got to surmount is to prevent the steam-rollers from breaking apart.

The simplicity of the device, if it succeeds, is its virtue. All that is required is a roller of sufficient breadth and with wheels properly fitted and an unscaleable bullet-proof house for the crew. Three or four men would be quite enough, and as the machine is only worked by night it might not be required to stand against artillery. In a fortnight I wish to see these trials.

The steam-roller project was a complete failure. Even when the rollers could be persuaded to move they failed to crush the trench but for the most part they remained bogged in soft earth.

Churchill was not to be discouraged by this initial failure. Whenever Murray Sueter had to see him on matters arising out of the Royal Naval Air Service, Churchill would bring up the problem of beating the trenches. "Now, D.A.D.," he would urge, "put your best brains into this." [1] D.A.D. did not quite see what trench warfare had to do with either the Royal Navy or the Air Service—but "Anything to help win the war" was a good motto. The ultimate responsibility was Churchill's, who could also see to footing the bill, a matter which was causing the Fourth Sea Lord to remonstrate. The Fourth Sea Lord had no liking for the Armored Car Force and its costly experimenting.

There is no doubt that but for the insistence of the First Lord the experiments would have been abandoned. Even the armored-car experts became weary of cracking hard nuts which were the proper concern of the Army. Churchill persisted and in February 1915 a test of a caterpillar truck was arranged for him on Horse Guards Parade. Hitherto in the contest of armored cars versus trenches, wheels had let the armored cars down. Caterpillar wheels were the alternative. For the Horse Guards test, a caterpillar truck was made to show its paces, drawn by a patient horse. Murray Sueter himself pushed a truck about to prove how easily it moved. Churchill pushed too, saw, and was convinced.

Although [writes Murray Sueter] Mr. Churchill does not shine at his best in dealing with mechanical matters, he has the sharpest brain for grasping a new idea that I have ever met and at once saw that my proposals were a better proposition than his steam-roller idea or Squadron-Commander Hetherington's giant wheel scheme. After considerable discussion it ended in Mr. Churchill being quite satisfied that our turreted armoured cars could be constructed with caterpillars instead of wheels, and gave me approval to build eighteen landships before any other department or firm came into the landship picture.

The immediate sequel was the appointment by Churchill of a committee to develop the idea of a superior armored car on caterpillar wheels. Sir Tennyson D'Eyncourt, the Director of Naval Construction, was the chairman and among the members were Colonel Crompton, the traction expert, and Squadron Commander A. C. Hetherington, representing the Director of Air Department. It was under naval auspices that the evolution of the tank was thus pushed forward—the term "tank" had not then been improvised—and the ideas of the senior service were reflected by the title chosen—the Landship Committee. The problem was looked upon as being that of producing a vessel to travel on land, for the stresses of a landship on bad terrain were similar to those of a ship in a rough sea.

Before Churchill left the Admiralty in May 1915, sufficient progress had been made for him to place a definite order for eighteen landships at a cost of £70,000. He acted on his own initiative without consulting the Board of Admiralty or the Army Council. He had little support outside his band of enthusiasts, and certainly no encouragement from military authorities. Those who heard of the new machines referred to them contemptuously as "Winston's folly."

When he left the Admiralty the naval authorities who had murmured against the "idiotic" caterpillar landships sought to have the experimental work wound up. Thanks, however, to the fight Murray Sueter put up the work was continued, though on a reduced scale.

In February 1916, when Churchill was in France, "Big Willie," as this first juggernaut was called, was given its official trials in the presence of King George V at Hatfield. Kitchener, seemingly aloof and skeptical, represented the Army with officers from General French's headquarters, and Lloyd George, keenly alive to the possibilities of this new weapon, was also present. "Big Willie" could raise a maximum speed of only two miles an hour with a

150-H.P. engine, but the tests were successful and on February 12 the War Office placed an order for forty of the machines, to be secretly manufactured. All embodied the large double cartwheel "rudder," which was one of "Big Willie's" most remarkable features. This was dropped when the adaptation of the caterpillar principle was completely mastered.

Once skepticism had been dispelled a remarkable enthusiasm for the new weapon developed. The War Office increased its order to 150 landships and a special section of the Machine Gun Corps, itself a wartime innovation, was formed to man them. In the meantime, the term "tank" had been adopted on the suggestion of a subcommittee of the Committee of Imperial Defense, to conceal the real purpose of the new engines of war.

Then came a major blunder. Churchill was out of office; his project had been taken out of his hands. He sought out the Prime Minister and urged that the tanks should not be disclosed to the enemy until they could be used in overwhelming force. But the military authorities were anxious for battlefield tests and declined to wait. So on Friday, September 15, forty-nine of the land ships were sent into action in the Battle of Thiepval, which opened the second phase of the battle of the Somme. They did everything expected of them and completely vindicated Churchill's enterprise. Haig reported that "A new type of heavy armored car proved of considerable utility," despite the fact that the attack was launched over a quagmire.

Fortunately for the Allies, the Germans did not profit by this premature disclosure of the new weapon. Twelve months later the tanks were employed in really adequate force, and their onslaught was devastating. Experience had led to the elimination of many primitive features when the tanks made their great attack at Cambrai, "a battle made for them," as Churchill himself declared. In all in this operation 378 fighting tanks and 98 auxiliary tanks were engaged. The Tank Corps had come into being albeit still called the "Heavy Machine Guns" and had proved itself the greatest offensive arm in modern warfare. The action was well staged. There was no preliminary artillery bombardment to apprise the enemy of the coming assault; the tanks led instead of merely supporting the infantry. The Canadian infantry, under General Byng, were the troops engaged. Says the official history of the

Tank Corps: "As the tanks moved forward with the infantry close behind, the enemy completely lost his balance and those who did not fly panic-stricken from the field, surrendered, with little or no resistance. By 4 P.M. on November 20th, one of the most astonishing battles in all history had been won."

Over the front of more than six miles the German trench system had been captured with 200 guns and 10,000 prisoners. The British losses totaled only 1,500 men. Thenceforth tanks were the decisive factor in the war. Ludendorff, discussing the German decision to ask for an armistice, said that one of the major influences was the unexpectedly large numbers of tanks which were employed against them.

"In cases where they have suddenly emerged from smoke clouds in huge numbers," he wrote, "our men have been completely unnerved. They broke through our foremost lines, making a way for their infantry, wrecking our rear and causing panic which entirely upset our control of the battle."

The 1940 blitzkreig began where the 1914 war had left off. Churchill had the mortification of witnessing how the invention he and the British Army had contributed to the craft of war was exploited by the enemy. The Germans had applied the lessons of 1917–18 which the French and British had neglected. Winston's folly! There was folly infinitely more calamitous in its consequences.

As a postscript to the chapter on tanks, it is appropriate to tell of Churchill's connection with the junior service and his personal experiences as airman. He was in control of one or other branch of the Air Service during the first eleven years of its existence. From 1911 to 1915, as First Lord he was responsible, as I have indicated, for the Royal Naval Air Service; in 1917 and 1918, as Minister of Munitions, he was in charge of the design, manufacture and supply of aircraft; and from 1919 to 1921 he was the head of the Air Ministry, combining the post of Minister with that of Secretary for War.

His sense of duty combined with his insatiable curiosity to make a practical airman of him. His first flight in a seaplane was taken in 1912. The conquest of the air had not then advanced beyond the stage when the sense of gambling with death imparted an additional piquancy to the thrill of flight. Winston was fascinated with the idea of flying and yet was conscious of "a dread of going into the air for the first time." His anxieties prevailed throughout the flight, on which he was piloted by Commander Spencer Grey. He confessed afterward that his imagination supplied him with the most realistic anticipations of a crash.

That his concern was no extravagant fancy was shown by a succession of lucky escapes. He took his first lesson as pilot one day; the next, his instructor was killed while flying the same machine. He took a flight in a new type of seaplane off Southampton and landed safely; on arrival by yacht at Sheerness he was informed that the seaplane had crashed, with the loss of life of all on board her.

Radical M.P.s became solicitous for his safety when he continued to make ascents in the perilous airplane. One member asked in the House whether the Prime Minister would use his influence to discourage members "whose lives are of value to the public, from exposing themselves to needless risk. "I regret," replied Asquith, "that valuable lives should be exposed to needless risks, but I have no reason to suppose that I have any such persuasive influence as the honorable gentleman suggests." So the First Lord went on flying.

During the latter stages of the war and the period of the Peace Conference, Churchill made use of the airplane as the means of journeying to and from Paris. On one occasion his machine caught fire in mid-Channel. Again his luck held. Another day his plane crashed while taking off, turned a somersault, and was smashed to pieces. He suffered no more than cuts and bruises and the same good fortune extended to the pilot.

One summer day in 1919, the margin of escape was less than ever. He himself was handling the controls and executing a turn 100 feet over Croydon Aerodrome, when the machine refused to respond to the guiding stick.

> We were [writes Churchill[2]] scarcely 90 feet above the ground, just the normal height for the aerial sideslip accident, the commonest of all. I saw the sunlit aerodrome and the impression flashed through my mind that it was bathed in a baleful yellowish glare. Then in another flash a definite thought formed in my brain. "This is very like death."
>
> There was no time for fear. The 'plane struck the ground with

terrific force. Its left wing crumpled and its propeller and nose plunged into the earth. I felt myself driven forward as if in some new dimension by a frightful and overwhelming force through a space I could not measure. There was a sense of unendurable oppression across my chest as my belt took the strain. I felt as a distinct phase the whole absorption of the shock. Suddenly the pressure ceased, the belt parted, and I fell forward quite gently on the dial board in front of me, safe.

Two hours later he contrived to speak at a House of Commons dinner.

From planes it is a natural sequence to bombs, and here again Churchill played his part. His contribution was little known until it was disclosed by Colonel Turner, former Superintendent of Design at Woolwich, who was the designer of practically all types of bombs used by British forces in the 1914–18 war: [3]

The drive of the First Lord of the Admiralty, Mr. Winston Churchill, played a prominent part in the development of our bombing equipment.

He took a deep personal interest in all trials, and was present at Kingsnorth in June, 1915, when the first 550 lb. H.E. bomb was dropped from the airship Astra Torres.

The attitude of the R.F.C. to bombing was well expressed by a Squadron Leader of that Corps, when in March, 1915, the writer visited his aerodrome in France. Asked whether the 112 lb. bombs were satisfactory, the R.F.C. Officer said: "We don't use them. We look upon bomb-dropping as the waste of a good pilot and a good machine. But if you care to go over the German lines and drop one, we will arrange for it."

Lord Trenchard later became known as a great protagonist of bomb attack, but it took a long time to convert him, and had it not been for the action of Mr. Churchill the material would probably not have been available.

BOOK FOUR

FIGHTING THE SOCIALISTS

I have done the State some service and they know it,
No more of that. I pray you in your letters
When you shall these unlucky deeds relate
Speak of me as I am; nothing extenuate
Nor set down aught in malice.
                              —SHAKESPEARE, Othello

CHAPTER ONE

WINDING UP THE WAR

1918–1920

ON THE NIGHT of November 11, 1918, Winston Churchill dined with the Prime Minister at 10 Downing Street. The dinner marked the crest of the wave in world events. Behind were the turbulent waters through which they had passed to victory. Before them, and unknown, lay the waters of transition, through which the course had then to be set. For a moment they were poised upon the crest. They could savor the satisfaction that comes from a task magnificently performed. It was but for a moment. The waves are never still. The problems a statesman solved yesterday form the new situation that creates the problems of tomorrow.

For Lloyd George and Winston Churchill the respite was the brief space of that Armistice night's dinner. The one must then bend himself to the making of the new world at the Peace Conference, the other must undertake the direction of the great reversal of gears as the industrial machine reverted to the functions of peace.

From the experiences that followed the end of hostilities in World War I, Churchill and members of the Coalition Government of World War II were able to profit. By taking the lessons of 1918 as their guide, they were able to avoid the mistakes that had been made a quarter of a century previously.

It was a fortunate circumstance that Churchill had had first-hand experience in 1919 of the change-over from war to peace production. By such and such measures, he was able to recall, we carried this thing through in 1919; here precedent could safely be followed; here difficulties in the past suggested that improvements must be made.

Over and beyond the knowledge of the machinery and practical aspects of demobilization, his experience of the past served to illuminate the dark problems of psychology—for it was the psychological factor that nullified the perfection of paper planning and sent things wrong in 1918. There were errors in psychology in carrying out the demobilization of the armed forces that led to unrest bordering on mutiny as men retained in the services were infuriated at the sight of more-favored comrades gaining priority in release and a better place in the scramble for jobs. Another psychological error—made in the blindest good faith—staged the maddest of all general elections within a few weeks of the war's ending and returned the most embarrassing majority to Parliament that has ever troubled a Prime Minister.

Wisdom and sanity were at a discount in the 1918 election. The Jingo ruled the hour. Even the patriotism of Lloyd George was not enough to satisfy the electors. "Hang the Kaiser," "Make the Germans pay," "Squeeze them till the pips squeak"—the people were in the mood to require the most perfervid declarations of patriotism.

At Dundee, Churchill found his electors roused from their customary Scottish restraint. His declarations failed to satisfy them until he had echoed the noisy clamor of the hour. His statesmanship doubted the wisdom of the "Hang the Kaiser" cry—raised, among others, by Mr. Barnes, Labour's representative in the War Cabinet. Dundee was not satisfied until Churchill had declared at least for bringing that Prussian figurehead to trial. He had the limited satisfaction of writing to some of his constituents letters that preserved balance of judgment at a time of general delirium. Even so he could only permit himself to hint his doubts on the wisdom of public demands by a series of interrogation marks. Do not let ourselves be robbed of the fruits of victory—but ought the terms Germany imposed on France in 1871 to be the best precedent to follow? Annex provinces of Germany—but would that not bring in its train a repetition of the evil of '71?

He had the satisfaction, too, in that month of November, 1918, of enunciating the dilemma that was to baffle Allied statesmanship. Make Germany pay—well and good; but how make Britain and the Allies accept? In gold or currency?—it was not practicable. In goods?—it would only mean putting our own workmen out of employment.

Churchill's was a clearer realization than was vouchsafed to many of the statesmen and economists. It would have saved much searching of heart during the decade to come had reparations then and there been written off as a largely unrealizable asset costing the victor even more to take than the vanquished to pay. But this needed ten years to prove.

The Khaki Election ended in the rout of the Anti-Coalition forces. Labour was represented by a handful of M.P.s; the Liberal Party was all but annihilated. Lloyd George was given a vast majority in the House in which Tory M.P.s predominated.

Before the election was over Churchill had wound up his work as Minister of Munitions. When the war ended nearly 5,000,000 workers, including 1,500,000 women, were under the Ministry's control. In preparation for the day when a stop would be called to the pouring out of implements of war, detailed plans had been drawn up by various committees. These measures worked smoothly when they were put to the test of operation. The production of guns and tanks and planes and all the vast paraphernalia of war was halted. By successive steps control was lifted from the country's industrial processes. The workers were released for the tasks of peace.

The first part of the great task of demobilization under Churchill's direction was efficiently achieved. Before he carried out the second and more difficult installment, there was a partial demobilization in the ranks of the Coalition Government following the general election. For Churchill a new place had to be found. He was offered the choice of War Office or Admiralty, with the Air Ministry as a subsidiary in either case. The Prime Minister had decided not to keep the Air Ministry as a separate department— strange lack of appreciation on the part of Lloyd George, who was swifter than most in realizing the importance of new discoveries.

Churchill plumped for the Admiralty—you can well imagine why. Reinstatement as First Lord would be proof to the world that his fall had been due to the machinations of his enemies. But even before his letter of acceptance had been received the offer was withdrawn. There was a difficult job to be done and he was directed to go to the War Office to face the anxious situation over demobilization.

As in the case of munitions workers, schemes had been prepared in advance; but though they were theoretically perfect they left out the human element. The plans were based on the release of "key men" first. In theory it was admirable: send the essential men back to provide the framework and get the wheels turning again; then industry would be in a position to absorb men by the thousands. But, alas for the imperfection of human reasoning, application of the scheme led to resentment which mounted to mutiny. The key men who were to be the first to leave had also been the last to reach the Army—men whose service was not longer than a few months, perhaps only weeks. Veterans of the war, men who had been at the front under Sir John French, men who had been wounded and gone back to the trenches two or three times, were expected to wait for their papers and watch the key men scurry back home to get the pick of the jobs. It was more than long-enduring manhood could tolerate.

For two months they had viewed this monstrous injustice with resigned indignation. By January 1919 when the new Minister took over the War Office, Army discipline, which had withstood all the assaults of the Hun, had been undermined. There were disorders on both sides of the Channel. At Folkestone there was mutiny not to be disguised as anything less. Even the august portals of the War Office had had to admit scores of angry demonstrators who had come along to tell authority what the common soldier thought in the common soldier's language.

It was with a certain relief, we may suspect, that Churchill found that peace hath her crises no less than war. The new Ministry was announced on January 10; the new Secretary for War took over at the War Office on January 15; within a couple of days he had summoned Sir Douglas Haig home from France for consultation; and on January 23 he crossed the Channel to obtain sanction for his proposals from the Prime Minister, then en-

Combine

Churchill, as Home Secretary, was criticized in January, 1911, for leaving his departmental desk to be at the scene of action of the famous "Siege of Sidney Street." Two desperados had entrenched themselves in a house and battled with armed police and soldiers before the house caught fire. Their charred bodies were found in the ruins.

Combine

Churchill learned to fly in 1914 and frequently flew between England and the Western Front in the closing years of World War I

Always fond of riding, Churchill excelled as a polo player and continued his active interest in this sport even after he reached the rank of Cabinet Minister

Combine

Combine

Seeking re-election in 1924, Churchill had active support from women
constituents but was defeated by a Unionist candidate

The Chancellor of the Exchequer, with his wife, the former Clementine Ogilvy Hozier walk toward the House of Commons with their eldest daughter, Diana, and their only son, Randolph, in 1925, when Churchill was to deliver the first of five Budget speeches

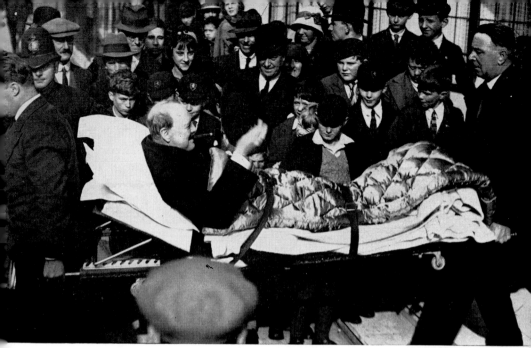

Combine

A sympathetic crowd looks on as Churchill leaves a nursing home in October, 1932, after he suffered a severe attack of paratyphoid

Churchill, his face partially covered with bandages, spent considerable time in Lenox Hill Hospital, New York, in December, 1931, after he had 15 bones broken and suffered other internal injuries when struck by a taxi cab on a New York street

Wide World

Churchill is shown with the Prince of Wales, later Edward VIII and now Duke of Windsor. The Prince consulted Churchill on his decision to abdicate in 1936 in favor of his brother, the late King George VI

Associated Press

Churchill began painting in his forties and this example—"The Blue Room, Trent Park, 1934"—was the first painting he ever sold. It was purchased at a London charity auction which was promoted by his wife, and was hung in the art museum of Sao Paulo, Brazil.

Fox

With war imminent, Churchill was summoned to 10 Downing Street
on September 1, 1939, by Neville Chamberlain, to be offered a seat
in the War Cabinet as First Lord of the Admiralty, the post he had
held in the opening months of World War I

gaged in conference in Paris in the complexities of remapping Europe. On the 24th, decisions were obtained from Lloyd George, and the Adjutant General, Sir George Macdonogh, was instructed to draw up the two Army orders to give effect to them. On January 29 the new orders were issued.

They met the Army's grievances. First they got rid of the hated "key man." Release was to be determined by length of service. For those who were retained there was the consolation of double pay to reduce the gap between military and civilian rates. Finally the maintenance of an army on the Continent was provided for without calling on the men who had borne the burden of fighting, by retaining for two years the young men who had completed their training but had not previously gone overseas.

It was well that Churchill worked with speed to produce his scheme. Even during the fortnight that elapsed, discontent was perilously intensified. In many places the men got out of control. There were riots at Glasgow and Belfast. At Luton a mob burned down the town hall. At Calais three or four thousand armed men took possession of the town and a couple of divisions had to be detached from the Army of Occupation to restore order. From the windows of his own department Winston watched anxiously as Grenadiers with fixed bayonets and men of the Household Cavalry rounded up a body of 3,000 demonstrators in Whitehall.

With the issue of the new orders there was a transformation. Discontent vanished from the air, discipline was restored, and the orderly process of demobilization proceeded uneventfully. At the end of six months a force of well over 3,000,000 men had been released and had been reabsorbed in civilian life. It was no mean feat of organization.

As Secretary for War, one further task in winding up the war fell to Churchill's lot—the liquidation of Allied commitments in Russia. In succeeding Lord Milner at the War Office he became "heir to the pledges and tragedies" of the Russian situation.

Russia at that time was the scene of civil war, or rather of several civil wars, of revolution and counterrevolution. Lenin and the Bolsheviks had a precarious hold on the capital and central provinces. In the outer provinces there were a number of anti-Bolshevik movements led among others by Admiral Denikin, General Koltchak and General Wrangel.

The anti-Bolshevik forces had been sustained by pledges of assistance of men and arms. Numbers of British and Allied troops were engaged on Russian soil. In North Russia, at Murmansk and Archangel, there were 12,000 British and 11,000 Allied troops. In the heart of the desolation of Siberia, Colonel John Ward, M.P., with two British battalions, was striving valiantly on behalf of the Omsk Government. At Vladivostok there were under British management training schools for 3,000 Russian officers. Shortly after the Armistice with Germany the War Cabinet decided to assist Denikin, in South Russia, with arms, to send officers and equipment to Siberia and to recognize the Omsk Government.

In the New Year of 1919 British commitments became a source of anxiety. With the ending of the long-drawn-out struggle against Germany, there was no liking for new adventures in Russia. The War Cabinet decisions of November had not, however, been annulled. A definite policy was lacking.

It was urgent that decisions should be taken—either to wind up the Russian operations or to press them with vigor. Only from the allied statesmen assembled around the conference tables at Versailles could the decision be obtained, and in February, Winston crossed once more to France to obtain authoritative instructions on the policy to be pursued. The occasion provided him with his only contact with President Wilson, then about to return to the United States after his labors to set Europe to rights. Churchill gave a lively account of the meeting:

> It was the very night that President Wilson was leaving on his first return journey to the United States. He had only a short time to get his dinner and catch his train to Cherbourg. He had actually risen from his place to leave the Conference, and there could not have been a less propitious moment for raising an extra, disagreeable and baffling topic.
>
> However, with the persistence born of my direct responsibilities upon the various Russian fronts, and with all sorts of cruel realities then proceeding, present in my mind, I stood up and made my appeal. "Could we not have some decision about Russia? Fighting was actually going on. Men were being killed and wounded. What was the policy? Was it peace or was it war? Were we to stop or were we to go on? Was the President going away to America leaving this question quite unanswered? What was to

happen while he was away? Was nothing to go on except aimless unorganized bloodshed till he came back? Surely there should be an answer given."

The President, contrary to my expectation, was affable. He turned back to the table and, resting his elbow on Clemenceau's chair, listened without sitting down to what I had to say. Then he replied frankly and simply to the following effect: "Russia was a problem to which he did not pretend to know the solution. There were the gravest objections to every course, and yet some course must be taken—sooner or later. He was anxious to clear out of Russia altogether, but was willing, if necessary, to meet the Bolsheviks alone (i.e. without the National Russians) at conference in Prinkipo. Nevertheless, if Prinkipo came to nothing, he would do his share with the other Allies in any military measures which they considered necessary and practicable to help the Russian armies now in the field." Then he left us.

The concentrated wisdom of the statesmen gathered at Versailles was not equal to the task of giving guidance on Russia. Even the setting up of a formal Commission to whom responsibility could be delegated was beyond their competence.

Churchill returned to London with his purpose unfulfilled. From Whitehall he sent appeals to the Prime Minister at Versailles pressing for definite decisions. Lloyd George replied with requests for estimates of costings. Churchill retorted that estimates were contingent on policy.

> With regard to your complaint [he wrote in one piquantly worded note] that the War Office have not furnished you with information, I must point out to you that the War Cabinet have long been accustomed to deal direct with the Chief of the Staff and other military authorities, and they know as well as I do the difficulties of obtaining precise plans and estimates of cost from military men in regard to this Russian problem. The reason is that all the factors are uncertain and that the military considerations are at every point intermingled with political decisions which have not been given.

By midsummer the Supreme Council of the Allies at length made up its mind. It would carry out its pledge to give aid in the shape of arms and money to Admiral Koltchak and his associates. This decision was definitely worded, but there definition ended.

By August Lord Curzon, then Foreign Secretary, in a memorandum was drawing attention to the confusion in Allied policy. He wrote:

> It cannot be said that an altogether consistent policy has been pursued. Even now the principles upon which that policy rests in the last resort are in some respects in dispute. Action is taken sometimes by the representatives of the Allied and Associated Governments sitting in Paris or by the institutions which they have set up, sometimes by the Governments themselves. The situation is so complex, and the difficulties of arriving at a decision which is acceptable to all are so great that, in some instances, it would be no exaggeration to admit that there is no policy at all.

There was nothing indecisive about the steps Churchill took to carry out the decision to evacuate the Allied forces from Russia. The manner of the accomplishment gave rise to misconceptions at home and Churchill was attacked by the Opposition parties, Liberal as well as Socialist, for embroiling the country still further in unpopular adventures in Russia.

Evacuations under enemy fire are difficult operations as we came to realize only too well from the tragic experiences of Dunkirk and Greece in World War II. In 1919 there was no such general appreciation of military commonplaces and when the Secretary for War announced that a volunteer force of 8,000 men was to be raised to cover the withdrawal there was a flurry of protest from the ill-informed and irresponsible.

The problem was not even confined to the military one of removing our own men. There were also the Russians with whom we had been cooperating, the men whose opposition to the Bolsheviks had been sustained and encouraged by British assistance and promises. As Churchill said in his defense in the House:

> Although to us who sit here at home in England it may seem very easy to say, "Clear out, evacuate, cut the loss, get the troops on board ship and come away"—yet on the spot, face to face with the people among whom you have been living, with the troops by the side of whom you have been fighting, with the Government which has been created by our insistence, with all the apparatus of an administration with all its branches and services —when you get our officers and men involved like that on the

spot, it is a matter of very great and painful difficulty to sever the ties and quit the scene. I do not disguise from the House that I had most earnestly hoped and trusted that it would be possible in the course of events for the local North Russian Government to have a separate life and existence after our departure; and with the fullest assent of the Cabinet and the Government, and acting strictly on the advice of the General Staff, we have been ready to hold out a left hand, as it were, along the Dvina River to Admiral Koltchak in the hope that he would be able to arrive in this district, and, by joining the local Russian forces, stabilize the situation and enable our affairs there to be wound up in a thoroughly satisfactory manner.

The soundness of the dispositions made was proved by the success of the operations. Behind the shield of the two additional brigades, the removal of British, American, French, and Italian soldiers, with their stores, was accomplished. General Rawlinson was dispatched to Archangel to conduct the evacuation there. General (later Field Marshal) Ironside made one final devastating assault on the enemy, to ensure that the withdrawal was not impeded, and when the time came the troops got aboard the transports almost without loss.

The decision to send Rawlinson to Archangel to conduct the withdrawal was an eminently wise one. I am indebted to my friend, the late Andrew Soutar,[1] for a memorandum, which describes how the decision was taken and gives a lively picture of Winston in action. Andrew Soutar had not then dismayed his Fleet Street friends by deserting journalism to devote himself to novel writing. He was attached to Ironside's force as special correspondent of *The Times,* and he returned to London to report. The sequel is told in his memorandum:

> I got back (touch of dysentery and other sickness) after eight or nine gruelling months—Murmansk, Archangel, and 250 miles up the river Dvina from Archangel where Ironside had his advanced headquarters. There would be about twelve thousand men up there, and as the river water was falling rapidly, the task of retreating to Archangel in order to embark and evacuate, was likely to be extremely hazardous.
>
> When I arrived at *The Times* office, I wrote a three-column dispatch on the situation, slept in the office that night, and was

informed next morning that Winston wished to see me at the War Office and lay any further details before him.

In England, at that time, there was keen resentment among the Labour Party. They refused to countenance the sending out of more troops to Russia, insisted that we should come out and leave the Bolsheviks alone, and actually threatened action if we persisted in fighting!

When I reached the War Office, on a beautiful summer evening (the newsboys were showing placards concerning the cricket scores, I remember), I was shown into about half a dozen rooms—moving like a piece on a draughts board—and being questioned in friendly, yet cautious manner by secretaries and under-secretaries attached to the Chief.

I realized that all this was procedure essential to high politics, it being the rule to go through a caller with a harrow before admitting him to the presence.

When, at last, I entered Winston's room, large, spacious, and certainly impressive, with his simple desk tucked away in a corner, he greeted me affably, placed a chair in position for me so that I should face him across it, and began:

"Now, tell me all about it."

On his writing-pad he had only a single sheet of paper and a lead pencil.

I began to describe the situation out there. His stolid expression conveyed to me the idea that he wasn't listening, that the names of Russian villages and trails and positions were simply blending themselves into a mournful song that came to him from a vast distance. I paused, I remember, frowned a little maybe at his apparent unconcern.

I said to him:

"Give me your pencil and I'll give you a rough sketch with the names of the places."

He smiled that bland smile of his, and said:

"I have them all in my head."

And to my surprise, he actually named village after village, point after point—villages with unpronounceable names. And the area covered thousands of miles! He knew his North Russia perfectly.

He listened. I talked. Never once did he question my statements; indeed, he was so tolerant that I expected him to say, of a sudden: "Thanks, you have added nothing to what I knew of the situation, and I'm sorry you've been troubled."

Instead, he got to his feet. The expression on his face had changed completely. The corners of his mouth came down to form that grim and decisive look so characteristic of him when he has made up his mind.

"Come and see Wilson," he said, and put an arm over my shoulder to hurry me across the floor.

I wasn't quite certain that I knew to whom he referred as "Wilson." We climbed the short flight of stairs to another corridor, and came to a comparatively small map room—a plain and unpretentious room, the walls of which were covered with maps. And walking about that room, talking to a staff officer, was the Sir Henry Wilson, Chief of the Imperial General Staff. A tall, angular man with a long, hooked, lean nose and a pair of those blue, Irish military eyes that look right through you, so that they can tell you the sort of back collar-stud you're wearing. There wasn't a chair in the room—we were all standing.

Said Churchill: "Listen, Wilson! This is Mr. Soutar, and he's just back from Archangel."

I told the C.I.G.S. of the situation. He was most charming, but I could see that he was in a difficulty.

He said to me:

"We cannot send another man out there. I don't think the situation is very serious—well, not so serious as you say."

I began to elaborate, pointing out the extreme difficulties of getting the troops out. In truth, I didn't hesitate to express the opinion that our men were "up in the blue" with only the river Dvina as a "road" back to Archangel; and the water was falling fast!

He protested: "I'm certain that Ironside and Maynard will get them out, and——"

Churchill's voice came in like the spit of a machine-gun:

"Listen to what he's telling you, Wilson!"

It was an embarrassing moment for me. Here was a mighty soldier being told to hold his tongue while I had my say. The fact that I was in uniform added to the embarrassment: I felt myself drifting back to my "Tommy" days and the longing, then, to tell a "Brass Hat" exactly what I thought of him!

Wilson became more charming than ever. He repeated that he simply couldn't ask for men to be sent out. He had arranged for the withdrawal of the troops, and he was still satisfied that the evacuation could be carried out without more than the usual risks attendant on such an operation.

"I really don't think . . ." he began to object, but that was as far as Winston allowed him to go.

He had been silent for a moment while Wilson was urging on me the utter impossibility of sending more men, then came his order:

"Wilson! Send Rawlinson out on a destroyer, to-night, and let him fetch them out!"

There it was—quick, decisive, unanswerable. No temporising, no argument. His word! Rawlinson did go out that night on a destroyer.

I went back with Winston to the private room. He talked of the campaign; he summoned back his affable manner; and so we parted. I was left with the impression of a Minister who could make up his mind in a flash. A Minister who knew his job from crown to boots, and . . . could prove it!

By autumn the Russian operations had virtually been wound up, but in the following summer the Labour Party critics were still trying to make political capital out of Russia when a document, known to fame as the Golvin memorandum, caused a minor Parliamentary storm. This memorandum was alleged to have fallen into the hands of the Soviet authorities after the allied evacuation of Archangel—we had not the same knowledge in those days of the technique of the production of this class of diplomatic thrillers. It was brought back from Russia by a Labour Party deputation.

It was dated May 6, 1919, more than a fortnight before the Supreme Council decision in favor of aid for the White Russians. It purported to convey to M. Sazonoff, last of the Czarist prime ministers, an account of an interview which Colonel Golvin, a White Russian emissary, had had with Churchill. The British War Minister, the document alleged, had promised the White Russian Government an indefinite postponement of the evacuation of the British forces and offered 12,500 volunteers who, while ostensibly covering the withdrawal, would constitute a new garrison.

The publication of this document created a sensation at Westminster. Churchill was assailed by Liberal and Labour critics who now accused him of having used his position to "gamble with lives and gold" in a "sneaking, underhand war." Scornfully he repudiated the allegations, pointing to the date of the document as evidence that the interview, which was "inaccurately and untruthfully recorded," had taken place before he received his instructions.

In winding up affairs in Russia in the manner I have described, Churchill was carrying out a policy which was not his own but rather that of the Prime Minister. Churchill and Lloyd George did not agree in their views on the Soviet. Lloyd George then (and later) was prepared to be more conciliatory in his dealings with the Bolshevik masters of Russia than was Churchill. In the years that were to come, Churchill was to use strong language in denunciation of Lenin and his associates, as he himself recalled when he made the dramatic announcement to the listening world in June 1941, promising British aid to the Russians in their fight against the Nazis.

His attitude to the Soviet was set out in a memorandum he submitted to Lloyd George in March 1920. In it he stated not merely his views on Russia, but the principles which he would have followed in dealing with the defeated German foe. The salient passages of this memorandum were:

> Since the Armistice my policy would have been "Peace with the German people, war on the Bolshevik tyranny." Willingly or unavoidably, you have followed something very near the reverse. Knowing the difficulties, and also your great skill and personal force—so much greater than mine—I do not judge your policy and action as if I could have done better, or as if anyone could have done better. But we are now face to face with the results. They are terrible. We may well be within measurable distance of universal collapse and anarchy throughout Europe and Asia. Russia has gone into ruin. What is left of her is in the power of these deadly snakes.
>
> But Germany may perhaps still be saved. I have felt with a great sense of relief that we may be able to think and act together in harmony about Germany: that you are inclined to make an effort to rescue Germany from her frightful fate—which if it overtakes her may well overtake others. If so, time is short and action must be simple.
>
> You ought to tell France that we will make a defensive alliance with her against Germany if, *and only if,* she entirely alters her treatment of Germany and loyally accepts a British policy of help

and friendship towards Germany. Next you should send a great man to Berlin to help consolidate the anti-Spartacist, anti-Ludendorff elements into a strong left centre block. For this task you have two levers: first, food and credit, which must be generously accorded in spite of our own difficulties (which otherwise will worsen); secondly, early revision of the Peace Treaty by a Conference to which new Germany shall be invited as an equal partner in the rebuilding of Europe. (This referred to the economic and financial clauses.) Using these levers it ought to be possible to rally all that is good and stable in the German nation to their own redemption and to the salvation of Europe. I pray that we may not be "too late."

Surely this is a matter far more worth while taking your political life in your hands for than our party combinations at home, important though they be. Surely also it is a matter which once on the move would dominate the whole world situation at home and abroad. My suggestion involves open resolute action by Britain under your guidance, and if necessary *independent* action. In such a course I would gladly at your side face political misfortune. But I believe there would be no misfortune, and that for a few months longer Britain still holds the title-deeds of Europe.

As a part of such a policy I should be prepared to make peace with Soviet Russia on the best terms available to appease the general situation, while safeguarding us from being poisoned by them. I do not, of course, believe that any real harmony is possible between Bolshevism and present civilization. But in view of the existing facts a cessation of arms and a promotion of material prosperity are indispensable: and we must trust for better or for worse to peaceful influences to bring about the disappearance of this awful tyranny and peril.

After winding up the Russian operations, Winston Churchill passed on to deal with another problem of the war's aftermath—the curtailment of British commitments in Mesopotamia. The occupation of that territory by a large British army was costing £40,000,000 a year and there was opposition to the policy of curtailment because of the many political interests involved by the creation of the new state of Iraq.

On Churchill's suggestion Lloyd George set up a special Middle East department of the Foreign Office to solve the difficulties, but it did not function as he had anticipated. So at the end of 1920 Churchill was invited to take over the post of Secretary for the Colonies.

It may be noted, in passing, that his under-secretary was the member for Ripon, who stood pre-eminent in the House by reason of his six feet five inches, and who was destined to make his reputation under three *aliases*—first as Edward Wood, Minister for Education, then (after he was raised to the peerage in 1925) as Lord Irwin, Viceroy of India, and later as Lord Halifax (which title he received in 1944), Foreign Secretary and Ambassador to the United States.

At the close of 1920 Churchill decided to go himself to Cairo to assist in unraveling the tangled skein in the Middle East. To win support of the Iraqis in the war, representatives of the Allied Governments had given varying pledges, some of which nullified others. Not all could be carried out. Some charge of betrayal was bound to arise. Churchill's conference decided to appoint an Arab king to rule over the Iraqis and Faisal was the choice made. The wisdom of the settlement reached under Churchill's guidance was testified to by T. E. Lawrence, who had as nice a sense of honor as any man. Lawrence, who had disowned his own government in disgust for having, as he thought, betrayed the Iraqis, paid the following tribute to Churchill in his *Seven Pillars of Wisdom:*

> Mr. Winston Churchill was entrusted by our harassed Cabinet with the settlement of the Middle East. In a few weeks at his conference in Cairo he made straight all the tangle, finding solutions fulfilling (I think) our promises in letter and spirit (where humanly possible) without sacrificing any interest of our Empire or any interest of the peoples concerned. So we were quit of wartime Eastern adventure, with clean hands, but three years too late to earn the gratitude which peoples, if not States, can pay.

Churchill also made an important innovation by entrusting the Royal Air Force with the responsibilities which the Army had been discharging. For policing such a country as Iraq, the RAF was equally effective and much more economical. Actually there was a saving of £35,000,000 to the British taxpayer. Even more important for the future was the concentration of a considerable body of our airmen in the Middle East.

Churchill was next involved in problems nearer home and the unraveling of Irish affairs.

CHAPTER TWO

IRISH PEACEMAKER

1921

H ISTORY WILL REMEMBER Winston Churchill as a great War
Minister. His particular aptitudes as man of action were
most prominently and successfully employed in directing warfare
against Britain's foes. But he had his achievements in constructive
statesmanship—in establishing a new constitution for South Africa
and in contributing a solution for the problem of Ireland that for
so long had defied British statesmanship.

The administration of the Lloyd George Coalition Government
from the 1918 election to its fall in 1922 has not earned much
praise. It should never be forgotten that it brought peace to Ireland. Lloyd George succeeded where Asquith and Gladstone
failed. Churchill played his part in the difficult negotiations that
led to the signing of the treaty. And it was only under his careful
nursing as Colonial Secretary that the birth pangs of the Irish
Free State were eventually completed. His work won from Michael Collins the simple tribute: "Tell Winston we could never
have done anything without him." It was the last message Collins
sent before he fell a victim to a fellow Irishman's bullet.

In 1921 Ireland seemed to have reached her darkest hour. The
country was given over to guerrilla warfare, which differed little
from murder and assassination. No time could have appeared to

offer fewer chances of peace. The Cabinet resolved, however, on one last attempt to negotiate an agreement before embarking on the unlimited exercise of force to suppress the rebels. In July an Irish delegation under Mr. de Valera came to London. It took until December to hammer out a treaty. On the Irish side the principal negotiators were Arthur Griffith and Michael Collins, whose exploits against the Black and Tans * had won him his place among the leaders of Sinn Fein.

There is an amusing passage in Churchill's recollections—one of the few amusing incidents in the long-drawn-out bitterness of the Irish negotiations—of a meeting between the two men who had had the experience of being hunted men—Churchill wanted by Boers and Collins by the English.

> I remember one night [Churchill wrote] when Mr. Griffith and Mr. Collins came to my house to meet the Prime Minister. It was at a crisis, and the negotiations seemed to hang only by a thread. Griffith went upstairs to parley with Mr. Lloyd George alone. Lord Birkenhead and I were left with Michael Collins meanwhile. He was in his most difficult mood, full of reproaches and defiances, and it was very easy for everyone to lose his temper.
>
> "You hunted me night and day," he exclaimed. "You put a price on my head."
>
> "Wait a minute," I said. "You are not the only one." And I took from my wall the framed copy of the reward offered for my recapture by the Boers. "At any rate yours was a good price— £5,000. Look at me—£25 dead or alive. How would you like that?" Actually no such reward had ever been offered for Collins by the British Government, but this I did not know at the time.
>
> He read the paper, and as he took it in he broke into a hearty laugh. All his irritation vanished. We had a really serviceable conversation, and thereafter—though I must admit that deep in my heart there was a certain gulf betwen us—we never to the best of my belief lost the basis of a common understanding.

There was universal relief on the signing of the treaty but the difficulties were not thereby ended. The treaty was only the halfway house to the final settlement and it was Winston, as I have said, who had to deal with the complexities of establishing the

---

* A special force recruited to assist the Royal Irish Constabulary. With khaki trousers and black caps and belts, they were nicknamed Black and Tans after a well-known type of hound.

new order the treaty had called into being. With the passing of the ancient office of First Secretary for Ireland, grave of many Parliamentary reputations, and the granting of dominion status, Ireland came within the sphere of his administrative responsibilities as Colonial Secretary.

Trouble had not ended in Ireland because a treaty had been signed in London. De Valera, implacable advocate of full rights of republic, intrigued against Griffith and Collins. The wild men had not put away their guns. The position of Ulster added to the difficulties of the situation. Southern Ireland boycotted Belfast. The frontier villages of the Six Counties were intermittently raided. The fixing of the boundary, in this embittered atmosphere, was a task of the utmost delicacy. Was the prospect of pacification to be blighted once again by the dreary steeples of Fermanagh and Tyrone?

Statesmen, a decade earlier, had been defeated by these same boundary lines, as Churchill recalled to the House in his speech moving the Irish Free State Bill:

> I remember on the eve of the Great War we were gathered together at a Cabinet Meeting in Downing Street, and for a long time, an hour or an hour and a half, after the failure of the Buckingham Palace Conference, we discussed the boundaries of Fermanagh and Tyrone. Both of the great political parties were at each other's throats. The air was full of talk of civil war. Every effort was made to settle the matter and bring them together. The differences had been narrowed down, not merely to the counties of Fermanagh and Tyrone, but to parishes and groups inside the areas of Fermanagh and Tyrone, and yet, even when the differences had been so narrowed down, the problem appeared to be as insuperable as ever, and neither side would agree to reach any conclusion.
>
> Then came the Great War . . . Every institution, almost, in the world was strained. Great Empires have been overturned. The whole map of Europe has been changed. The position of countries has been violently altered. The mode and thought of men, the whole outlook on affairs, the grouping of parties, all have encountered violent and tremendous changes in the deluge of the world, but as the deluge subsides and the waters fall we see the dreary steeples of Fermanagh and Tyrone emerging once again. The integrity of their quarrel is one of the few institutions that

have been unaltered in the cataclysm which has swept the world. That says a lot for the persistency with which Irishmen on the one side or the other are able to pursue their controversies. It says a great deal for the power which Ireland has, both Nationalist and Orange, to lay her hands upon the vital strings of British life and politics and to hold, dominate and convulse, year after year, generation after generation, the politics of this powerful country.

There were grave misgivings in the House over the bill, which for so many Conservatives marked the surrender of principles they had fought for much of their political lives. At the behest of their leaders, they did their duty in the division lobbies and the bill got an overwhelming majority. But their anxieties were not allayed by the continuance of lawlessness.

The troubles of Ireland which for a hundred years had vexed First Secretaries now bore down upon the head of the Colonial Secretary. There were outrages on the border, vendettas in Belfast, reproaches from Sir James Craig, premier of Ulster, protests from Collins in Dublin. Winston's capacity for peacemaking was taxed to the uttermost. He sent message after message to the men in Dublin, counseling, advising, encouraging and restraining. They were in the frankest terms—not the communications of one minister to another, but the outspoken letters that pass between friends who are men of affairs.

As an example I choose at random a letter dated April 29, 1922, addressed to Michael Collins. It starts on a note of congratulation on the courage Collins and Griffith had shown in confronting enemies of free speech and fair play, and proceeds:

> Altogether I see many sober reasons for hope. This makes me wonder all the more why you adopt such a very harsh tone in dealing with Sir James Craig. I am sure he has made a very great effort to fulfil the agreement in the letter and in the spirit, and that he is continuously and will continue striving in that direction. Of course, no one expected that everything could be made right immediately or that the terrible passions which are loose in Ireland would not continue to produce their crop of outrages dishonouring to the island and its people, and naturally you have many grounds of complaint against him. He, too, has furnished me with a long set of counter-complaints, and the Protestants also have suffered heavily in the recent disturbances. Belfast goods of

very great value, running into millions, have been destroyed, debts owing to Belfast have been collected illegally and intercepted, and the boycott, I am assured, is more injurious in fact than ever before.

Instead of these rough communications, I should have thought that the Irish leaders, North and South, would have found it much better to meet together, to take stock of the position, to record what has been achieved, to mark what has fallen short in the working of the late agreement, and to decide on new steps to complete its execution.

As I have frequently pointed out, the interest of your opponents, North and South, Orange or Green . . . is to provoke the worst state of feeling between the two parts of Ireland; and they would cheerfully welcome every step and every event which led up to a definite civil war between the two Governments. Your opponents in the North hope to see a Republic in the South because it will bring about *inter alia* such a civil war, in which they know they will have the whole force of the British Empire behind them. Your opponents in the South hope to use antagonism against Ulster as a means of enabling them to snatch the power from the hands of the Provisional Government or else involve them in a series of events so tragical that they will break up under the strain. And on both sides the wreckers dread any approach to the idea of a united Ireland as the one fatal, final blow to their destructive schemes.

All this seems perfectly simple to me, and I think these people judge rightly according to their own tactical view. What I do not understand is why you should let yourself be drawn into the quarrel. I know Craig means to play fair and straight with you, and I do not think you will find such another man in the whole of the North; and it perplexes and baffles me when I see you taking up such a very strong, and even aggressive, attitude against him in your public utterances. Although perhaps you get some political advantage for the moment by standing up stiffly against the North, yet every farthing of that advantage is drawn and squandered from the treasure chest of Irish unity.

Griffith and Collins had one great handicap in dealing with the wild men. They had scarcely any armed forces of their own on whom they could confidently rely to suppress them. The provisional nature of things in Ireland was not limited to the Government. In April, Dublin's historic seat of justice, the Four Courts, was seized by a band of fanatics, who proclaimed themselves to be the Republican Government of all Ireland. The Provisional Government had perforce to leave them there for the time being. On the Ulster border two townships were seized by the Republicans, and M.P.s in London became aware of the wrongs of Pettigo and Belleek.

It was when Tory feelings were thus perturbed that an event occurred which brought home the realities of the Irish situation to Londoners, and threatened to wreck the recent settlement. On June 22, Field Marshal, Sir Henry Wilson, who had just completed his term of office as Chief of the Imperial General Staff, was shot dead on the steps of his house in Eaton Square. The assassins, two in number, were caught on the spot almost with their pistols smoking in their hands. They were Irishmen. Sir Henry was one of the most prominent living Ulstermen, and the horror of the crime was heightened by the fact that he had just returned from a war memorial unveiling ceremony. It was established that, though Irishmen, the assassins had not acted under orders from Republicans in Dublin. The crime was due to their own murderous initiative.

Parliament was in session. Conservative members were roused to a new pitch of misgiving over the treaty that was not bringing peace to Southern Ireland and that was fulfilling the predictions of men in the North. A debate was demanded.

Churchill rose to speak in a House charged with emotion. He had to convince the House that the reign of outrage would be ended by the government that had been established in Dublin. He had to warn the Free State Government and yet could not use language that would undermine such authority as that Government had contrived to gain. He said:

> I should not be dealing honestly and fully with this subject
> if I left in the minds of the House the impression that all that is
> required is patience and composure. No, sir. Firmness is needed
> in the interests of peace as much as patience. The constitution
> which has been published, satisfactorily conforms to the treaty.
> It has now to be passed through the new Irish Parliament. There
> is no room for the slightest diminution of the Imperial and Constitutional safeguards and stipulations which it contains.
> That is not all. Mere paper affirmations, however important,

unaccompanied by any effective effort to bring them into action, will not be sufficient. Mere denunciations of murder, however heartfelt, unaccompanied by the apprehension of a single murderer, cannot be accepted.

Hitherto we have been dealing with a Government weak because it had formed no contact with the people. Hitherto we have been anxious to do nothing to compromise the clear expression of Irish opinion. But now this Provisional Government is greatly strengthened. It is armed with the declared will of the Irish electorate. It is supported by an effective Parliamentary majority. It is its duty to give effect to the treaty in the letter and in the spirit, to give full effect to it, and to give full effect to it without delay.

A much stricter reckoning must rule henceforward. The ambiguous position of the so-called Irish Republican Army, intermingled as it is with the Free State troops, is an affront to the treaty. The presence in Dublin, in violent occupation of the Four Courts, of a band of men styling themselves the Headquarters of the Republican Executive, is a gross breach and defiance of the Treaty. From this nest of anarchy and treason, not only to the British Crown, but to Irish people, murderous outrages are stimulated and encouraged, not only in the Twenty-six Counties, not only in the territory of the Northern Government, but even, it seems most probable, here across the Channel in Great Britain. . . .

If either from weakness, from want of courage, or for some other even less creditable reasons, it is not brought to an end, and a very speedy end, then it is my duty to say, on behalf of His Majesty's Government, that we shall regard the treaty as having been formally violated, that we shall take no steps to carry out or to legalize its further stages, and that we shall resume full liberty of action in any direction that may seem proper and to any extent that may be necessary to safeguard the interests and rights that are entrusted to our care.

The measure of success Churchill achieved on that occasion may be judged from the comment that Bonar Law made to him in the lobby after the debate. Speaking with suppressed passion he said: "You have disarmed us today. If you act up to your words —well and good. If not——" The prospective consequences were left to the imagination.

Churchill had dealt with the political situation. It remained to Griffith and Collins to do their part in Dublin, where O'Connor and his men, sallying forth from their citadel, had kidnaped the Commander in Chief of the Free State Army, General O'Connell.

Collins mustered such forces as could be relied on. But he lacked the essential aid of artillery. So General Macready, the British Officer in command, received a request from the Irish authorities for the loan of a couple of 18-pounders. Macready referred the request to the Government, and the necessary sanction was given. There was only one gunner in the Irish loyalist ranks that day, and on him the fate of Ireland rested. Had the Four Courts not been reduced, and had English soldiery once again intervened in an Irish quarrel, there is no telling what the end might have been. But the fates had exhausted the malice of their sport with Erin. The gunner was spared to fire shot after shot against the walls of the Four Courts.

In the afternoon two more guns were requested and supplied; by evening all the ammunition was exhausted and General Macready did not deem it within the limits of his own safety to reduce his reserves of 10,000 shells by supplying the Irish loyalists with 200 rounds more. Happily the attackers had gained just enough advantage. After two days, in which men on both sides had displayed the bravery of Irishmen in a fight, the defenders surrendered. The parturition of the Irish Free State was almost over. Having begun the task of rounding up the wild men, Collins and Griffith did not pause in their work of making the authority of their government supreme in the land.

On July 7, Churchill sent Collins a message of congratulation and encouragement. It was his final appraisement of the progress that had been achieved:

I feel this has been a terrible ordeal for you and your colleagues, having regard to all that has happened in the past. But I believe that the action you have taken with so much resolution and coolness was indispensable if Ireland was to be saved from anarchy and the treaty from destruction. We had reached the end of our tether over here at the same time as you had in Ireland. I could not have sustained another debate in the House of Commons on the old lines without fatal consequences to the existing governing instrument in Britain, and with us the treaty would have fallen too. Now all is changed. Ireland will be mistress in her own house, and we over here are in a position to safeguard your Treaty rights and further your legitimate interests effectually.

The history of Eire and Ulster—and indeed the course of the unforeseen Battle of the Atlantic—might well have been different had Churchill for the Imperial Government and Collins and Griffith on the Irish side continued to guide affairs. But within a few weeks the workings of destiny had removed the two Irishmen from the scene.

The succeeding month of August had not run half its course when Griffith died of heart failure. Another ten days and Collins met a fate he had foreseen—a victim at last of the guns of the extremists. Another six weeks and the Coalition Government had fallen, and Churchill was relieved of his ministerial responsibilities. By then the infant state of Eire had passed the danger period. Churchill, in the political wilderness, could look back upon the results of his anxious hours of nursing and Michael Collins' verdict on his work: "Tell Winston we could never have done anything without him."

CHAPTER THREE

CHANAK AND CRISIS

1922

THE FIRST Coalition Government came into being because of
the Dardanelles crisis. The second Coalition went out of office
because of the Chanak crisis. In 1922 Chanak was a name that hit
the world's headlines. The place lies in the Straits opposite the
peninsula of Gallipoli. The Turks precipitated the Dardanelles
operations. It was the Turks again whose operations led to the
passing of the Lloyd George Government. In both of these crises
Winston Churchill played a leading part.

Long since the fame of Chanak had faded, fame gained in those
anxious hours when the fate of war with the Turks depended
upon the conduct of a slender force of British troops behind
Chanak's barbed-wire defenses.

The full story of the clash between Greeks and Turks and the
conflict between rival diplomacies, of the march of armies and the
intrigues of statesmen, does not belong to the life story of Winston
Churchill. He took part in events only in their final phase.

Peace had long been concluded in Europe before its blessings
were shared by the Turks. A peace treaty, the Treaty of Sèvres,
was signed in 1920, but its terms were repudiated by Mustapha
Kemal and his Nationalists, founders of the New Turkey. They
took to arms and the Allies, having by this time no troops at their

disposal, authorized the Greeks to apply against the Kemalists the force they could not bring to bear themselves. The Greek Army drove the Kemalists back into the fastnesses of Anatolia, to the last line of their defenses. It appeared that this, too, must fall and the cause of Turkish nationalism be lost. For fourteen days Mustapha Kemal fought at Sakkaria; his sorely tried forces won the day; Ankara was saved and the Nationalists survived.

Hostilities were suspended and armistice negotiations were begun. The Turks made it a condition that the Greeks should evacuate Asia Minor, and while the negotiations hung fire they began to liquidate the Greek population of western Anatolia. At this the Greeks, withdrawing a couple of divisions from Asia Minor to Thrace, threatened to occupy Constantinople. Against this the Allied Powers entered a caveat—the Greeks must not take the city of Constantine. This sealed the fate of the Greek Army in Asia Minor. Mustapha Kemal launched an attack and the Greeks, weakened by the withdrawal of the two divisions, were routed.

Winston Churchill had been no supporter of Lloyd George's fervid pro-Greek policy. He had protested against the continued bolstering up of the Greeks and hostility to the Turks as inimical to British interests as a ruler of Moslem peoples and an ally of France. But the spectacle of a Turkey, sole master of Asia Minor, threatening a new invasion of Europe was more than he could accept. What would be the consequences of a new Turkish inrush into Europe? The flames of Smyrna and the hideous massacres gave an indication of what might be the sequel. With the Turks in Thrace, the Balkans would be menaced. Was it to that end that the Allies fought the Turk in Gallipoli, in Palestine, in Salonika, and in Mesopotamia?

Only a slender force of Allied troops—French and Italian as well as British—occupying the neutral zone (a narrow strip along the Dardanelles) stood in the way of the Turkish armies. A few hundred troops at Chanak, and a few at Constantinople, that was all to halt Turkish soldiery in the full flush of victory.

The British Cabinet met in anxiety on September 15, 1922. What was to be done? If the Turks, seeking a way to cross the Straits, were to violate the neutral zone, were they to be resisted, seeing that resistance meant war? Lloyd George, supporter of the Greeks, favored resistance. Churchill found himself now wholeheartedly at one with him. Balfour was of the same mind, so were Austen Chamberlain, Birkenhead, and Laming Worthington-Evans.

"We made," Churchill wrote, "common cause. The Government might break up, and we might be relieved of our burden. The nation might not support us; they could find others to advise them. The Press might howl; the Allies might bolt. We intended to force the Turk to a negotiated peace before he set foot in Europe."

From Constantinople there came a warning from Lord Plumer, on a visit to Sir Charles Harington, the Allied Commander. On the spot Plumer telegraphed his opinion that the Kemalists intended to gain their way by threat of force if that sufficed, by force if force was unavoidable.

Churchill was instructed on behalf of the Government to send a warning telegram to the Dominions informing them of the critical situation and inviting their aid if force had to be met with force. "Are you willing," he telegraphed to the head of each dominion government, "to associate yourselves with our action and do you desire to be represented by a contingent?"

This summoning of the clans proceeded in decent privacy on the night of Friday the 15th. On Saturday, Ministers met again— a conspicuous absentee being Curzon, the Foreign Secretary, who had retired for the week-end to his country seat at Hackwood. It was decided that the urgency was so great that the country had best be informed of the critical nature of events and of the greater crisis that might have to be faced. At the request of the Prime Minister and his leading colleagues, Winston drew up a communiqué for publication:

> The approach of the Kemalist forces to Constantinople and the Dardanelles and the demands put forward by the Ankara Government . . . if assented to, involve nothing less than the loss of the whole results of the victory over Turkey in the late war. The channel of deep salt water that separates Europe from Asia and unites the Mediterranean and the Black Sea affects world interests, European interests, and British interests of the first order.
>
> The British Government regard the effective and permanent freedom of the Straits as a vital necessity for the sake of which

they are prepared to make exertions. They have learnt with great satisfaction that in this respect their views are shared by France and Italy, the other two Great Powers principally concerned.

The question of Constantinople stands somewhat differently. For more than two years it has been decided that the Turks should not be deprived of Constantinople and Ankara. Turkish Governments were informed of the intention of the Allies to restore Constantinople to the Turks, subject to other matters being satisfactorily adjusted.

The wish of the British Cabinet is that a Conference should be held as speedily as possible in any place generally acceptable to the other Powers involved, at which a resolute and sustained effort should be made to secure a stable peace with Turkey. But such a Conference cannot embark upon its labours, still less carry them through with the slightest prospect of success, while there is any question of the Kemalist forces attacking the neutral zones by which Constantinople, the Bosphorus, and the Dardanelles are now protected.

The British and French Governments have instructed their High Commissioners at Constantinople to notify Mustapha Kemal and the Ankara Government that these neutral zones established under the flags of the three Great Powers must be respected.

However, it would be futile and dangerous, in view of the excited mood and extravagant claims of the Kemalists, to trust simply to diplomatic action. Adequate force must be available to guard the freedom of the Straits and defend the deep-water line between Europe and Asia against a violent and hostile Turkish aggression. That the Allies should be driven out of Constantinople by the forces of Mustapha Kemal would be an event of the most disastrous character, producing, no doubt, far-reaching reactions throughout all Moslem countries, and not only through all Moslem countries, but through all the States defeated in the late war, who would be profoundly encouraged by the spectacle of the undreamed-of successes that have attended the efforts of the comparatively weak Turkish forces.

Moreover, the reappearance of the victorious Turk on the European shore would provoke a situation of the gravest character throughout the Balkans, and very likely lead to bloodshed on a large scale in regions already cruelly devastated. It is the duty of the Allies of the late war to prevent this great danger, and to secure the orderly and peaceful conditions in and around the

Straits which will allow a conference to conduct its deliberations with dignity and efficiency and so alone reach a permanent settlement.

His Majesty's Government are prepared to bear their part in this matter and to make every possible effort for a satisfactory solution. They have addressed themselves in this sense to the other Great Powers with whom they have been acting, and who jointly with them are associated in the defence of Constantinople and the neutral zones.

It is clear, however, that the other Ally Powers of the Balkan Peninsula are also deeply and vitally affected. Roumania was brought to her ruin in the Great War by the strangulation of the Straits. The union of Turkey and Bulgaria would be productive of deadly consequences to Serbia in particular and to Yugoslavia as a whole. The whole trade of the Danube flowing into the Black Sea is likewise subject to strangulation if the Straits are closed. The engagement of Greek interests in these issues is also self-evident.

His Majesty's Government are therefore addressing themselves to all these three Balkan Powers with a view to their taking a part in the effective defence of the neutral zones. His Majesty's Government have also communicated with the Dominions, placing them in possession of the facts and inviting them to be represented by contingents in the defence of interests for which they have already made enormous sacrifices and of soil which is hallowed by immortal memories of the Anzacs.

It is the intention of His Majesty's Government to reinforce immediately, and if necessary to a considerable extent, the troops at the disposal of Sir Charles Harington, the Allied Commander-in-Chief at Constantinople, and orders have also been given to the British Fleet in the Mediterranean to oppose by every means any infraction of the neutral zones by the Turks or any attempt by them to cross the European shore.

The consequences of that communiqué were considerable. It was read by the people at home that September Sunday and raised fears of a recurrence of 1914. It was read by Curzon in his retreat at Hackwood and aroused his outraged mind to a high pitch of indignation. It was read by Poincaré, the French Premier in Paris, and prompted him to send a telegram withdrawing the French contingent from the neutral zone; Poincaré was not going to embroil France in war to save the face of the Allies. It was read in the Dominions and caused the maximum disquiet in official circles, for its publication preceded the decoding of the warning to premiers dispatched almost twenty-four hours earlier.

It was also read by Mustapha Kemal in Asia Minor—and Mustapha Kemel was struck as Lord Curzon was struck at Hackwood by the bellicosity of the language employed. Curzon was indignant; Mustapha Kemal was impressed. He ordered his troops away from Chanak. It might have been bellicose, but it was a success. Churchill's bellicosity was supported by General Harington's diplomacy. The Allies were able to extricate themselves from the Turkish imbroglio without loss of face even if honor did not shine too brightly.

Churchill could claim a large share of the credit for keeping the Turk out of Europe. Let Harold Nicolson, the diplomatist who left the Foreign Office to become author and Member of Parliament, testify on this point, one on which he pronounced with his customary deftness in his memoir of Curzon: [1]

"It is sad for any admirer of Lord Curzon to have to admit that he himself can claim no share in this reckless and triumphant gesture. To Mr. Lloyd George and above all to Mr. Churchill is due our gratitude for having at this juncture defied not the whole world merely, but the full hysterical force of British public opinion."

Lloyd George and Churchill kept the Turk from Europe, but there were no bouquets at the final curtain. The bellicose communiqué might deter Mustapha Kemal in Asia Minor but it also alarmed the Conservatives at home and infuriated Liberal and Socialist opinion. Bonar Law's declaration that Britain could not act alone as world policeman was the keynote of a popular outcry which was raised in Britain and was echoed in the Dominions, loyally though their governments had pledged themselves in response to the appeal. Churchill bore the brunt of the attack for attempting, as the critics alleged, to "dragoon the Empire into war." Even Lloyd George was not so furiously assailed as his Colonial Secretary.

The Conservatives were alarmed. Uneasiness had been increasing at the Lloyd George methods of government. The Irish settlement had been a grievous burden to bear. Chanak was the final straw.

CHAPTER FOUR

THE COALITION FALLS

1922

I N BRITISH POLITICAL HISTORY, World War I is the great divide
which, like the Atlantic, separates the old world from the new.
The spacious days of the past, so comfortable in retrospect, when
Tory Government succeeded Liberal, and Liberal gave place to
Tory, ended with 1914.

The new force of socialism, (or Labour *) so disturbing to the
timorous, so menacing to the idle rich, had begun to manifest itself while the century was young. After the war the Labour Party
took second place in the state. In the first postwar election in 1918
the Liberals were relegated to third place. They have contrived to
preserve the existence of their historic party, but the slow process
of attrition has reduced the numbers of their representatives at
Westminster, though Liberalism exerts an influence far greater
than is proportionate to its Parliamentary forces.

In this simplification of politics and progression from a three-
party back toward the traditional two-party alignment, Winston
Churchill played a leading part. This involved him in a second
transfer of his political allegiance, thereby giving a new handle
to his critics.

---

* I plead guilty to the common inaccuracy that makes the two terms—Labour
and Socialist—indescriminately applicable to the principal party of the Left. Neither
name is accurate as a description. Many besides those belonging to the party
are guilty of labor and by no means are all of the faithful socialists.

With a vision picturing in black and white without gradations of greys, his vision of post-war politics was of the simple opposition of socialism and antisocialism. Looking on socialism as only a shade less detestable than the virulence of Bolshevism, he conceived it the duty of all antisocialists to unite to face the peril from the Left.

During the closing months of the Lloyd George Ministry, he worked for the promotion of a Centre Party, under which the existence of the Coalition would have been perpetuated. Two of the most able Tory ministers supported him—Lord Birkenhead and Austen Chamberlain, leader of the Conservative Party. Conservative members, in the majority, did not feel inspired by the idea of a Centre Party. The Conservative Party, so far as they were concerned, was the most effective organization for the combat of socialism, and they began to yearn for the delights of the party game. The Conservative Central Office (party headquarters) campaigned against the continuance of the Coalition in any form.

By 1922 there was not much magic left in the name of Coalition. Even the fame of Lloyd George, the "man who won the war," was beginning to burn dim. Men who had gloried in the brilliance of his leadership were now questioning the unavowed opportunism and unorthodoxy of his methods. A formidable indictment was made against the Coalition ministers. They talked of economy, it was said, and spent money like water; they pretended to support industry and piled on taxation; they dallied with Bolshevism and supported campaigns against it; they coquetted with Germany and played fast and loose with France. "As a result of their inconsistencies," *The Times* acidly observed, "the word of England lost currency throughout the greater part of the world as the word of an upright land."

The Chanak crisis brought the Conservative mutineers against the Coalition into open revolt. Bonar Law, the former leader who was highly respected by his party, precipitated events by a letter to *The Times,* protesting that Britain should not alone assume the burden of action in resistance to the Turks. "We cannot," he wrote, "act as policemen of the world." The letter was published on October 7, and such was its effect on Conservative opinion, already exacerbated, that on October 12 Austen Chamberlain found it necessary to summon a meeting of Conservative ministers to discuss the situation, and then to convene a full meeting of Tory M.P.s and peers to be held at the Carlton Club on October 19. The fate of the Coalition Government and the course of politics between the wars was to be determined.

The intervening seven days were a period of activity for Tadpole and Taper. Either the Coalition was to continue as a Centre Party against Socialism, or the Conservatives were to throw off their allegiance and a reversion to party politics would ensue. It was an anxious week for Winston Churchill. He was the advocate of the Centre Party but as a Liberal was barred from attendance at the meeting. Nothing could be more vexatious to the spirit of a man of action than to have to await the determination of his fate by a jury before whom he was not permitted to plead. What was possible to rally his colleagues to the cause he did. The leading Tory ministers met at his house to dine. Lloyd George was also at the party. Loyalty to the Coalition was pledged. Curzon, who was one of the guests, in common with his colleagues, agreed that the Coalition should appeal to the electors for a further lease of life.

A second dinner party was arranged to be held at Churchill's house, but the guests assembled without George Nathaniel Curzon. In the interval "George wobbled" as the wits said, handed in his resignation, and allied himself with the Anti-Coalition group. George Nathaniel, Lord Curzon, was an imperiously minded man. He had served in the exalted position of Viceroy of India. In the coalition government, he was nominally Foreign Minister, but Lloyd George conducted his own foreign policy. At this crisis Curzon revolted. No longer would he tolerate the "garden suburb," that rival secretariat, housed in huts in the garden of 10 Downing Street, which the Prime Minister employed in preference to the Foreign Office, its minister and staff, for his personal incursions into the field of diplomacy and international affairs.

Curzon's defection was a blow for the Centre Party group. But when the Carlton Club meeting was held it was Stanley Baldwin, President of the Board of Trade, who delivered one of the two decisive speeches. His description of Lloyd George as a dynamic force has its place in history—"a dynamic force is a terrible thing; it may crush you, but it is not necessarily right." Bonar Law pronounced the final sentence that "the Coalition must end." Austen

Chamberlain and his fellow Coalitionists argued in vain. The Carlton Club meeting decided by 187 votes to 87 to withdraw from the Coalition.

It was the end of Lloyd George's premiership and the end of Churchill's schemes for a Centre Party. Bonar Law, the hand of death already upon him, formed a government without the cooperation of the leading members of the party—a government of "second-class brains," in Birkenhead's phrase. A general election immediately followed.

Despite the Carlton Club verdict, it was as a Centre Party man in spirit, though not in name, that Churchill for the fifth time invited the suffrages of the electors of Dundee.

"I stand," he assured them in his address, "as a Liberal and Free Trader, but I make it quite clear that I am not going to desert Mr. Lloyd George or the high-minded Conservatives who have stood by him.

The principles of Liberalism were now menaced by two opposite dangers. On the one hand were the unprogressive Conservatives, and Churchill portrayed Bonar Law's ministry as being super-reactionary. "It is a Government which stands on far too narrow a basis to be capable of securing political stability. Four out of the five great Secretaryships of State are held by members of the House of Lords. Out of 37 ministers, 19 are peers or sons or brothers of peers. The diehard elements are very strongly represented.

"But if the character and composition of the Government reminds us of the days of King George III rather than of King George V, the policy that has been announced by the new Prime Minister carries us back to the Middle Ages." He stigmatized Bonar Law's policy as one of negation—a do-nothing policy, saying that over the portals of 10 Downing Street the Premier had inscribed Dante's phrase: "All hope abandon ye who enter here."

"I will never stifle myself in such a moral and intellectual sepulcher." It was folly to suppose that socialism, communism and other revolutionary doctrines could be corrected by a do-nothing policy.

He drew no distinction between Socialists and Communists, who formed the second menace to liberalism. "Mr. Gallacher," he declared, "is only Mr. Morel [one of the Socialist leaders of the day] with the courage of his convictions and Trotsky is only Mr.

Gallacher [the Communist leader] with the power to murder those whom he cannot convince."

Menaced on the one side by stagnation and on the other by revolution, where was the elector to turn for salvation? "We have," Churchill assured him, "a national conception as opposed to the rule of any class. We have the principles of liberalism and the great mass of the Liberal Party. We have very large numbers of moderate-minded Conservatives. We have distinguished statesmen like Lord Balfour, Mr. Austen Chamberlain, Lord Birkenhead and Sir Robert Horne, resolved to pursue the middle course of wisdom and safety."

Churchill would have developed his thesis of the "middle course for wisdom and safety" in a series of masterly speeches had he been able to pursue the campaign, but three days before the contest opened, his health, which hitherto had supported him magnificently, suddenly failed. He had to undergo an operation for appendicitis and was kept out of the fight until two days before the poll. Mrs. Churchill with loyal friends conducted his campaign on his behalf.

On the eve of polling day he faced a meeting of the electors in Dundee Drill Hall. They were evidently hostile and it was equally apparent that their hostility was pronounced. From the looks of passionate hatred he received he concluded that it was only his helpless condition that prevented them from attacking him. His opening remarks were the signal for the Scottish heckler to exercise his prerogative, and heckling gave place to continuous interruption and uproar. "You are beaten," "You'll be at the bottom," were the only articulate sounds to rise above the increasing volume of discordant noise. The candidate, a sick man, had no chance of making himself heard a few feet beyond the edge of the platform. A seething crowd took possession of the building, chanted the dreary refrain of the "Red Flag" and gave a conclusive demonstration of their dislike of free speech. The power of massed lungs triumphed. The meeting was abandoned.

When the declaration took place, Churchill was not placed among the elect. His majority of 15,000 at the Victory Election was transformed into a deficit of over ten thousand. Dundee returned at the top of the poll a prohibition candidate, Mr. Scrymgeour, who at last gained the reward of persistency. Five times before he had stood for Dundee: five times before he had been beaten by decisive majorities. At his first attempt he gained the support of fewer than 400 voters; now he claimed over 32,000.

So Churchill found himself, as he said, "without an office, without a seat, without a party, and without an appendix." At least he had the saving grace of humor. He could reproach fate for having brought so sorry a conclusion to a year which had been the most successful in his ministerial career, marked by his work on the delicate problems of Iraq, Palestine and Ireland. There was one consolation—defeat set him free to nurse himself back to strength. He left for the South to recuperate in the milder climate of Italy and Spain. Political affairs could wait until the spring. He solaced himself with the pleasure of painting.

CHAPTER FIVE

IN THE WILDERNESS

1923

Winston Churchill did not sit in the Bonar Law Parliament. Before he again stood before the electors, death had terminated Bonar Law's brief premiership. Stanley Baldwin had succeeded to the inheritance, a man less known to the country at his accession than any Prime Minister for a hundred years—a fact that added to the bitterness of soul that afflicted his rival, Lord Curzon, at losing the prize he thought was to have been his. "A man of no experience," faltered Curzon between his tears, "and of the utmost insignificance." Curzon had confidently expected the premiership. He suffered an agony of mortification.

Mr. Baldwin—the simpler title seems more fitting to the man than the later dignity of the earldom—began his premiership by seeking to appoint the Free-Trader, Reginald McKenna, as Chancellor of the Exchequer. In this he was not successful. A few weeks later he dissolved Parliament to seek from the country a mandate to embark upon a policy of protection and imperial preference.

An election fought on free trade was a boon to the Liberals. Baldwin had repeated the service to the disunited Liberal Party that Joseph Chamberlain had performed a quarter of a century earlier. The rival wings of the party, Asquithians and Lloyd Georgites, could coalesce, leaving the Prime Minister with the consolation of having achieved what was beyond any other person's competence. "I never thought," he quaintly admitted, "there was a sufficiently large bed to hold Mr. Asquith and Mr. Lloyd George, but they have climbed into the same one and I think we will wait to see which kicks the other out."

For the moment Lloyd George and Asquith made up their differences and Churchill, too, acknowledged his old leader. Churchill had the choice of a number of constituencies. He decided to accept the invitation to stand for West Leicester, where his opponent was a socialist-pacifist, Pethick-Lawrence (who, with a peerage, was to take office with the Socialists in 1945, as Secretary for India). Leicester electors not long before had inflicted ignominious defeat on the Labour Party leader, Ramsay MacDonald, who throughout the war had been steadfast to the cause of pacifism.

Churchill's first public appearance after the announcement of the election was in the traditional Liberal citadel of Free Trade Hall, Manchester. Here (November 16, 1923) he denounced the futile and inglorious Parliament that was terminating its brief existence by the attempted assassination of free trade. He passed on to probe the mystery of Stanley Baldwin's conversion to the faith in tariffs.

> Mr. Baldwin, [he said] is a very honest man; he tells us so himself [laughter] and I for one am quite ready to believe him. It is a fine thing to be honest, but it is also very important for a Prime Minister to be right.
>
> I am forced to ask: when did Mr. Baldwin reach this extraordinary conclusion that the free import of foreign goods into the home market is the cause of existing unemployment? It was certainly not in his mind a year ago at the General Election when, as Mr. Bonar Law's principal lieutenant, he appealed for five years' tranquillity and supported Mr. Bonar Law in saying that a disturbance of our fiscal system would be the cause of more loss than gain.
>
> It was certainly not his opinion when he became Prime Minister, for his first act was to send for Mr. McKenna and ask this eminent Free Trade financial authority to be his right-hand man as Chancellor of the Exchequer. All through the summer he was beseeching Mr. McKenna to come to his aid. Right down to the month of August he was still urging Mr. McKenna to join him. He was appealing to him just as earnestly—and just as honestly—

as he has appealed to those protectionist and imperial defence politicians, Lord Birkenhead and Mr. Austen Chamberlain, to join him to-day.

Obviously it must have been a very important event, something so compulsive and urgent that made him feel it his duty as an honest man [laughter] to jeopardize his Prime Ministership, to destroy the Parliament, newly elected, which had acclaimed him, to plunge this unfortunate country into the sterile waste and turmoil of a most unpopular election.

We have evidently witnessed a sudden mystic process of almost miraculous conversion. You will remember how Paul was going down to Damascus when he saw a light shining on the way. And you will also remember the case of Balaam's ass [laughter] who saw something in his path not visible to the mundane eye [laughter]. What was this revelation?

Churchill was looking forward to smiting his opponents hip and thigh on a battleground so familiar as the tariff issue provided. He reckoned without his Socialist opponents. They shared his opposition to tariffs. They fought him with the weapon of personal prejudice. The uproar at Dundee Drill Hall twelve months before had been much publicized. Followers of Trotsky might not have the power in this country to "murder those they cannot convince," but they could still shout down the man they could not defeat in an argument.

Throughout the election Churchill was the victim of an organized campaign of rowdyism. The methods of Dundee were imitated and improved upon. Meeting after meeting ended in scenes of disorder. Winston was frequently in danger of personal assault. In one strongly Socialist area a police escort had to be provided for him, and it was thought advisable to warn Mrs. Churchill not to speak at the same place.

Politics were largely left out of this Socialist campaign. His opponents played on personal prejudice existing in the uninformed popular mind against his part in Antwerp and Gallipoli. A curious time-lag in opinion facilitated these tactics. During the war, when the Conservatives in the House were campaigning against him, popular opinion was unaffected. When Churchill went to France, men of the forces who recognized him greeted him with cheers. Now, eight years later, the old slanders were rehashed to inflame the electors.

Churchill would rise to speak about the evils of tariffs and the voice of the heckler would be heard: "What about the Dardanelles?" He would refer to the benefits of free trade and the familiarly raucous voice would shout: "What about Antwerp?" As days and nights passed, and the taunts were continued, he was forced to answer the detractors.

"I have heard," he said, "there is a campaign of defamation going on in the highways and byways and in holes and corners, destined to prejudice the electors against me on account of the Dardanelles. In the whole of the findings of the report of the Royal Commission there is not one word of detraction of what I did. . . . The Dardanelles might have saved millions of lives. Don't imagine I run away from the Dardanelles; I glory in it."

From Sir Ian Hamilton, Churchill received a personal message of triumphant vindication on the Dardanelles. The pity was that it should have been necessary. The silence of Asquith eight years before was still exacting its penalty. From Asquith he received a message of support declaring: "Upon your success depends in no small degree the fate of the fallacious protectionist proposals." A message on the Dardanelles would have been more to the point at that juncture, but the Asquithian silence was preserved.

There was no resisting the tide of obloquy. After the mockery of a democratic contest, West Leicester rejected him by 13,000 votes to 9,000.

There was small consolation for any of the party leaders on the results of the 1923 election. Baldwin lost the majority Bonar Law had won, Conservative representation being reduced from 347 to 255 seats. Asquith and the reunited Liberals, 158 strong, still ranked as third party in the House. MacDonald and the Socialists claimed 191 seats and had to face the dubious prospect of forming a government without a voting majority to back it—office without power.

Only one thing emerged clearly from the poll—free trade was saved. But whether Conservatives, Socialists or Liberals were to rule was no longer in the hands of the electors. Any two parties in combination could outvote the third. Asquith and the Liberals were numerically the weakest but they held the balance of power. In a speech of characteristically Asquithian phrasing, the Liberal leader pronounced for Ramsay MacDonald. He would install the

Socialists on the Treasury bench. Labour for the first time was to rule—but only so far as the Liberals would permit.

Asquith's decision brought Churchill and the Liberals to the parting of the ways. Since the break-up of the Coalition, Churchill had developed his simplification of the political issues. On the one hand he saw socialism and revolution, on the other the anti-Socialist forces that alone could save the country from anarchy. His constant aim had been to unite the anti-Socialists under the progressive banner of a middle party. Now the Liberals were leagued with the forces of revolution. This was not his conception of what the Liberal policy should be. He took up his pen to make an emphatic protest. He was almost the only considerable figure in politics who could offer a detached judgment on Asquith's decision. The Liberals were committed by it, the Socialists were exalted and the Conservatives reduced. Churchill was in no way involved. On January 17, 1924, a letter above his signature appeared in the public press. Asquith had by then pronounced against the Conservatives, but the death sentence had not been carried out.

> The currents of party warfare [Churchill wrote] are carrying us all into dangerous waters. The enthronement in office of a Socialist Government will be a serious national misfortune such as has usually befallen great states only on the morrow of defeat in war. It will delay the return of prosperity, it will open a period of increasing political confusion and disturbance, it will place both the Liberal and Labour parties in a thoroughly false position.
>
> The Liberal party will be led into supporting Socialists whom they have just been fighting in hundreds of constituencies throughout the country, and who will still be attacking them and undermining them in those constituencies with ceaseless activity.
>
> The Socialist party will be called upon to conduct and administer the business of this immense community without the reality of power which springs from the will of the majority, or the sense of responsibility which arises from the reality of power. They will be invited to cure the distresses of the time on the express condition that they use none of the remedies which they have advocated and in which they believe, and under the threat that if they have recourse to these remedies they will be immediately dismissed.

They will be invited to continue in office on sufferance in order
that if they are violent they may be defeated and if they are
moderate they may be divided. And this is called giving Labour
a fair chance to govern. It is no fair chance to Labour; it is no
fair chance to Britain. It is only a fair chance to faction and
manœuvre. . . . Strife and tumults, deepening and darkening, will
be the only consequence of minority Socialist rule.

The letter went on to make suggestions by which the calamity
Churchill foresaw might be averted. It produced no immediate
effect. The newspapers which a few mornings later recorded the
death of Lenin, also announced the advent of the first Labour
Government to office.

Churchill decided that he could no longer continue to support
the Liberal cause, now tarnished by association with Socialism.
For him as anti-Socialist, the only course was co-operation with
the Conservatives, the party whose resistance to Socialism could
alone be effective. He looked for an opportunity to invite the
verdict of the electors. The chance was not long delayed.

In February a vacancy occurred in the Abbey Division of Westminster caused by the death of the member, Brigadier General
Nicholson. Feelers were put out to the Conservative Party leaders
and it appeared that Winston would become the official party
candidate, but when the matter had almost been arranged, the
local association complicated the situation by adopting a candidate—Captain O. W. Nicholson, nephew of the late member.
Baldwin had favored Churchill's candidature, but had perforce to
support the choice of the local party.

It was an embarrassing position for Churchill. If he stood he
would have to oppose the official nominee of the party to which
he was offering his allegiance. Many prominent Conservatives,
however, urged him to proceed and he resolved to stand inde-
pendently as a Constitutionalist.

Churchill was now to become the target of political brickbats
for having deserted both Conservatives and Liberals. Inconsistency is a convenient stick with which to beat the political dog.
And when high office followed his second change of party, he was
accused of sacrificing his principles to gain position, or charged
with being a careerist without having a principle to sacrifice.
Read the speeches he made at the time and you will find that he

left the Liberals to rejoin the Conservatives under the pressure of strong convictions. In his speech announcing his decision to stand for the Abbey Division he said:

> My candidature is in no way hostile to the Conservative party or its leaders. On the contrary I recognize that that party must now become the main rallying ground for the opponents of the Socialist party. In the King's Speech of the late Government the Conservative leaders announced a broad progressive policy in social matters and have made declarations which in their main outline might well have served as the King's Speech of a Liberal Government.
>
> Only a week ago Mr. Baldwin made it clear that he accepted the verdict of the electors on the question of a general tariff and he appealed in consequence for Liberal support. Indeed anyone can see that a large measure of Liberal support must be won by the Conservatives if there is to be an effective resistance in the big struggle that is coming and coming soon.
>
> It is only by co-operation on independent and honest lines that a foundation can be built strong enough to sustain a stable and efficient Government in these critical times, and rescue us from the increasing confusion of a three-party system and minority rule. I am sure that in the coming contest throughout the country, however many differences of opinion there may be, or however many schools of political thought there may be, there will be only two sides.

As to the immediate campaign, he submitted that a great constituency such as the Abbey Division ought to have a strong view of its own on the grave issues of politics and should exert a proper influence in national affairs.

> If I thought that the present Conservative candidate really represented the force of character of the constituency I should not have come forward as a candidate. An important public principle is involved. The days of family preserves and pocket boroughs ought not to be revived. It is not right that the Westminster Abbey division should be passed on from hand to hand as if it were a piece of furniture—handed on from father to son, or from uncle to nephew.

A statement had appeared that he had declined to join the Conservative Party. On this he observed:

I do not think it would be right of me to make a change like that for the purpose of securing an easy entry into Parliament. I have lived the last twenty years of my life in a certain political position, opposed both to protection and to Socialism. Almost every election I have fought has been on these two points and if I am able to co-operate cordially with the Conservative Party at this juncture it is not because I have changed my position. It is because they have very wisely and rightly returned or are in process of returning to a broad and progressive platform.

I can unsay nothing that I have said in praise of Liberalism as a great and modifying influence on public affairs.

Coalition was killed at the Carlton Club. The idea of a Centre Party grounded around Liberalism perished with the decision of the Liberal leaders to put the Socialists into power. There remains only a united and intact Conservative Party in co-operation with a Liberal Wing. Such a Liberal Wing would modify Conservative policy in proportion to its members and strength and would afford the nation the guarantee that it requires against retrogression. Thus and thus alone will a line be formed strong enough and broad enough to resist the oncoming attack of the Socialist party with its old heresies and new prestige.

Of all the elections in his parliamentary career, Churchill found his greatest enjoyment in the fight for the Abbey Division. He had a new cause to fight for. He was leading the first campaign of the Rest versus Socialism. There was no Centre Party but he was giving an indication to the country of how the Centre Party would have fought. He was the Centre Party personified. You can savor the zest he felt in his speeches. The old Churchill was brought to life anew. There was no repetition of the hackneyed catchwords against free trade, but a vigorously proclaimed new gospel.

"Westminster," he declared, "has it in its power to send to our Dominions beyond the seas, to our friends and allies an important message. It will be a message that a new current has begun to flow—that party squabbles will not obstruct the reassertion of the national consciousness of Britain and that the British people to whom the whole world looks for example and guidance is not going to slide and slither weakly and hopelessly into Socialist confusion.

The Socialists had begun their administration in the mildest-mannered fashion, but Churchill warned the electors not to be deceived. "How well," he said, "the Socialist Government is doing. How moderate, how gentle they are. How patriotic Mr. Thomas's speeches. How lofty Mr. MacDonald's views of his functions. How pious is Mr. Henderson. How prudent is Mr. Snowden, how careful of the State. I say there is no correspondence between this glossy surface and the turbulent currents that are flowing beneath. These leaders can never restrain their followers."

Ultimately these same Socialists would make a tremendous bid to secure an absolute majority and unfettered power. "They can place before the electorate a program of bribes and doles the making good of which would ruin the credit of the state, but which would not have to be paid for till after it has been voted on."

Churchill started out with the initial handicap that he had no organization. He had to face three opponents, nominees of the parties, who had the advantage of long-established, efficient organizations. He had, however, the benefit to be gained from the London press—support from the major part and publicity from all of it, and publicity in an election campaign is almost as valuable as support. He had the backing, too, of an enthusiastic band of workers, and the aid of a number of Conservative M.P.s. Ladies of Mayfair canvassed on his behalf; the chorus girls of Daly's, the famous theater opened by an American in the nineties, sat up all night to send out his election address.

One thing was lacking—a message endorsing his candidature from one of the leaders of Conservatism. His old friend, Arthur Balfour, now the eldest statesman in the party, and a member of the upper house with the title of earl, agreed to write a message of recommendation. He made it a condition that before publication Baldwin's consent, as leader of the party, should be obtained. The Conservative leader did not consider himself free to give his consent seeing that he had to recommend Captain Nicholson to the electorate. He did, however, permit himself to agree to publication of this Balfour note if any other Conservative leader were to intervene on behalf of Captain Nicholson.

The Conservative leaders were disobligingly reticent. None was moved to enter the lists as champion of the Captain. Polling day drew near and the Balfour note was unpublished. Then, when it appeared that the message was to remain undisclosed, a letter was discovered in a newspaper in which Leo Amery gave it as his opinion that the Conservative cause would be strengthened if the Abbey electors returned Captain Nicholson. There was some uncertainty whether Mr. Amery came within the requirements of the Baldwin proviso—a leader of the party. Still, he was a member of the Shadow Cabinet, and Conservatives hurried off to take Baldwin's opinion. They need not have been in doubt. Their leader, although it was then only breakfast time, had already released the Balfour note. It was broadcast throughout the constituency and had an immediate influence on the electors, securing for Churchill the support of progressive Tories and permitting his old coalition associates, Austen Chamberlain and Lord Birkenhead to range themselves with him.

Balfour, in his note, wrote as a private individual "untrammelled by administrative rules which when dealing with party organization every party leader must unswervingly follow." It was a neatly phrased suggestion that but for the rules, Baldwin might also have written expressing the personal hopes and wishes to which Balfour gave expression:

> These are inevitably and I think rightly influenced by my strong desire to see you once more in the House of Commons, once more able to use your brilliant gifts in the public discussion of the vital problems with which the country is evidently confronted. On these you and many others who are associated with you think as we do. And where matters of great moment are in debate those who think alike should act together. Your absence from the House of Commons at such a time is to be deplored and since I believe that your convictions on fundamental questions, whether Imperial or social, are shared by the majority of the electors in the Abbey Division, your return for that historic seat would be warmly welcomed by men of moderate opinion throughout the country and by no one more than yours sincerely —BALFOUR.

Polling day found Churchill confident of victory. The count was close and as the last packet of votes was carried to the table someone said: "You're in by a hundred." This news was actually telegraphed around the world, to be followed within a few moments by a correction. Churchill was beaten by the narrow margin of 43 votes in a poll of 22,000. The figures were:

Captain Nicholson (Conservative) 8,187
Rt. Hon. Winston S. Churchill (Constitutionalist) . . . 8,144
Fenner Brockway (Socialist) 6,156
Scott Duckers (Liberal) 291

There was general regret that Churchill had not won the day. This feeling was aptly expressed by the *Daily Telegraph,* the same journal that twenty years before had gloated over his reverse at Manchester. Now the newspaper found it regrettable that Winston was out.

"We had hoped," the *Daily Telegraph* observed, "Winston Churchill would win because he was incomparably the best man in the field, because his presence was badly required in the House of Commons where his debating force and volcanic energy would be of the greatest value to the principal opposition." Disappointed in this, the leader, in passing, turned a few acid phrases at the expense of the Asquithians whose poll was "derisory." The Liberal vote had in the main been split between the Socialist and the anti-Socialist; what was left was the mere drainings of Liberalism.

Churchill was defeated but he had staged a magnificent comeback. Fortune, relenting, had begun to smile once again. Churchill could feel gratified that his conception of the union of anti-Socialist forces had received an endorsement.

A few months passed and, before the year had run its course, Parliament had been dissolved and another general election was in progress—the third within two years. Churchill was engaged upon his fourth campaign in a similar period and on this occasion he stood for a rural constituency, the West Essex, or Epping, division.

The Red Letter Election of 1924 was caused by the withdrawal of Liberal support from the MacDonald administration. The Liberals had tired of the role of "patient oxen" (in the Lloyd George phrase) pulling the Socialist car. Baldwin's dry assurance that he did not envy his neighbor's ox expressed the oxen's own feelings. So, when the decent pretext of a trade agreement with Russia, coupled with a £30,000,000 credit from the British government, offered itself, the Liberals announced the withdrawal of their support.

Ramsay MacDonald appealed to the country to free himself from the necessity for aid from the Asquithians. Churchill's prediction had come true sooner than he had himself imagined. Labour sought unfettered power. Labour's opponents fought the campaign on the lines Churchill had followed in the Abbey Division. The celebrated Red Letter facilitated their task.

To this day it has never been established whether Zinoviev, head of the Bolshevik Third International, wrote or did not write the letter attributed to his authorship calling on the British Communist Party to organize armed revolt in England. It was issued as a genuine document by MacDonald's own department of the Foreign Office—and forgery or no forgery, he could not escape from its consequences.

There is no need to dwell on Churchill's campaign at Epping. He restated the case he had set before the electors of Westminster. He was commended to West Essex by Lord Birkenhead as "the greatest House of Commons man now living." Austen Chamberlain in a message of good wishes added the recommendation: "Your return as Constitutionalist candidate will be the first step in the decisive movement of public opinion. The old quarrels of Liberal and Conservative belong to the past."

Churchill won Epping in a canter, 6,000 votes ahead of the combined poll of his Liberal and Socialist opponents. The Conservatives were returned to power with the massive majority of 211 over all parties. The Liberals were almost extinguished, winning a paltry forty seats—a sorry reward for the patient oxen. Asquith himself went down at Paisley to a Socialist.

When Stanley Baldwin announced the composition of his second administration the name of Winston Churchill was found to be included. This had been predicted by the press. But the office he received was that of Chancellor of the Exchequer—and that was anything but in accordance with expectation. The appointment was declared to be a courageous one for the Prime Minister to have made, not because of any doubt over Churchill's adequacy for the post, but because it was notorious that he was not equally acceptable to all sections of the Conservative Party.

The general surprise was indicated by the story that went the rounds of the interview between the Premier and Winston Churchill. Summoned to receive the offer of a ministerial post, Churchill heard the words—so at least it was related: "I can offer you the job of Chancellor," to which he innocently inquired, "Of the Duchy?" "No," Baldwin was made to say, "of the Exchequer."

Churchill's comeback had been magnificently achieved. He had returned to the Tory fold to receive the highest honor. The Chancellor of the Exchequer by custom is regarded as the prospective successor to the Premier. It is a post that could never have been his had Bonar Law still been alive. Under Bonar Law's leadership there would have been no future for Churchill in the Conservative Party.

CHAPTER SIX

CHANCELLOR OF THE EXCHEQUER

1924–1929

THE RETURN of the political wanderer to the Tory fold was the
topic of the hour. The public was startled, the Conservative
Party dumbfounded. For twenty years the name of Churchill, the
man who had ratted on them, had been anathema to the faithful
rank and file. But now the prodigal was back in triumph. He had
deserted them for the flesh-pots of Liberalism. It was satisfactory
to know that he had seen the error of his ways. But was there need
to reward him with one of the choicest bones in the Prime Minister's cupboard.

There was much speculation over the motive that lay behind
his appointment. It was the result of one of the more shrewd of
Stanley Baldwin's calculations. He saw the chief danger to his
premiership to lie in a new partnership between the coalition allies, Churchill and Lloyd George. In the public eye these old
campaigners were the outstanding figures of the day. United they
would be formidable in force. It would be worth the price of a
seat in the Cabinet to detach Churchill from his old allegiance
and so the offer was made. Churchill's acceptance was a permanent bar to the renewal of the old partnership.

In the light of after-knowledge there is something incongruous
in the close association of Winston Churchill and Stanley Baldwin. In the thirties they were antagonists over rearmament. At the

bar of history, Baldwin was to stand arraigned by Churchill for his failure to prepare the country against the challenge of Hitler. In the twenties these developments were hidden. Men were concerned to recover from the last war, not to prepare for the next. Nevertheless, there was no easy association between the two men.

Churchill had to get on terms and, after a year's effort, he persuaded himself that he had advanced towards an understanding— "We know each other better than we did and I have been happy under your leadership." It was the expression of an aspiration rather than the record of an accomplished fact. Churchill was less in accord with Baldwin than with any of the four Prime Ministers in whose Cabinets he served. In character and outlook there were differences that made the great divide between the man of action and the contemplative idealist, a visionary of sensitive understanding. Baldwin was said to be "all antennae and little more." It was a critic's judgment, but it conveyed something of the truth.

Baldwin had an acute awareness of the state of the public mind. By experience drawn from his early years in the family manufacturing business, he knew what the working man was thinking. He came to the premiership with two deep-seated purposes—the first was to restore the decencies of English public life after the debasements of the Lloyd George coalition. The second was to heal the rifts in the nation and check the progress of the class war.

The twenties were years of transition. There was a changed order in society. The Liberals were passing as a parliamentary force. The Labour Party had arrived. The Mother of Parliaments, that wondrously adaptable matron, had absorbed Labour's representatives as other firebrands of the Left had been absorbed down the years. But, there was the extra-Parliamentary force of organised labor. The vast potential of Trades Union strength was so far uncommitted. How was it to be applied? This was the question mark of the twenties—anxious, disturbing. In Russia the force of the proletariat had been exploited for the overthrow of Czarism and the setting up of the new Communism (Bolshevism in the twenties) with all the excesses of the French Revolution. Was Britain to be sent the way of Russia? Would London, Birmingham and Glasgow furnish British Soviets? Would the Mother of Parliaments be replaced by a dictatorship of the proletariat?

Prime Minister and Chancellor of the Exchequer were alike

concerned by the question mark. They differed in their appreciation of the prospects.

Churchill, inclined by nature to see the sharp contrasts of black and white, took the apprehensive view. The spirit of unrest was abroad. Europe was surging with ideas born of the Russian Revolution. Lloyd George, noting the signs, had pronounced that there was in Britain a deep sense of revolt against the conditions of life and work that prevailed up to 1914. Churchill concurred.

The cries of the class war were not to be ignored. The Trades Unions began to toy with the dangerous notions of direct action—the employment of their strength and the weapon of the general strike, as a means of imposing their will. There were hotheads on either side. Reactionary Tories were ready for a show-down, eager to put the workers back in their place, their old place of subjection.

It was then that Stanley Baldwin rendered his service to the State. He imposed his tranquillizing influence over the forces of unrest. In the House of Commons he made his emotionally charged appeal for good will in industry, with its passionate close, "Give peace in our time, Oh Lord!" It was the spirit of his premiership. It smothered the class war.

Churchill made no such contribution to the needs of the time. No one ever mistook him for a tranquillizing influence. He was out of tune with the twenties, out of sympathy with Baldwinism. His qualities were not those needed in the twenties. His challenging leadership, giving a sharper turn to differences, could have added to the dangers of class war. Before 1914, under Lloyd George's influence, he had taken a hand in social reforms, but, divorced from his old partner, his sympathies with Labour waned. He did not know the working man as Baldwin, or Lloyd George, knew him, from the close contact of everyday life. He shared the anxieties of those who looked with alarm at the designs of the wild men of the Trades Unions with their talk of direct action. He looked at Russia, at the Bolsheviks with their tyranny and their bloody crimes against humanity. Alarmed by the fear that the states of Europe might follow Russia into the abyss, he found cause to praise Mussolini and the Italian Fascists—"the necessary antidote to the Russian poison." *

* *The Times* of London, January 21, 1927.

These matters were put to the test when the Trades Unions staged their General Strike in 1926. To the observer abroad it seemed that Britain was poised for Revolution. It was the turning point of the twenties. As a provoker of this strike Winston Churchill received criticism beyond his deserts, but in the widest sense it may be said that the strike was the consequence of his handling of the nation's finances. His was an uneasy Chancellorship. He was involved in a continuing struggle against the economic consequences of his own policy at the Exchequer.

His first considerable measure was to restore Britain to the gold standard at the pre-war value of the pound sterling. Thereby he determined the course of his chancellorship—and much besides. It was as if he wound up a financial and economic clockwork machine, capable of producing effects throughout the whole fabric of the nation's existence. Once set in motion it went on ticking out its consequences. The man who had wound it could do nothing but seek to alleviate the worst effects.

Five years in the toils of the gold standard—it was a hard fate even if it was of his own choosing. But why did he choose it? He chose it because it was predetermined for him. The City of London expected it; the Treasury experts recommended it; his predecessor in office, the Socialist Philip Snowden, had paved the way for it. There was no escape except by challenging financial orthodoxy—and for a Conservative Chancellor that would have been greater heresy than for a bishop to repudiate the Thirty-nine Articles of the Church of England.

The question of the gold standard which faced Churchill in 1925 was almost the greatest financial problem left over from World War I. Because of the war Britain had gone off gold. The value of the pound had fallen so that it was worth only 90 per cent of its value in 1914 (about $4.90). The enactment which put Britain off gold set a limit to the term of the relaxation of the gold standard, and in 1925 * that term had nearly run out. Britain had either to go back on gold again at the prewar parity or let the world know that the pound sterling was to be allowed to sink to a lower value.

Britain's prosperity is based upon two main planks—her credit and her export trade. London in pre-1914 days was the recognized

* In 1925 the pound was worth about $4.80. It was devalued to $2.80 in 1949.

financial center of the world—a pre-eminence founded upon her credit. To the financial center of the City of London it was essential that nothing should be done to undermine the credit on which that pre-eminence had been built. There must be no playing about with the gold standard. To maintain British credit the old-time value of the pound must be restored.

For exporters the problem was not so simple. Even with the pound sterling at its lower level they were having difficulty in selling their goods in markets where competition was fierce and where they were being undercut by manufacturers in other countries. If the pound worth 18 shillings were suddenly to become worth 20 shillings, their difficulties would be intensified; for the customer abroad would have to pay 20 shillings for the goods that had been costing him 18 shillings. In trades where competition was fiercest, the British exporter would be able to continue his sales only by reducing his price, and the corollary of this would be that his production costs would have to be reduced by that amount. Of the costs of production the principal are the wages paid to labor. It follows that for the export trades, return to the gold standard on the old parity of exchange inevitably involved the reduction of wages.

Eventually, when all the consequential adjustments had taken place, labor would be no worse off; their wages would be lower, but their money would buy more. But until the new equilibrium had been reached, there would be industrial dislocation, labor disputes, strikes, and not a little suffering.

Were the benefits of returning to the old gold standard value of the pound sterling so great as to outweigh the consequences that must follow? This was the problem that faced Churchill on becoming Chancellor. He took the advice of the Treasury Committee on Currency, and their advice was unequivocal. Their report marshaled the arguments which convinced him as Chancellor and convinced his colleagues in the Government.

Looking back, now, we may dissent from the reports of the experts. The parity to which the pound was restored in 1925 had to be abandoned in six years' time under the pressure of the world economic blizzard. Labor and industry, reflecting the strains and stresses and hardships of the six years between, might well be disposed to question—like Sam Weller's charity boy reaching the end of the alphabet—whether it was worth while to go through so much to gain so little. In retrospect it is easy enough to say it was ill-advised, but Winston's contemporaries were scarcely in a position to claim the luxury of criticizing him.

Financial experts and economists (with the notable exception of Professor Keynes) supported the decision. Among those who gave it their endorsement was Philip Snowden. Snowden, indeed, did move the Opposition amendment of criticism, declaring that while the decision was sound, the actual moment was inopportune, but that was no more than the discharge of the Opposition's duty to oppose.

Professor Keynes was clear-sighted enough to warn the Chancellor of the effects of his policy. He had made his reputation with the book *The Economic Consequences of the Peace,* and he now published a criticism of the gold policy under the title of *The Economic Consequences of Mr. Churchill.* It was an exposure, and the author poured scorn on the report of the Treasury experts—"vague and jejune meditations" was the phrase he applied to their arguments. In a passage scintillating in its simplicity he set out what, in his view, they should have told the Chancellor.

The first to experience the consequences of the return to the old gold-standard parity of the pound was the mining industry. Things were difficult enough for the coal-exporter beforehand, but afterward coal could not be sold abroad unless prices were cut, and the coal owner saw no way of reducing prices but by lowering wages.

The miners said, "We strike if you do," and, what is more, they said, "If we strike, all our friends in other jobs, like the railwaymen and the transport people, they will strike, too." To put off the evil day of a strike all round, the Government gave the coal owners a subsidy to enable them to go on paying the old wage rates, and while the subsidy kept things going a long inquiry was held. This merely left the matter where it was before. The mine owners said it showed they could not pay and the miners said it proved the need for nationalization of the industry.

So the strike had to be, and the cynics said that it at least would prove who would starve first, the masters or the men.

Organized labor downed its tools. The railways stopped, the docks stopped, the buses stopped. Volunteers ran the country.

Newspaper workers joined the strikers and this gave Churchill his chance.

It was Churchill and the printers who set the events in motion. Indeed, Churchill was afterward to be charged with applying the match to the powder and causing the explosion of the strike, but that was an exaggeration.

It was the evening of the first Sunday in the month of May, the year, of course, being 1926. The strike was still in the balance. Strike notices had gone out. The government was ready for the emergency. Hyde Park was to be a military camp and milk depot. Troops were about in Whitehall. While the nervous-minded braced themselves for calamity, last minute peace moves were proceeding in Downing Street. The Trades Union leaders were at Number 10 closeted with the Cabinet negotiators, the Prime Minister and Lord Birkenhead. They were striving for a formula that would save the industrial peace and save the faces of the uneasy Trade Unionists, anxious to avoid striking.

For long enough the talks had gone on. It was past eleven in the evening. Next door, at 11 Downing Street, the Chancellor of the Exchequer's house, the rest of the Cabinet awaited the outcome of the talks. There was some impatience in the air, some Ministers holding that the limit had been reached and that the time had come to teach the Labour hotheads a lesson. Neville Chamberlain, for one, was set against any concessions for a compromise. Churchill, a man rarely known to "walk about with an oil can in his hand," was prepared for the worst eventualities.

The negotiators joined their fellow ministers. They reported that a formula has been found satisfactory to the Trades Unionists. If the miners accepted it, all would be well and the strike called off. At this point the telephone rang. A fateful message was received, its terms imparted to Churchill. He placed them before the Prime Minister and his colleagues: a situation developed at the offices of the *Daily Mail*. The compositors declined to set the type of the lead editorial headed "For King and Country."

At Churchill's report, opinion among the ministers hardened. Already, it seemed, the printers were resorting to direct action, endangering the freedom of the press. It turned the scale. Instead of negotiations being resumed, the Labour leaders were given an ultimatum. The Cabinet members departed, the Prime Minister went to bed. The lights went out in Downing Street. The printers had begun the General Strike.

Among the many consequences of the strike, the least expected was that it installed Churchill in the editorial chair of an improvised national newspaper—*The British Gazette.*

With their printing staffs on strike, the London daily papers were reduced to a shadow of their normal selves. They carried on, but their issues were slight affairs, news sheets not newspapers, turned out by small-scale jobbing printers in the London suburbs. To meet the emergency a government newspaper was established and the Prime Minister appointed Churchill to run it.

He turned editor with relish. His chair was pitched just off the Strand, in the building of the old *Morning Post,* where production and printing proceeded for the term of the *Gazette*'s seven issues. The editor made his bow in a lead editorial in which the vigor of Churchill's phrasing is clear to mark.

A few words are needed to explain the appearance of *The British Gazette* . . .

Nearly all the newspapers have been silenced by violent concerted action. And this great nation, on the whole the strongest community which civilisation can show, is for the moment reduced in this respect to the level of African natives dependent only on the rumours which are carried from place to place. In a few days, if this were allowed to continue, rumours would poison the air, raise panics and disorders, inflame fears and passions together, and carry us all to depths which no sane man of any party or class would care even to contemplate.

The government have therefore decided not only to use broadcasting for spreading information, but to bring out a newspaper of their own on a sufficient scale to carry full and timely news throughout all parts of the country.

The British Gazette is run without profit on the authority and if necessary at the expense of the government. It begins necessarily on a small scale and the first issue cannot exceed 700,000 copies. It is proposed, however, to use the unlimited resources of the state, with the assistance of all loyal persons, to raise the circulation day after day, until it provides sure and sufficient means of information and a guide for action for all British citizens.*

* *The British Gazette,* May 5, 1926.

In the matter of circulation the *Gazette* fulfilled its editor's hopes. The first day's issue at 232,000 copies fell far short of the promised 700,000, but a week later the figure had risen to 1,801,-400. The paper gave a salutary lesson to those who are concerned with the British press and its freedom. Under the direction of editor Churchill it emerged not as a newspaper but as a propaganda sheet. No self-respecting Fleet Street editor would have permitted his news columns to be so perverted no matter how strong his opinions, or how extravagant the language he might employ to express his editorial opinions in his editorials.

Even during the stress of the emergency, protest was made against the "poisoning" of public opinion and the departure from the standards of truthfulness and impartiality of a daily newspaper. Geoffrey Dawson, as editor of *The Times,* was able to make a direct protest to the Prime Minister at the manner in which the *Gazette* was being mishandled. At Baldwin's suggestion, Dawson wrote a memorandum on the subject for submission to the Cabinet, but this produced no effect. Appointed editors (as Dawson's own career suggested) are not easy to control when they decide to take their own line.

In the House of Commons, Churchill was attacked for his distortions. Lloyd George added his voice to the criticisms of the Socialists, complaining that the *Gazette* suppressed news that was not to the editor's liking. Churchill was impenitent. His aim was to beat the strike and he was not over-squeamish about the means. Views not news might have been his motto. The *Gazette* remains as a monument and a warning against the enormities of a state-controlled Press.

Even more galling to the hard-pressed regulars of Fleet Street were Churchill's ways with newsprint. He was a pirate, highhanded and unscrupulous. Newsprint, that essential commodity for newspaper production, was in desperately short supply. To maintain the *Gazette,* he commandeered what he required. Dawson, striving to keep *The Times* going, had to fight to maintain his paper's existence. Despite his resistance a quarter of the available paper stocks had to be yielded up by *The Times.*

Protests against these "wild commandeering raids" were made to the Cabinet, but before action was joined the General Strike had ended, and the editor of *The British Gazette* had resigned his editorial chair, to forget the episode amid the pressure of Exchequer affairs. There were memories in Fleet Street. In the thirties references in *The Times* to Churchill suggested an imperfect sympathy on the part of the newspaper. Geoffrey Dawson was to work closely with Neville Chamberlain and it may be that his influence contributed to Churchill's exclusion from office in the years immediately before the war.

Churchill could find cause for satisfaction in his editorship. So, too, did the Prime Minister, although for different reasons.

"The cleverest thing I ever did," Baldwin once said, "was when I put Winston in a corner and told him to edit *The British Gazette.*" *

His attention engaged by his newspaper, Churchill had the less time to intervene in the Cabinet to press for the strong measures that he favored. Baldwin was not incisive enough for the liking of a man of action, but when the strike was over, Baldwin's policy was rewarded.

The Trades Unionists had put direct action to the test. It had failed. Thereafter the Trades Unions were content to take their place in the constitutional order of British society.

After weeks of bitterness, the miners were starved out.

The stoppage in the pits was one of the longest and most disastrous in the unhappy annals of British labor disputes. It involved vast losses while the pits were idle, and even when work was restarted the tale was not ended, for many consumers abroad who had gone for their supplies elsewhere did not renew their orders to British collieries.

Churchill's difficulties at the Treasury were rendered the more difficult by this dislocation of industry. The restoration of trade, particular of trade abroad, and the reduction of unemployment were the main problems of the day. The return to the gold standard had handicapped all exports; they must not be burdened with additional taxation. In considering Churchill's administra-

---

* In the days that followed Churchill's political opponents took the *British Gazette* rather more seriously than he did. Some time after its disappearance, on an occasion quite unconnected with the General Strike, feelings were running high in the House. Churchill was rebuking the Opposition amidst angry interruptions, when his manner suddenly became ominously threatening. The Government would not flinch. Let the Opposition take care or extreme measures would be used. "We will give you—yes, we will give you another—*British Gazette!*" Tension relaxed amid laughter.

tion as Chancellor the problem that beset him must be borne in mind: how to find the money for various social schemes without calling on the taxpayer to pay more. His expedients were many and ingenious. They enabled him to solve the problems, but by their combined effect they gave him the appearance of being a Chancellor of brilliant improvisations rather than of sound and solid finance.

Occupying the office which his father had resigned in an attempt to stem the ever mounting tide of state spending, Churchill was in a position to raise the tattered flag of economy. But the world had moved on since Lord Randolph quit office. The war had revolutionized financial values. In 1885 the Chancellor had been able to run the country by demanding £73,000,000 from the taxpayers. In 1925 he had need to take £683,000,000.

It was not easy in 1925 to enforce economy. There were speeches enough advocating it, lip service to an ideal, but at the stage pious hopes should be translated into administrative action it was found that the odium to be borne by the economizer was an effectual deterrent to action. By 1931 another £50,000,000 had been added to the taxpayer's annual burden, and it required the urgency of the world financial crisis to put into practice the painful policy of economy.

In his first budget speech, Churchill expressed regret that time had been too short to permit the comprehensive review of expenditure required to produce economies, but he permitted himself the forecast that £10,000,000 a year might be saved. He promised that a searching inquiry should be made into all branches of public spending by a Cabinet committee. The results were seen in an economy bill presented in 1926. Out of a total expenditure of roughly £600,000,000, a saving of less than £10,000,000 was to be made. And when the second Churchillian budget was introduced, it was found that an actual increase in taxation of £9,000,000 was involved. The Chancellor was faced with an expenditure which was "not only undiminished but seems to be undiminishable."

With the 1926 Economy Bill, Churchill gave up pursuit of the unattainable. The best he could do was to maintain expenditure at roughly the same level. Even this he was able to do only by resorting to a variety of expedients and the gathering of financial windfalls.

As a speaker Churchill added to his reputation during his period at the Treasury. The sobering influence of finance did not dim his wit but it added a deeper note of responsibility and authority. Oratorically his first budget was a brilliant success. Sir Robert Horne, former Tory Chancellor, in epigrammatic phrase, assured him that he had demonstrated that figures need not be dull and that a Budget need not be drab. Snowden allowed that Churchill's rhetorical achievement must have given high satisfaction to Lord Randolph, "if the spirits of former occupants of the Treasury bench still hover round the scene of their earthly conflicts."

Churchill's wit garnished his budget speeches, and his clashes with Snowden enlivened the debates. The encounters between the financial rivals were the best parliamentary duels of their time. Snowden would excel himself in acerbity. The Chancellor would find a devastating phrase as retort.

"Twelve months ago," said Snowden in 1926, "I described the Budget as a rich man's budget. Today I describe this budget as the budget of a profligate and a bankrupt."

"Parliamentary Billingsgate," Churchill retorted.

Snowden, assuming a tone of superiority, affected to look down on these rhetorical duels, but in truth the reputation they gained pleased him well enough. His satisfaction emerged from behind the mask of superiority he assumed in his reference to them in his autobiography:

> It would be tiresome if I were to deal at length with the innumerable encounters between Mr. Churchill and myself in the Budget debates of this year and of succeeding years. As an Ex-Chancellor it fell to me to lead the Opposition in the Budget debates, and I found Mr. Churchill a foeman worthy of my steel. The debates between us became quite a Parliamentary entertainment. They were regarded as the best show in London. When it was expected that we should both be speaking, the public galleries were invariably crowded. After a time I ceased to take very much interest in these duels, but I was expected to play the Parliamentary game of opposition and to provide entertainment for my supporters.

Mr. Churchill, during these years, gradually developed as a Parliamentary debater. He learnt to rely less on careful preparation of his speeches and more upon spontaneous effort. However much one may differ from Mr. Churchill, one is compelled to like him for his finer qualities. There is an attractiveness in everything he does. His high spirits are irrepressible. It was said of a French monarch that no one ever lost a kingdom with so much gaiety. Mr. Churchill was as happy facing a Budget deficit as in distributing a surplus. He is an adventurer, a soldier of fortune. An escapade has an irresistible fascination for him.

Five successive budgets were opened by Churchill. There is not much profit in recalling details of the melancholy achievements of the tax-extortioner-in-chief in bygone years, but the highlights of the Churchillian statements are still entertaining in retrospect.

First Budget (April 28, 1925)—Apart from the decision to return to the Gold Standard, the principal announcement was the institution of pensions for widows. Relief was granted to super-tax payers, and the income tax rate was reduced from 22½ per cent to 20 per cent. Snowden called it the rich man's budget, but Sir Alfred Mond, as a rich man, thought it was robbing Peter to pay Paul; for though income tax was reduced by £20,000,000 to stimulate industry, £14,000,000 was taken back in contributions to pensions. Under the Safeguarding of Industries Act, a silk duty was imposed and a duty on lace.

Second Budget (April 26, 1926)—Introduced under the shadow of the miners' strike and the impending General Strike, it contained no major announcements. The most controversial measures were the decisions to devote £7,000,000 from the revenue motorists contributed to the Road Fund to the purpose of general taxation (raiding the Road Fund) and the institution of a betting tax of 5 per cent on every stake on a race track or through a credit bookmaker. The latter provision was one of the most unpopular ever introduced by a Chancellor and resulted in the unexpected spectacle of a strike of bookmakers. The public bore this with the fortitude to be expected in a country inured to stoppages by the greater calamities of the miners' strike and the General Strike. Curiously enough, religious sentiment was for once ranged on the side of the bookmaker, not out of sympathy but as Snowden, expressing what he believed to be the sacred feelings of a vast number of people, explained—because the vice of betting was thereby accorded a respectability and prestige it did not possess. What a sight for the gods the Chancellor presented falling "between the angels who disapproved of betting and the devils who got their living from it."

Third Budget (April 11, 1927)—The Chancellor thought himself fortunate, following the financial havoc brought by the General Strike and the miners' strike, to be able to report that the revenue, though mauled and wounded, had survived the "shocking breakdown in our island civilization." No major fiscal changes were announced, and the Chancellor gave a dexterous exhibition of meeting a prospective deficit of £35,000,000 by a variety of ingenious expedients which avoided the imposition of new taxation. A further raid on the Road Fund to the tune of £12,000,000 was the chief. Wines, motor tires and tobacco were called upon to help the Chancellor bridge the "formidable precipice" of his prospective deficit.

Fourth Budget (April 24, 1928)—The Chancellor allowed himself to survey the financial position in a spirit of restrained optimism—the future finance of the country was "freer of difficulty and stringency" than in any of his preceding budgets. Only minor changes were announced—a new duty on British wines, a duty on mechanical lighters (to protect the revenue from matches) were the chief of the proposals that were estimated to make a difference of only £200,000 a year to Exchequer receipts. The principal announcement was that the rating system of the country was to be reformed. The object was to readjust rating burdens as between productive industries—which were unjustly burdened—and the distributing trades—which escaped their just dues. Relief was to be given by reducing the rates on all premises used for production and on freight-carrying railways, docks and canals. Agricultural land would be freed of the last remaining 25 per cent liability for rates. Local authorities were to receive government aid under a new system of block grants. Exposition of this vast de-rating scheme involved the Chancellor in a speech of three and one-half hours, and he was allowed the courtesy of a break of half an hour. The speech was admitted by Snowden to be a Parliamentary triumph, and it received the cordial congratulations of Lloyd George. The bill carrying out the de-rating plans was piloted through the House by Neville Chamberlain, Minister of Health.

Fifth Budget and last (April 15, 1929)—It was opened on the eve of the general election to the imminence of which it was unashamedly correlated. The changes were very slight—repeal of the betting duty which had been nullified by evasions, and the remission of the duty on tea, an impost which had furnished a subject for protests for a couple of centuries. In place of the betting tax, a licence duty of £10 on bookmakers was proposed, but the bookies escaped, for the Socialists came into office, and Snowden was financially too virtuous to seem to be taxing vice. The Chancellor wound up with a survey of his administration at the Treasury. Since he had taken office, he claimed, savings by the smallest class of investor had increased; employment in the insured trades had gone up; the cost of living index had decreased by eighteen points while money wages had remained almost exactly at the level of 1924; there had been a notable decline in the consumption of alcoholic liquor and a progressive diminution of drunkenness; the consumption of working-class indulgences, motor bicycles, excursions and popular amusements, had shown a general increase; and, further, the consumption of tea and sugar had reached record figures. Finally, the balance of trade had sensibly improved; foreign investment, new capital issues for home investment, and bankers' deposits had all made steady growth since 1924.

He dwelt on the "rewards" of the returning to the gold standard, in making inflation impossible; in regaining for Britain her position as the greatest international market; and in its effects on the world-wide operation of credit and commerce, on which nearly one-quarter of the British population depended, and for which the stability of sterling was essential. Not the least of the attractions of this policy had been the decline in the cost of living which it had brought about and which he calculated as equivalent to a remission of indirect taxation of £160,000,000 a year by increasing the purchasing power of consumers.

There was one last passage of arms between the Chancellor and his Socialist critic chief. During a discussion of the war debt settlement with Italy, Snowden disowned the Balfour Note. This statement had governed Britain's policy on war debts and reparations in accordance with the pledge that no more would be demanded by Britain from debtors more than was sufficient to pay what was due from Britain to the United States.

In words spoken on the spur of the moment Snowden somewhat injudiciously declared: "We [Socialists] have never subscribed to the principle of the Balfour Note. I think that was an infamous note." The Socialists would hold themselves open, if circumstances arose, to repudiate the conditions of that note.

Churchill, seeing political possibilities in this threat in view of the imminence of the election, at once challenged Snowden on his statement. It was important, he declared, because the note embodied the principle on which British agreements with France and Italy had recently been reached.

The matter was brought before the Cabinet the following morning and in the afternoon a Government statement was read to the House. It declared that Snowden's threat was a wanton and reckless act, capable, if it were credited abroad, of doing the utmost injury to British interests. Ramsay MacDonald, as Socialist leader, was invited to state whether he endorsed the Snowden declaration and whether it constituted the official policy of the party. After an unrepentant Snowden had reiterated his threat, Churchill again attacked him.

MacDonald could not avoid a statement, and his embarrassment was evident. He was placed in the dilemma of repudiating Snowden, or the debt settlements. His statement was a model of Parliamentary evasiveness; amidst the welter of words, his meaning was, as he intended, as obscure as a mist on his native heaths of Scotland.

Churchill pressed him for an explicit declaration, submitting categorical questions for his reply. MacDonald refused to be drawn. With a scornful gesture the Chancellor leaned across the table and exclaimed: "I commend to the attention of the country the fact that the Leader of the Labour Party and the ex-Prime Minister of the country is incapable of answering plain and simple questions. He sits there and does not open his mouth."

There the incident ended for MacDonald did not unseal his lips. It was exciting while it lasted and Churchill exploited the situation to its utmost. But it must be confessed that this Snowden indiscretion was unproductive of any political consequences.

In the election that followed, the Conservatives chose to fight under the unattractive catchwords of tranquility and safety first. The electors did not respond, and when the next House of Commons met, the Socialists were installed on the Treasury bench and the member for Epping sat in opposition.

Despite his satisfaction so intensely felt to take up his father's old post, Churchill's five years at the Exchequer were the least successful of his career as Minister of the Crown. Finance was his weakest point. Lord Randolph had inquired with exaggerated ignorance as to the meaning of the "damned decimal dots." Winston was a class or two ahead of his father, but he was not given the qualities of an economist. In the twenties there was need for a bold and imaginative financial policy. Insufficiently informed, himself, Churchill had, for once, to submit to the views of the experts. He followed the course of financial orthodoxy, which was to end in the catastrophe of the economic crisis in 1931.

CHAPTER SEVEN

OUT OF STEP

1929–1931

WINSTON CHURCHILL'S term at the Exchequer caused him to lose ground in the political race. With his leader and his party he lost favor. Tories demanding tariffs to keep out the imports flooding in from abroad, regarded his chancellorship as a disaster. The raising of the value of the pound had not merely handicapped British exporters. It had given a price advantage to foreign manufacturers whose cheaper priced goods were putting British factories and British artisans out of work. The protectionists fretted and fumed against the dead hand of Churchill the free trader.

Nor was Stanley Baldwin encouraged by the experience of five years of Churchill's drive. There was one acceptable result—the Lloyd George-Churchill partnership had been for ever broken. But otherwise Baldwin had rueful memories. A Cabinet meeting, when Churchill was present, could not proceed with the appointed agenda for invariably the Chancellor had a clever memorandum for consideration on the work of some department other than his own.

The Chancellor of the Exchequer is considered to be the Prime Minister's right hand man, and political heir apparent. Churchill was certainly not so regarded when the Tories left office in 1929.

Indeed, the word got round that he had fallen so far in his leader's estimation, that were Baldwin again to form a Ministry there would be no place in it for the ex-Chancellor. The whisperings of the malicious are never long in going their rounds. Anticipating the pendant sword, Churchill himself made the break. While the Socialist Government still continued, he parted company with Baldwin. It kept him out of office for the ten years following and, under the workings of a beneficent providence, it spared him from contaminating association with appeasement. It was the decisive step towards his own premiership. India was the immediate cause of his break with the party.

On the face of things it appeared that he was seizing upon the India reforms as the means for attacking Baldwin and wresting the party leadership. There was the precedent of Disraeli's campaign against Peel over the Corn Laws a century before. Appearances suggested that Churchill was leading a factional fight for which place and not principle was the motive force. One could not but compare his tactics with those of Dizzy,* to Churchill's disadvantage. Churchill could not strike as effectively as Dizzy struck, could not aim such shafts as were discharged by that master of flouts and jeers. There were things, it appeared, to which Winston would not stoop in order to conquer.

As the campaign against the India Bill came to be viewed in perspective, the conception of Churchill as leader of a faction fight was no longer tenable. His differences with the Conservatives on India were seen as the beginning of his revolt against the spirit of surrender that marked ministries and people in the thirties.

Baldwin's mild liberalism and Ramsay MacDonald's pacifism reflected the prevailing national mood. Churchill's revolt was against the lack of decisiveness in the conduct of affairs. He pilloried MacDonald as the "boneless wonder of his age," and it was against the general bonelessness of the age that he revolted.

Members who were privileged to be present long remembered the speech in which Churchill taunted Ramsay for his bonelessness. It was one of the brightest of the quips and gibes with which he enlivened the dreariness of debate.

* Nickname for Benjamin Disraeli, first Earl of Beaconsfield, Prime Minister (1867-68, 1874-80).

When Churchill, the parliamentary impresario, introduced the "boneless wonder," the piece on the political stage was known by the unlively title of the "Trade Disputes and Trade Unions (Amendment) Bill." At that date—January 28, 1931—Ramsay and his Socialist Government were in office, maintained by the votes of Lloyd George and the Liberals. The Amendment Bill had been introduced to remove some of the restrictions imposed on trade unions after the 1926 general strike.

It was a delicate matter for the Liberals. If they opposed the bill they would turn the Socialists from office; if they supported it they would seem to be condoning oppressive trade union practices. After much searching of heart they decided on equivocal support. MacDonald stated that committee consideration of the measure would not be taken on the floor of the House but in the greater seclusion of the committee room upstairs.

Churchill denounced this procedure as a Parliamentary disgrace, and he passed on to reproach Lloyd George and the Liberals for not safeguarding Parliamentary procedure and the means by which discussion in public should be assured for questions arousing public feeling:

> Mr. Lloyd George told us the other day on a question of the same kind, on another measure, what were his doctrines on procedure. They were very remarkable. They were expressed with his usual candour. It all depends on these questions of procedure whether you like the Bill or not.
>
> If you like the Bill—I am not quoting him any more—then, of course, away with Parliamentary forms and cumbersome debate, slap it through by the quickest and most expeditious method possible. If you do not like it, then out will come all the constitutional arguments about the rights of Parliament and the interests of minorities of which the Liberal Party have always been the champions. Then will be the time for the peroration about 'the cause for which Hampden died on the field and Sidney on the scaffold.' These are the ethics of Parliamentary procedure as expounded by the leader of the Liberal Party.
>
> I must ask a further question. How do you decide whether you like it or not? No one can deny that Mr. Lloyd George and the Party which he leads take infinite pains in coming to a decision whether they like or whether they dislike any particular measure. Although we are not permitted to take part in these

discussions, the House has resounded with the echoes of their conclaves and perturbations. Once they have decided to like a Bill that is the end of Parliamentary procedure so far as the minority in the House of Commons is concerned.

But in this case the Liberal Party and their leader seemed to have very great difficulty in deciding whether they liked or disliked the Bill, so they came to a compromise by agreeing, so far as I can make it out, not to dislike it too much here, but to hate it like poison hereafter. Mr. Birkett [a Liberal M.P., later a High Court judge] was deputed to explain what was to be done to the Bill. The execution is to be in private and it is to be ruthless. After I had listened to his account, which is fresh in the minds of those who have followed these debates, I could not see that anything was left of the Bill except possibly the Title. That is what they have decided on.

What are the Government, and the Labour Party, going to do about it? What is the Prime Minister going to do about it?

I spoke the other day, after he had been defeated in an important division, about his wonderful skill in falling without hurting himself. He falls, but up he comes again, smiling, a little dishevelled but still smiling. But this is a juncture, a situation which will try to the very fullest the particular arts in which he excels.

I remember when I was a child being taken to the celebrated Barnum's Circus which contained an exhibition of freaks and monstrosities, but the exhibit on the programme which I most desired to see was the one described as "The Boneless Wonder." My parents judged that the spectacle would be too revolting and demoralizing for my youthful eyes, and I have waited 50 years to see the Boneless Wonder sitting on the Treasury Bench.

We have made our protest against the Bill. We have made our protest also against the procedure for which the Liberal Party bear a keen responsibility, but it seems to me that the real grievance lies with the Trade Unions. They seem to me, after all has been said and done, the parties who are being deceived in this matter.

I was not invited to the Conference which took place last week in Downing Street between the Prime Minister and the leader of the Liberal Party, but my Hon. Friend the member for Treorchy gave me a shrewd account of the interview between the two party leaders.

After the usual compliments, the Prime Minister said, "We

have never been colleagues, we have never been friends—not what you would call holiday friends, but we have both been Prime Ministers and dog don't eat dog. Just look at the monstrous bill the Trade Unions and our wild fellows have foisted on me. Do me a favour and I will never forget it. Take it upstairs and cut its dirty throat."

It is not to be imagined that Ramsay MacDonald would have welcomed Churchill as a Cabinet colleague.

It was a couple of days after the "Boneless Wonder" speech that Churchill disclosed that differences had developed between himself and Baldwin over India and that, as a consequence, he was withdrawing from the Conservative Shadow Cabinet. The split was most amicably arranged. Churchill wrote to his leader regretting that sincere and inevitable differences had developed; expressing the hope that the friendship of the previous six years would not be impaired thereby, and conveying the assurance that he would on all other matters continue to cooperate with the party in the defeat of the Socialists. His leader, equally regretting the divergence, did not consider that there was anything in a difference of opinion "on a single policy, however important," to prevent close and loyal cooperation in future. "Our friendship," he added, "is now too deeply rooted to be affected by differences of opinion whether temporary or permanent."

Churchill had embarked on a long campaign. He came to assume the leadership of the right-wing or Diehard group of the party, and the persistence of his challenge to Baldwin's leadership must have placed a severe strain on their friendship. It was the anti-Brodrick campaign of twenty-five years before repeated and intensified, but this time he fought in vain.

A volume the size of this book would not suffice to record all the speeches he made. Many were devoted to technical points which require for their appreciation detailed examination of the processes of the long-drawn-out procedure over the India reforms. There is an illuminating example here, of the business of Empire administration and constitution-making, but it scarcely comes within the scope of this biography.

Churchill's main position can be briefly stated. He was not opposed to the extension of the participation of Indians in their own government. His opposition was to the sudden step of dominion status and federal government. He protested against surrendering India to Gandhi, the agitator who combined a capacity for leadership, a sense of religious devotion and a political shrewdness of a high order. From the address he delivered to a demonstration at the Albert Hall on March 18, 1931, I make the following extracts, to convey the main burden of an argument that was developed in a score of speeches:

> What spectacle could be more sorrowful than that of this powerful country casting away with both hands, and up till now almost by general acquiescence, the great inheritance which centuries have gathered? What spectacle could be more strange, more monstrous in its perversity, than to see the Viceroy [Lord Irwin, afterward Lord Halifax, Foreign Secretary and Ambassador to Washington] and the high officials and agents of the Crown in India labouring with all their influence and authority to unite and weave together into a confederacy all the forces adverse and hostile to our rule in India? One after another our friends and the elements on which we ought to rely in India are chilled, baffled and dismissed, and finally even encouraged to band themselves together with those who wish to drive us out of the country.
>
> It is a hideous act of self-mutilation, astounding to every nation of the world. The Princes, the Europeans, the Moslems, the Depressed classes, the Anglo-Indians—none of them know what to do nor where to turn in the face of their apparent desertion by Great Britain. Can you wonder that they try in desperation to make what terms are possible with the triumphant Brahmin oligarchy?
>
> I am against this surrender to Gandhi. I am against these conversations and agreements between Lord Irwin and Mr. Gandhi. Gandhi stands for the expulsion of Britain from India. Gandhi stands for the permanent exclusion of British trade from India. Gandhi stands for the substitution of Brahmin domination for British rule in India. You will never be able to come to terms with Gandhi.
>
> If at the sacrifice of every British interest and of all the necessary safeguards and means of preserving peace and progress in India, you come to terms with Gandhi, Gandhi would at that self-same moment cease to count any more in the Indian situation. Already, Nehru, his young rival in the Indian Congress, is preparing to supersede him the moment that he has squeezed his last drop from the British lemon. In running after Gandhi and trying to build on Gandhi, in imagining that Mr. Ramsay MacDonald

and Mr. Gandhi and Lord Irwin are going to bestow peace and progress upon India, we should be committing ourselves to a crazy dream, with a terrible awakening.

No! Come back from these perilous paths while time and strength remain. Study the report of your own Statutory Commission headed by Sir John Simon and signed unanimously by the representatives of all the three parties in the State. Let us take that as our starting-point for any extensions we may make of self-government in India.

I repudiate the calumny which our opponents level at us that we have no policy but repression and force. Do not be deceived by these untruths.

We take our stand upon views almost universally accepted until a few months ago. We believe that the next forward step is the development of Indian responsibility in the provincial governments of India. Efforts should be made to make them more truly representative of the real needs of the people. Indians should be given ample opportunity to try their hand at government in the provinces; and meanwhile the central Imperial executive, which is the sole guarantee of impartiality between races, creeds and classes, should preserve its sovereign power intact, and allow no derogation from its responsibility to Parliament.

Is that Diehardism? That is the message of the Simon report, unanimously signed by the representatives of the three parties. That is the purport of the alternative scheme submitted a few months ago by the Viceroy himself.

After all, it opens immediately an immense and fertile field for Indian self-government. The provinces of India are great states and separate nations comparable in magnitude and in numbers with the leading powers of Europe. The responsible government of territories and populations as large as Germany, France, Poland, Italy, or Spain is not a task unworthy of Indian capacity for self-government, so far as it has yet been displayed.

It is a task the successful discharge of which would certainly not conflict with the ultimate creation of a federal system. On the contrary it is the indispensable preliminary without which no federation, desirable or undesirable, is possible. Why, the very word "federal" signifies a *foedus,* or treaty made between hitherto sovereign or autonomous states. All federations have arisen thus. In the United States of America, in Canada, in Australia, in South Africa, in every case the units have first been created. Why should these unpractised, unproved, unrepresentative, self-chosen groups of Indian politicians disdain the immense possibilities offered within the limits of the Statutory Commission's report, and demand an immediate setting up of an United States of India, with themselves in control, and the British army at their orders?

Before a federal system for India could be set up there must be first the self-governing constituent provinces; and secondly, far greater, more real, more representative contact between the Indian political classes and the vast proletariat they aspire to rule. Even Europe cannot achieve such a united organization. But what would be said of a scheme which handed the federal government of the United States of Europe over to political classes proportionately no larger than the inhabitants of Portugal, and no more representative of the needs and passions of a mighty continent than the inhabitants of a single city like Rome? Such are the follies we are forced to expose. . . .

In India far more than in any other community in the world moral, political and economic considerations are outweighed by the importance of technical and administrative apparatus. Here you have nearly three hundred and fifty millions of people, lifted to a civilization and to a level of peace, order, sanitation and progress far above anything they could possibly have achieved or could maintain. This wonderful fact is due to the guidance and authority of a few thousands of British officials responsible to Parliament who have for generations presided over the development of India. If that authority is injured or destroyed, the whole efficiency of the services, defensive, administrative, medical, hygienic, judicial; railway, irrigation, public works and famine prevention, upon which the Indian masses depend for their culture and progress, will perish with it. India will fall back quite rapidly through the centuries into the barbarism and privations of the Middle Ages.

To abandon India to the rule of the Brahmins would be an act of cruel and wicked negligence. It would shame for ever those who bore its guilt. These Brahmins who mouth and patter the principles of Western Liberalism, and pose as philosophic and democratic politicians, are the same Brahmins who deny the primary rights of existence to nearly six millions of their own fellow countrymen whom they call 'untouchable,' and whom they have by thousands of years of oppression actually taught to accept this sad position.

Side by side with this Brahmin theocracy and the immense Hindu population—angelic and untouchable castes alike—there dwell in India seventy millions of Moslems, a race of far greater physical vigour and fierceness, armed with a religion which lends itself only too readily to war and conquest. While the Hindu elaborates his argument, the Moslem sharpens his sword. Between these two races and creeds, containing as they do so many gifted and charming beings in all the glory of youth, there is no inter-marriage. The gulf is impassable. Over both of them the impartial rule of Britain has hitherto lifted its appeasing sceptre. Until the previous reforms began to raise the question of local sovereignty and domination, they had got used to dwelling side by side in comparative toleration. But step by step, as it is believed we are going to clear out or be thrust out of India, so this tremendous rivalry and hatred of races springs into life again. It is becoming more acute every day.

Were we to wash our hands of all responsibility and divest ourselves of all our powers, as our sentimentalists desire, ferocious civil wars would speedily break out between the Moslems and the Hindus. No one who knows India will dispute this.

But that is not the end. The Brahmins know well that they cannot defend themselves against the Moslems. The Hindus do not possess among their many virtues that of being a fighting race. The whole south of India is people with races deserving all earnest solicitude and regard, but incapable of self-defence. It is in the north alone that the fighting races dwell.

There can be no doubt that the departure of the British from India, which Mr. Gandhi advocates, and which Mr. Nehru demands, would be followed first by a struggle in the North and thereafter by a reconquest of the South by the North, and of the Hindus by the Moslems.

This danger has not escaped the crafty foresight of the Brahmins, It is for that reason that they wish to have the control of a British Army, or failing that, a white army of janissaries officered, as Mr. Gandhi has suggested, by Germans or other Europeans. They wish to have an effective foreign army, or foreign-organized army, in order to preserve their dominance over the Moslems and their tyranny over their own untouchables. There is the open plot of which we are in danger of becoming the dupes, and the luckless millions of Indians the victims.

It is our duty to guard those millions from that fate. It will be a sorry day when the arm of Britain can no longer offer them the protection of an equal law.

There is a more squalid aspect. Hitherto for generations it has been the British policy that no white official should have any interest or profit other than his salary and pension out of Indian administration. All concession hunters and European adventurers, company-promoters and profit-seekers have been rigorously barred and banned. But now that there is spread through India the belief that we are a broken, bankrupt, played-out power, and that our rule is going to pass away and be transferred to the Brahmin sect, all sorts of greedy appetites have been excited, and many itching fingers are stretching and scratching at the vast pillage of a derelict Empire.

I read in *The Times* newspaper only last week of the crowd of rich Bombay merchants and millionaire millowners, millionaires on sweated labour, who surround Mr. Gandhi, the saint, the lawyer, Lord Irwin's dear colleague and companion. What are they doing there, these men, and what is he doing in their houses? They are making arrangements that the greatest bluff, the greatest humbug and the greatest betrayal shall be followed by the greatest ramp. Nepotism, back-scratching, graft and corruption in every form will be the handmaidens of a Brahmin domination.

Far rather would I see every Englishman quit the country, every soldier, every civil servant embark at Bombay, than that we should remain clutching on to the control of foreign relations and begging for trading facilities, while all the time we were the mere cloak of dishonour and oppression.

Churchill's campaign allied him with men it was strange for a former member of the Liberal Party to be working with, the diehards of Conservatism, the section to which his own chief critics in former years had belonged. It estranged him from his former friends. It even involved him in leveling a charge against the Earl of Derby—a charge that was referred to the judgment of the Committee of Privileges of the House of Commons. The committee reported that Lord Derby and Sir Samuel Hoare, Secretary for India, who was also involved, had committed no breach of privilege as was alleged against them. Churchill retorted on the report that the committee, to avoid declaring that a breach of the law had been committed, had proclaimed a new reading of the law. It was a lively if inconclusive interlude.

After months of argument, the India Bill was passed through the Commons. In a final speech of denunciation Churchill recapitulated all his forewarnings of imperial disaster. The effect was rather spoiled by Mr. Amery, who followed him in debate.

Leo Amery was at Harrow in Churchill's time, and Churchill once had the temerity to push him into the water in a sudden and unprovoked assault. Young Amery did not exact immediate chastisement, but he had perhaps been saving it up. When Churchill had brought to a close his prophecy of woe on India, Leo Amery rose and said, "Here endeth the last chapter of the Book of the Prophet Jeremiah."

Amery had pronounced the epitaph that was acceptable to the British electors.

They did not wish to be troubled over India. They had had Ireland around their necks for a century and they did not intend to be involved on a larger scale over India. Churchill harangued in vain. He was using arguments that would have been effective in the year of Queen Victoria's Diamond Jubilee, but the captains and the kings had long since departed, the sense of imperialism of the Diamond Jubilee had evaporated. The British people no longer had faith in their imperial destiny. They looked almost apologetically on the hacking that had gone to the making of the Empire. Occasionally they might feel a glow of pride at what had been achieved in the past, but they had no intention in their generation of shouldering the white man's burden; it was as much as they could do to earn their living at home. Certainly they were in no heroic mood. Churchill's orations over India came a generation too late.

No politician, however forceful or eloquent can make headway against the prevailing tide of opinion. The time-servers do not try. They are content to watch the cat of politics and jump just a shade ahead. The man with faith, or a creed, or a message will make no immediate progress if he is out of tune with the mood of the moment, but it does not follow that he pleads his cause in vain. The stone the builders rejected is not necessarily forgotten even in politics. British electors are accustomed to treat their politicians as a pool into which they can dip at will, pulling from the reservoir the one that serves the purpose of their prevailing fancy. In the first war Ramsay MacDonald, the pacifist had been the most hated man in the country, but by the late twenties Britain's militancy had evaporated. The people were anti-war and MacDonald was whistled up to serve them. The wind that caught his sails was dead against Winston. Through the thirties he was as much out of favor as a politician can be, but the moment the emergency of war came, there were cries for "Churchill." He was swept into power to be as suddenly dismissed when danger was passed.

When the struggle on the India Bill began, the Socialists were in office. Before it was ended the political scene had been transformed. Under the pressure of the economic blizzard the Socialist Government passed from the scene. A National Government was formed under Ramsay MacDonald with Baldwin taking the second place and the Liberals coming in as well. Churchill did not miss the opportunty to recall that one of the destroyers of the Coalition in 1922 had now taken a prominent part in coalition-promoting.

"During the years," he said, "when I worked so closely with the right honorable gentleman—we were then almost 'a pair of brothers working together'—I always was alert to catch his inspirations and to profit by the sterling qualities for which he is renowned. If there was one doctrine which he inculcated in me more than any other it was his hatred of coalitions. Why, he even spoke in public rebuking some of the younger members of this House, warning them of the dangers of hunting with other packs besides their own; and therefore it is certainly surprising now to find him the champion coalitionist, though doubtless for a very good reason. I am sure no one is more aware of the danger of such a course than my right honourable friend, and I am sure he will be reminded of those dangers whenever he should chance to walk across the portals of the Carlton Club."

This was a well-loosed arrow, for it was Stanley Baldwin's part at the Carlton Club meeting in 1922 that was largely responsible for bringing down the Lloyd George coalition.

The National Government had taken office to deal with the particular financial crisis of 1931; having coalesced, its constituents did not find the occasion for separating. Baldwin replaced MacDonald, Neville Chamberlain succeeded Baldwin, the National Government persisted. Full-blooded protection replaced free trade, some Liberals dissenting and some resigning. Hitler came to power in Germany; disarmament became the international preoccupation.

BOOK FIVE

FIGHTING THE DICTATORS

. . . Faithful to his trust,
In the extremest points of justice, just;
Well knowing all, and loved by all he knew;
True to his king, and to his country true;
Honest at court, above the baits of gain;
Plain in his dress, and in his manners plain,
Possessing much, and yet deserving more;
Deserving those high honours which he wore
With ease to all, and in return gain'd fame
Which all men paid, because he did not claim;
When the grim war was placed in dread array,
Fierce as the lion roaring for his prey.
                    —CHARLES CHURCHILL, Independence

CHAPTER ONE

WARNINGS OF THE WASTED YEARS

1931–1936

T HE THIRTIES—the nightmare years. The years of Britain's decline, of the supremacy of the dictators. The wasted years, years of disarmament, of appeasement, of Munich. The years of Hitler's triumphs.

The thirties ended with Winston Churchill stepping onward toward his destiny as leader of Britain at war. The place was his by right of his exertions throughout the years when Britain was allowed to drift to peril and disaster. Others, irresolute and misguided, had then been in charge of affairs. Denied the opportunities of office, he had had to stand by in agonized frustration. He could do no more than raise his voice in warning and expostulation. From crisis to crisis he was heard, somber and magnificent in his phrases, denouncing, exhorting, persuading, seeking always to raise the people and their leaders to exert themselves in time to save the country from the dangers he could perceive ahead.

Europe, throughout the thirties, was disturbed by the re-emergence of the vanquished Germans. Deprived of their overseas possessions after 1918, denied the right to army, navy, or air force, Germany in the twenties had been a negligible factor in Europe's affairs. But it was not possible to keep a nation of seventy

million people indefinitely in subordination. Victors had to prepare to meet vanquished on terms of equality. The French, realistic always, looked to their armed forces. British governments,
pursuing the elusive phantom of peace, based their policies on
disarmament through the League of Nations and appeasement.
It was to the opposition of the irresolute courses of appeasement
that Churchill devoted himself.

Looking back, it is easy enough to pronounce that Churchill
was in the right, and to exclaim against the tranquilizers who
held office. How regrettable that Churchill was not in charge of
the Foreign Office! What mistakes would have been avoided, what
calamities Europe would have been spared had he been responsible for the conduct of affairs! But though afterward he was
seen to have been in the right, he gained at the time a minimum
of support. His speeches, for all their eloquence, were powerless
to deflect the tranquilizers from their course, for the electors
favored international tranquility. Ramsay MacDonald, the pacifist; Stanley Baldwin, advocate of peace in our time; Neville
Chamberlain, apostle of appeasement, were strongly supported
in the House and in the country. At variance with his party,
Churchill was out of sympathy with the times.

It has been consistently represented that Britain in the thirties
was pacifist. This, to my recollection, is a partial and misleading
description. There were few thoroughgoing pacifists, men like
George Lansbury, the Labour leader. The mass of the people were
anti-war, not on the moral ground that it was always wrong to
fight, but because they had been convinced by the experience of
1914–18 that war was folly, cruel and futile. The mud, the filth,
the squalor, the degradation of the trenches, the slaughter of
Passchendaele and the lesser Passchendaeles had left searing memories. The people were nauseated by the idea of war.

It was against the dead weight of opinion that Churchill had
to contend. "Better to be frightened now than to be killed hereafter," he said, but for long his warnings went unheeded. War-
mongers were not in favor, nor "jitterbugs," to use the later term.
The British people, their war fever cooled, wanted no more than
to let bygones be bygones and to settle down, with their late
enemies in untroubled industry and contentment. In Germany
there were bitter memories, wrongs to be avenged.

It was a national misfortune that British zeal for disarmament should have coincided with the upsurge of German nationalism, and that a succession of conciliators should have occupied Downing Street when Hitler and the Nazis were thrusting forward.

In the twenties the treaties of Locarno had been hailed as the beacons of a new era in which war would forever be abolished from the comity of nations. By the thirties the bright beams of Locarno had faded. A world slump in trade had brought financial disaster in its train. Currencies were shaken, dollar as well as sterling; national bankruptcy was threatened on both sides of the Atlantic. In Germany trade and industry collapsed and ten million workers were thrown out of employment. In the despair of their privations the Germans came to look on Hitler and his National Socialists as their salvation from Bolshevism and chaos.

In Britain the business slump swept the Socialist Government from office. It left Ramsay MacDonald, the Labour leader, as an inheritance to the new administration, the National Government. The Tories had the voting strength, but Baldwin was content to take second place in the Ministry to Ramsay MacDonald. Easygoing to the point of indolence, he was well satisfied to escape the irksome burdens of the premiership.

Politics, which makes strange bedfellows, has produced no association more quaint than that of MacDonald and the Tories. During the 1914–18 war, which he opposed, he was the most hated politician in the country. Times had changed, and his pacifism was in tune with the anti-war feeling of the thirties. It did not recommend him to the Tories, but they were glad enough to have him on their side in the 1931 election to lead in the fight against his former Socialist followers. Thereafter his pacifism and their zeal for economy marched together. The businessmen, financiers and industrialists had been badly shaken by the trade slump that rocked Britain off the gold standard.

When the spendthrift Socialists were sent packing at the polls, rigid retrenchment became the order; and while economy ruled there could be no money to spend on armaments. MacDonald could pursue his work for peace with the support of the Tories, who were anti-war because it was bad for business, for industry and for employment. So MacDonald strove zealously to bring about universal disarmament down to the German level, exerting pressure on the French to cut down their forces.

With contrary purpose, the Germans sought to arm. The old Teuton spirit was stirred by dreams of recovery and revenge. Artifice and deception were employed to evade the restrictions of the peace treaties. Soldiers were trained and so too were airmen under the cloak of civil aviation.

When Churchill last held office in 1929 it was an accepted principle that Britain would not for ten years be involved in a major war. By 1932 the situation had changed. A resurgent Germany was clamorous for equality with the nations who had defeated her. Churchill raised the note of warning.

"The demand is," he said in a speech in the House, "that Germany should be allowed to rearm. Do not let the government delude themselves by supposing that which Germany is asking for is equal status. All those bands of splendid Teutonic youth marching to and fro in Germany, with the light of desire to suffer for their Fatherland in their eyes, are not looking for status. They are looking for weapons and when they have weapons, believe me, they will then ask for the restoration of lost colonies, and when the demand is made it cannot fail to shake, and possibly to shake to their foundations every country in the world."

The German nation could not permanently be deprived of the right to arm. What policy should Britain pursue? He gave the answer in a prophetic passage:

> The bringing about of anything like equality of armament while grievances are unredressed will appoint the day for another European war. It is far safer to re-open questions like Danzig, the Corridor and Transylvania, with all their delicacies and difficulties, in cold blood, and in a calm atmosphere, while the victor nations still have ample superiority. It is far better to do this than to drift from stage to stage until once again vast combinations, equally matched, confront each other face to face. Great Britain will run far less risk in pressing for the redress of grievances than in pressing for disarmament. The road of pressing for disarmament leads us deeper into the European situation. The removal of grievances will remove the cause of danger, or lead us out of danger itself.

His policy was never put to the test. Instead, MacDonald

pressed forward with his disarmament plan. Hitler came to power in Germany as Chancellor and then, in succession to the veteran Hindenburg, as President of the Reich, Fuehrer of the German people. German democracy ended in the flames that destroyed the Reichstag in February 1933. Democrats, Jews, and Communists perished in the terror. The Nazi steam roller obliterated opposition, the concentration camps confining those who were not killed. The Night of Knives (June 30, 1934) completed Hitler's triumph. The blood bath of the purge removed leaders of his own Nazi Party who might challenge his authority. The ex-corporal, son of the minor official in Braunau, reached the highest place, sole master of the German people. Once established, he speeded up the process of rearming.

While the Germans were so engaged, and while MacDonald preached disarmament, Churchill gave thanks to Providence for the existence of the French Army. Through his own channels of information, he received perturbing reports of the extent of German rearmament, in particular in the air. The RAF was being left behind in the race for supremacy. He gave warning in the House (July 1934) of what was proceeding.

> Germany has already, in violation of the Treaty, created a military air force which is now nearly two-thirds as strong as our present home defence force. By the end of 1935 the German Air Force will be nearly equal in numbers and efficiency to our home defence air force at that date.
>
> I do not believe that war is imminent or inevitable, but it seems difficult to resist the conclusion that if we do not begin forthwith to put ourselves in a position of security it will soon be beyond our power to do so. Germany is re-arming. She has now equipped herself again with the practical apparatus of modern war and is instilling into the hearts of her youth and manhood the most extreme nationalism and militaristic conceptions. What concerns us most is the re-armament of Germany in the air.

He spoke of the vulnerability of Britain to air attack, with London the greatest target in the world. "We are a rich and easy prey. If the government have to admit at any time in the next few years that the German air forces are stronger than our own they will be held to have failed in their prime duty to the country."

Some strengthening of the RAF was resolved upon, and even this drew protests from Liberals and Socialists. Those were the times when the young men of Oxford assembled in the Union, passed their resolution: "That this House refuses to fight for King and Country." Abroad, exaggerated importance was attached to this piece of emotional ebullience by those who wished to believe that the British people were decadent. Six years later the Union reversed its decision by voting in favor of conscription in which the decision of the House of Commons was anticipated.

There now took place the celebrated exchanges on air strengths between Winston Churchill and Stanley Baldwin. Baldwin had stated that Britain should not be in a position of inferiority in the air, "to any country within striking distance of our shores." That November (1934), Churchill challenged the government in a resolution declaring that the strength of Britain's defenses, particularly in the air, was no longer adequate to ensure the safety of the country. He repeated his assertion that the German Air Force was approaching equality with the RAF. This drew from Baldwin a flat denial: "So far from the German military air force being at least as strong as our own, we estimate that [next year] we shall still have a margin in Europe alone of nearly fifty per cent."

In Germany they must have smiled at Baldwin's denial. A few months later the truth was disclosed by Hitler himself. John Simon, the Foreign Secretary, was on a mission to Berlin and to him the Fuehrer declared that the German Air Force had already reached equality with the RAF. It was a shock for British ministers. It made nonsense of the assurance that had been given to the House. Baldwin owned up to his mistake with a candor that disarmed criticism—he had been wrong, completely wrong, he had been misled. He was forgiven. His opponents of the Labour Party were more concerned to press for the abolition of all armaments than to attack Baldwin and his colleagues for not providing the RAF with planes. The price would one day have to be paid in the battle of the skies, but that belonged to the future. Churchill, brooding on the consequences to come, grew more anxious.

The uneasy months went by. Hitler, with pretenses cast aside, decreed conscription for Germany. In Britain some steps were taken to expand the RAF and to provide the Royal Navy with new battleships. Churchill was gratified to be able to place his experience at the disposal of the services as member of the Committee on Air Defense Research and as unofficial adviser to the Admiralty.

In 1935 Mussolini gave a new turn to Europe's affairs by invading Abyssinia. At Geneva, member-states of the League of Nations, made a show of preparing to suppress the aggressor. Anthony Eden, Minister for League Affairs, took the lead in advocating sanctions against Italy. It seemed that British warships in the Mediterranean, under the authority of the League, would blow Italian hopes to the skies. Churchill was astonished by the reckless foolhardiness of Mussolini.

"To cast an army of nearly a quarter of a million men, embodying the flower of Italian manhood, upon a barren shore two thousand miles from home against the goodwill of the whole world and without command of the sea, and then in this position embark upon campaigns against a people and in regions which no conqueror in four thousand years ever thought it worth while to subdue, is to give hostages to fortune unparalleled in all history."

Mussolini offered the hostages but the forfeit was not claimed of him. The members of the League had loudly proclaimed their intentions, but when the hour for action came they hesitated and drew back. Sanctions in half measure, halfheartedly applied, were insufficient to sustain the Abyssinians fighting to defend their ancient kingdom.

In Britain, while opinion against the Italian aggressors was at fever heat, a general election was held. The National Government, led now by Stanley Baldwin, was returned to power with a majority of 242 seats. Since he had made the League of Nations the keystone of his policy, Baldwin was expected to take a strong line against the Italians. Instead, discouraged by the French, he allowed the sham of sanctions to continue, so that the Abyssinians faced defeat. At this stage the two Foreign Ministers of Britain and France, Samuel Hoare and Laval, agreed upon a plan to divide Abyssinia between its people and the invaders, designed to preserve something for the Abyssinians. The compromise evoked a howl of execration in Britain. Electors who had voted for Baldwin and the League, were outraged by what they considered a betrayal. To save the government, Hoare with his compromise was jettisoned. He resigned, to be followed as Foreign Secretary by Anthony Eden.

Abyssinia was subjugated by the Italians in its entirety. Mussolini had brought off his bluff. "Fifty nations led by one" had lacked the resolution to stop him. Britain and France suffered a diplomatic setback in the eyes of Europe.

Despite the fiasco over Abyssinia, faith in the League of Nations continued in Britain. In France it was different. With their natural skepticism, the French had looked on the League with cold mistrust. The simple British had accepted the idea that the League was going to make war impossible by acting as the police force of the world. That it had failed over Abyssinia was attributed by the British not to any shortcomings in the institution, but to lack of backing by its supporters, in particular the French. Indeed, little effort would have been needed to check the Italians and send Mussolini toppling from his Fascist seat. A splendid chance was lost for lack of nerve. Later, when the test of war showed the weakness of the Italian regime, the exaggerated respect that had been paid to Fascist pretentions was seen to have been grotesquely misplaced. British conduct over Abyssinia was grotesque throughout, beginning with the trumpetings at Geneva, and ending in ultimate acquiesence in Italian conquests. Winston, who had watched the proceedings with scorn and dismay, passed censure on the failure of the government in a speech to his Essex constituents:

> No one is compelled to serve great causes unless he feels fit for it, but nothing is more certain than that you cannot take the lead in great causes as a half-timer. Mr. Baldwin said that sanctions meant war. Then he led us into sanctions with a thoroughly virtuous resolve against war. What was the result? The economic sanctions had to be confined within limits which would not lead to war.
>
> As far as I can make out, Signor Mussolini let it be known that he would submit to any economic sanctions which merely inflicted privations upon the Italian people. He would not submit

to any economic sanction which prevented him from conquering Abyssinia. He would treat an economic sanction which had the effect of crippling his aggressive armies as if it were a military sanction—that is to say, an act of war. It also seems to me that the League of Nations submitted to this position from the outset.

If you examine the sanctions which the League of Nations, under our leadership, imposed upon Italy, you will see that they all conform to this condition. For instance, the import of aluminum into Italy was prohibited. But that happened to be almost the only metal of which Italy has a larger domestic supply than she requires. Again, the import of iron ore or scrap-iron into Italy was forbidden. But as they were allowed to import as much pig iron or steel as they wanted, it made no difference at all to them.

If oil sanctions had been imposed at the outset, it might have produced a fatal effect upon the operations of the Italian armies. But that might have led to war. If our leaders had definitely decided that they would not go into war to stop Mussolini conquering Abyssinia, it seems to me that they ought to have sung a very much smaller tune.

The conclusion which I think we should draw is that we should be scrupulously careful not to involve the word and honour of Britain upon the Continent of Europe in any business which we are not prepared, if the worst comes to the worst, to carry through, whatever the cost, with all our force and strength.

I have tried to support the Government and Mr. Baldwin in their policy upon the League of Nations and about Abyssinia. I found it very difficult to keep in step with all their zigzags. First, we had Mr. Baldwin's statement, "Sanctions mean war." Then we had the policy of sanctions without war. Then the sudden reinforcement of the British Fleet in the Mediterranean. Then came Sir Samuel Hoare's magnificent speech at Geneva, which was heard and hailed as a trumpet-call to the world.

There followed a moment in which it seemed as if war might come and that we must be attacked. At that moment it was the duty of everyone to rally to the national cause. The Labour Party and the Trade Unions rallied. They turned Mr. Lansbury out of their Labour leadership for his pacifism. They became seriously divided among themselves. They suffered at the General Election because of their divisions.

No one could deny that this support of valiant idealism played a great part in the votes that were given by so many millions of our people. But what followed? All of a sudden, over a week-end, we were confronted with the agreement between Sir Samuel Hoare and M. Laval to give Italy a large part of Abyssinia. Everyone can see now that this agreement was a very shrewd, far-seeing agreement, which would have saved the Emperor of Abyssinia from ruin before his army was destroyed. The serious thing against it was that it should have been made by the same Sir Samuel Hoare who had sounded his wonderful trumpet-call to the League of Nations scarcely three months before.

It was this violent revolution of policy, however sagacious in itself, which threw Parliament into confusion. But no one did it throw into more confusion than Mr. Baldwin. He and his Cabinet agreed with Sir Samuel Hoare. But such a storm arose, and he felt the force of such a great tide of public opinion, that he had to turn round and sacrifice Sir Samuel Hoare, tear up the Hoare-Laval agreement, and start off again on the old policy of "Sanctions which mean war," coupled with the proviso that there was to be no war. It has been very difficult to keep pace with all these chops and changes.

After a few weeks of hesitation, the Government decided on the lifting of the halfhearted sanctions that had been so ineffectively applied. The Prime Minister confessed to a feeling of bitter humiliation.

Churchill pointed to the root cause of the humiliation which had reduced Britain's prestige throughout the world. "It is," he said, "the lamentable weakness in which our defenses have been allowed to fall. Errors, feebleness, vacillation there have, no doubt, been in the current policy of the Government, but the underlying cause of our impotence is the improvident neglect of our defensive strength in years when every other great nation was arming sternly and resolutely.

In re-forming the Baldwin Government it seemed that a place might be found for Churchill. By the mid-thirties, the portents were no longer to be ignored. Disarmament down to the German level was no longer to be recommended even by the most zealous pacifist, seeing that the Germans were arming fast. A government White Paper, calling a halt to disarmament, announced that "additional expenditure on the three Defence Services can no longer be postponed."

It was decided to set up the new post of Minister for the Coordination of Defense. Here was the task for Churchill, so obviously marked by his long experience for the position. Of all posts it was the one he coveted. There he would have the opportunity of doing something to catch up on ground that had been lost in the wasted years, the years the locusts had eaten. His prospects were canvassed in the Press, his chances were rated high, but to his chagrin he was passed over. Thomas Inskip (later Lord Caldecote, Lord Chief Justice), an elderly churchman-lawyer, was chosen. Churchill was rejected on the ground that Hitler might have reckoned his appointment provocative. It might have been supposed that the Englishman the Germans denounced would be the one a British Premier would pick, but other views prevailed in those irresolute days.

At the time, Churchill keenly felt his disappointment. Looking back in after years, however, he could discern the workings of a kindly Providence that kept him from office, and spared him from the contaminating association with the misfortune of appeasement and Munich.

By then he was drawing all the fire of the Nazis. Not even his famous ancestor was more execrated on the Continent as "Malbrouk" than Churchill by the propagandists of the Third Reich. When things were dull in Berlin, Goebbels turned the jet of his venom against Winston for a day's diversion.

Churchill—German-hater, was the parrot cry. "For years now," Goebbels wrote, "Churchill has painted not landscapes but a picture of the German danger. He is the leader of the implacable haters of Germany in England, and even if he is somewhat less dangerous than those sinister wire-pullers in the half-darkness of the Secret Service and of many ministerial quarters, yet nevertheless he sets in motion those waves of gall which are not to be taken too light-heartedly."

The organ of the Wilhelmstrasse, the official *Diplomatic Correspondence*, accused him of desiring the encirclement and suppression of Germany. Churchill, it was declared, was fond of coming forward as the ever ready spokesman of the circles in which it was customary to give the appearance of justification for personal dislike of an honorable understanding with Germany by suspicions of Germany's will for peace.

Thenceforth the dictators of Berlin and Rome were coupled

against the democracies. Mussolini had hitherto sided with the French, but the opposition to his Abyssinian adventure caused him to change his adherence. The Axis came into being, the catchword originating in the Duce's remark that the line between Rome and Berlin was not a division but an axis. This reorientation disturbed the balance of power in Europe to the disadvantage of the democracies.

Hitler now took offensive action. He had noted the signs over Abyssinia. The German generals warned him against any rashness before the Reichswehr had developed in strength. He ignored them. What need to trouble about the League in its impotence and the democracies of Britain and France, effete and irresolute? The troops were ordered to march. The Rhineland was occupied.

Under the Versailles Treaty the Rhineland had been established as a demilitarized zone. The Germans were barred from fortifying an area fifty miles wide. By sending in his marching columns Hitler challenged the French and British to enforce the treaties he had torn up. The French, alarmed by the threat to their security, pressed for immediate action. Baldwin and his colleagues applied the brake. The French had hung back over Abyssinia. The Rhineland was no matter of great concern to the British. Why should not the Germans move soldiers into their own country? They were only going into their own back garden. After days of paralyzed uncertainty, the breach of the peace treaties was remitted to the League. It was the equivalent to no action being taken. Hitler's coup had succeeded. Britain and France had lost their chance of unseating him before the advantage of greater strength passed over to the Germans.

Vast consequences were to flow from the Rhineland occupation. They scarcely entered into the British reckoning. Winston, however, saw in it a menace that exposed Holland, Belgium and France. Hitler had barred his front door, a protection for the day when he should decide to move to the attack in other directions. Evaluating the strategic results in a speech in the House (April 6, 1936), Churchill said:

> The creation of a line of forts opposite to the French frontier will enable the German troops to be economised on that line and will enable the main forces to swing round through Belgium and Holland, and then look east. There the consequences of the

Rhineland fortification may be more immediate. The moment those fortifications are completed and in proportion as they are completed, the whole aspect of Middle Europe is changed. The Baltic States, Poland and Czechoslovakia, with which must be associated Jugoslavia, Rumania, Austria, and some other countries, are all affected very decisively the moment that this great work of construction has been completed.

Strategic insight and prophetic appreciation have rarely been so penetrating. The moves on the checkerboard of Europe had been accurately foretold. Hitler, with the barricades up at his front door, pursued his preparations. Europe's attention was next engaged by the civil war in Spain, which developed into an international free-for-all, Germans, Russians and Italians taking a hand and trying out their weapons. At home in England the disturbances of the Continent were forgotten in the crisis of the Abdication.

CHAPTER TWO

THE ABDICATION

1936

HOW DIFFERENTLY events appear when time has placed them in perspective. In 1936 the abdication of King Edward VIII roused his subjects to an emotional peak from which they seemed to be viewing one of the climaxes in their island history. For a while the King's marriage absorbed the attention of his Ministers to the exclusion of other matters, such as the designs of the dictators. For a while that exceeded the nine-day limit of a wonder it was the talk of the town and the sole topic of the newspapers.

Twenty years and a world war later, and the abdication, under the corrective influence of time, had dropped in the scale of values. Public opinion that had been brought to the full froth of effervescence, soon subsided. The war put the affair out of men's minds. By the fifties, the change in Kings seemed to have produced no more than a ripple in the pool of English history. King Edward's abdication, like his reign, was ephemeral in its influence.

Winston Churchill's part in the abdication crisis was a minor one. He was called in to be adviser to his sovereign. His intervention was without effect on the course of events.

The King's mind had been made up. His choice had been narrowed down—to marry or to reign. Resolutely resolved to marry he passed from the scene. Churchill, who had pleaded for delay in the hope that the extremity of abdication might be avoided, was powerless to avert an outcome that he deplored, but which he recognized to be inevitable.

The tale of the King who was prepared to surrender everything so that he might win his love will appeal to the romantics down the ages. It will live as a diversion in the volumes of sober historians, a twentieth-century variation on the theme of King Cophetua, with a twice-married American woman in the role of beggar-maid. King Cophetua was suffered to indulge his gracious condescension. Not so King Edward. His subjects might conceivably have accepted a beggar-maid, pretty and prattling in her youthful inexperience. King Edward's choice had fallen on a lady of quite other qualities. The affair that began as a romance, developed into a political and constitutional crisis. As politician King Edward fell below the level of his royal predecessors, who in their varying fashion, had always contrived to manage their love affairs without endangering their crowns.

It was on December 1, 1936, that Britain learned of the existence of what was termed the constitutional crisis. The news came with the shock of surprise, intense as to be almost stunning. Abroad surprise was lacking. In almost every country in the world, the King's infatuation for the wife of a United States citizen, Ernest Simpson, had been the subject of dispatches from London. In the United States newspaper readers had been titillated by accounts of what was afoot and speculation as whether a new link between Britain and the United States was to be provided in the person of an English Queen. In Britain, by self-denying ordinance, no reference was made in the newspapers to the royal romance. The name of Mrs. Simpson appeared in the Court Circular as one who had dined with the King. Mrs. Simpson was reported to be sharing the King's holiday cruise on the yacht *Nahlin* off the Dalmatian Coast. But, as most newspaper readers knew nothing of the Simpsons, the reports conveyed little to them.

Among members of the government, in court circles and among the well-informed there was no such ignorance. The Prime Minister, Stanley Baldwin, was deeply concerned. His anxiety spread through the nation with the breaking of silence in the press. All regretted the dilemma in which King Edward was placed, but beyond this opinion was divided. The young and the romantically minded supported him. But for the greater part his subjects deplored the fact, in varying degrees of indignation, that he should be permitting the pursuit of his private happiness to bring the monarchy into disrepute.

The King and the Prime Minister discussed the situation in a series of interviews. It became established that Edward was determined to relinquish his throne rather than the lady. As a possible escape from the impasse, it was suggested that a morganatic marriage might meet the difficulty and that the King should have a wife but not a Queen. This proved to be no solution. Not one of the governments of the Dominions was prepared to accept Mrs. Simpson on any terms. From Australia the opinion was received that in view of the scandal that had arisen the King could not re-establish his prestige or again command the confidence of his peoples. The Prime Minister shared the views of the Dominions. He and his Cabinet were not prepared to introduce the legislation necessary to permit of a morganatic marriage, a device unknown to English law.

It was at this stage that Winston Churchill became involved as counsellor to the King—there were not many on whom His Majesty could call.

In the brief period of his reign he had contrived to alienate those whose support was essential to him were he to have any prospect of realizing his hopes. He wished to have both his crown and his queen—the suggestion made at the time that he had never wished to reign was no more than a stupid invention. But, he had made the realization of his hopes the more difficult by antagonizing, in turn, the court, the parliament and the church.

On his succession he began to change the old ways of the court and displace the men his father, King George V, had trusted. His informality, as he strolled the London streets with bowler-hat and umbrella displeased those who considered that a divinity should hedge a King. He made it plain that he found it hard to tolerate the social round and the ceremonies of the Court. Leaders of society, debutantes and their mothers, were dismayed. Church people could find no sign of conformity in the sovereign, titular head of the Established Church. Bishops began to pray that Edward might become aware of the need for a greater manifestation of divine grace. The politicians were alarmed that his Majesty in his tours about the country, was winning the sympathy of the poorer classes by identifying himself with the cause of the workless, assuring them that something must be done to help them. This was intrusion into their own sphere that the politicians resented. As Prince of Wales, Edward had been by far the most popular man in the country. Eight months on the throne, and he was one of the least popular of sovereigns.

There were about him few on whose judgment and loyalty he felt he could rely. No King had stood in greater need of faithful counsel and he asked that he should be permitted to consult with Winston Churchill. This, in itself, raised a minor constitutional issue, for the sovereign's adviser in all matters political is his Prime Minister. In this case, however, no objection was raised. The Sovereign and his first Minister being at variance, there was reason for him to obtain independent and disinterested advice.

Churchill was summoned to the King's home. It was natural that the choice should have fallen upon him. Outside the Government he was the outstanding figure in politics. He was prompt to answer the royal call. An ambitious, calculating politician might have hesitated. Opinion in parliament was so hostile that any attempt to put forward the King's case would rouse strong resentment. These were considerations that Churchill ignored. His Sovereign had need of him and in unquestioning loyalty he answered the call.

His intervention did damage to his reputation. His motives were suspected. He was accused of seeking to exploit the crisis for the promotion of his personal ambitions, by leading a King's Party, and of seeking to supplant Baldwin as chief minister by offering to accomplish for the King what Baldwin had declined to undertake. This was fantastic nonsense, founded on suspicions that are quick to form when the public mind is inflamed. His friends warned him at the time. He took no heed. The Sovereign in his hour of need sought his services and as a loyal subject he was proud to do his duty. In so doing he received one of the angriest manifestations ever directed against any man in the House of Commons.

It has since been accepted, that there was no ground for the accusations made against him. Indeed, there was never a possibility of carrying out the proposal of a morganatic marriage. There would have been little influential backing for a King's Party even had a misguided attempt been made to form one. Nor did Churchill himself differ from the view that abdication was the only possible end once events had reached their final phase. His intervention was confined to pleading for time that might have provided another solution, avoiding the extremity of the loss to the country of a King who as Prince of Wales had made so splendid a reputation in his country's service. For the purpose of the record I give the appeal to the people that Winston Churchill made with impassioned force while the issue was still in doubt:

> I plead for time and patience. The nation must realise the character of the constitutional issue. There is no question of any conflict between the King and Parliament. Parliament has not been consulted in any way, nor allowed to express any opinion.
>
> The question is whether the King is to abdicate upon the advice of the Ministry of the day. No such advice has ever before been tendered to a Sovereign in Parliamentary times.
>
> This is not a case where differences have arisen between the Sovereign and his Ministers on any particular measure. These could certainly be resolved by normal processes of Parliament or dissolution.
>
> In this case we are in presence of a wish expressed by the Sovereign to perform an act which in no circumstances can be accomplished for nearly five months, and may conceivably, for various reasons, never be accomplished at all.
>
> That, on such a hypothetical and supposititious basis the supreme sacrifice of abdication and potential exile of the Sovereign should be demanded, finds no support whatever in the British Constitution. No Ministry has the authority to advise the abdication of the Sovereign. Only the most serious Parliamentary processes could even raise the issue in a decisive form.
>
> The Cabinet has no right to prejudge such a question without having previously ascertained at the very least the will of Parliament. This could, perhaps, be obtained by messages from the Sovereign to Parliament, and by addresses of both Houses after due consideration of these messages.
>
> For the Sovereign to abdicate incontinently in the present circumstances would inflict an injury upon the constitutional position of the monarchy which is measureless and cannot fail to

be grievous to the institution itself, irrespective of the existing occupant of the Throne.

Parliament would also fail entirely in its duty if it allowed such an event to occur as the signing of an abdication in response to the advice of Ministers without taking all precautions to make sure that these same processes may not be repeated with equal uncanny facility at no distant date in unforeseen circumstances. Clearly time is needed for searching constitutional debate.

The next question—What has the King done? If it be true, as is alleged, that the King has proposed to his Ministers legislation which they are not prepared to introduce, the answer of Ministers should be not to call for abdication, but to refuse to act upon the King's request, which thereupon becomes inoperative.

If the King refuses to take the advice of his Ministers they are, of course, free to resign. They have no right whatever to put pressure upon him to accept their advice by soliciting beforehand assurances from the Leader of the Opposition that he will not form an alternative Administration in the event of their resignation, and confronting the King with an ultimatum. Again, there is cause for time and patience.

Why cannot time be granted? The fact that it is beyond the King's power to accomplish the purpose which Ministers oppose until the end of April [the final decree in Mrs. Simpson's divorce suit would not be issued until that month] surely strips the matter of constitutional urgency.

There may be some inconvenience, but that inconvenience stands on a different plane altogether from the grave constitutional issues I have set forth.

National and Imperial considerations alike require that before such a dread step as a demand for abdication is taken, not only should the constitutional position be newly defined by Parliament, but that every method should be exhausted which gives the hope of a happier solution.

Lastly, but surely not least, there is the human and personal aspect.

The King has been for many weeks under the greatest strain, moral and mental, that can fall upon a man. Not only has he been inevitably subjected to the supreme stress of his public duty, but also to the agony of his own personal feelings.

Surely, if he asks for time to consider the advice of his Ministers, now that at length matters have been brought to this dire culmination, he should not be denied.

Howsoever this matter may turn, it is pregnant with calamity and inseparable from inconvenience. But all the evil aspects will be aggravated beyond measure if the utmost chivalry and compassion is not shown, both by Ministers and by the British nation, towards a gifted and beloved King torn between private and public obligations of love and duty.

The Churches stand for charity. They believe in the efficacy of prayer. Surely their influence must not oppose a period of reflection. I plead, I pray, that time and tolerance will not be denied.

The King has no means of personal access to his Parliament or his people. Between him and them stand in their office the Ministers of the Crown. If they thought it their duty to engage all their power and influence against him, still he must remain silent.

All the more must they be careful not to be the judge in their own case, and to show a loyal and Christian patience even at some political embarrassment to themselves.

If an abdication were to be hastily extorted the outrage so committed would cast its shadow forward across many chapters of the history of the British Empire.

It is regrettable to have to record that as sequel to the issue of that statement Churchill was charged with trying to make political capital out of the crisis for his own personal ends.

On Thursday, December 7, the Prime Minister made to the House a partial disclosure of the situation in carefully chosen words. Its effect was that the King was engaged in reaching a conclusion on the course he would take. He deprecated the asking of supplementary questions as the matter was of such gravity and the answers would have to be improvised.

Winston, however, rose to repeat the request he had made before—that no irrevocable step be taken before a formal statement was made to Parliament. The reception he received must be described by an observer at the time. "When Mr. Churchill, who had been leaning forward in his corner seat below the gangway, rose to put a further question, the House became impatient. As he uttered the first mystifying and familiar words of his now usual request that 'no irrevocable step should be taken,' there were cries from all sides of 'No' and 'Sit down.' It was the most striking rebuff of modern Parliamentary history. It is to be regretted that

Mr. Churchill did not attempt to move an adjournment so that the House would have been able to see for the first time the insignificant dimensions of the section which was following him."

In fact Parliament was not vouchsafed a full statement before the final and irrevocable step had been taken. The abdication of King Edward VIII was announced by the Speaker to the House of Commons on December 10. Thereafter a statement was made by the Prime Minister, and in the brief debate that followed Churchill said:

Nothing is more certain or more obvious than that recrimination or controversy at this time would not only be useless, but harmful and wrong. What is done, is done. What has been done, or left undone, belongs to history, and to history, so far as I am concerned, it shall be left. I will, therefore, make two observations only.

The first is this: It is clear from what we have been told this afternoon that there was at no time any constitutional issue between the King and his Ministers, or between the King and Parliament. The supremacy of Parliament over the Crown; the duty of the Sovereign to act in accordance with the advice of his Ministers; neither of those was ever at any moment in question. I venture to say that no Sovereign has ever conformed more strictly or more faithfully to the letter and spirit of the Constitution than his present Majesty. In fact, he has voluntarily made a sacrifice for the peace and strength of his realm, which go far beyond the bounds required by the law and constitution. This is my first observation.

My second is this: I have, throughout, pleaded for time; anyone can see how grave would have been the evils of protracted controversy. On the other hand it was, in my view, our duty to endure these evils, even at serious inconvenience, if there was any hope that time would bring a solution.

Whether there was any hope or not is a mystery which, at the present time, it is impossible to resolve. Time was also important from another point of view. It was essential that there should be no room for aspersions, after the event, that the King had been hurried to his decision. I believe that, if this decision had been taken last week, it could not have been declared that it was an unhurried decision, so far as the King himself was concerned, but now I accept whole heartedly what the Prime Minister has proved, namely, that the decision taken this week has been taken by his Majesty freely, voluntarily and spontaneously, in his own time and in his own way. As I have been looking at this matter, as is well known, from an angle different from that of most members, I thought it my duty to place this fact also upon record.

That is all I have to say upon the disputable part of this matter, but I hope the House will bear with me for a minute or two, because it was my duty as Home Secretary, more than a quarter of a century ago, to stand beside his Majesty and proclaim his style and titles at his investiture as Prince of Wales amid the sunlit battlements of Caernarvon Castle, and ever since then he has honoured me here, and also in war time, with his personal kindness and, I may even say, friendship. I should have been ashamed if, in my independent and unofficial position, I had not cast about for every lawful means, even the most forlorn, to keep him on the Throne of his fathers, to which he only recently succeeded amid the hopes and prayers of all.

In this Prince there were discerned qualities of courage, of simplicity, of sympathy and, above all, of sincerity, qualities rare and precious which might have made his reign glorious in the annals of this ancient monarchy. It is the acme of tragedy that these very virtues should, in the private sphere, have led only to this melancholy and bitter conclusion. But, although to-day our hopes are withered, still I will assert that his personality will not go down uncherished to future ages, that it will be particularly remembered in the homes of his poorer subjects, and that they will ever wish from the bottoms of their hearts for his private peace and happiness, and for the happiness of those who are dear to him.

I must say one word more, and I say it especially to those who here and out of doors—and do not underrate their numbers—who are most poignantly afflicted by what has occurred. Danger gathers upon our path. We cannot afford—we have no right—to look back. We must look forward; we must obey the exhortation of the Prime Minister to look forward. The stronger the advocate of monarchical principle a man may be, the more zealously must he now endeavour to fortify the Throne, and to give his Majesty's successor that strength which can come only from the love of a united nation and Empire.

With this speech Churchill's part in the abdication was completed and with it must end this strictly objective record. The rest, as his speech put it, must be left to history.

Churchill was one of the last to bid farewell to the late King, now Duke of Windsor, as he began the journey into exile. Bareheaded, he stood on the steps of Fort Belvedere, watching as the Duke was driven away. His eyes were wet with tears and he tapped out with his stick the rhythm of the lines as he recited:

> "He nothing common did, nor mean
> Upon that memorable scene."

It was characteristic of the man that Winston Churchill should have stood by the King in his hour of need. It was a human gesture, but he suffered for it in loss of popularity. To the accusations that his actions had been calculated to further his personal ambitions, he disdained to reply. He had done his duty as he conceived it, actuated, as his friends knew, by no motive other than that of serving his sovereign.

CHAPTER THREE

OPPONENT OF APPEASEMENT

1937–1938

Winston Churchill's fortunes were now at their nadir. Discredited by his opponents for the part he had taken over the Abdication, mistrusted for his brilliance, his judgment suspect, it seemed that his fate would be that of the politician who has outlived his day. He was over sixty and they began to speak of him as one of the Elder Statesmen. Elder Statesman—was the splendid past to fizzle out in this? He was becoming, like Lloyd George, a link with the Parliamentary past of which they had each been an ornament. His place in the House was the corner seat below the gangway, the retreat of members out of step with their party. Was this to be his niche until, in the fullness of time, he lapsed into the ultimate seniority of Father of the House? Or, perchance, it might be his fate to crumble into senectitude in the House of Lords. It was a dismal prospect for one who had been the right-hand man of Prime Ministers, and who had played his part in the fashioning of history.

Lesser men, more supple politicians, were installed in office and lorded it on the Treasury bench. There were few who acknowledged him as leader. He had not the graces and crafts by which the masters of politics attract followers. He appeared to be too indifferent to the claims of others to induce them to support his. In his robust indifference he followed his own line, and he had to pay the penalty for what was termed his own uncompromising self-sufficiency.[1] His supremacy in debate was galling to men of lesser parts, who were rarely flattered by his interest in their views. They complained that he did not listen to any speeches but his own, that he had usurped a position in the House "as if he had a right to walk in, make his speech, walk out and leave the whole place as if God Almighty had spoken." [2]

A stranger inquiring concerning the character of Winston Spencer Churchill would have formed an unfavorable opinion had he relied on the popular estimation of the man. The Churchill of those days was mistrusted on every hand, by members of his own party as well as his opponents. He was looked on as one who would serve or abandon any cause for the promotion of his own ambition. His essential unsoundness was seen in a succession of incidents. I remember, for I listed them at the time, how Winston was saddled in the public mind with responsibility for a succession of mistakes—the failure of Antwerp, the catastrophe of Gallipoli, the ill-conceived campaigns against the Bolsheviks, the saber-rattling over Chanak, the ill-advised return to the gold standard involving the disaster of the General Strike. It was a considerable catalogue. Trade unionists spoke bitterly of him as strikebreaker. Left-Wingers denounced him as anti-Russian, pacifists as warmonger. There were both Liberals and Conservatives who detested him for ratting. It was true enough that no lover was more fickle than Churchill had been in his political affiliations. According to their individual fancies men despised or admired him for the flexibility of opinions that had carried him from political pole to pole and back again—first Conservative, then Liberal, a Radical and opponent of a strong Navy, then First Lord and champion of the strongest Navy afloat, Coalitionist, Constitutionalist and plain Conservative once again. Having boxed the political compass, he still could not remain loyal to his leader, it was said, but must needs have sought to exploit prejudice over India to overthrow and replace Stanley Baldwin. Noting how opportunely, in the past, high office had followed his change of party allegiance, his critics identified him with the politician of a former generation whose tergiversation inspired the lines:

A side I chose and on that side was strong
Till time hath proved me fairly in the wrong.
Convinced I changed, can any man do more?
And have not greater patriots changed before?
Changed I at once, can any man do less?
Without a single blush that change confess,
Confess it with a manly kind of pride,
And change the losing for the winning side.

Churchill was the politician most mistrusted in the country. The others might not be brilliant, but with them you knew where you were—at least they were safe. With Churchill the man in the street felt he never knew—Churchill was incalculable, his changes unpredictable. It was a burden of prejudice that must have proved fatal to Churchill's prospects, but for the emergency of war.

After the crowning of King George VI there was a change in the premiership. Baldwin, after fifteen years' leadership of the Conservative Party, resigned office and retreated to the House of Lords in the mellow afterglow of praise for his handling of the abdication crisis. His fame was to be fleeting. Within a few years he had been made the national scapegoat for neglect of the country's defenses and failure to suppress Hitlerism in its infancy. He must, as leader, bear his share for the failure of a party, a Parliament and a people. But to him is due the credit for enabling Britain to escape the embittering differences of the class war that in the twenties and thirties rent the peoples of the Continent, causing civil strife in Germany, Italy and Spain. The least partisan of premiers, Baldwin gave a tone to public life that was the source of national strength when war eventually came.

His successor, Neville Chamberlain, was a man of greater capacity in a narrower sphere. He applied the industry and efficiency of the businessman to state affairs. Though he strove for peace he was not able to inspire it. Rousing his followers by his partisan leadership he enraged his opponents to the pitch of passionate antagonism. He took office with the purpose of a man with a mission—the establishment of world peace. To its accomplishment he brought the eager faith of one who follows the gleam and the methods of a martinet. His judgment, so shrewd in politics, was not adequate for the role he assumed in world affairs. He underestimated the Russians, overestimated the Poles, and misestimated Mussolini. Matching himself against Hitler in person he was beguiled by a wickedness that was beyond his reckoning. Dedicating himself to the cause of peace, he was fated to be remembered as the Premier of Appeasement.

There could be no place in the Chamberlain Government for Winston Churchill. He, no less than the other, was dedicated to a cause, which he pursued with equal tenacity of purpose. Convinced that the policy of appeasement was an encouragement to aggression, he was in continuing conflict with the Prime Minister, but he did not act in a partisan spirit nor seek personal advantage. It was the country's cause that he pleaded, for arms and allies. On other questions he was not at variance with his party and he claimed the right to second Neville's election as Conservative Party leader. Praising his work as Chancellor, Churchill said that it was his careful financial administration that made it possible for the country to bear the burden of the vast sums needed for national defense.

> Any Chancellor of the Exchequer [Churchill went on] naturally finds as his normal business that he should resist and criticize and canvass expenditure, particularly expenditure on what are called unproductive channels. But when the late Government were at length convinced—you will pardon my 'at length' —of the urgent need to re-arm against the danger in which we stood and still stand, no one was more active than Mr. Chamberlain. . . .
>
> We feel sure that the leader we are about to choose, as a distinguished Parliamentarian and House of Commons man, will not resent honest differences . . . which must inevitably from time to time arise among those who mean the same thing.
>
> I will also say that I feel sure that his great experience of the party and all its branches, and all its organisation, will make it certain that party opinion will not be denied; that if subordinate it will still have its rightful place in the mind of the leader. We have to combat the wolf of Socialism, and we shall be able to do it far more effectively as a pack of hounds than as a flock of sheep.

On the following day, in the House of Commons, Churchill assisted the new Prime Minister to extricate himself from an embarrassing predicament. Neville, as Chancellor, had introduced the budget and had included a special tax as a National Defense Contribution that aroused wide opposition. By the time the proposals came to be debated in detail, he had handed over the N.D.C. as a legacy to the new Chancellor, Sir John Simon. When the clause came up for consideration, Conservative backbenchers plainly indicated their dislike. It was a dilemma for the new Prime Minister. Was he, at the outset, to suffer in prestige by abandoning one of the outstanding features of his final budget?

Churchill made the way of retreat easy in a speech in his happiest vein of wit. He began with the confession that he took a friendly interest in this new government without quite knowing why he did so. "I would not go so far as to call it a paternal interest because, speaking quite candidly, it is not the sort of Government I would have bred myself. But if it is not paternal, at any rate I may call it avuncular."

A chuckling House then heard canons of financial orthodoxy quoted, each of which hit the Defense Contribution. Excellent motives were allowed to Mr. Chamberlain, but his tax had been shown to be unworkable. Face-saving was not important. Avowal of mistakes used to be one of Mr. Baldwin's most successful weapons in discomfiting those who with much toil pointed out his errors. This smiling, rueful reminiscence of old-time conflicts set the House roaring.

Various precedents for withdrawal were quoted. Finally, with gusto, Churchill took a case of his own. He had been in trouble when he was Chancellor of the Exchequer, over the kerosene tax —"a very good tax." The Chief Whip telegraphed to him in the country, "All our fellows against it and all the others too." Had there been any similar communications recently?

"I acted with great promptitude. In the nick of time, just as Mr. Snowden was rising with overwhelming fury, I got up——" [roars of laughter drowned the rest of the sentence].

"Was I humiliated?" Churchill cried. "Was I accused of running away? No! Everyone said, 'How clever, how quick, how right.' Pardon me referring to it, Mr. Speaker. It was one of my best days."

Shaking with mirth, the House recovered to hear a serious argument that long Cabinet examination, "a good knocking about behind the scenes," should be given to proposals for new taxes. So, after grave insistence that Government supporters must not vote against the Finance Bill as a whole, Churchill appealed earnestly to Mr. Chamberlain to drop the Defense Contribution, "drop the whole thing, and drop it now." His counsel was taken.

Parliamentary observers contrasted Churchill's achievement that day with his experience only a few months before when he made his interventions during the abdication crisis almost to be shouted down. That was in December. Then everyone said that he would never recover from the blow to his reputation. Now in June he had delighted the House.

At least the proposal to raise a tax specifically allocated as a contribution to defense was an indication of a growing realization of the need for rearmament. Churchill's long campaign had not been without avail. The Government proposed to expend £400,-000,000, financed by means of loans on a five-year defense program. The Government was roused to the needs of the times even if the Socialists still lagged in the locust years. The Labour Party, indeed, puzzled its friends by calling for the maximum of vigor in British policy and insisting on the minimum of expenditure on defense.

Large as were the sums voted, there could be no catching up with Germany. There the catchword was: "Guns not butter." In England the restrictive influences still lingered, of the times when the country was to be defended without an adequate defense budget. In Treasury circles the dangers of a financial crash were reckoned to be greater than a military one. To plunge in with the order to "re-arm at all costs and damn the expense" was recklessness not to be dared.[3]

Churchill was dismayed that under the new Prime Minister greater effort was not being made, and he sought to galvanize the Government into a supreme endeavor. "The months slip by; if we delay we may be forbidden by superior power to complete the process." It was his perpetual theme. "Let men of goodwill get together in face of the growing menace of Hitlerism."

Chamberlain did not share these forebodings. Churchill, he considered, overpainted his picture. The dictators were not as black as was represented—"They are too often regarded as though they are entirely inhuman. I believe this idea to be quite erroneous."[4] He was eager to meet them in person as a first step to establishing better relations.

Again it must be insisted that it was Chamberlain, not Churchill, whose policy commanded the support of public opinion. He was at one with those who looked on war as the worst of futilities —"It wins nothing, cures nothing, ends nothing." Chamberlain thought, as many others thought, of the seven million young men on both sides cut off in their prime between 1914 and 1918 and of the thirteen million who were maimed and mutilated. "In war there are no winners but all losers." He had, too, the businessman's abhorrence of war for its wastefulness.

The shock of national bankruptcy, narrowly escaped in the depression of the early thirties, left a persisting apprehension in commercial and industrial circles. Neville Chamberlain, as Chancellor of the Exchequer, had been the careful husbandman under whom the national recovery was staged. He protested—and he spoke for the business community—at the thought of having to dissipate the people's hard-won savings on weapons of war. It was hateful and damnable. His business instincts were revulsed.[5]

"If," he reflected, "we were now to follow Winston's advice and sacrifice our commerce to the manufacture of arms, we should inflict a certain injury on our trade from which it would take generations to recover . . . and we should cripple the revenue."[6]

Among the Socialists the no-more-war sentiment was quickened by their class consciousness. They would give no support to the wars of capitalism. They called, still, for security through the League of Nations, but were opposed to armaments that would give Britain the strength effectively to back the League.

There was yet another facet of opinion that acted as a deterrent to the kindling of strong feelings against Hitler's moves. With their characteristic notion of fair play and their sympathy for underdogs, the British people persuaded themselves that the Germans had been given a raw deal at the Peace Conference and that, under French influence, the Versailles Treaties had been oppressively drafted. The strength and influence of this unfortunate example of British emotionalism was accentuated by Lloyd George, one of the authors of those treaties. Lloyd George met Hitler in 1936 and came under his spell. He pronounced that this "born leader of men," "the greatest living German," was without aggressive intentions, a testimonial that had its effect on British opinion. From his meetings with the Fuehrer, Lloyd George came off rather worse than Neville Chamberlain, the opponent he despised.[7]

Churchill had had no illusions about the limitations of the League of Nations. He had supported it not as an organization powerful enough to bring about the outlawry of war, but as an instrument for the promotion of collective security and the forming of a united front against the dictators. He watched with approval as Anthony Eden made his stand against Mussolini's Abyssinian adventure.

The fall of Anthony Eden was the first milestone in the crisis-charged year of 1938. He was the first minister to be sacrificed in the cause of appeasement. As Foreign Secretary under the easy-going Baldwin, Eden had had a fairly free hand. Chamberlain came to the premiership resolved to direct foreign affairs according to his own conceptions. A Foreign Secretary seeking collective security in face of the dictators must clash with a Prime Minister bent on coming to terms with them. In a hurry to apply his own ideas, Chamberlain sighed for a more conformable occupant of the Foreign Office. He chafed at the delay in opening discussions with Mussolini. Eden protested that the Italians should fulfill some of their existing obligations to show their good faith before negotiations were started. On this issue Chamberlain forced Eden's resignation, together with that of his under-secretary, Lord Cranborne (Lord Salisbury of later years). They left office rather than submit to Italian blackmail.

Churchill was profoundly shocked by the news of Eden's departure and for once he was robbed of sleep by his anxieties. All night long he lay brooding over the hazards of the future, his fears heightened by the fall of the one strong young figure who had stood against the tide of drift and surrender.[8] A few days later (February 22) he expressed his sense of disquiet in the debate in the House.

"The Italian dictator," Churchill said, "has carried his vendetta with Mr. Eden to a victorious conclusion. The conflict between them was long. There is no doubt that Signor Mussolini has won. All the majesty, power and dominion of the British Empire have not been able to secure the success of the courses that were entrusted to the late Foreign Secretary by the general will of Parliament and the country."

In Italy jubilation was undisguised. Press and public cheered the news, so that the Italian papers were instructed not to be too triumphant lest Eden were transformed into a martyr of Fascism.[9]

There was a further aspect of Eden's resignation, not made public at the time, that roused Churchill's indignation. A few weeks previously, when Eden had been absent abroad, a message was received from President Roosevelt suggesting that he might take a hand in the affairs of Europe. As a contribution to easing the tension, he was considering summoning at Washington a conference of the lesser European states, a preliminary to a meeting of the major powers to discuss a general international settlement. It was a bold step for the President to propose in view of the strength of isolationist opinion in the United States. He wished to know what view Britain would take of his proposal.

Neville Chamberlain replied in Eden's absence. Without consulting his colleagues, even without informing them of the President's proposals, he answered that Roosevelt's intention would cut across his own efforts to reach an understanding with Germany and Italy. The President at once abandoned the idea.[10]

Churchill lamented this lost opportunity. There was nothing that could have been more calculated to make for peace than American intervention in the affairs of Europe. He was at a loss to understand how Chamberlain could have waved away the proffered hand from across the Atlantic. It was the last frail chance to have saved the world from war and it was thrown away.

For the vacancy at the Foreign Office, Chamberlain chose his closest friend in politics, Edward, Lord Halifax, ex-Viceroy of India, High Churchman, Master of Foxhounds. The appointment was attacked by the Labour Party, on the ground that the Foreign Secretary should be a member of the House of Commons. Again Churchill defended Chamberlain against the critics, recalling Salisbury, Rosebery and Lansdowne, Foreign Secretaries of the past fifty years who had been members of the House of Lords.

"When we have the Prime Minister here, what is the good of worrying about the Foreign Secretary?" Churchill asked. "What is the use of crying for the moon when you have the sun?"

Halifax had barely settled down at his desk in the Foreign

Office, before Hitler struck. German troops and Nazi blackshirts advanced into Austria. For Hitler the occasion was marred by the breakdown of tanks that blocked the road to Vienna. That mishap gave no relief to the Austrians, who were subjected to a reign of terror. Austrian democrats in their thousands were plundered, imprisoned or killed. Austrian independence was ended, the state absorbed into the Reich.

From his seat below the gangway, Churchill again pointed the lesson for the democracies. Europe, he said, was plainly confronted with a program of aggression. Not merely was Austria lost, but the mastery of Vienna had given the Nazis economic and military control of southeastern Europe. There was now, in particular, a threat to Czechoslovakia. His warnings were little heeded. The easygoing resented the disturbance of their complacency.

"Winston," said one hostess, "spoiled my dinner party last night with his terrifying stories of war that is to come—so boring!" [11]

In the House they shrugged their shoulders at his words—the "old war horse" was at it again.

To the East the Russians had been watching Hitler's moves with Churchill's sense of mounting concern. They now came forward with their proposals for countering German aggressiveness. They had an agreement with the French to go to the aid of Czechoslovakia. This pact, they proposed, should be extended within the framework of the League. Here again Neville Chamberlain was unresponsive. He placed little value on the support of the Red Army and he suspected the intention of the men of the Kremlin. With Machiavellian duplicity they were, he believed, scheming to embroil Britain in war with Germany. He rejected the Russian suggestion with the curt reply that it must be inimical to the prospects of European peace.[12] It was the gesture of an improvident isolationist. First the American President and now Stalin had been rebuffed.

Churchill, seeking closer cooperation with the French and the establishing of a Grand Alliance against the dictators, crossed the Channel for a series of meetings with the French political and military leaders. He met M. Blum, the Premier, M. Daladier, War Minister, and General Gamelin, Chief of the Defense Staff. In his private capacity he was able to make a frank statement on

British policy, voicing the views of his few, immediate associates on the need for maximum cooperation between the two countries. He stressed the necessity for concerted measures both in the development of the air forces of the two nations and in their operations. During his visit he met Paul Reynaud, with whom he was to have fateful discussions a few months later. Each man was impressed by the other's personality.

On his return to London, Churchill reported to Halifax at the Foreign Office on his discussions. The visit paved the way for an ultimate understanding regarding the pooling of the resources of the two Allied Powers.

Churchill put forward his own alternative foreign policy, in a public speech at Manchester (May 1938):

> Arm, and stand by the Government of the League. If the League of Nations has been mishandled and broken we must rebuild it. If the authority in the Covenant is divided we must reinforce it.
>
> Here is the practical plan. Britain and France are now united. Together they are an enormous force, which few countries would dare to challenge. I should like to see these two countries go to all the smaller States that are menaced, who are going to be devoured one by one by the Nazi tyranny, and say to them bluntly, "We are not going to help you if you are not going to help yourselves. What are you going to do about it?"
>
> If we could rally even ten well-armed States in Europe all banded together to resist an aggression upon any one of them, then we should be so strong that the immediate danger might be warded off and a breathing-space be gained for building later a still broader structure of peace. To the east of Europe lies the enormous power of Russia, a country whose form of government I detest, but which, at any rate, seeks no military aggression upon its neighbours, a country profoundly menaced by Nazi hostility. We should certainly not go cap in hand to Soviet Russia, or count in any definite manner upon Russian action. But how improvidently foolish we should be, when dangers are so great, to put needless barriers in the way of the general association of the great Russian mass with the resistance to an act of Nazi aggression.
>
> We are told we must make a special pact with Nazi Germany. I want to know what that pact is going to be and at whose ex-

pense it is to be made. Undoubtedly the Government could make an agreement with Germany. All they have to do is to give her back her former colonies or such others as she may desire; to muzzle the British Press and platforms by a law of censorship; to give Herr Hitler a free hand to spread the Nazi system and dominance far and wide through Central Europe.

There is the alternative foreign policy. It is one which in my view would be disgraceful and disastrous. In the first place it leads us straight to war. The Nazi regime, elated by this triumph and with every restraint removed, would proceed unchecked upon its path of aggression. We should be helpless, silent, gagged, apparently consenting spectators of the horrors which would spread through Central Europe.

The Prime Minister rejected the idea of the Grand Alliance. He discussed the matter with his Foreign Secretary, and took the advice of the Chiefs of Staff. Having weighed up the possibilities he pronounced: "It is a very attractive idea; indeed there is almost everything to be said for it until you come to examine its practicability. From that moment its attraction vanishes." [13] He was not even prepared to join in the guarantee the French had given to the Czechs.

It was a relief for Churchill in those dismal times to meet men of the services and to go afloat, as in the old days, to mingle with the sailors as they went about their tasks untroubled by the tides of politics. That June he was invited to visit the submarine hunters at Portland. He had expressed his doubts about this aspect of the Navy's work, so Chatfield, First Sea Lord, asked him to come along to see for himself. He jumped at the chance to go afloat again. Aboard the battleship *Nelson,* as the guest of Admiral Roger Backhouse, he was splendidly entertained. A submarine hunt was arranged for his benefit. He was greatly impressed and returned to London with his doubts removed, and his sprits restored by contact with men of the greatest service in the world.[14]

Steadfast in his self-sufficiency, Chamberlain continued his endeavors for peace. Hitler, with Austria absorbed, whipped up his campaign against the Czech Government. On the ground that two million Sudeten Germans were inhabitants of Czech territories, he demanded that Sudetenland be restored to Germany. By late summer of 1938, the world waited in suspense as Britain and France were seen to be nerving themselves at last to make a stand against the dictator. German troops were concentrated on the Czechoslovak border. The Czech defenses were manned, and so was France's Maginot Line. In Britain defense precautions were taken.

It seemed that war must be the outcome, when Neville Chamberlain ("the man with the umbrella") flew to Berchtesgaden to meet Hitler in person. Having obtained Hitler's terms, he flew back to London and sought the acquiescence of the Czechs in the dismemberment of their state. Pressed by Britain and France, the Czechs gave their reluctant, heartbroken assent.

On his return to Germany for a second meeting, at Godesberg, Chamberlain was informed that he was too late—Hitler had put up the price. Vaster demands were advanced. It was more than Chamberlain was prepared to stomach. He came back home profoundly shocked, prepared to face the worst rather than acquiesce in anything so outrageous.

It was announced that were Czechoslovakia to be invaded, the French would fulfill their obligations to the Czechs and that Britain and Russia would support the French—an assurance given without consultation with the Russians. The Czechs ordered mobilization. The French leaders crossed the Channel for discussions and staff talks. An exodus from London began. Air-raid wardens distributed gas masks, shelters were improvised in the parks, the Fleet was mobilized. Hitler announced his ultimatum, five days in which his requirements must be met.

Churchill, in a public statement, protested against submission to Hitler's demands. "The menace," he urged, "is not solely to Czechoslovakia but to the cause of freedom and democracy in every country. The idea that safety can be purchased by throwing a small state to the wolves is a delusion. The German war power will grow faster than the British and French can complete their preparations for defense."

Still the Prime Minister continued his efforts for peace. He was ready, if it would contribute to a settlement, to cross to Germany for a third time. The summons came as he was reporting to the House of Common on the course of events. Joined now by Daladier, the French Premier, he met Hitler at Munich, Mussolini being in attendance as mediator. The terms rejected at Godesberg were presented with little amendment and were now accepted by Chamberlain and Daladier. Czechoslovakia was sacrificed in the cause of appeasement. Hitler was accorded the territories he demanded. The Czechs were left only the rump of their state. Chamberlain returned home to be greeted by cheering crowds. He brought with him the scrap of paper that was Hitler's pledge, a reciprocal declaration that the peoples of Britain and Germany would never go to war with one another again.

"Peace with honor . . . peace for our time," declared the Prime Minister to the crowd in Downing Street as he waved his scrap of paper.

One Cabinet minister, Duff Cooper, First Lord of the Admiralty, resigned from the Government in protest at what had been done.

"It was 'peace with honor' I could not stomach," he explained. "If he'd come back from Munich saying 'peace with terrible, unmitigated, unparalleled dishonor' perhaps I would have stayed. But 'peace with honor'!"

The House of Commons was invited to adopt a testimonial to the Government for the policy which "averted war in the recent crisis." Members joined in acclaiming the Prime Minister. The man of appeasement was the hero of the hour. He was applauded at home and abroad, even by sober-minded Germans, to the vast annoyance of Hitler. Peoples who had been spared the ordeal of war rejoiced over their deliverance.

Winston Churchill rose to address a House that was out of sympathy with his warnings of disaster. He passed judgment on what had been done in a speech of somber foreboding. Even now his phrases fall mournfully on the ear:

> All is over. Silent, mournful, abandoned, broken, Czechoslovakia recedes into the darkness. She has suffered in every respect by her association with the Western democracies and with the League of Nations, of which she has always been an obedient servant. She has suffered in particular from her association with France, under whose guidance and policy she has been actuated for so long. I venture to think that in future the Czechoslovak state cannot be maintained as an independent entity. I think you will find that in a period of time which may be measured by years, but may be measured only by months, Czechoslovakia will

be engulfed in the Nazi regime. Perhaps they may join it in despair or in revenge. At any rate, that story is over and told.

But we cannot consider the abandonment and ruin of Czechoslovakia in the light only of what happened last month. It is the most grievous consequence of what we have done and of what we have left undone in the last five years—five years of futile good intentions, five years of eager search for the line of least resistance, five years of uninterrupted retreat of British power, five years of neglect of our air defences. Those are the features which I stand here to expose and which marked an improvident stewardship for which Great Britain and France have dearly to pay.

We have been reduced in those five years from a position where the very word 'war' was considered one which could be used only by persons qualifying for a lunatic asylum. We have been reduced from a position of safety and power—power to do good, power to be generous to a beaten foe, power to make terms with Germany, power to give her proper redress for her grievances, power to stop her arming if we chose, power to take any step in strength or mercy or justice which we thought right—reduced in five years from a position safe and unchallenged to where we stand now.

So far as this country is concerned the responsibility must rest with those who have had the undisputed control of our political affairs. They neither prevented Germany from re-arming, nor did they re-arm ourselves in time. They quarrelled with Italy without saving Ethiopia. They exploited and discredited the vast institution of the League of Nations, and they neglected to make alliances and combinations which might have repaired previous errors, and thus they left us in the hour of trial without adequate national defense or effective international security.

We are in the presence of a disaster of the first magnitude which has befallen Great Britain and France. Do not let us blind ourselves to that. It must now be accepted that all the countries of Central and Eastern Europe will make the best terms they can with the triumphant Nazi power. The system of alliances in Central Europe upon which France has relied for her safety has been swept away, and I can see no means by which it can be reconstituted.

What will be the position, I want to know, of France and England at the close of this year and the year afterwards? What will be the position of that Western front of which we are in full authority the guarantors? The German army at the present time is more numerous than that of France, though not nearly so matured or perfected. Next year it will grow much larger, and its maturity will be more complete. If the Nazi dictator should choose to look westward, as he may, bitterly will France and England regret the loss of that fine army of ancient Bohemia which was estimated last week to require not fewer than 30 German divisions for its destruction.

Can we blind ourselves to the great change which has taken place in the military situation, and to the dangers we have to meet? We are in process, I believe, of adding in four years, four battalions to the British Army. No fewer than two have already been completed. Here are at least 30 divisions which must now be taken into consideration upon the French front, besides the twelve that were captured when Austria was engulfed. Many people, no doubt, honestly believe that they are only giving away the interests of Czechoslovakia, whereas I fear we shall find that we have deeply compromised, and perhaps fatally endangered, the safety and even the independence of Great Britain and France. This is not merely a question of giving up the German colonies, as I am sure we shall be asked to do. Nor is it a question only of losing influence in Europe. It goes far deeper than that. You have to consider the character of the Nazi movement and the rule which it implies.

The Prime Minister desires to see cordial relations between this country and Germany. There is no difficulty at all in having cordial relations between the peoples. Our hearts go out to them. But they have no power. But never will you have friendship with the present German Government. You must have diplomatic and correct relations, but there can never be friendship between the British democracy and the Nazi power, that power which spurns Christian ethics, which cheers its onward course by barbarous paganism, which vaunts the spirit of aggression and conquest, which derives strength and perverted pleasure from persecution, and uses, as we have seen, with pitiless brutality the threat of murderous force. That power cannot ever be the trusted friend of British democracy.

What I find unendurable is the sense of our country falling into the power, into the orbit and influence of Nazi Germany, and of our existence becoming dependent upon their good will or pleasure. We do not want to be led upon the high road to becoming a satellite of the German Nazi system of European domination.

I have been casting about to see how measures can be taken to protect us from this advance of the Nazi power, and to secure those forms of life which are so dear to us. What is the sole method that is open? The sole method that is open is for us to regain our old island independence by acquiring that supremacy in the air which we were promised, that security in our air defences which we were assured we had, and thus to make ourselves an island once again. That, in all this grim outlook, shines out as the overwhelming fact. An effort at re-armament the like of which has not been seen ought to be made forthwith, and all the resources of this country and all its united strength should be bent to that task.

I do not grudge our loyal, brave people, who were ready to do their duty no matter what the cost, who never flinched under the strain of last week—I do not grudge them the natural, spontaneous outburst of joy and relief when they learned that the hard ordeal would no longer be required of them at the moment; but they should know the truth. They should know that there has been gross neglect and deficiency in our defences; they should know that we have sustained a defeat without a war, the consequences of which will travel far with us along our road; they should know that we have passed an awful milestone in our history, when the whole equilibrium of Europe has been deranged, and that the terrible words have for the time being pronounced against the Western democracies: "Thou art weighed in the balance and found wanting". And do not suppose this is the end.

This is only the beginning of the reckoning. This is only the first sip, the first foretaste of the bitter cup which will be proffered to us year by year, unless by a supreme recovery of moral health and martial vigour, we arise again and take our stand for freedom as in the olden time.

There was no burst of cheering for Churchill when he brought his long speech to an end. Again he was out of tune with the temper of the House. For long enough, now, the indictment he presented against the appeasement of Munich has passed into common acceptance, but the opinions that came to be commonplaces thereafter aroused vigorous dissent at the time. Chamberlain's endeavors that had saved the peace won the approbation of members of all parties. Churchill addressed himself to an unsympathetic House. His declaration that the democracies had met with a total defeat at the hands of Hitler aroused a hubbub of protest, and he was forced to pause until the clamor had died down. Undeterred he persisted until his denunciation was concluded.

The final ironical comment on the pacification of Munich came, some years later, with the disclosure that Chamberlain's intervention had been responsible for saving Hitler from deposition by his own generals.[15] Alarmed by the grandiose scheme of the mad Fuehrer, who seemed to be leading Germany to destruction, the Army chiefs had laid their plans to arrest him. The day fixed for their coup was that on which Chamberlain flew to Berchtesgaden. It was an intervention they had not provided for. The generals' plans were disorganized. Their utter discomfiture was caused by Anglo-French capitulation at Munich. What validity was left in their direful warnings? They had prophesied ignominious defeat if war came over Czechoslovakia. Instead, without a shot fired, Hitler had been accorded all he had sought. Chamberlain, by his personal intervention, had saved Hitler from arrest for criminal irresponsibility and installed him on a pinnacle of prestige.

Munich bought a year's grace for the democracies. When the policy of appeasement lay in ruins about its author, the claim was made that the breathing space worked out to the advantage of Britain and France. It was an argument Churchill contested. The debate has continued, but the world's judgment on what was done was reached without regard to the balancing of material gains and losses. It was tersely conveyed. Munich—the name became a term of obloquy, two syllables to carry the stigma of a diplomatic betrayal.

CHAPTER FOUR

MAYBE TO FIGHT—MAYBE TO DIE

JANUARY–SEPTEMBER 1939

AT LENGTH THE YEARS of frustration were coming to their close.
There is no greater mortification for a politician with a purpose than to be perpetually denied the opportunity of office and the chance to translate his ideas into practice. Mortification becomes almost beyond bearing for the man who believes that on the adoption of his ideas depends the safety, the very survival of his country.

During the appeasement Winston Churchill had been an onlooker and critic, powerless to check the course of events, as Britain had been brought down from security to the direst peril. He had longed to lay his hands on the military machine. Instead, he had had to stand by while the milestones were passed on the road of Britain's decline.

In those years he found escape from the pressing anxieties by withdrawing into the past and playing the historian. Having chronicled the career of his illustrious ancestor, the Duke of Marlborough, he took as his subject the history of his forebears on both sides of the Atlantic, the English-speaking peoples. He drew inspiration and comfort from the achievements of those famous men, the founding fathers of England and America. He found, too, the minor satisfaction of censuring the shortcomings of the present as he related the failures of statesmen of generations gone by.

Early in 1939 he had reached the reign of William the Dutch-man, who ruled as William III.* The Tory Party leaders of the last years of the seventeenth century were compared, in his scorn, with the Tories of the appeasement. Acting in the name of peace, economy and isolation, they had undermined the strength of the country at a time when war on the Continent was to be renewed.

> Their action, [wrote Churchill with a certain grim relish] has been largely imitated in our own times. No closer parallel exists in history than that presented by the Tory conduct in the years 1696–1699 with their similar conduct in the years 1932–1937. In each case short-sighted opinions, agreeable to the party spirit, pernicious to national interests, banished all purpose from the State and prepared a deadly resumption of the main struggle of Continental war. These recurring fits of squalor in the Tory record are a sad counterpoise to the many great services they have rendered the nation in their nobler and more serviceable moods.[1]

While the historian was engaged among the books of his library, the days of 1938 ran out without further disturbance to Europe's peace. As the weeks of 1939 passed, ministers began to preen themselves. From well-informed circles (as they are termed) it was conveyed that the international outlook was more than usually serene. The Prime Minister let it be known that disarmament talks might begin before the year 1939 was out.[2] It was ill-timed optimism, voiced as the price of Munich was about to be exacted. That same week—the Ides of March were near—Hitler struck again. Conceiving the time to be ripe for taking what at Munich had been denied him, he sent his troops into Prague. The sham of Munich was swept away. Without offering a pretext to excuse his action, he annexed the country as a German protectorate. The independence of Czechoslovakia was ended, the armies disbanded, munitions and factories taken over.

At Easter, Mussolini, following Hitler's example, seized Albania. It was the end of appeasement. Outraged by the deceptions of the men who had duped him, Neville Chamberlain set about organizing a front of resistance to aggression. Poland was the danger spot. The Poles were given a pledge of British support in the event of attack, and this was followed by guarantees to Greece and Romania.

* Publication of this history, delayed by the war, was not started until 1956.

In a halfhearted manner, the Prime Minister made approaches to the Kremlin. Mistrustful of Russian purposes, dubious of Russian strength, apprehensive of the effect on opinion in the Dominions and the United States of an alliance with the Communists, he set the negotiations going with no incisive direction. Already it was too late. Rebuffed in the past, ignored at the time of Munich, without faith in the purpose of Britain and France, Stalin was preparing to make a deal with Hitler.

There was reason enough for the observer, German as well as Russian, to find resolution lacking in Britain. Chamberlain might pledge his guarantees, but little was being done to give them the effective backing of force. Some steps were taken. It was decided to double the Territorial Army. A Ministry of Supply was set up in embryonic form. Compulsory military service, falling far short of conscription, was announced. They were measures that could not yield immediate results. A modern army is not to be produced by the magician's wand and an Act of Parliament. Doubling the Territorials is easily accomplished on paper, but to produce the men and the equipment is a task for months, if not years.[3]

Over these laggard measures there was cast an apologetic aura. Let it not be imagined that there was any provocative intention in Britain—what was being done was purely defensive in its purpose. Appeasement was over but hopes still lingered on. Hitler might denounce the Poles with mounting truculence; arms might pour into the city of Danzig; Goebbels might rouse his propagandists to fury. Nevertheless, Chamberlain would not despair. If only the Germans would be patient it might well be that the means would be found for meeting their claims against Poland.[4]

Reluctant to take any measure that could give provocation to Hitler, it was inevitable the Prime Minister should decline to strengthen his Cabinet by inviting Winston Churchill and Anthony Eden to join him. It was a step urged upon him by colleagues and advisers, official and unofficial.[5] British public opinion had been transformed. By mid-summer the so-called pacifism of the past had evaporated. Churchill, opponent of appeasement, was seen to have been indisputably justified by events. The warnings of those somber speeches, though neglected at the time, had not fallen on heedless ears. Their effect was seen in the swift dispersal of the miasma of appeasement. Now that his predictions were fulfilled, was not Churchill's place in the Government? Billboards and posters carried the slogan: "Winston must come back." Lord Camrose backed his claims in the *Daily Telegraph.* Lord Beaverbrook's papers were favorably disposed. *The Times,* however, did not forget the past, the editor Geoffrey Dawson, noting in his diaries:

> "The *Daily Telegraph* joined the hue and cry for the inclusion of Winston in the Cabinet to impress the Germans. We continued the more effective process of calling attention to the growing strength of the British Army."

Dawson was gratified to learn at first hand that Chamberlain had "no intention of being bounced into taking back Churchill," [6] although the Prime Minister had a different estimate of the effect Churchill's recall might produce. "The nearer we get to war, the more Churchill's chances improve and vice-versa," was Chamberlain's reflection. "If there is any possibility of easing the tension and getting back to normal relations with the dictators, I wouldn't risk it by what would certainly be regarded by them as a challenge." [7]

Prejudice dies hard. Even at that late hour there were strong influences at work against Churchill's return to office. A considerable body of Tory M.P.s looked on him as erratic and lacking in judgment, a potential source of danger. Government whips used the prejudice to their advantage by suggesting to their followers that the reappointment of Winston Churchill would bring a declaration of war from Germany. It was suggested that among Dominion governments, there was opposition to Churchill's inclusion in the Cabinet.[8]

In August the House of Commons rose for the summer recess. So menacing were the prospects that many M.P.s hesitated to separate for as long as two months. There was mistrust of the Government and apprehension that, with Parliament in recess, Chamberlain might be persuaded into a second Munich. Churchill joined with members of all parties in advocating that the adjournment be limited to three weeks. The Prime Minister, flippantly partisan, made mockery of their anxieties—his critics showed themselves to be badly in need of a holiday, their reasoning faculties "wanting a little freshening up at the seaside." He was reproved by one of his own supporters for "jeering, pettifogging party speeches that divide the nation."

"We are in a situation," declared young Ronald Cartland in a tragic forecast, "that within a month we may be going to fight, and we may be going to die. [A member: "Oh."] It is all very well for the honorable gentleman to say, 'Oh.' There are thousands of young men at the moment in training camps and giving up their holiday. The least we can do here, if we are not going to meet together from time to time and keep Parliament in session, is to show that we have faith in this democratic institution."

Within a year the prophecy was fulfilled and Ronald Cartland had fallen in the fighting at Mont Cassel, splendid in spirit until the last. His words, in all their poignancy, are the ultimate verdict on appeasement, with its fumblings and evasions, and compromisings with the dictators. Argument and counterargument might continue, but when all the words had been said there remained the ineluctable fact: "We may be going to fight, we may be going to die." The young M.P. and his generation had to take over the responsibility for redeeming the errors of the past. Appeasement, however well-meaning, had not been enough.

The business of debating concluded, Winston Churchill at the invitation of the French, crossed the Channel to inspect the fortifications of the Maginot Line, the rampart that was to have provided France with security against any weight of attack. He was accompanied by Major General Spears, who in World War II was to continue the service he had rendered to the Allied cause twenty years before as head of the British Military Mission to Paris. The visitors went everywhere and were shown everything. There were meetings with the two leading French generals—the able Georges who was to be Commander in Chief in the field and the spruce Gamelin, supreme generalissimo. Churchill was impressed by the fortifications—they were impregnable—but not by the men manning them. He was dismayed by the defensive attitude of the French officers; they were Maginot-minded.

At last the visitors came to the point where the Maginot Line ran out. On the farther side were the forests of the Ardennes extending from Belgium into the state of Luxembourg. At this point the French had provided field works far less impressive than the fortifications of the Maginot Line. On another occasion, another English visitor, Sir Samuel Hoare, halted at this point during his tour of inspection.

"Look at that terrain!" said a French general, pointing toward the forests. "No German army can get through there."

Churchill was invited to form a similar opinion. He drew his own conclusions in a sense contrary to the complacency of the Frenchman and voiced his concern in a warning that was to be recalled by the time another summer was running its course. The Germans, he replied, were concentrating on forming armored forces in great strength.

"Forests," he said, "will be particularly tempting to such forces since they will offer concealment from the air."

So it was to prove. The Forests of the Ardennes were to be the German route to victory, the graveyard of the French strategists. Churchill returned home anxious at heart. He had no doubt that Hitler would attack the Poles—he calculated that the first fortnight of September was the critical period. It was time to make his own personal preparations. When the fighting began there was reason enough to suppose that Nazis in England might make him the object of their attentions. He drew his weapons from the cupboard in which they had been put by. He summoned his old detective from retirement to serve as his bodyguard, with the order that he should bring his pistol with him.

The pact between Stalin and Hitler (August 23) was the last rumble before the storm. It was a deal between foes. Hitler signed the non-aggression agreement to buy off the Russians, while he dealt with the Poles, Stalin to gain a share in the loot. There was no mistaking Hitler's purpose. Neville Chamberlain and his colleagues, anxious only that the Germans should not deceive themselves over Britain's intentions, announced that despite the new pact Britain, with the French, would fulfill her obligations to the Poles. To establish the matter beyond the shadow of a doubt, the Prime Minister wrote in clear terms to tell Hitler that Britain would keep her word.

"If the need should arise the Government are resolved and prepared to employ without delay all the forces at their command and it is impossible to foresee the end of hostilities once engaged."

Disappointed in his expectations of a second Munich, Hitler released his waiting armies. It was then that the call came to Winston Churchill. As champion of the free peoples he advanced to the climax of his life's service, the fulfillment of his destiny for which the years of preparation had magnificently fitted him.

BIBLIOGRAPHICAL NOTES

BOOK ONE

CHAPTER II

1. Winston Churchill, *A Roving Commission: My Early Life* (New York: Charles Scribner's Sons, 1939).
2. Churchill, *The Story of the Malakand Field Force* (New York: Longmans Green, 1898).

BOOK TWO

CHAPTER IV

1. Sylvia Pankhurst, *The Suffragette Movement* (Woodford Green, Essex: Lalibela House, 1931).

CHAPTER V

1. Eileen Baillie, *The Shabby Paradise* (London: Hutchinson & Co., 1958).
2. Sir Nevil Macready, *Annals of an Active Life* (London: Hutchinson & Co., 1924).

BOOK THREE

CHAPTER II

1. Norman Macmillan, *Sir Sefton Brancker* (London, Toronto: W. Heinemann, Ltd., 1935) is a mine of information on the development of aviation from the earliest days.

CHAPTER IV

1. Brig. Gen. C. F. Aspinall-Oglander, *Military Operations, Gallipoli* (London: W. Heinemann, Ltd., 1929).

CHAPTER V

1. Lord Beaverbrook, *Politicians and the War* (Garden City, N. Y.: Doubleday, Doran and Co., Inc., 1928), I, 109.

CHAPTER VI

1. Beaverbrook, *op. cit.* I, 106.
2. *Ibid.,* p. 111.
3. Blanche E. C. Dugdale, *Life of Arthur James Balfour* (London: Hutchinson & Co., 1936), II, 184.

CHAPTER VII

1. J. A. Spender and Cyril Asquith, *Life of Lord Oxford and Asquith* (London: Hutchinson & Co., 1932), II, 163.
2. Beaverbrook, *op. cit.,* II, 74.

CHAPTER VIII

1. Macready, *op. cit.*

CHAPTER IX

1. Beaverbrook, *op. cit.,* II, 105.
2. George Allardice Riddell, *Lord Riddell's War Diary 1914-1918* (London: Nicholson and Watson, Ltd., 1933), p. 242.

CHAPTER X

1. Rear Admiral Sir Murray Fraser Sueter, *The Evolution of the Tank* (London: Hutchinson & Co.; Toronto: Ryerson Press, 1941) is a complete and authoritative account of the birth pangs of the tank.
2. Churchill, *Amid These Storms* (New York: Charles Scribner's Sons, 1932).
3. A letter to the *Daily Telegraph,* May 20, 1938.

BOOK FOUR

CHAPTER I

1. Andrew Soutar, *With Ironside in North Russia* (London: Hutchinson & Co., 1940).

CHAPTER III

1. Harold Nicolson, *Curzon, the Last Phase* (New York: Harcourt, Brace & Co., 1939), p. 272.

BOOK FIVE

CHAPTER III

1. Anonymous, *Right Honourable Gentlemen* (London: Right Book Club, 1940), p. 102.
2. George Lansbury, Budget Debates, 1932.
3. Lord Chatfield, *Autobiography of Admiral of the Fleet Lord Chatfield* (London: W. Heinemann, Ltd., 1947), II, 163-4.

4. Keith Feiling, *Life of Neville Chamberlain* (New York: Macmillan, 1946), p. 324.

5. *Ibid.*, p. 320.

6. *Ibid.*, p. 314.

7. Frank Owen, *Tempestuous Journey—Lloyd George: His Life and Times* (New York: McGraw-Hill, 1954), pp. 734-6.

8. Churchill, *The Gathering Storm* (New York: Houghton Mifflin Co., 1948), p. 201.

9. Count Galeazzo Ciano, *Ciano's Hidden Diary: 1937-1938* (New York: E. P. Dutton & Co., Inc., 1952), p. 78.

10. Lewis Broad, *Sir Anthony Eden: The Chronicle of a Career* (New York: Thomas Y. Crowell Co., 1955), pp. 101-108.

11. Barbara Cartland, *Isthmus Years* (London: Hutchinson & Co., 1943), p. 171.

12. Feiling, *op. cit.*, p. 347.

13. *Ibid.*, p. 347.

14. Chatfield, *op. cit.*, p. 139.

15. John W. Wheeler Bennett, *Nemesis of Power* (New York: St. Martin's Press, Inc., 1953) should be referred to for a full account.

CHAPTER IV

1. Churchill, *The New World (History of the English Speaking Peoples,* Vol. II) (New York: Dodd, Mead & Co., 1957).

2. L. S. Amery, *My Life* (London: Hutchinson & Co., 1955), p. 307; Duff Cooper, *Old Men Forget* (London: Hart Davis, 1954), p. 252.

3. Chatfield, *op. cit.*, pp. 168-171.

4. Feiling, *op. cit.*, p. 407.

5. John Evelyn Wrench, *Geoffrey Dawson and Our Times,* (London: Hutchinson & Co., 1955), p. 393.

6. Feiling, *op. cit.*, p. 406.

7. Churchill, *The Gathering Storm,* p. 280; Lord Templewood, *Nine Troublous Years* (London: Collins, 1954), p. 385; Barbara Cartland, *Life of Ronald Cartland* (London: Hutchinson & Co., 1942), p. 130; Sir E. Spears, *Assignment to Catastrophe* (London: W. Heinemann, Ltd., 1954), I, 19.

8. Churchill, *The Gathering Storm,* pp. 300, 313; Spears, *op. cit.*, p. 17; Templewood, *op. cit.*, p. 342.

CHURCHILL'S ELECTION RECORD
1899–1935

OLDHAM

1899	A. Emmott *(Lib.)*	12,976
	W. Runciman *(Lib.)*	12,770
	Winston Churchill *(Cons.)*	11,477
	J. Mawdsley *(Cons.)*	11,449
1900	A. Emmott *(Lib.)*	12,947
	Winston Churchill *(Cons.)*	12,931
	W. Runciman *(Lib.)*	12,709
	C. B. Crisp *(Cons.)*	12,522

MANCHESTER NORTH-WEST

1906	Winston Churchill *(Lib.)*	5,639
	Joynson Hicks *(Cons.)*	4,398
1908	Joynson Hicks *(Cons.)*	5,417
	Rt. Hon. Winston Churchill *(Lib.)*	4,988
	D. D. Irving *(Soc.)*	276

DUNDEE

1908	Rt. Hon. Winston Churchill *(Lib.)*	7,079
	Sir G. W. Baxter *(Lib. Un.)*	4,370
	G. H. Stuart *(I. Lab.)*	4,014
	E. Scrymgeour *(Ind.)*	655
1910 (Jan.)	Rt. Hon. Winston Churchill *(Lib.)*	10,747
	A. Wilkie *(Soc.)*	10,365
	J. S. Lloyd *(Unionist)*	4,552
	J. Glass *(Unionist)*	4,339
	E. Scrymgeour *(Prohib.)*	1,512

1910 (Dec.)	Rt. Hon. Winston Churchill (*Lib.*)	9,240
	A. Wilkie (*Lab.*)	8,957
	Sir G. Baxter (*Unionist*)	5,685
	J. S. Lloyd (*Unionist*)	4,914
	E. Scrymgeour (*Prohib.*)	1,825
1918	Rt. Hon. Winston Churchill (*Lib.*)	25,788
	A. Wilkie (*Lab.*)	24,822
	E. Scrymgeour (*Ind.*)	10,423
	J. S. Brown (*Soc.*)	7,769
1922	E. Scrymgeour (*Ind.*)	32,578
	E. D. Morel (*Lab.*)	30,292
	D. J. MacDonald (*N. Lib.*)	22,244
	Rt. Hon. Winston Churchill (*N. Lib.*) . .	20,466
	W. Gallacher (*Com.*)	6,681

LEICESTER WEST

1923	F. W. Pethick Lawrence (*Soc.*)	13,634
	Rt. Hon. Winston Churchill (*Lib.*)	9,236
	Captain A. Instone (*Unionist*)	7,696

ABBEY DIVISION OF WESTMINSTER

1924	O. W. Nicholson (*Unionist*)	8,187
	Rt. Hon. Winston Churchill (*Ind.*) . . .	8,144
	A. F. Brockway (*Soc.*)	6,156
	J. Scott Duckers (*Lib.*)	291

EPPING DIVISION OF ESSEX

1924	Rt. Hon. Winston Churchill (*Constitutionalist*) . .	19,843
	G. G. Sharp (*Lib.*)	10,080
	J. R. McPhie (*Soc.*)	3,768
1929	Rt. Hon. Winston Churchill (*Cons.*) . .	23,972
	G. G. Sharp (*Lib.*)	19,005
	J. T. W. Newbold (*Soc.*)	6,472
1931	Rt. Hon. Winston Churchill (*Cons.*) . .	35,956
	A. S. Comyns Carr, K.C. (*Lib.*) . . .	15,670
	J. Ranger (*Soc.*)	4,713
1935	Rt. Hon. Winston Churchill (*Cons.*) . .	34,849
	G. G. Sharp (*Lib.*)	14,430
	J. Ranger (*Soc.*)	9,758

HIS GOVERNMENT OFFICES

1906–08   Under-Secretary for the Colonies
1908–10   President of the Board of Trade
1910–11   Home Secretary
1911–15   First Lord of the Admiralty
1915   Chancellor of the Duchy of Lancaster
1917–18   Minister of Munitions
1918–21   Secretary of State for War and for Air
1921–22   Secretary for the Colonies
1924–29   Chancellor of the Exchequer
1939–40   First Lord of the Admiralty

CHURCHILL'S BOOKS
1898–1939

The Story of the Malakand Field Force, New York: Longmans Green, 1898.
The River War, New York: Longmans Green, 1899, 1902.
Savrola (a novel), New York: Longmans Green, 1900.
London to Ladysmith via Pretoria, New York: Longmans Green, 1900.
Ian Hamilton's March, New York: Longmans Green, 1900.
Lord Randolph Churchill, New York: Macmillan, 1906.
My African Journey, London: Hodder & Stoughton, 1908.
Liberalism and the Social Problem, London: Hodder & Stoughton, 1909.
The World Crisis (4 vols.), New York: Scribner's, 1923–29, 1931.
A Roving Commission: My Early Life, New York: Scribner's, 1930, 1939.
The Unknown War: The Eastern Front, New York: Scribner's, 1931.
The Aftermath, New York: Scribner's, 1929.
Amid These Storms, New York: Scribner's, 1932.
The Great War, London: Newnes, 1933–34.
Marlborough (6 vols.), New York: Scribner's, 1933–38.
Great Contemporaries, New York: Putnam, 1937.
While England Slept (speeches), New York: Putnam, 1938.
Step by Step (articles), New York: Putnam, 1939.

INDEX

THE AUTHOR AND HIS BOOK

CHARLES LEWIS BROAD, *journalist, author and fruit farmer, was born in 1900 in the village of Marston, Oxford, England, and makes his home at Podkin Farm, High Halden, in the county of Kent. He was educated at Perse Grammar School, Cambridge, and began his writing career at the age of nineteen when he joined the staff of one of the oldest newspapers in England, The Hertfordshire Mercury. After serving his apprenticeship he moved to Fleet Street, London's newspaper row, and eventually joined the staff of one of the city's leading newspapers, the Daily Telegraph. He became Night Editor of the Telegraph, and later joined the Norman Kark magazine chain where he served as Editor-in-Chief for two years. As a newspaperman and author he has written many millions of words—mostly in longhand—and he estimates that more than one million have been on Sir Winston Churchill whose activities he first began covering while a reporter in London. His various books on Churchill have been the result of twenty-five years of research into this controversial figure in British politics, and his works have been translated into many languages, including French, German, Italian, Spanish, Czechoslovakian and Danish— "but never into Russian," he adds. Since 1948 he has lived on his farm, growing fruit and writing—"and it always seems to be about Churchill." His other books include* The Bernard Shaw Dictionary *(A & C Black, 1929);* Trunk Crimes Past and Present *(Hutchinson, 1934);* The Way of the Dictators *(in collaboration with Leonard Russell) (Hutchinson, 1935);* Crowning the King *(Hutchinson, 1937);* A B C of the Coronation *(Hutchinson, 1937);* Crisis Year

(1938) in Story and Picture *(Hutchinson, 1939);* Ming the Panda *(Hutchinson, 1939);* Pets of Pets Corner *(Hutchinson, 1939);* Winston Churchill: Man of War *(Hutchinson, 1940);* The Innocence of Edith Thompson: A Study in Old Bailey Justice *(Hutchinson, 1952);* Queens, Crowns and Coronations *(Hutchinson, 1952);* The Friendships and Follies of Oscar Wilde *(Hutchinson, 1954);* Sir Anthony Eden: The Chronicles of a Career *(Hutchinson, 1955);* The Adventures of Sir Winston *(Hutchinson, 1957);* Advocates of the Golden Age *(John Long, 1958). He is currently preparing the second volume of this biography—*Winston Churchill: The Years of Achievement.

WINSTON CHURCHILL: THE YEARS OF PREPARATION *(Hawthorn, 1958), was designed by Sidney Feinberg and completely manufactured by American Book-Stratford Press, Inc. The body type was set on the Linotype in Baskerville, a modern reproduction of the type cut in 1760 by John Baskerville, of Birmingham, England, reflecting the style of stone inscriptions.*

HAWTHORN   BOOKS,   INC.